How to Invest in Gold Stocks
And
Avoid the Pitfalls

DONALD J. HOPPE

HOW TO INVEST IN

GOLD STOCKS

And

Avoid the Pitfalls

ARLINGTON HOUSE   *NEW ROCHELLE, N. Y.*

To Bonnie Jean,
Sunshine and Gold

Contents

Figures

List of Illustrations

1. Smelting and working gold in ancient Egypt
2. Gold panning in California, 1849
3. The rush to California, 1849
4. California placer mining, 1850
5. El Dorado gambling saloon, Sacramento California, 1850
6. Gold prospectors in Australia, 1852
7. The great greenback controversy, 1862–1879
8. Greenbacks drive out gold and silver, 1862–1879
9. Gold mining in Colorado, 1880
10. Gold is discovered in South Africa, 1886
11. Going down the Victoria shaft—1887
12. Prospectors ascending Chilcoot Pass, Alaska—1897
13. Fiat money inflation in Germany, 1919–1923
14. Coal used as money, Germany—1923
15. Unemployed at mass demonstration, New York—1930
16. General view of the Homestake Mine, 1971
17. Loading an ore car at the Homestake Mine
18. Ball mills at the Homestake Mine
19. Yield per ton at the Homestake Mine
20. Aerial view of Dome Mines
21. Underground drilling at the Dome Mine
22. Pouring a gold bar at the Dome Mine
23. The Campbell Red Lake Mine
24. Aerial view of Madsen Red Lake Mine
25. Giant gold dredge in South America
26. Johannesburg—city of gold
27. General view of Western Deep Levels Mine
28. Drilling an ore seam in South Africa
29. Ore reduction works at the Buffelsfontein Mine
30. Athletic recreation for Bantu mineworkers

31. Sinking a new shaft at Southvaal
32. Gold bullion in the South African Reserve bank

Preface

In modern times, the ownership of gold mining shares has, on many occasions, provided not only safety for capital but opportunities for profit far in excess of that obtained from the possession of gold bullion itself. The evidence of history, both ancient and modern, unfailingly substantiates the view that a gold oriented investment portfolio offers the best defense against the following economic calamities:

RUNAWAY INFLATION

DEVALUATION

DEPRESSION

The United States has been in a condition of more or less continuous monetary crisis since 1958, and as I write this the end is nowhere in sight. Chronic, worldwide inflation has become the prime financial characteristic of our age. In addition, gold has once again assumed a central role in world monetary affairs, despite every effort by four successive U.S. administrations to reduce its importance.

Work on this book commenced at the beginning of 1971, a period of relative calm in international monetary affairs, with gold selling only a few dollars above its old par of $35 per troy ounce on the London market. But when the writing was completed in April of 1972, the situation was anything but calm and the world price of gold was beginning a startling advance which would soon carry it to historic high levels above $50 per ounce.

Much had happened in the interim and the author was hard pressed to keep up with the dramatic events that were coming to pass; an unexpected amount of revision and rewriting became necessary to keep the book current and make it as complete as possible. And although I did not plan it that way at the beginning, I found that the historic events of 1971 (and the extra labors they involved for the writer) had enabled me to present the complete story of the United States gold exchange dollar, from its creation on January 31, 1934 to its demise on August 15, 1971. Since, for better or for worse, the author has the historian's passion for dividing the stream of human experience into readily identifiable eras with a precise beginning and a specific end, such a result was not without its personal rewards.

Actually, I had correctly forecast the monetary events of 1971 in previous publications and was in the process of reviewing and ex-

panding on these prior predictions, as well as developing further projections for the future, in the manuscript at hand. Nevertheless, it was
disturbing to see so many of my initial forecasts become reality (and
so much sooner than I had anticipated), because such a development
obviously gave additional support to my financial and socio-economic
projections for the United States over the remainder of this decade,
which are, unfortunately, not very comforting.

The only bright spot in this situation, at least for the author, is that
through both personal counseling and publication I have been able to
help a great many people not only protect their capital but, in many
cases, to considerably increase it. And I have no reason to feel that I
may not continue to do so. In the past at any rate, judging from the
response of readers of my previous book, which dealt with the investment potential of gold coins, there were many who increased their
wealth by a far greater percentage than did the author in the two years
since its publication! But I have no complaints; one does not and
should not measure success entirely in terms of dollars and cents.
Beneath all good writing lies the law of service to the reader. A good
book, a successful book, is one that provides such service.

Nevertheless, a writer of books giving investment advice cannot
altogether avoid a feeling of anxiety upon their publication, for at that
point the opportunity to revise or reverse one's analyses and opinions
is irretrievably passed. There is obviously no way to recall thousands
of books, should the author suddenly have a change of mind concerning the merits of a particular strategy or specific investment. Consequently, great care has been taken to eliminate or at least greatly
reduce the possibility that coming events could significantly alter any
of the basic conclusions, suggestions or recommendations presented
in this book.

However, we are compelled by the nature of our inquiry to attempt
to penetrate the future, regardless of the possibility of error. Actually,
it is generally far more dangerous to ignore the future than to try,
however imperfectly, to anticipate it. Like it or not, we are all proph-
ets, for the great majority of our actions are determined on the basis
of some anticipated future result. Success in speculation or investment is almost entirely dependent on a correct evaluation of the future. However, we seldom need to know the exact details of coming
events, but only their basic pattern and direction.

Investment is not a science, but an art. And the only areas of certainty in any art are its basic rules and principles; the ultimate forms
can be endlessly variable. In this book I have attempted to provide the
reader with a basic guide to the historic role of gold as money and have

tried to show that the laws of economics and finance regarding gold remain as significant today as they were in the days of Julius Caesar. The rules and principles outlined for gold-oriented investment are those developed by the author and several associates from direct experience in the market place. And those rules and principles were used to review current and future investment opportunities in specific stocks and situations.

At any rate, I believe an investment book should cover a lot more ground than just what stocks to buy. It is not my intention merely to tell you what to do, but to help you determine for yourself what to do, regardless of what specific circumstances or events come to pass in the years ahead. This requires the inclusion of a considerable amount of background material, which I hope will be entertaining as well as instructive. But the results obtained thus far by many readers of my previous book, *How to Invest in Gold Coins* (Arlington House, 1970) have reinforced my belief that this is a practical and successful approach for an investment book and that such books can retain their usefulness for a considerable period of time. I certainly feel that this one could, because I believe we are just beginning an era of direct conflict between gold and paper money, between monetary conservatives and inflationists.

It is generally forgotten now, but through much of the 19th century such a conflict dominated the United States both politically and economically. For thirty years the "greenbackers", inflationists and "Free Silver" advocates fought the rule of gold and sought to debase the currency, until their most persuasive and final champion, William Jennings Bryan, went down to defeat in the Presidential election of 1896. Are we in for a struggle of similar duration? The modern greenbackers, the Keynesian inflationists, are far more numerous, more sophisticated and more powerful than their 19th century predecessors and consequently have already caused vastly more damage to the economic, financial and political health of the United States and to the world. Unfortunately, they will undoubtedly do a great deal more harm before their delusion is finally discredited and the rule of gold is once again recognized by all the governments of the world.

During the 1960's, the struggle between the advocates of standard gold money and the inflationists was largely a secret affair, confined to the panelled and carpeted meeting rooms of central bankers. But that phase of the conflict was ended on August 15, 1971. Henceforth, the struggle will not only be more direct and more open but far more intense, leading to even more extreme changes in the price of gold and the value of the dollar.

The central economic event of 1971 was of course the formal announcement by President Nixon on August 15, that the international convertibility of the dollar into gold was from that date officially ended. This action amounted to a unilateral abrogation of the Bretton Woods agreement of 1944 by the U.S. Government, which had pledged to keep the dollars held by other nations freely convertible into gold at $35 per ounce. Since then, the price of gold has steadily increased in international markets and the myth of a U.S. paper dollar standard for the world has been utterly destroyed. The neo-Keynesian economists and politicians who had loudly proclaimed that the U.S. credit dollar was as good as gold—or even better than gold—have for the time being retreated into an embarrassed silence. However, I do not think for a moment that they have abandoned their efforts to force upon the U.S. and the world a completely managed fiat currency system and a completely managed world economy to compel its acceptance.

In the past, the policy of the U.S. Treasury has been one of desperate expediency, and with the reluctant cooperation of the central banks of our principal military and political allies, Washington managed to keep the patchwork IMF gold-dollar exchange standard at least superficially alive through crisis after crisis. Even as late as the Smithsonian meeting of December 18, 1971, which "theoretically" devalued the dollar from $35 to $38 per ounce of gold and readjusted world currency parities, the old policy or rather non-policy of simply trying to delay the collapse for a little while longer and meanwhile hoping for a miracle apparently had not changed.

But in the face of the obvious ascendency of gold in 1972, I would not at all be surprised to see the fiat money forces suddenly undertake a reckless offensive. All pretense at international monetary cooperation would then be abandoned. The U.S. may unilaterally (again) announce the "demonetization" of gold, that is, officially sever even any theoretical link between its dollar and gold. The entire U.S. national debt of some $450 billion or more may be "cancelled" and replaced with more printed greenbacks or with Federal Reserve bank credit. The U.S. Government may then finance future deficits only through direct "borrowing" from the Federal Reserve banks at an arbitrarily fixed low rate of interest and secured only with non-maturing, non-callable Treasury notes, thus completing the perversion of the Federal Reserve System into a captive engine of inflation.

In short, be prepared for bold and desperate acts from the U.S. Government, regardless of what administration is in power for the next five to ten years. Any or all of the preceding steps will of course require that the yoke of totalitarian economics, with its wage, price and exchange controls, be made a permanent feature of American life. In the long run, however, I believe that all such actions will prove to be self-defeating and that the dollar will eventually have to be returned to a genuine convertibility into gold, at whatever price or ratio is appropriate at the time. But, as Baron Rothschild used to say, blood will probably run in the streets first.

At the University of Toronto in May of 1972, Dr. Franz Pick, the internationally recognized world currency and banking expert from Switzerland, held one of his frequent monetary seminars. The good doctor, who is famous for his monumental faith in gold and his similar lack of faith in the U.S. fiat dollar, pointed out that the "two-tier" gold system established in March of 1968 was already dead and buried. It was self evident, he noted, that governments holding gold nominally valued at $US38 per ounce would hardly be willing to "spend" it at that price to settle international payments deficits when the open market price for gold was near $US60. They would simply pass the dollars they hold, which are constantly depreciating in value, and hang on to their gold which is obviously gaining in value.

Dr. Pick made it plain that he was still a real bull on gold and that he did not believe the rise would stop at $100 or even $140 per ounce. "In the future," he said, "I can visualize $175." So can the author, although I don't think it will get there overnight and I look for numerous corrections and setbacks along the way, which should provide further opportunities for gold-oriented investors and traders.

The Swiss monetary expert also strongly supported the author's long-held and previously published view that Western Europe will evenually have a common currency (Dr. Pick thinks in 1973) and that such a currency will be based on and convertible into gold. And since Dr. Pick is convinced that inflation will eventually reduce the present U.S. fiat dollar to scrap paper, he favors only those investments that have historically survived such debacles. Among these he includes:

Gold and gold coins

Mineral wealth in the ground
(including non-producing oil fields)

Works of art

The author's view is that works of art are suitable only for investors with some degree of sophistication in this area and furthermore, while moderately severe inflation often encourages a speculative boom in such items, an extreme or runaway type inflation generally brings about depression-like conditions, in which artworks and antiquities may not do as well as the more necessary and traditional articles. In the European hyper-inflations of the 1920's, there was no boom, only one long, continuous bust. Artworks, jewels and antiquities were not much in demand when the majority of people were desperately trying to obtain just food, clothing and shelter. The aristocrats and formerly wealthy were sometimes forced to trade their treasures and heirlooms for the necessities of life at what amounted to absurdly low values.

The author's investment policy therefore takes into account that depression conditions could follow or even accompany the coming world monetary debacle. Therefore I recommend portfolios consisting of:

> Gold coins
> Gold mining stocks
> Common silver coins

Gold buillion is not on the above list, because it is presently illegal for Americans to own or possess it.*

Although this book is concerned primarily with gold mining stocks, the other two recommended areas are also briefly examined. However, for reasons that will subsequently be revealed to the reader, the author does not recommend two other popular inflation-devaluation hedges: silver bullion (including futures) and silver mining stocks. Some investment advisers suggest adding vintage wines and liquors to the list on the grounds that if all else fails, you can still have the pleasure of drinking them. I would like to end this preface on a more positive note, but the only consoling thought that comes to mind is that the declining phase of the Roman Empire was probably the most fun.

At any rate I can very positively thank the many nice people who generously and often indispensably assisted the author in the preparation of this work. However, there are some who furnished statistical information and other data whose names, regretfully, I had better not mention; the author's views may not exactly be popular at their places of employment and I surely do not want to risk rewarding their kindness by exposing them to any sort of embarrassment or criticism. But I can gratefully mention Mr. L.C.G.C. Williams, editor of the *Quarterly Review of South African Gold Shares* and others on the staff of that

---

*Without a license from the Treasury Department and such licenses are granted only to commercial and industrial users.

worthy publication, as well as members of the editorial department of the *Mining Journal* of London, who responded with unfailing courtesy and promptness to my sometimes desperate requests for assistance.

For the arduous but vital task of typing the final manuscript, Elaine Harrington deserves a special thanks for her steadfast performance.

I am also greatly indebted to Arlington House, not only for their willingness to publish controversial books on the issues of our day, but for the obvious dedication and enthusiasm of their staff and for their determination to design and produce volumes that are unfailingly a tribute to the book maker's art. Their editors provided, as always, sagacious editorial judgment and personal encouragement, both indispensable to the final realization of this work.

And finally, I would have been utterly lost without the frequent assistance and constant support of my wife Joan, who is not only a woman of incomparable charm, but a first rate copy editor.

Mr. Donald P. Howe, Director of Services, Homestake Mining Company, Mr. C.P. Girdwood, Vice President and General Manager, Dome Mines Ltd., M. M. Masterson, Secretary-Treasurer, Madsen Red Lake Gold Mines Ltd., Mr. D. Hallam, Secretary, Pato Consolidated Gold Dredging Ltd., and Mr. Charles P. van Niekerk, Senior Information Officer, Information Service of South Africa, all graciously contributed photographs which add so much to the content and interest of this book. Mr. Joseph Karzen, Director, Historical Pictures Service, provided the fascinating glimpses of the past found among the photo-illustrations. The artwork which now and then finds its way onto these pages is just another vanity of the author.

May you get as much pleasure out of reading this book as the author had in the writing of it. And may it profit you in every other way.

DONALD J. HOPPE
Crystal Lake, Illinois

Part 1

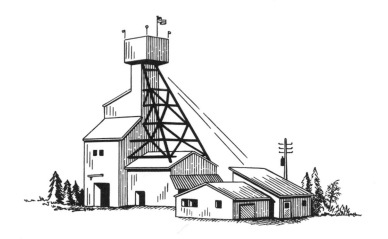

The Case for Gold

I

GOLD, MAN AND HISTORY

"History is the only true philosophy and the only true psychology."
—NAPOLEON

"The earliest and oldest and longest still has the mastery of us."
—GEORGE ELIOT

IF there is one single element around which civilizations have risen or fallen, it is gold. Since the very beginnings of organized society, untold legions of men have toiled for it, fought for it, and all too often died for it. Great nations, and even whole civilizations, have been known to wither and die for the lack of it. Like it or not, gold has occupied a central place in the affairs of man throughout his recorded history and, like it or not, it may yet decide the future of the United States, or even the ultimate destiny of Western Civilization itself.

The ancient Mediterranean kingdom of Lydia rose to its zenith with the pure gold coins of Croesus. The Persians, led first by Cyrus and then by Darius, conquered Lydia and made the Persian gold *daric* the symbol of wealth and power in the eastern Mediterranean. Alexander the Great eventually struck down Persia and seized its arduously accumulated golden hoard. Alexander built his world empire upon captured gold as well as upon his unmatched military and political genius.

A loss of gold and a chronic debasement of its currency were cited by the historians Gibbon and Mommsen as being among the chief causes of the collapse of the Roman Empire. And after the fall of Rome, the Byzantine Empire led an almost miraculous existence for 800 years, primarily because of its determination to maintain the purity and value of its gold coinage. Only after it failed to honor the world's trust in its money did the Byzantine Empire succumb to foreign conquerors.

The gold of Mexico and Peru made Spain the world's most powerful nation for two centuries, but, when the gold ran out, imperial Spain declined into impotence.

The past indeed furnishes countless examples of the power and importance of gold, but current history is, most assuredly, not without such lessons. In the early 1960's, the Soviet Union used gold laboriously extracted from its Siberian mines to make massive purchases of wheat from the United States. Russia was thus saved from famine and possible internal uprising, and the United States in turn was rescued (albeit temporarily) from a dangerous predicament concerning its balance of payments.

China also used gold to facilitate its enormous wheat purchases from Canada.[1] Gold is still the world's most acceptable international money, and without it (or gold-backed foreign exchange) Red China would have found herself either faced with mass starvation and collapse or forced to appeal to the Western powers for credit, perhaps in exchange for extensive political and military concessions.

But gold is far more than a mere index of raw commercial power. It has also been one of the most persistent and dynamic civilizing forces known to man. The history of gold is literally the history of civilization. The unhappy occurrences of greed, brutality and warfare that have accompanied the historic quest for gold have been more than offset by the enormous benefits this noble metal has conferred upon us. Gold has been, and still is, the supreme metal of the arts, the world's most effective and useful money and an industrial commodity of inestimable value.

Gold is an extremely dense, soft, bright yellow metal with a rare lustrous beauty. It is the most stable and imperishable of the metallic elements. It is immune to the effects of weather and oxygen. It does not tarnish, rust or corrode. It withstands the attack of most acids and alkalis, and survives immersion in salt or fresh water indefinitely, without alteration. It is also, without a doubt, the most easily worked and fabricated of all metals. As any artisan or jeweler will testify, working with gold is a most delightful experience.

Because of its brilliant lustre, imperishability and geologic occurrence in the natural state, gold was one of the first metals to attract the attention of man. It may quite possibly have been the first—at least we have scriptural authority for that assumption. Gold is not only the first metal, but the first element and the first specific substance mentioned in the Bible.[2]

Archaeological evidence overwhelmingly supports the conclusion that, from the earliest dawning of the ancient civilizations, gold made a profound impression on the mind of man. Long before gold came to be regarded as the ideal money, in fact long before the very concept of money was firmly established in the ancient world, gold was universally and unquestionably recognized as the ultimate form of wealth.

Natural gold, in the form of nuggets and crystals, was probably worked to make jewelry and ornaments before the use of bronze (and consequently the technique of melting) was established. The oldest known objects of gold are some beads found in excavations of the earliest Sumerian cultures of the Tigris-Euphrates valley. They are thought to date from about 4000 B.C.[3]

By the time the capital of a recognizable Sumerian civilization was firmly established at Ur (3500–2500 B.C.), a profusion of gold amulets, jewelry and small objects appears to have come into general use. Gold figurines and statuettes of frogs and apes were also common. The local god was represented by a small golden bull wearing a beard. Casting techniques were highly developed during this period.

Whenever one attempts to recall the wealth and splendor achieved by some of the ancient civilizations—Egypt, Assyria, Crete, the Etruscans, Minoans or early Greeks—one thinks almost immediately of their fabulous ornaments of gold. At the beginning of the Egyptian dynastic period (about 3200 B.C.) gold was already in general use in the Nile valley for artistic purposes. Much gold jewelry was found when the royal tombs at Abydos (1st and 2nd dynasties) were excavated, but no silver was discovered. Later, silver was referred to in Egyptian hieroglyphics as "white gold," indicating the prior use of gold. Because the Egyptians strongly adhered to the ancient custom of burying personal adornment and the most valuable personal possessions with their dead, the amount of ancient gold jewelry and treasure that has been discovered in Egypt is very large and nearly always shows the highest degree of craftsmanship and artistic ability.

The deep lode mines of Abyssinia (Ethiopia) were the most productive of ancient Egypt, but they were worked by slave miners who were cruelly mistreated. Extensive placer operations (panning, washing and sluicing) were also carried out in the rivers and streams of the empire. Egyptian gold mining and processing techniques were quite advanced, and are well illustrated and described in both wall paintings and hieroglyphics. The earliest such mural dates from 2900 B.C.

Whenever gold was available to premonetary cultures it had no rival as the ultimate symbol of wealth, power, beauty and prestige. When Cortés and the Spanish *conquistadores* looted the palaces, temples and graves of Central and South America, they also found a treasure of gold and jewels, a hoard so rich that it unbalanced the entire economy of Europe and propelled Spain abruptly into preeminence among world powers.

It is easy to understand the ancient feeling for gold as wealth. Gold is attractive to look at, difficult to obtain, and has many exciting and unusual qualities, not the least of which is its mysterious permanence. Man did not have to be taught to value gold. He has demonstrated throughout his history, in countless cultures and societies, that he has an innate sense of the worth of things. Beneath even the most savage human breast lies the soul of an artist; it is one of the more redeeming features of our species. In the author's opinion, the modern Keynesian economist who proclaims that gold is a valueless, useless fetish, not worth the effort it takes to mine and process it, understands neither the nature of gold nor the nature of man.[4]

The role of gold as the premier metal of the arts quite obviously remains intact to this day and therefore consumption of gold for jewelry and artistic uses is still an important part of the total supply-demand situation. As such, it will be examined in the course of subsequent chapters. But for now, let us sum up the cultural debt we owe to gold. The goldsmith was undoubtedly the world's first professional artist. Gold has been the wellspring of art in every major culture and civilization, no matter how completely they were isolated from one another in time or space. The lure of gold repeatedly inspired dangerous and difficult explorations and led to the settlement of new lands. In addition, the original contributions of gold seekers and goldsmiths to the technologies of mining, metallurgy and manufacture are beyond calculation. Gold was indeed a powerful civilizing force in the early societies and it continued to be so in the modern era, particularly through its role as money.

GOLD BECOMES MONEY

We could easily devote the remainder of this volume to investigating man's powerful affinity for the esthetics of gold. However, it is the use of gold as money that is the most vital concern of modern man.

The concept of money is without a doubt one of the most significant of human inventions. Without it no social organization can evolve much beyond the herd-nomad stage. Even in the savage-tribal state some sort of money seems to be a necessity. Brides must be purchased, and cattle, weapons and other articles need to be exchanged frequently, without undue complication or delay. Direct barter soon becomes awkward and unsatisfactory and its inefficiency increases as the size of the socio-economic unit grows and the needs of its members multiply. Apparently money is one of those elementary human requirements, like language, that seems to have been satisfied in every human culture at some stage in its development, and usually at quite an early stage.

Broadly speaking, money can be anything that is generally agreed upon to be an acceptable medium of exchange. Cattle, axe-heads, seashells, jars of wine or oil, baskets of grain, slaves, animal skins and similar items have all been used at one time or another as money. Occasionally, even advanced societies find themselves in situations where they are unable to obtain their usual money or where the existing monetary mechanism has completely broken down. In such cases, they too quickly revert to primitive forms of commodity money and thus are able, at least, to survive economically.

Notable and successful examples of this type of monetary retrogression are to be found in the colonial era of North America. The early colonists were often unable to obtain sufficient coined money from Europe and had to resort to such things as tobacco bundles, beaver skins, musket balls and even the native Indian wampum, or strings of colored seashell beads, to carry on their commerce. All of these items mentioned were at one time or another used as legal tender in different parts of North America. A far more recent case was that of post-World War II Germany. From the military collapse in 1945 and its accompanying monetary-financial failure to the economic and currency reforms of 1948, the common money of Germany consisted of American cigarettes, sugar and coffee.

But although common commodities can thus serve as quite useful monies, they are by no means ideal mediums of exchange, let alone reliable and imperishable stores of value. For one thing they lack universality. Tobacco may have been the most negotiable commodity in colonial Virginia and so came to be used as money, but, at the same time, beaver skins were performing the identical function in Canada. The colonists of New England, however, were then finding musket balls and Indian wampum more practical.

The only commodity that has ever acquired a truly universal acceptance as money has been gold. Silver has been its rival, off and on, for many centuries, and even copper has played an important part in the historical development of money, but, considering the overall span of history, the triumph of gold has been complete.

It must also be recognized here that gold derives its worldwide acceptance and value from the fact that it is considered by nearly all men to be one of the highest forms of *luxury*. And whereas demands for the most prosaic commodities are sooner or later exhausted by the requirements of consumption, human demands for luxuries are unlimited. Luxury therefore is the ultimate form of utility. Luxury goods are always in demand

and consequently always negotiable. Gold has not only proved to be the most desired luxury throughout the course of history but the most practical, because, in addition to providing intense esthetic and emotional satisfactions, it is exceptionally durable, portable, homogenous and readily divisible into small parts having a high unit value. It is, in short, the ideal commodity money.

Most modern economic theory, however, tends to deny the necessity of a commodity basis for money. The dominant Keynesian and monetarist viewpoints are not only openly hostile to the idea of gold (or any other commodity) as a principal money, but hold that *any link* between "money," as a deliberate creation of government, and an actual commodity, such as gold, only serves to place unnecessary and often dangerous restrictions on the government's ability to properly "manage" the national economy. Contemporary economic theory relies heavily on mathematical analysis and an implied faith in the managerial abilities of government economic and financial technicians. The Keynesians, in particular, give little credence to the phenomena of mass psychology or the evidence of history.

But this lesson of history is plain: man likes gold. He would much rather have a gold pen and pencil set than one of steel or plastic. His wife wants gold jewelry. If her spouse could afford it, she would hardly wear anything else. As far as money is concerned, nothing gives people more confidence in their economic arrangements, regardless of their race, creed or color, than having money made from gold or related to gold in some obvious way.

All previous attempts to base money solely on intangibles, such as credit or government edict or fiat, have ended in inflationary panic and disaster. People have no confidence in such money and, when people do not have confidence in the value and stability of their money, they quickly lose confidence in the government that issued it. Consequently the general employment of fiat money—that is money unrelated to any commodity —brings about political, social and economic breakdown in a very short time. It has always done so in the past *and it is doing so today*, virtually all over the world.

But whenever an overall breakdown of a monetary or financial system occurs, a return to gold always restores order, revives confidence and brings back prosperity. It has done so many times in the past and it may eventually do so again. In any case, gold is not going to fade away and become just another useful metal. The evidence of history and the forces of mass psychology overwhelmingly indicate exactly the opposite. Gold has had far too important a role in the fundamental development of civilization for it to be arbitrarily dismissed by economic theorists or political opportunists. Whatever the future of gold may be, it will be dramatic and exciting, just as its past has been.

The general adoption of metals as commodity monies became possible only upon the introduction of practical systems of weights and measures. Those very clever people the Babylonians are accorded the honor of being the first to perfect a sound system of metallic money, based on their invention of the steelyard scale, or balance, and an accompanying development of standard weights. The Babylonian system of weights included the *mina* (roughly equivalent to the pound), the *shekel*, and the grain, and its general introduction allowed small ingots of gold, silver and copper to be passed by weight as uniform mediums of exchange. The *shekel* of gold and the *half-shekel* of silver became the most common monetary units.[5] About 1925 B.C., the renowned Babylonian king Hammurabi offered his subjects the option of paying their taxes either in kind, as was traditional, or in the stamped metal ingots.[6]

The commercial domination of the Babylonian-Assyrian civilization was assured by this uniform metallic money. For the first time, the world had a monetary system that would provide not only the function of a medium of exchange, but would also serve as a reliable store of value and furnish effective units of account. This last possibility opened the way for the development of banking and allowed a much more complex system of commercial contracts and credit to function.

There is also some evidence that the ancient Chinese used small ingots of gold, about one inch square, as their standard of value and as a principal medium of exchange.[7] Small transactions were facilitated with round copper discs cast with a square hole in the center. The earliest we could date this usage would be around 1200–1000 B.C. and China was completely isolated from the Western world at that time.

The second stage in the evolution of gold into money was through the invention of coinage. This feat was accomplished by the Lydian Empire, a small, dynamic, but short-lived kingdom of Asia Minor.[8] About 700 B.C., King Gyges of Lydia established the world's first mint by having the seal of the Lydian kingdom stamped on uniform-sized lumps of a natural-gold alloy the Greeks called "electrum" (usually about 75% gold and 25% silver). Silver coins were being struck by the Ionian Greeks a few years later, most notably on the silver-rich island of Aegina.[9] Another Lydian monarch, the legendary Croesus (560–546 B.C.), struck the first coins of pure gold. These first gold coins were simply bean-shaped lumps of the metal stamped with the heads of a lion and a bull facing each other on one side and a double incuse square on the reverse. Crude as they were, they began a monetary revolution that has yet to be completed.

The wealth of Croesus was derived principally from extensive sluicing and washing operations in the Pactolus River, and it proved to be too tempting a target for the neighboring Persians. Croesus hardly had time to spend his prized gold coins before he and his kingdom were swallowed up forever by the great Persian Empire of Cyrus and Darius I.

The use of coin spread with great rapidity and within a century or two virtually the entire commerce of the civilized world (the Mediterranean Middle-East area) was being conducted with coined money. In the East, the Persian gold *daric* was the favored coin, while in the Greek city-states silver was preferred, primarily because extensive deposits of the white metal were found in the Greek territories. The Greeks, and indeed all the ancient peoples, had a high regard for coin, and by 400 B.C. the design and engraving of coins had reached an artistic level that has yet to be surpassed.

After the Macedonian conquests, Phillip II put the Greeks more or less on the gold standard with his small gold *staters*. His renowned son, Alexander the Great, completed the work of making gold coins the primary money of the world by spreading the use of the gold *stater* as far as India.

MONEY CONQUERS THE ROMANS

The Romans did not get coined money until rather late in their development and when they did they made a pretty thorough mess of it. The early Romans used a one-pound bar of copper as their basic monetary unit, and from the beginning they seemed unable to resist the temptation to cheat one another on the weights. Perhaps that is one of the reasons why they suffered so continuously from internal disorder and civil war. The original Roman copper *as*, or one-pound ingot, was gradually whittled down until it eventually weighed no more than half an ounce. Silver coins were introduced from the Greeks but, unlike the logical Greeks, the Romans simply could not, or would not, maintain their value.

I have always found it absolutely amazing that the Romans, for all their enormous contributions to civilization, and despite their capacity for intense disciplined effort, could not master the institution of money. They were forever tinkering with the coinage—reducing, diluting and debasing it, ultimately to the point of uselessness. And whenever new coinage was introduced to revive confidence, it soon embarked on the same dismal course of debasement that had destroyed its predecessors.

The Romans were, in a sense, the world's first Keynesians, because they too tried to create the ability to purchase without a corresponding exchange of values. The Greeks and the Eastern peoples, the great traders of the world, by contrast appeared to recognize the basic principle of economics, which is that, in any commercial transaction, a true exchange of values must take place or else it is mere embezzlement: one person depriving another of property or services without a just or balancing compensation. And no economy can prosper under conditions amounting to perpetual embezzlement by the monetary authorities. At any rate, the Greeks, Persians and Orientals had, overall, a surprisingly good record of maintaining the purity and value of their coinages.

When Julius Caesar came to power on the ruins of the Roman Republic, he was quick to recognize that sound money was one of the essentials if chronic civil disorder was to be ended. So, in effect, he put Rome on the gold standard by making his newly introduced gold coin, the *aureus*, the standard of value.

Caesar's monetary reform, completed by his successor Augustus, was surprisingly effective, and it gave the Romans a period of financial tranquility for about 75 years.[10] The new imperial Roman coinage was based on the old Roman *libra* or pound measure. The *aureus* initially contained 126 grains of fine gold and was minted at the rate of 40 to the *libra*. The old Republican silver *denarius* was reestablished at the rate of 84 to the *libra* and valued at 25 to the *aureus*. Small copper pieces were also provided for.

Fittingly enough it was the infamous Nero who was responsible for the first devaluation of the imperial era. He reduced the *aureus* from 40 to 45 to the *libra* and the *denarius* from 84 to 96 to the *libra*. Moderate as was this devaluation, it opened the door once again to the old evil.

During the reign of Trajan the purity as well as the weight of the coinage was reduced, although this action is somewhat hard to comprehend. Trajan was in many ways an able and intelligent administrator. He was also responsible for the conquest of Dacia (Roumania) in 105 A.D. And the occupation of Dacia brought the rich gold mines of Transylvania under Roman control.[11]

The history of Rome after Trajan bears a remarkable resemblance to our own time. Like the present, there was more gold available than ever before, yet the debasement of the monetary system continued at a sickening pace.[12] Inflation ravaged the Roman Empire at the height of its political and military power, and at the very time when the means to prevent it were at hand. It was not that the Roman authorities were exceptionally dishonest as a group, although there were certainly those among them who were, but rather that they were extraordinarily ignorant when it came to economics and finance. They profited not at all from the previous half-millenium of experience with coined money in the Mediterranean world. The Romans were accustomed to getting their way with the sword, and it did not occur to them that the cultivation of honor and trust would be much more effective.

Despite the great influx of gold from the Dacian mines, the Romans made little attempt to put their financial system in order.[13] Instead, they continued in their old ways of plundering, robbing and enslaving friend and foe alike. The rich colonies and provinces were kept under tribute, and huge ransoms of grain, wine, cattle and timber continued to be taken at the point of a sword. The Roman administrations could just as easily have bought these things with good coin and gained the unswerving loyalty of their citizens and subjects but, as it was, they all too often earned only their undying hatred and contempt. The Byzantine or Eastern half of the empire was to prove the superiority of honest commerce and sound money somewhat later, but, unfortunately for the Latins, they let their own finances languish in the hands of embezzlers, cheats and economic ignoramuses.

Under the Emperor Severus (A.D. 193–211) the depreciation had reached such a point that the *denarius* was only 50 percent silver. Caracalla (A.D. 215) officially devalued the *aureus* from 45 to 50 to the *libra*, but this was little more than an academic exercise as the imperial mints had already debased the purity of the *aureus* by as much as 40 to 50 percent. Caracalla also introduced a new silver coin, the *antoninianus,* that was intended to restore public confidence and replace the now almost worthless *denarius.*[14] The new *antoninianus* was introduced at 84 grains of fine silver, half again as heavy as the old *denarius*, but it soon embarked on the same downward spiral that had destroyed its predecessor. By the end of the rule of Gallienus (A.D. 268) the *antoninianus* had the honor, or rather the dishonor, of becoming the world's first clad coinage, as it was then being issued as an all copper coin with only a thin plating of silver.

As one might expect, gold and silver fled the boundaries of the empire at every opportunity, and what could not escape was hidden from the rapacious tax collectors. For the Roman authorities were fond of demanding that taxes be paid to Caesar in good gold or silver, while they made their own payments in debased coin, or brass or copper tokens.

In A.D. 273 the emperor Aurelian apparently grew weary of fending off the attacks of the Eastern barbarians and ordered the complete abandonment of Dacia. In the fashion of some modern generals, he may have regarded this move as a "strategic" retreat that would favorably shorten his lines of defense.[15]

Whatever the reason, the end result was that there was no longer any possibility of effectively rebuilding the crumbling financial structure of the empire. The loss of the Dacian gold was a further economic disaster.

From then on the political and military decline of the empire was as rapid as that of its monetary system. Commodities began replacing money as the chief instruments of commerce. Farms and shops were deserted and ships rotted in the harbors. Few people were willing to exchange valuable goods for the worthless Roman coinage, and the old power of the legions to compel its acceptance declined with each passing day. The soldiers themselves were angry and rebellious at being continually defrauded of their wages through the issuance of debased or worthless coin.[16] The commerce and trade of the Mediterranean area, what there was left of it, looked to the East, to Persia and the Orient, where good coin was still available.

It should be of interest to the modern Keynesian economists that, although the emperors of Rome tried frantically to "manage" their economies, they only succeeded in making matters worse. Price and wage controls and legal tender laws were passed in abundance, but it was like trying to hold back the tides. Rioting, corruption, lawlessness and a mindless mania for speculation and gambling engulfed the empire like a plague. With money so unreliable and debased, speculation in commodities became far more attractive than producing them. Thus, shortages of even the most common articles accelerated the inflationary illness.

At last, after floundering in economic and financial chaos for more than a century, the Romans got an emperor, the great Constantine, who had some grasp of economics as well as the military arts. Constantine succeeded in arresting, for a time at least, the disintegration of the empire, but only at the cost of destroying the last vestiges of freedom remaining to the population. But, in addition to Constantine's draconian rule, three historic events stand out: the ending of religious persecutions and the placing of Christianity on the same basis as the other religions of the empire, the founding of a new Eastern capital at Byzantium, and the minting of the gold *solidus* or *noumisma*, which was intended to return Rome once again to a sound gold standard.

In 324, after finally defeating his rival Licinius, who had held the Eastern or Greek provinces of the empire for eleven years, Constantine laid out the site for a new capital on the ruins of the ancient Greek city of Byzantium. He called it Constantinople and thought he was only establishing a new headquarters from which he could more effectively control the Eastern territories. In reality, he was founding a whole new nation that would survive the Western Roman Empire by a thousand years. He also hoped his new gold coin would help rebuild the shattered economy of the Western Empire, but it could not; there was no longer enough gold left in the Western provinces to mint gold coin in sufficient quantities. Nonetheless, Constantine's *solidus,* in the hands of the Byzantine Greeks, was to rule the commerce of the world for the next 800 years.

GOLD TRIUMPHS IN THE EAST

The so-called Byzantine Empire was a curious historical phenomenon.[17] Roman by law and tradition, but Greek in language and customs, it rose like a phoenix in the East just as the Latin Roman Empire was being swept away forever in the West. But there was nothing odd about the Byzantine regard for sound money. The *solidus* introduced by Constantine became the basic monetary unit of the Byzantine Empire. Perhaps in an attempt to recapture something of the Eastern tradition of sound money, Constantine had based his new gold coin on the Greek silver *drachma* of the Hellenic period, giving the *solidus* the same weight, 66 grains, but minting it in gold instead of silver.[18]

The *solidus* was immensely popular in Byzantium and under the Greek name of *bezant* was minted for the next 800 years without alteration. It remains, perhaps, the most remarkable achievement in the history of money. Gold *bezants* circulated freely throughout the world during this period, bringing much trade and great wealth to the Byzantine Empire. And it is worth noting that throughout these eight centuries there was never any "shortage" of gold in the Byzantine treasury. The producers and owners of bullion were always willing to exchange it for the prized *bezants*.

Anyone who counterfeited, clipped, filed or otherwise debased a *bezant* was apt to pay for it with his head. At the very least, one of his hands was cut off. For the peoples of the Levant, of the East and of the Orient have a depth of feeling for gold money that persists to this day and is virtually incomprehensible to most of the ivory-tower economic dreamers of the West. The Easterners know firsthand of the security afforded by the possession of this strange fascinating metal. Gold is virtually indestructible, but the boasts and promises of emperors, kings and populist politicians alike are all too often written on the wind. At any rate, it is a fact that as long as the Byzantine Empire unfailingly maintained the purity and value of the *bezant* it never succumbed to a foreign invader.

It is generally acknowledged, even among noneconomic historians, that the long survival of the Byzantine Empire, surrounded though it was by hostile forces, was primarily due to its greatly superior economic organization, an organization made possible mainly because of the reliability and soundness of the financial structure underlaying it.

During the reign of Alexius Comnenus (1081–1118), however, the eight centuries of trust and confidence were irreparably damaged. Alexius devalued the *bezant* in order to help pay off his private debts. Modest though this first devaluation was, it opened a Pandora's box of evils. The Byzantine Empire was never the same thereafter. Further devaluations and other official dishonesties followed with increasing frequency and with them came military impotence and political and economic chaos. For the next 250 years the Byzantine Empire managed a precarious existence, but it became a shadow of its former wealth and splendor. The fall of the Byzantine Empire parallels the collapse of its Western predecessor a thousand years earlier. By the time the Vandals sacked Rome, there was hardly a trace of a viable commercial economy left. The same could be said of the Byzantine Empire when Constantinople fell to the Ottoman Turks in 1453.

Another outstanding example of the successful employment of standard gold coin as the primary money occurred in the great Arab empire founded by Mohammed. This empire, which coexisted (in time at least) with the Byzantine state, eventually extended from Baghdad to Barcelona, and at its height enjoyed a civilization that rivaled that of its Byzantine neighbor and even the Rome of Augustus. The coin of the Arab empire was the gold *dinar,* which was minted at approximately the same weight as the *bezant.* The imperial Arabs were great admirers of classic Greek culture and philosophy, and consequently had readily adopted the Greek attitude toward sound money and honest commerce. Because the *dinar* was almost identical in value to the *bezant,* the two coins could circulate side by side and were frequently exchanged.

The *dinar* was established about 692 by the great Caliph Abd-el-Malik at 65 grains, .979 fine, and it was thereafter issued as the standard coin from all mints of the Arab empire. It circulated for about 450 years without alteration, and during that time the Saracen Arab civilization flourished with an astounding brilliance, while Europe languished in darkness, ignorance and despair. Ultimately the Arab civilization also collapsed (and with almost the same rapidity as it had been formed), but its demise was due largely to religious quarrels and factions rather than to any economic or financial delinquency.

These historic examples are cited and the general history of gold is briefly reviewed in *Part One* of this book in order to refute the widely accepted, but highly misleading, Keynesian economic doctrines regarding gold. It is constantly proclaimed by Keynesian-oriented economists, bankers and monetary officials that faith in gold is "barbaric," but quite the opposite is indicated by history. The record of history reveals that the maximum use of gold as standard money occurs during peak eras of civilization rather than in the formative years or during periods of decline and decadence. Thus, the use of gold appears to be a reliable index of prosperity and civilization, but hardly one of barbarism. In fact, it is almost a law of history that the more widespread the use of gold, and most particularly the more extensive the use of gold as money, the greater the degree of social, economic and political stability, and the more pronounced the cultural advancement of the society concerned.

Another pervasive fallacy of neo-Keynesian economics is

that the use and importance of gold as money has been gradually declining throughout the course of history. This is also a gross distortion of fact, because a truly universal and effective international gold standard did not become a reality until the beginning of the twentieth century, and then only as the result of 4,000 years of monetary evolution! Furthermore, there is more gold *per capita* now than at any other period of recorded time, and the total monetary holdings of governments and private individuals continue to establish new records.

But despite the obviousness of both the historical record and day-to-day events, we continue to be bombarded with the sophistries and deceptions of those who, for their own reasons, would indeed like to see their imaginary death-of-gold-wish become a reality. The gold-oriented investor must, therefore, attain a degree of sophistication regarding the role of gold in economics and finance, in order to see through the deluge of misleading propaganda put forth by powerful antigold interests. A grasp of the historical development of gold-based money, as well as of its present status, will help give the investor that sophistication.

Therefore, we must next turn to Europe, which began to awaken, after its long hibernation, just as the Arab and Byzantine empires were slipping into oblivion.

Notes:

CHAPTER I

1. The 1970 sale of some 98 million bushels, valued at $160 million, was the largest single wheat contract in Canada's history up to that time. From 1963 to 1971, Canada sold more than 500 million bushels of wheat to China. The terms of the 1970 sale were similar to those of previous transactions: 25 percent in cash as each vessel is loaded and the balance, also in cash, in 18 months, with interest. And "cash" in international monetary parlance meant gold or gold-backed currencies. (Contract details reported in *Wall Street Journal,* October 28, 1970.)

2. See Genesis 2:10–12.

3. Sheldon Cheney, *A World History of Art* (New York: Viking, 1947), p. 38.

4. It must be recognized of course that what the Keynesians are actually objecting to is the gold standard or the use of gold as money. However, the nature and tone of their attacks are sometimes so general and so excessive that one wonders if they do not have some deep-seated emotional aversion to the metal itself.

5. The *shekel* eventually evolved into a rather famous Hebrew coin, but at the time of the Babylonian ascendancy it was just a specific weight of metal.

6. It was so stated in the famous *Code of Hammurabi,* one of the world's oldest known compilations of civil and criminal law.

7. From Chinese documents written several centuries after the fact.

8. Ancient Lydia was located in what is now south-central Turkey.

9. Most numismatic scholars consider only metallic money entirely struck or stamped from dies to be coin. There were circular bits of cast copper, such as the Assyrian "tree money," in use before 700 B.C., but these are not generally regarded as true coinage.

10. Caesar's *aureus* did not do as well as the U.S. gold dollar, the British gold pound of 1816 or the French gold franc of Napoleon

Bonaparte, each of which survived about 100 years before encountering its first official devaluation.

11.   Some of the mines of Transylvania are still producing gold today.

12.   Before the conquest of Dacia the Romans obtained the bulk of their gold from Spain, Dalmatia and the Middle-Eastern provinces.

13.   Much as the United States ignored the opportunity to return to the full gold standard in the early postwar years, an opportunity made possible by the tremendous influx of gold to Fort Knox from 1935 to 1949.

14.   The *denarius* had sunk so low by the time of Caracalla that it was no more than a copper penny, without any silver content at all.

15.   One can hardly criticize Aurelian for this action however, because on the whole he was one of the ablest and most energetic of Roman commanders. In a series of brilliant campaigns he forced the return of Spain, Gaul and Britain to the empire. At the same time, except for Dacia, he held off the barbarians in the East. But his attempts to reorganize the monetary system were generally ineffective.

16.   It eventually became the Roman custom to pay the salaries and wages of state officials and soldiers in rations or in kind, in order to maintain their loyalty.

17.   The term "Byzantine Empire" was invented primarily for the convenience of historians. Theoretically, the Greek provinces remained the Eastern Roman Empire. The emperors and citizens of the Byzantine state continued to regard themselves as Romans. But in reality their culture and development were vastly different from those of the Latin or European part of the Empire, and they survived as a separate national identity long after the fall of Rome itself.

18.   Despite the monetary debacle of the West, Greek silver *drachmas* of original purity were still being minted occasionally for local use at Antioch and Alexandria.

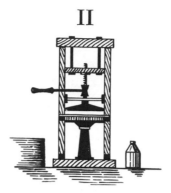

II

THE WESTERN EXPERIENCE: GOLD, PAPER MONEY AND THE GOLD STANDARD

"Money has little value to its possessors unless it also has value to others."
—LELAND STANFORD

THE final destruction of Greco-Roman civilization left Western Europe in a state of social, political, cultural and economic anarchy for the better part of six centuries. And although modern scholars no longer believe these "Dark Ages" were quite as bleak as was formerly thought, they were grim enough to reduce most of society to a primitive subsistence economy. Europe was totally fragmented, and nearly all traces of an orderly or uniform monetary system had been lost since the latter days of the Roman Empire. Barbarian chiefs, feudal lords and early medieval princes sometimes made use of *bezants* or Arab *dinars* for the infrequent financial arrangements of the time. Local coinages, although still fairly numerous, were generally limited to crude copper pieces of uncertain value.

But in the ferment of the Dark Ages and the medieval period are the roots of what we now call Western civilization. By the eleventh century, economic and social conditions had become stable enough so that the revival of the city as a center for trade and commerce could begin. Among the first to acquire importance were the city-states of Northern Italy: Venice, Genoa, Pisa and Florence.

In 1252, the Republic of Florence began minting the first significant gold coinage in Europe since Caesar's *aureus*. The Florentines made this new coin, the *"fiorino d'oro,"* or gold *florin,* their basic monetary medium, thus placing themselves on a *de facto* gold standard.* Twenty-eight years later, the Republic of Venice followed suit by minting its gold *ducat* to the same weight and value as the *florin.* By the end of the century, nearly all other cities in northern Italy, and several beyond the Alps, were issuing gold coins in *florin/ducat* denominations.[1]

The availability of a reliable gold coinage brought a period of great commercial success and prosperity to the Italian city-states and eventually to most of Western Europe. Consequently, gold money was instrumental in the coming of the Renaissance. Culture flourishes under conditions of wealth, not of poverty, and the power of gold once again propelled men forward to a higher civilization.[2]

During the fourteenth century, a monetary-commercial economy was virtually reestablished throughout Europe. Several centuries still had to pass before the debilitating remnants of feudalism and medievalism were completely cast off but, in essence, the pattern of our modern commercial-industrial civilization was irrevocably established at this time. The general return of money to Europe was, of course, a welcome and beneficial development, but it hardly meant that henceforth all would be well.

In many ways it is unfortunate that Western civilization has derived more from the Latin tradition than from the Greek. This is particularly true in the realm of money and finance, for the revival of a monetary economy in Europe was accompanied by a return of the old evils of currency debasement and inflation. In addition, as the pace of commerce advanced well beyond the limits established by the ancient kingdoms, the monetary structure encountered a variety of difficulties un-

---

*The florin was never made the official monetary unit of Florence.

known even to the Romans, although it might well be said that these new problems stemmed from a similar inability to understand, philosophically, the institution of money.

From the minting of the *florin* to the present day, our Western monetary and financial system, which is now the world financial system, has been plagued by six major deficiencies:

1. Chronic currency debasement and monetary inflation.
2. Bimetallism: the attempt to make both gold- and silver-standard money at the same time.
3. Banking insolvency: the issuing of banknote currency in excess of the ability to redeem it.
4. Unwarranted and unwise interference, by governments, in the monetary-financial system for political and military considerations.
5. The excessive use of bank credit as money.
6. The general employment of noncommodity, nonredeemable government fiat money and money substitutes.

There is no need to examine in further detail the ruinous practice of coin debasement, except to note that it continued to be a major problem in Europe until well into the seventeenth century. The fragmented political condition of the Continent during this period allowed a horde of petty princes and dukes to rule and issue local coinages of their own.

The right to clip, file and debase these coinages, and arbitrarily to alter the monetary unit itself, was considered to be an inalienable privilege of the sovereign. The *seigniorage* or profit from such official dishonesties was often a major source of revenue for the crown.

So pervasive was this vice that even the powerful kings of England, France and Spain frequently succumbed to it. At times it seemed that all Europe was going down the same path and would therefore eventually descend into the same financial ruin that had destroyed the Romans. It was only the discovery and exploitation of the Americas that brought about a new opportunity for Europe to return to the economic salvation of sound money.

But although Europe was tremendously revived and stimulated by the seemingly limitless wealth of gold and silver found in the Americas, the unfortunate practices and follies of the past were never really corrected. They remain a hereditary disease of the Western economic body that continues to take its toll to this day, and which may yet destroy us if we do not take the classical medicine. A return to a reliable and immutable gold standard restored and preserved the Eastern half of the collapsing Roman Empire for a thousand years. It may yet do the same for our desperately ill Western society—or at least for part of it.

It has been said that when Columbus stepped ashore on the island of Hispaniola his first words were to ask the frightened Indians for gold. His successors (much to the sorrow of the natives) later found it elsewhere in great quantities, and thus began an economic revolution that was to lead eventually to our present dilemma. In the premodern era, the perpetual contest had been between sound (gold and silver) commodity money and debased commodity money. But, ironically, by the time the first treasure-laden galleys were arriving in Spain, the primary struggle was already beginning to evolve into one between the ideal commodity money (gold) and noncommodity money substitutes: banknotes, bank credit and government promises. The invention of paper money, the rise of commercial banking and the insatiable demands of the new dynastic states for complete control over the power of money combined to challenge the leadership of gold even before it could be securely reestablished.[3]

BIMETALLISM AND THE RATIO PROBLEM
In the historic contest for monetary leadership, gold has often been unfairly handicapped by the so-called "ratio problem." Ever since the rise of the West began with the minting of the *florin* in 1252, the monetary authorities of virtually every nation have tried at one time or other to establish a satisfactory ratio between the values of gold and silver, so that both types of coins could circulate side by side as *equal* partners in the monetary system. The purpose of bimetallism is of course to provide more units of money for general circulation, and laudable though this intention appears, it nearly always fails in practice.

Bimetallism defeats one of the basic criteria for a reliable money system, which is to have one single commodity (and gold has historically proven to be the most suitable commodity) established as the standard by which all other commodities and services may be measured and valued. You fix the monetary value of a specific weight of gold and let everything else fluctuate in relation to it. This is the essence of the gold standard. An *international gold standard* occurs when a number of nations agree to define their monetary unit, whether it be the dollar, pound, franc, or mark, etc., in terms of a specific weight and purity of gold, thus making these currencies interchangeable.

Bimetallism prevents the operation of a true system of standard money, except in terms of a *de facto* standard. Such a standard comes into being when the real value of one metal falls sufficiently below the other, regardless of the officially stated price, so that the obviously higher-priced coin (in terms of actual intrinsic value) becomes the commonly accepted standard money. The United States for example, although legally on a bimetallic standard from 1837 to 1900, operated for all practical purposes on a *de facto* gold standard. The real value of silver fell well below its official price during much of that era.

Despite the rather obvious evidence that bimetallism works neither in theory nor in practice, monetary technicians spent some 650 years after the introduction of the *florin* in futile and often destructive attempts to make it effective. Somehow, it is difficult to understand how so many people have been deluded for so long into believing it was possible to establish a fixed ratio between two commodities of widely varying *availability*. No matter how carefully one would attempt to calculate a ratio, any new ore discovery or unexpected industrial or commercial demand for one metal or the other would immediately upset the balance and Gresham's Law would go into effect, and the coin with the highest real value would be hoarded or melted at the expense of the other.[4]

It is quite possible, however, to have a workable *silver* standard, and this type of standard has been used by China, India, Mexico and, off and on, by several European countries. Under a true silver standard, the price of gold is allowed to "float" against a monetary unit denominated only in terms of a fixed weight of silver. But you cannot have a fixed official price for both metals without serious trouble—as the U.S. Treasury was still finding out as late as 1965.[5] Nevertheless, silver can be used effectively under a gold standard, but it must be kept in a subsidiary role. To do this, the intrinsic value of silver coin must be set low enough so that it cannot reasonably be expected eventually to exceed its face value.

Silver has never had the monetary prestige accorded to gold. It has never gained equivalent international recognition as a standard money. Its reputation is that of a "poor man's money," more useful in China and India than anywhere else. For most of its modern existence as money, the price of silver had to be artificially supported by Western governments, attempting (unsuccessfully) to perpetuate bimetallic standards. Therefore I do not recommend the purchase of either silver bullion or silver shares *as a hedge against monetary upheaval.* Silver appears to me to have very little future as a monetary metal. President Roosevelt's abysmally unsuccessful attempts to revive a major role for silver in the 1930's were, I believe, the last gasp of the ancient and troublesome philosophy of bimetallism.

When silver lost its final monetary function as a subsidiary coinage, in 1965, it became solely an industrial commodity. In fact, one might argue that subsidiary coinage use itself was little more than just another industrial outlet for the metal. In any case, it seems to the author that the future of silver, as an investment, rests completely on industrial and commercial supply-demand factors. Silver would probably be a satisfactory hedge against runaway inflation, although I would hardly consider it to be the best holding under such conditions, but it is also my belief that today's investor needs insurance against currency devaluations and economic depressions. I do not feel that silver stocks or silver bullion offers significant protection against the latter two situations.

Any idea that the ancient theories about a fixed ratio between the price of silver and the price of gold might still become operable is, to say the least, unrealistic. One cannot assume that a rise in the price of gold, brought about by monetary and financial conditions, will somehow affect the price of an industrial commodity like silver, any more than it would the price of copper. In the early 1930's, the price of gold and the price of gold-mining stocks soared in anticipation of the devaluations that were to come in 1934, but the price of silver dropped like a stone on the world markets.

Bimetallism has been a colossal nuisance throughout the centuries of striving for a trustworthy monetary system.[6] But the trouble it has caused, serious though it may have appeared at times, has been trivial when compared to the damage wrought by unsecured paper money.

PAPER MONEY AND CREDIT

The era of gold production that followed the discovery of the Americas was the greatest the world had witnessed to that time. During the period from 1492 to 1600, total world production of gold exceeded 23 million ounces, and about half this amount came from the mines of Mexico, Colombia and Peru. The overall rise in the production of silver was equally impressive. Yet, in the words of Adam Smith, no complaint was more common than that of a scarcity of money.

Again there is a remarkable parallel to our own time, for despite the record gold production of the past decade we also hear the constant laments about the "shortage of gold," the "lack of liquidity" and a general scarcity of money. No matter how many trillions of paper banknotes, bonds, bills, SDR's or other monetizations of debt we put into circulation, there is never enough "money." There is never enough "purchasing power" or "investment capital" or "mortgage funds." We have not yet learned what has been demonstrated over and over in the course of history, that increasing the number of monetary units cannot, by itself, increase the liquid wealth of the nation (or the world for that matter). The only true *liquid* wealth or money is gold, and our present difficulties will not be overcome until that elementary fact is once again universally recognized.

Nevertheless, the popular cry has always been for more and ever more "money." For centuries, man has used every ingenuity in vain attempts to satisfy this understandable but essentially irrational demand. But you cannot give what you do not have. You cannot possibly distribute more wealth than you possess. You may borrow what you do not have, or borrow what you need in advance, but only to the extent that you can reasonably expect to recover from the future sufficient wealth eventually to repay the debt. In any case, you cannot loan or borrow *permanently* what you do not have and do not ever expect to acquire, any more than you can give away what is not possessed. Yet our modern debt-based economy attempts to function on just such a system.

The devices employed to produce more monetary units and thus create the illusion of an increase in wealth have already been outlined. The first of these, and the most time-honored, that of diluting the coinage by debasing its weight and purity, is so obvious a fraud that it is recognized by even the most unsophisticated, thus bringing rapid ruin to the economy dependent on such coinage.

Devaluation, that is reducing by law the amount of precious metal that constitutes a theoretically established monetary unit or unit of account (such as the dollar, the franc, the pound, etc.) is merely a more sophisticated and modern version of the ancient fraud of monetary debasement. It is not quite as obvious as directly degrading intrinsic-value coinage, but the end result is a similar loss of confidence and of value in the circulating currency.

The second of these devices, bimetallism, although inefficient and often disruptive, is at least an honest attempt to increase the supply of money. Perhaps this is why it persisted for so long, despite the rather obvious impossibility of ever finding a successful ratio, and in spite of the overwhelming psychological preference for gold.

The third device, the use of banknote currency, is also an honorable method of giving wider circulation to money, providing it is kept within reasonable bounds. But, more often than not, the printing press, as a provider of money, has proved to be more a tyrannical master than an efficient slave.

True paper money did not make its appearance in Europe until early in the seventeenth century, although, long before that time, promissory notes, redeemable in coin or bullion, had been issued on leather, parchment and even paper.[7] The use of such notes, however, was limited to periods of emergency, such as war or siege, when it was temporarily impossible to obtain sufficient coin. The first widely circulated paper money appears to have been the goldsmith's receipt. In the early part of the seventeenth century, merchants and gentlemen of wealth acquired the habit of depositing their coin and plate with local goldsmiths, who usually had safe storage facilities for precious metals. The receipts obtained from these deposits were often widely circulated and accepted as payment for goods, services and obligations.

The goldsmith's receipts, being actual warehouse certificates for gold or silver on deposit, were actually no different than the gold-certificate or silver-certificate currency issued by the U.S. Government in the nineteenth and twentieth centuries. Such money is the ideal currency, in that it combines the greater general utility of paper money with the proven virtues of pure commodity money. The only weakness of this type of paper currency is that it depends entirely on the integrity and honesty of the person or authority issuing it. In the case of the goldsmiths, the temptation to issue (for their own profit) receipts for which there was no corresponding deposit of specie, or to issue more than one receipt for the same deposit, was sometimes more than the flesh could bear. As for the U.S. Government, I do not know of any time when gold-certificate currency was issued in excess of gold on deposit. This was small comfort, however, when all such notes outstanding were repudiated in 1933.[8]

Charles II of England issued paper "exchequer orders" beginning in 1665, which were made full legal tender by Parliament. These orders, however, could only be transferred by endorsement and were redeemable only after a specified date of maturity. Thus they were not true paper money of unlimited circulation, but neither were they merely bank checks, because they were made legal tender. The bank draft itself, or "bill of exchange" for the payment of a sum of money at a distant point to its bearer, was known to the Assyrians as early as the ninth century B.C., although of course they wrote them on clay tablets instead of on paper. Many of the mechanisms of modern banking, the use of checks, drafts, money orders, promissory notes, and the granting of credit, are almost as old as metallic money itself.

For some time after the return of a money economy to Europe, the lust for liquid wealth, especially on the part of the rulers and monarchs, was so great that it could not be satisfied by the time-hallowed practice of filing, sweating or clipping the coinage. Furthermore, the ungrateful peasants were prone to hide the good coinage and circulate only the bad, which had already been thoroughly debased. Taxes were usually oppressive to the point of no further return, so there remained only the more direct interventions in the economy. The most oppressive of these measures was the forced loan. The king's inspectors visited every house to collect the appointed sums, and history suggests that their methods were seldom gentle. And as might be expected, history also records that these "loans" were invariably defaulted.

After having bled their subjects to the point where it was impossible to extract another copper, many prominent rulers turned next to the Italian bankers. The results of these ventures were all too frequently of little benefit to the banking system. Edward III of England defaulted on a loan of 1,355,000 gold *florins* due the Peruzzi and Bardi firm in 1339. The King of Sicily failed to repay a loan of 200,000 *florins,* and Phillip II of Spain repudiated all his debts on no less than three separate occasions.

Such financial anarchy brought both the banking and monetary systems of Europe to virtual ruin only three centuries after the commercial renaissance brought about by the introduction of the *florin* had begun. In 1584, the great Venetian banking house of Pisani and Tiepolo failed, owing their depositors 500,-000 *ducats,* an enormous amount of money for the time. In 1596, the largest bank in Genoa collapsed. Numerous smaller banks also failed or were in trouble all over northern Italy. In times that were in many ways similar to our own banking crisis of the 1930's, the Venetian Senate resolved to establish a state bank to take over the deposit business formerly conducted by the private banking houses.

The new state bank, the *Banco della Piazza del Rialto,* was to be operated strictly as a safe-deposit operation. The bank was not to make loans or extend credit, but merely to keep the money of its depositors in safety, for a fee, and to pay it out and transfer it on demand. As Venice was one of the leading ports in Europe, the bank soon became the most important commercial institution in the Republic. Foreign coinage was accepted and discounted, and bills of exchange and drafts were issued.

The *Banco della Piazza* prospered until 1619. But in that year the Venetian Government, embarrassed for funds, hit upon the idea of paying off an overdue contract with bank credit. To do this, they created another bank, the *Banco del Giro,* and started it off with a state credit (i.e., a claim upon the government) entered on its books as an asset, without any corresponding deposit of specie.[9] Thus the bank could issue drafts against this credit, and these drafts could be deposited in other banks or otherwise used as money. From that time on, the concept of banking as strictly a warehouse and deposit institution, which could not loan what it did not possess, began to disappear.[10] Henceforth, with increasing frequency, and often with the encouragement and collusion of governments, banks embarked on the dubious practices of manufacturing fiat credit and monetizing debt. And paper money is, unhappily, also the perfect medium for exploiting these little-understood phenomena.

By 1718, the theory and practice of credit creation had reached such an advanced state that a Scottish adventurer named John Law managed to get control of the entire banking system of France. He then flooded the country with unsecured paper money and set off one of the classic hyperinflations of economic history.[11]

Law's theories and practices have a curiously modern ring. By the very act of issuing his paper banknote currency (in unlimited quantities), he had promised to make the country rich. A state, he said, must have a currency that could be increased in proportion to the growth of its people and its commerce. What was needed, he insisted, was simply a greater availability of money and credit, and further, that no modern nation should suffer from the unfair and obsolete restrictions imposed by the use of metallic money.

Law's banking and currency manipulations only resulted in a wild and uncontrollable inflationary boom, followed by a colossal bust. The prestige of the French monarchy, which had

enthusiastically supported Law's delusions, never really recovered from this debacle. Some of the seeds of the French Revolution were thus planted by this strange stateless gambler, John
Law, destined to die a penniless outcast in Venice in 1729.

In time, however, the general economy of France did recover,
as human enterprises always do, but only after a return to the
exclusive use of metallic currency. Time also tends to erase
memories and, by 1790, the new Revolutionary government of
France was led to repeat the financial insanity of Law and the
old monarchy on an even grander scale. But, unlike John Law's
unsecured bank note currency, the new Revolutionary paper
money was to be strictly a government issue, supposedly based
on the value of the lands and properties recently confiscated
from the Church. However, very much like Law's currency, it
was to bear absolutely no binding relation to metallic money or
specie. The results were predictable, only this time the catastrophe was so complete that it took a Napoleon to rescue France
from itself.

From 1790 to 1797, some 40,000 million francs worth of paper
assignats (literally, land mortgage notes) were put into circulation, along with 2,600 million francs in *mandats* (which were
supposed to replace the depreciated *assignats!*). The French
economy was totally prostrated by this experience, and once
again man was taught the painful lesson that a nation cannot
print its way to prosperity. At the height of the *assignat* inflation, one gold franc was worth 600 francs in paper.[12]

THE RISE OF THE GOLD STANDARD

Napoleon Bonaparte, like all dictators, came to power following a period of massive political, social and financial anarchy.[13]
His rule was accepted because he restored order and discipline
to a democratic society that had proved incapable of controlling or disciplining itself. Nowhere is the presence or lack of a
voluntary internal self-control more evident in a nation than in
the way it manages its monetary system. The French Revolution had gone mad in its latter days, and nowhere was this
madness more obvious than in the delusion that the printing
and issuing of paper money in unlimited amounts would bring
wealth and prosperity to all.

As soon as he had restored the precarious military situation then prevailing in France and had consolidated his leadership beyond challenge, Napoleon turned his attention to the desperate financial plight of the country. Although advised to issue some new form of paper money himself, Napoleon absolutely refused. "Never", he replied, "I will pay cash (gold and silver) or nothing." He never broke this promise, not even in the emergency of the Hundred Days.

In 1803, Napoleon restored France to a full specie basis, which was to be preserved by all succeeding French governments until 1914, although it began as a bimetallic standard. The basic monetary unit, the franc, was established as a silver coin of 5 grams, .900 (90 percent) fine or pure. But gold coins of 20 and 40 francs were also authorized, thus providing for a "defined" gold franc of .32258 grams, .900 fine.[14] It was this defined gold franc that remained inviolable until 1914; the intrinsic value of silver coins was altered several times in later years to put France on a *de facto* gold standard.

Two questions may be asked here. One: Why didn't Napoleon arrange for a full gold standard in the first place? And, two: Where did all the gold and silver come from to enable France to resume a full metallic monetary system after both the John Law and *assignat* inflations? The answer to the first question is that Napoleon was only following the tradition of bimetallism that had dominated Europe since the minting of the *florin* and the general revival of coinage as money. Furthermore, when we consider that Napoleon at last gave France a system of dependable and honest metallic currency, after four or five centuries of royal profligacies, debasements and embezzlements, not to mention two of the most destructive paper-money inflations in history, that is achievement enough.

As to where the gold and silver came from, one must remember that these metals, and particularly gold, are virtually indestructible. Precious metals are not destroyed during periods of great political, social or economic unrest; they are merely put into hiding. Precious metals are the only practical (and concealable) forms of liquid wealth, and one does not unnecessarily expose one's liquid assets when the risks of theft or official confiscation are high. Gold is thus said to be the world's greatest coward: it always flies from danger and hides. The hoarding of gold becomes very intense during times of great trouble. That is why the prices of gold *and gold mining stocks* soar at the slightest hint of genuine political, economic or military difficulty. However, when the trouble passes, the hidden gold readily comes forth to resume its role as the guarantor of honest commerce.

In Napoleon's case, it must also be admitted that he did not hesitate to "liberate" much treasure from the vaults and palaces of his defeated opponents. But in spite of this, and despite all the battles and bloodshed caused by this astounding man, despite Spain, the terrible winter in Russia, and Waterloo, one can only say in the end that he found France in ruins and left it a modern nation.[15]

The world's first true gold standard, like so many other notable social and economic achievements of modern times, was primarily a British invention. As early as 1666, the principle of "free coinage" had become law in Britain, thus taking the right of coinage from the monarch or government and placing it where it belongs, in the hands of the people. Under the rule of free coinage, the state exercises no more than supervision over the minting process. Private citizens may, at their own volition, bring the bullion they have mined or otherwise acquired to state-operated mints and receive for it in exchange, coinage of equal intrinsic value in the metal presented, less a small *seigniorage* or minting charge.

Consequently, England had solved the first problem, that of assuring a pure and dependable metallic currency, well in advance of the Continental nations. In 1693, the Bank of England was established, and although hardly a perfect institution, it was good enough eventually to serve as a model for the central banks of virtually all modern nations. However, it should also be noted that the creation of a central bank of issue and discount did not solve the problems brought about by the use of bank credit as money. There were general bank failures and crises due to the overextension of bank credit and bank note currency in 1695, 1720, 1745, 1793, 1797 and 1825. It was not until 1844 that a banking act was passed that seriously attempted to curb unsound banking practices and halt the flagrant misuse of bank note currency.

In 1816, the victorious conclusion of the Napoleonic Wars seemed a propitious moment for Great Britain to inaugurate a full gold standard. In that year, the British pound sterling (which had originated as a pound weight of silver) was made equal by law to the new standard gold coin of the realm, the *sovereign,* containing .2354 of an ounce of fine gold. Thereafter, all British money, whether coin or banknote, could be redeemed in gold at any time in amounts as small as one-half pound (the smallest gold coin authorized was the *half-sovereign*). Larger amounts could also be redeemed on demand in bullion as well as coin, at the rate of .2354 ounces of gold per pound sterling. Thus, all British money was made, theoretically, as good as gold. I say theoretically, because on several occasions between 1816 and 1914 the Bank of England was forced to suspend redemptions, temporarily, due to war or economic crisis. Nevertheless, it was a historic step forward and did much to reinforce London's position as the banking and trading center of the world.

On the Continent, the bimetallic tradition lingered on, although one by one the European countries unceremoniously drifted over to *de facto* gold standards, while legally remaining bimetallic. The main resistance to the gold standard came from some of the big banking and trading houses who, for centuries, had profited by "arbitrage" operations, that is by buying and selling one metal or coin against the other, as the interminable fluctuations in the real versus official ratios offered opportunity.

Among the forces irrevocably thrusting the world toward an international gold standard were the opening of great new goldfields both in California and Australia during the 1850's. The effect of this new supply of gold on the world's markets was to distort severely the established ratios, causing gold to depreciate in relation to silver and tending to force silver out of circulation and into hoarding. Subsequent major discoveries of silver had the opposite effect. Clearly the time had come when bimetallic standards could no longer function at all.

However, the solution to the problem of bimetallism was not achieved, as it should have been, in the wise counsels of statesmen and financial experts, but by the repeating rifles and

Krupp cannon of the Prussian Army. Bismarck's Prussia, in the brief but bloody Franco-Prussian War of 1870, invaded and decisively defeated the incompetent France of Emperor Louis Napoleon.[16] At the treaty of Frankfurt, in 1871, the victorious Prussians and their Germanic allies levied an idemnity of five billion gold francs* upon the helpless French, and then went on to Versailles to unite formally as a new German Empire.

With all that French gold in its pocket, the German Empire could well afford to proclaim, as one of its first official acts, its adherence to a full and unrestricted gold standard. The mark, which also had originated centuries before as a weight of silver, was defined as 5.532 grains of fine gold. From then on there was no serious resistance to the complete acceptance of gold as the standard international money. In 1872, the Scandinavian countries followed the lead of Germany. By 1877, the Netherlands had suspended the free coinage of silver. In 1876, France and Belgium ended free silver coinage as well, and, in 1878, the rest of the Latin Monetary Union, Italy, Switzerland, Roumania and Greece did likewise. Austria-Hungary and Russia followed suit in 1879. Thus, all Europe at last abandoned silver, which had enjoyed at least official equality with gold since the beginning of metallic money.[17]

But if the age-old problem of the ratio was finally solved, the problems arising from the growing dependence on paper currency and bank credit for internal use, despite the disasters they had already caused, were only beginning. Nevertheless, new discoveries of gold in South Africa in 1886 and in Alaska and the Canadian Yukon in 1896, inaugurated an era of gold production that was to dwarf all previous such epochs in world history. More gold was to be taken from the earth and processed into coins and monetary bullion after 1886 than had existed in all prior historic time. It seemed as though nature herself was giving unqualified approval to the advent of a new golden age.

Even the United States, which had already been the world's major producer of gold for half a century, elected formally to adopt the gold standard, by Act of Congress, in 1900. Of the

*About one billion dollars (at 1871 exchange rates).

major nations, only China and Mexico remained on silver, and Mexico opted for gold in 1905.

ACHIEVEMENT AND DISASTER

The beginning of the twentieth century was welcomed with sincere enthusiasm by the peoples of the Western world. And while poverty and other social ills had not yet been completely banished, there was little doubt in the minds of most intelligent men that a time would inevitably come when they would be. Surely no one suspected that this new century would bring the greatest trials to mankind since the collapse of the Roman world, and that these trials and challenges would threaten the very survival of Western civilization itself.

But beneath the dynamic and peaceful exterior of the commerical world, two poisonous evils were festering. The first of these was militarism. France still thirsted to revenge herself on Germany for the humiliation of 1870. The Germans, in turn, armed themselves in paranoid fear of a revived France and a power-hungry Russia. The government of Austria-Hungary feared and mistrusted just about everyone, and England watched the increasing naval power of imperial Germany with growing apprehension.

The second of these evils was a constant financial manipulation. Despite the triumph of the gold standard, little was done to correct the unsound banking and financial practices that had begun when the *Banco del Giro* fictitiously manufactured a deposit credit for the bankrupt Venetian government. In fact, the granting of dubious credit, the floatation of unsecured bank notes, the virtually uncontrolled issue of questionable stocks and bonds, and, worst of all, the insidious monetizations of government debts were well established during the golden age, and the latter, in particular, made possible the financing of one of the most insane wars in history.

In 1914, when the blow fell, it destroyed not only a large part of the enormous material wealth created during the previous 50 years, but the world's hard-won financial freedom as well. All of the belligerent nations suspended gold convertibility at the outbreak of hostilities and proceeded to finance the war through bond sales to the public (thus borrowing what the public really did not have) and by enormous issues of unsecured fiat paper currency.[18]

The end of World War I found Europe utterly prostrate. Financially, the damage was far greater than even the awesome physical ruin would indicate. France numbered herself among the victors, yet she owed a war debt to her allies (particularly to the United States) that was more than four times as great as what she had been forced to pay the Germans for losing the war of 1870. Germany, which had entered the war as the economic giant of Europe, was almost totally paralyzed. Austria-Hungary, once a major economic unit of the Continent, was fragmented into six hopelessly disorganized smaller nations. Yet the Allies clung to the delusion that somehow Germany and the former Central Powers could be forced to pay vast sums in reparations and thus relieve the financial crisis afflicting Europe as a result of the war. From Germany alone they hoped to get some $40 billion (plus interest) despite the fact that people were starving in Berlin and Vienna. In the end, the Allies (meaning mostly the United States) had to loan Germany and Austria money and credit just to ensure their survival.

Russia was out of it for good, as far as European or international monetary cooperation was concerned, and England was struggling desperately to restore stability to the pound. Only the United States was able to maintain a full gold standard (for a time) in the post-World War I era. Nevertheless, although the United States had emerged from the war as the most powerful economic unit of the world, its financial structure had been seriously weakened. However, this was hardly noticed by the exuberant America of the 1920's.

Actually, all major currencies, including that of the United States, should have been devalued after World War I; the international price of gold should have been raised and world currency parities should have been adjusted to reflect the realities of the time. Such an action, in the author's opinion, could have led to an early restoration of the pre-1914 international gold standard. It would also have allowed for a rational settlement of the reparations question and of inter-Allied indebtedness.

But, most important of all, an immediate postwar general devaluation and a return to a genuine international gold standard might have prevented, or at least mitigated, the economic tragedies that were to follow: catastrophic inflation in Germany and Eastern Europe, a rapid deterioration of the French franc and other Allied currencies, economic stagnation in England, an unhealthy speculative boom in the United States and, finally, the total world economic collapse of the 1930's. The first of these events, the postwar inflation in Germany, was a shockingly dramatic forecast of how sick the world's financial system had become since the general abandonment of the gold standard.

THE NIGHTMARE GERMAN INFLATION, 1919–1923

The Germany of 1919 furnishes a particularly appropriate example that we as individuals can learn from, although it is too much to hope that governments ever will. The old imperial German government had not wanted to remind its people of the true burden of war by the imposition of heavy taxes. Furthermore it expected only a short war and hoped to make its defeated enemies pay for it, as had been done so successfully in 1870. Consequently, Germany financed her war expenses primarily by floating and monetizing government debt through the Reichsbank.

By the end of the war, the amount of paper currency issued had increased by more than 1100 percent, but less than half of that was in general circulation. Strict wartime rationing and controls and the absence of a large part of the working population, who were then serving in the armed forces, effectively prevented the price level from reflecting the actual state of monetary deterioration. A large part of the wartime currency and credit issued remained inactive, awaiting the return of peace, when there would be, hopefully, better opportunities to spend it and more goods to spend it on.

By December of 1918, the Consumer Price Index had risen only by a modest 150 percent over the 1914 level. This was an unhealthy increase to be sure, but hardly an alarming one. In fact, it was no worse than what had occurred in other belligerent nations, including the United States and Great Britain. But the real danger was the debt of the Reichsbank, which had soared from 0.3 billion marks in 1914 to 55 billion at the end of 1918.

This mass of debt either had to be cancelled, reduced to manageable proportions or redeemed. There are no other ways to dispose of debt. Unfortunately for them, the Germans had reached the point where they could no longer redeem maturing bonds by the now universal expedient of selling more bonds. The loss of the war, the threat of harsh reparations and the postwar political turmoil had virtually destroyed the credit of the new democratic government, even before it could become fully organized. But instead of asking for forbearance and further sacrifice on the part of the public until financial and political order could be restored, the new democratic-socialist leaders sought instead to restore confidence by promising increased wages, shorter hours, an expanded educational system, improved pensions and a great variety of other social benefits.

The postwar Weimar Government of Germany was unquestionably faced with awesome problems and responsibilities, but it compounded these problems by a disastrous series of political and economic mistakes. It not only made no real attempt to deflate or even stabilize the precariously overextended monetary and financial structure it had inherited, but instead committed itself to spending thousands of billions more in paper marks for unemployment compensation, veterans' benefits and subsidies of all kinds.

In the early stages of the inflation, the rise in the price level continued to lag well behind the rate of creation of *ersatz* money. But Germany's political and economic problems continued to multiply in the early postwar years and the government seemed unable to find any effective response to these difficulties, except to provide ever larger amounts of currency. It soon became apparent to everyone, both in and out of Germany, that the inflation itself was a leading cause of the very unrest it was attempting to relieve. But by then Germany was caught so completely in this trap of her own making that she was helplessly unable to extricate herself; the madness would have to run its course.

Fiat money inflation is a monetary disease that feeds upon itself; more money means cheaper money, and cheap money brings higher prices, and higher prices require more money, and so it goes. The disease may have a lengthy incubation period, but once the virus is activated it moves with relentless and ever-increasing velocity to a final terrifying climax, wherein the victim and virus together eventually succumb in exhaustion. The recovery is invariably long and painful—if the victim survives.

The climactic stage began early in 1923, when French and Belgian troops occupied the industrial Ruhr district of Germany in an attempt to collect more reparations in kind. The Weimar Government responded to the occupation with a policy of passive resistance and ordered a general strike in the Ruhr, thus assuring another huge addition to the unemployment and relief roles. By this time, the general price level was rising so fast that the most frantic efforts were required to provide sufficient currency just to keep up with it.

Denominations in thousands of marks were soon replaced by notes in the millions, and finally in the hundreds of millions. It was the wildest inflation in history, up to that time, and it consumed the economic and social fabric of a whole generation, and perhaps affected their sanity as well. Bread rose to 200 billion marks a loaf, a newspaper cost 100 billion and 3 billion marks were required just to mail a letter. Workmen who were formerly paid by the month had to be paid by the week, then every day, and finally by the hour. At the end of each hour, payroll clerks pushed currency-laden carts through those German plants that were still trying to operate and deposited bundles of thousand- and ten-thousand-mark notes on every desk and bench, but by the time the next hour came around prices had doubled again.

The printing presses hummed day and night around the clock, seven days a week, trying to keep up with the mindless, voracious demand for more and more money. Yet there was in those days, believe it or not, a constant complaint of a shortage of currency. Although it was never officially admitted, some of the larger German industrial plants were reported to have received plates for large denomination notes from the government and to have set up printing presses in their basements, so that they could meet their worker's demands for more money, to meet higher prices, without delay. It is very doubtful whether an accurate accounting was kept of this deluge of note issuing during its climactic stage.

But habits of mind are strong, and the hapless Germans kept clinging to the illusion that the old familiar Reichsbank notes were somehow still usable money, long after the point of hopelessness had been passed. They just could not grasp what was happening; it was like some gigantic Kafkaesque nightmare. How does one accept the fact that after a lifetime of hard work and thrift one's savings would not buy a single slice of bread? Even the bare statistics are hard to comprehend. On July 31, 1914, there were approximately 2 billion (2,000,000,000) marks worth of paper currency circulating in Germany, or at least that amount had been issued. But on November 20, 1923, when it all ended, the Reichsbank admitted that the amount of paper currency issued had grown to 500 *quintillion* (500,000,000,000,-000,000,000) marks, give or take a few billion. The table, *Fig. 1,* illustrates the rate of this descent into fiscal insanity.

13   *Fig. 1*

INFLATION OF THE GERMAN MARK

1914–1923

Date	Exchange Value of Mark*		
July 31, 1914	4.2 M	=	$1.00
Dec. 31, 1918	8.4		
Dec. 31, 1919	28		
Dec. 21, 1920	74		
Dec. 31, 1921	162		
Dec. 31, 1922	7,000		
July 31, 1923	160,000		
Oct. 1, 1923	242,000,000		
Nov. 20, 1923**	4,200,000,000,000		

*Per U.S. dollar, based on official quotations; black-market rates were considerably higher after 1920.

**Last official quotation for old mark; conversion rate established November 30, 1923, at one *trillion*-to-one with new Reichsmarks:

1,000,000,000,000 M	=	1 RM
4.2 RM	=	$1.00

On November 20, 1923, the issue of mark notes was at last suspended. The new German Chancellor, Stresemann, had decided to abandon the policy of resistance in the Ruhr and to reopen negotiations with the Allies on the reparations question. The time seemed propitious also to attempt a reorganization of the monetary crisis. A temporary emergency currency, the *Rentenmark,* was introduced in strictly limited quantities, to get the country through the reorganization period, and the financial destiny of the nation was entrusted to a rising young banking expert, Dr. Hjalmar Schacht, who would soon earn international fame as the economic "wizard" of Germany.[19] The key to Dr. Schacht's wizardry consisted of the certain knowledge that somehow the German monetary system had to be returned to a firm gold basis.[20]

The new "Commissioner for National Currency," and soon thereafter President of the Reichsbank, Herr Schacht achieved his goal in a remarkably short time. After only a month in office, he was able to persuade Montagu Norman, the enigmatic Governor of the Bank of England, to grant a substantial loan of gold-backed foreign exchange to Germany, to be used as capital for a new subsidiary to the Reichsbank. This new bank, the *Golddiskontbank,* was then given the task of returning Germany's foreign-exchange operations to the prewar gold-standard basis. As for the Reichsbank itself, Schacht demanded, and eventually got, a law establishing its independence from government control.

The terms for exchange of old mark notes were set at one-*trillion*-to-one for new *Reichsmark* notes. This meant that the old mark was stabilized at its November 20, 1923, cut-off quotation of 4,200,000,000,000 to the dollar, even though the black-market rate had climbed to 12 trillion to the dollar by the end of the month. By holding to the last official quote, Schacht not only surprised and ruined a great many German and foreign currency speculators (who had only helped to perpetuate the chaos), but also greatly simplified the bookkeeping problem: all the Germans had to do was drop all the zeros and they were back to the 1914 gold-standard rate.[21]

The currency-stabilization program devised by Dr. Schacht was successful enough so that the Reichsbank was able to maintain the external gold parity of the new *Reichsmark* until the world banking crisis of 1931. German economic recovery, however, was slow and painful. In essence, financial order was restored in Germany by simply wiping out virtually all of the existing currency and debt. But it was done too late; virtually the entire middle class of Germany had been financially destroyed. The German people would have suffered a severe loss in any case, but it would have been much easier to take the step in 1919, while it was still bearable, than to allow it to get completely out of hand. But socialist politicians are inclined to take short-range views. They search for simple panaceas for complex problems, and the simplest of all is to borrow and spend today with no thought of tomorrow.

Although the German currency inflation of 1919–1923 was a classic example of the disease in its purest and most virulent form, it is by no means unique in the twentieth century. Similar episodes, although not quite so extreme, also occurred after World War I in Austria, Hungary, Poland, Roumania and Russia. After World War II, inflations, at times even exceeding the original German example, again ravaged Eastern Europe, particularly Hungary and Roumania. The Germans themselves fared somewhat better after World War II than after the earlier war, but still the *Reichsmark* had lost 96 percent of its value by 1948, when it was exchanged for the postwar *Deutschmark*.

Nationalist China was decimated by runaway inflation from 1946 to 1949, and this disaster contributed heavily to the ultimate Nationalist collapse and defeat during the civil war with the Communists. In the final days, the Nationalist *yuan* currency was being quoted at 50,000 to the dollar. Brazil, Chile, Uruguay and Indonesia, in addition to China, are just a few of the modern nations that have endured inflations, in recent years, serious enough to bring about major political and social problems, as well as profound economic dislocations. In fact, outside of North America, few areas of the world have escaped the curse of fiat-money inflation, in its more extreme stages, at one time or other. The twentieth century has indeed been, in the words of Jacques Rueff, an *Age of Inflation*.

SOME LESSONS FROM HYPERINFLATION

While American investors are certainly familiar enough with the more gradual type of inflation (which destroyed nearly 70 percent of the purchasing power of the 1934 dollar by the end of 1971), they have yet to experience the runaway or uncontrollable stage of the disease, which can completely wipe out the value of a currency in a relatively brief period. Nevertheless, history now suggests that the possibility of such an inflation in the United States is no longer as remote as was previously assumed.

The demonetization of gold, or the *de facto* suspension of all gold-standard limitations, marked the beginning of every known hyperinflation in the past. Since 1968, when the legal requirement for a 25 percent gold backing of Federal Reserve currency was eliminated, the United States has had no direct relationship between its money system and gold. And on August 15, 1971, even the final (theoretical) link was cut when the right of foreign central banks to convert their surplus dollar holdings into gold at the U.S. Treasury was suspended. This last action, however, was merely an official acknowledgment of a long-standing reality, as the dollar had been, in fact, a nonconvertible currency since the mid-1960's, when foreign-held dollars first began substantially to exceed the amount of gold available for their redemption.

A monetary system under which a government may deposit its bonds with a central bank in exchange for bank note currency or bank credit, at the government's pleasure, can be expanded without limit, as long as there are no gold "cover" requirements or redemption privileges on such currency. Since the United States has had such a system for some time, one of the most significant preconditions for a hyperinflation has been established. If gold is to be forever demonetized in the United States, and perhaps abroad as well, the dollar will rest entirely upon the fragile reed of public confidence, no less than did the German mark of 1919. And if that confidence should ever be severely shaken by some future economic, political or social crisis, such as a major war, an atomic war scare, an economic depression or any widespread political or social unrest that demands a large increase in deficit spending, a chain reaction type of hyperinflation could easily be set in motion.

I am not making any flat prediction that the present U.S. fiat dollar is inevitably doomed to a final inflation "blowoff" following the German example; it may just continue to suffer the agony of gradual or "creeping" inflation for another decade or so until its total ruin is accomplished. Nevertheless, there are enough historical similarities and parallels to warn us that a runaway breakout, at any time, is no longer beyond the realm of possibility, despite what our bankers, economists and politicians would like to have us believe. Of course it can be argued that severe wage and price controls would be invoked during any emergency condition. *But all previous hyperinflations actually occurred while strict economic and financial controls were supposedly in force.* History shows, rather conclusively, that wage and price controls are almost totally ineffective without strong public support. Once public confidence in a currency is lost, no amount of official coercion or threat is able to force its acceptance at fixed rates.

Of all the major economic catastrophes, hyperinflation is undoubtedly the most difficult for the individual to cope with. Preserving capital under such a condition becomes a truly herculean task. But since runaway inflations are inevitably arrested by a genuine return to a new fixed gold parity, one can assume that gold investments offer the safest and most effective hedge against such hazardous times. Historically, this has proven to be the case, virtually without exception. But the difficulties of holding gold or a claim on gold during such periods are considerable, to say the least.

Obviously, gold coins, if they are available, offer an excellent way to preserve capital at such times, and they have the great advantage of being easily concealed. Stocks in sound gold mining companies operating in other countries (presumably not affected by serious inflation) represent a claim on gold, in the form of ore reserves in the ground and bullion and other assets held above ground, as well as a share in current earnings. The problem lies in the fact that governments experiencing severe economic or financial distress sometimes make it difficult or illegal to own them.

Nearly all belligerent governments attempted to induce or

coerce their citizens into surrendering both gold and silver coin during World War I, but such measures proved difficult to enforce and substantial quantities of such coin remained in private hands. Great Britain called in foreign securities during both World Wars. Curiously enough, the imperial German government made no effort to seize foreign securities in the hands of private citizens, but after the war the Allies pressured the Weimar Government into trying to do so in the hopes of using the cash thus obtained for a reparations payment. German investors, however, found it easy to slip across their borders into neutral Holland or Switzerland to deposit or register their shares in these countries.

In recent years, an enormous amount of private American capital has been (legally) sent abroad for safety as well as investment, most of it going to Europe (mainly Switzerland) and Canada. Unquestionably, some of this capital has been invested in Canadian or South African gold shares that have been registered abroad. Although I haven't the slightest doubt that the future will bring exchange controls to the United States, which will make it difficult, if not actually illegal, to export private capital for investment, I do not believe that this practice can be entirely eliminated. The enterprising will always find ways (legal or otherwise) of getting around financial controls or restrictions.

Actually, there is really very little one can do *during* a hyperinflation except wait until it is over. One still has to provide for daily needs and expenses, of course, and this requires arrangements for a continuing source of income that will, hopefully, keep pace with the rate of currency depreciation. But any investment capital or surplus accumulated beyond immediate needs would be best employed in the purchase of tangible nonperishable items or commodities of intrinsic or recognized value, which should be retained, as far as possible, until the acute stage of inflation has been decisively ended by a complete currency reorganization and a return to a meaningful gold standard.

All types of antiques and artworks have merit, but gold coins are ideal, because of their direct monetary relationship with the price of gold. Common silver coins would be an acceptable holding, although not nearly as trustworthy as gold coins because the price of silver is entirely dependent on industrial demand. If a period of depression or business stagnation follows the reorganization crisis after a hyperinflation (and this is likely), the holders of silver, in all forms, could actually lose a part of their capital, in terms of preserved purchasing power. In any case, silver bullion is unacceptable as an inflation hedge, in the author's opinion, because of the danger of government confiscation.

Whenever there is an obvious threat or manifestation of hyperinflation, such as a rise in the general price level at a rate of 10 percent or more per year, all forms of securities—stocks, bonds, warrants, debentures, etc.—and all types of monetary instruments—bank accounts, bills, notes, mortgages and the like—should be completely avoided. The one exception is, of course, stocks in sound gold-mining companies located abroad. It probably would be an added safety factor if such stocks could be registered and held in some form of safekeeping or trust account outside of the country suffering from runaway inflation.

Hyperinflations are, historically, ended by a "reorganization crisis," at which time all of the outstanding inflated currency is either voided or called in to be exchanged for a new and presumably stable currency. However, unless a genuine gold parity can be established for the new currency, the reorganization will be ineffective and a new outbreak of inflation will occur. But assuming that a reasonable degree of monetary stability is achieved, gold coins will reach their peak value almost immediately after the reorganization establishes a new fixed gold price, and they can be sold anytime thereafter. However, the profits from gold stocks, in the form of both dividends and capital gains, will be realized over a period of from two to five years following the reorganization. Some clues as to when to sell gold stocks following a major monetary reorganization will be outlined in a subsequent chapter, but the major point is not to sell them too soon.

Notes:

CHAPTER II

1.   Some European countries still mint gold coins (primarily for numismatic purposes) in *florin/ducat* denominations.

2.   It is significant to note here that the rise of northern Italy as a major commercial and banking center, with its own trusted gold coinage, followed almost immediately after the downfall of the *bezant.*

3.   But gold money always wins in the end, although much damage has been done by foolish attempts to replace it or assign it an inferior role.

4.   See Glossary definition of Gresham's Law.

5.   In 1965, rising industrial demand for silver reached a point where the intrinsic value of U.S. subsidiary silver coins exceeded their face value. Consequently, these coins were hoarded in the usual response to Gresham's Law, causing major shortages of small change. The inept response of the U.S. Treasury to this situation is richly detailed in William F. Rickenbacker's *Wooden Nickels* (New Rochelle, N.Y.: Arlington House, 1966).

6.   The ancient people also had their troubles with the ratio. The problem became particularly acute after Alexander the Great introduced great quantities of captured Persian and Oriental gold into the silver-standard economy of the pre-Hellenistic Mediterranean world. Aristotle apparently originated the still-persisting belief that 15:1 is the ideal ratio for monetizing gold and silver.

7.   Paper was little used in Europe before the fourteenth century. Prior to that time it was a luxury import from China and the Arab empire. European production of paper did not become widely available until after 1300.

8.   Specifically, their gold convertibility was cancelled. Gold certificates were allowed to be exchanged for (nonredeemable) Federal Reserve notes.

9.   *Banco del Giro* means literally "circular," or circulating, bank, from the new (in 1600) custom of transferring funds or credit

from the books of one bank to the books of another, without the necessity of any actual specie changing hands.

10.   In 1637, the *Banco della Piazza* was absorbed into the *Banco del Giro* and its deposit functions were no longer exclusive.

11.   The full and fascinating story of John Law and the first great paper-currency inflation of modern times may be found in Charles Mackay, *Extraordinary Popular Delusions and the Madness of Crowds* (London, 1841. Reprint ed., New York: L.C. Page Co., 1932; 11th printing, 1960) Chapter I.

12.   For the complete story of the *assignat* debacle (and everyone should read it for the light it sheds on our present dilemma) see, Andrew Dickson White, *Fiat Money Inflation in France* (New York: Foundation for Economic Education, 1959). It is a small book, but very valuable.

13.   As did Julius Caesar, Mussolini, Hitler, Franco, V.I. Lenin, and perhaps even Charles de Gaulle.

14.   This works out to a 15.5 to 1 ratio between silver and gold.

15.   Quite unlike Hitler, who took over a modern nation and left it, and the rest of Europe, in ruins.

16.   Also known as Napoleon III, but he was hardly the man his uncle was.

17.   As a standard coinage. Subsidiary coinage of silver was continued (except for war periods) until the middle 1960's.

18.   That is, they paid their workers and soldiers with fiat paper money and then cajoled or coerced them into loaning part of it back. Such are the miracles of modern finance, that governments can not only pay with unfulfillable promises, but borrow them as well.

19.   The *Rentenmark* was backed only by mortgage bonds on German landed property. In this respect it closely resembled the disastrous French *assignat* of 1791. Fortunately, the early success of the stabilization program and the introduction of the Reichsmark made it unnecessary to submit the *Rentenmark* to a prolonged test.

20.   Hjalmar Schacht, *My First Seventy-Six Years* (London: Wingate, 1955) p. 180.

21.   *Ibid,* p. 186.

III

THE UNITED STATES AND GOLD

"The power of coining money and of regulating its value was delegated to Congress by the Constitution for the very purpose, as assigned by the framers of that instrument, of creating and preserving the uniformity and purity of such a standard of value."

—UNANIMOUS OPINION OF THE UNITED STATES SUPREME COURT—1850

THE Spanish adventurers who first came to the New World were looking for gold. They found their gold, and silver as well, in quantities that exceeded even their most avaricious expectations. The exploitation of this treasure became the foundation of a great Spanish empire that soon dominated the Americas. However the British colonists, who began the settlement of the North American coastal area more than a century later, had no thought of gold or silver; they were looking for land, and for a greater freedom to work out their individual destinies. They too found what they were looking for.

The Spaniards established a mint at Mexico City in 1536, only fifteen years after Cortés had seized the capital from the Aztecs. The Mexico City mint, which still survives as the oldest operating mint in the Americas, produced one of the most famous coins of history, the Spanish milled* silver dollar, or "piece of eight," so called because it was valued at eight Spanish *reales*

*Refers to the practice of milling or reeding the outside edge of a coin to prevent filing.

and divisible (as a monetary unit) into eight parts, or "bits."[1]
Fractional coins in silver were also struck, as were a great
variety of gold coins with such historic identities as *escudos,*
pistoles and *doubloons,* but it was the *8-reales* silver dollar that
became the *de facto* standard coin of the New World and served
eventually as the model for the monetary unit of the United
States.[2]

Despite its rapid growth and prosperity, British colonial
America was never given an adequate monetary structure.
From beginning to end, the English government made little
effort to provide its North American colonies with an adequate
supply of coined money. Consequently, the colonists had to rely
on pure commodity monies, such as animal pelts, tobacco, musket balls and even Indian wampum, in the early years, and on
whatever foreign coin they could obtain in trade as they became more advanced commercially. At the time of the Revolution, a great variety of foreign coinage—Spanish, French, Portuguese and Dutch—as well as a few English pieces, comprised
the colonial circulating medium, but one could hardly charac-
terize this haphazard accumulation as a monetary system.[3]
The most popular and most available coin, however, was the
Spanish *8-reales* silver dollar.[4]

Even before the Revolution, some of the colonies had passed
laws giving legal-tender status to Spanish coins, so it was quite
natural for the Second Continental Congress to declare, in 1775,
that its debts and obligations would henceforth be denominated and payable in "Spanish milled dollars, or the value
thereof in gold or silver." Unfortunately, they were unable to
put this laudable intention into practice, beyond making the
Spanish silver dollar the standard of value and the unit of
account. One of the main tasks facing the Congress was to find
a means of financing the Revolutionary War. However, the
credit of the new government was too poor to permit foreign
borrowing, and its cause was not yet popular enough to allow
the imposition of heavy taxes. As a result, the United States
began its existence with a monetary system of unsupported
paper currency.[5]

During the course of the war, some $240 million worth of
continentals, as these notes came to be called, were put into

circulation. In the usual response to Gresham's Law, all coins were soon driven into hiding and the Continental paper money became the sole currency of the people. Theoretically, these notes were to become redeemable after the war, but the Continental Government had no coin or bullion at the time, and everybody knew it. Consequently their notes were regarded as pure fiat money from the beginning and depreciation was rapid. By 1780, flour was $150 a barrel and coffee and butter were each $12 a pound; other prices rose in proportion. Merchants and others who accepted and held large amounts of *continentals* were financially ruined. Even the Continental troops eventually refused to accept them, and by 1781 they had ceased entirely to circulate as money.

Speculators later bought up *continental* notes with coin at rates ranging from 400 to 1 to 1,000 to 1. In 1791, an act was passed by the First United States Congress allowing for the redemption of *continentals* in coin at the rate of $100 to 1. Some $6 million worth (face value) were eventually turned in to be redeemed at this 100 to 1 rate; the rest were apparently lost, discarded or destroyed.[6]

The unhappy experience of the *continentals* was aggravated by the concurrent issue of fiat paper money by the individual states. Such state paper was issued in amounts that exceeded, in total, the circulation of *continentals*. Severe measures were taken to keep both the state notes and the issues of the Continental Congress at par value. As early as 1776, committees were set up to prosecute vigorously persons charged with discriminating against paper money. Among the penalties meted out for this offense were confiscations of goods and property, floggings, and public declarations naming the offender as a traitor to his country.

The various state conventions of the time passed a profusion of price-fixing laws and regulations and made speculation in goods or commodities a capital offense. Arrangements to pay rents or wages in produce or merchandise were regarded with great hostility and suspicion. But it was all to no avail; such draconian measures only served to accelerate the inflation. By 1780, the Army itself was at the point of open rebellion, and Washington was unable to move his troops to Yorktown until

Congress could borrow sufficient hard money from France to meet their back pay. Thus it was that French gold, in the end, saved the American Revolution.[7]

This first, but now almost forgotten, American experience with fiat-money inflation provides lessons that should be memorized by every contemporary economist. They should know, for example, that fiat money can bring starvation and poverty in the midst of plenty. During the course of the Revolution, the major cities in the hands of the patriots came close to famine, as a result of runaway inflation. Also, the sufferings of Washington's Army at Valley Forge were in no way due to the disruptions of war or to a breakdown of the Continental economy, but to the lack of an acceptable currency with which to obtain the necessities of life. By contrast, the British army, then comfortably quartered in Philadelphia, was able to supply its needs lavishly from the surrounding countryside by simply paying for them with an unlimited supply of hard money. Thus, it was demonstrated that there were no significant shortages of food or other necessities to account for the patriots' difficulties and privations, but only a shortage of good coin or specie.

Legal-tender laws, price and wage controls and severe penalties, including death, are not sufficient to keep a fiat currency from depreciating, no matter how worthy the cause for which it is issued. This has surely been demonstrated often enough in history. Economic laws are derived from the natural order of things and cannot be overturned by legislations of man. At best, man's laws can only delay the inevitable. In the long run, governments can only set the stage upon which the economic forces play. To do more, to try to turn economics into a puppet show, with bureaucratic managers pulling the strings, will always result in chaos and collapse. Men are not puppets to be manipulated; they are free.

THE CONSTITUTION ESTABLISHES A METALLIC CURRENCY

After the war, seven states again issued fiat paper money and only succeeded in prolonging the dismal financial paralysis of the wartime era. By the time the Fathers of our country had agreed upon the provisions of a Federal Constitution in 1787, the country had seen enough of paper money. The new Constitution specifically denied the states the right to *"coin money, emit bills of credit; make anything but gold and silver coin a tender in payment of debts."*[8] Since the states were prohibited from issuing money, and since all Federal powers were delegated by the Constitution, and since the Constitution contained no provision or power granting the right to issue paper money, the framers of that noble document thought they had freed the country from the dangers of unsecured or fiat paper currency.[9] Unfortunately, the protections afforded by the Constitution in this regard were challenged repeatedly in subsequent years and finally nullified completely by the Gold Reserve Act of 1934.

The Constitution of the United States, ratified by all existing states as of January 10, 1791, delegates to Congress the sole responsibility for the nation's financial affairs and, under this charge, specifically grants it the right and duty:[10]

"To lay and collect taxes, duties, imposts and excises, to pay the debts and provide for the common defense and general welfare of the United States."

"To borrow money on the credit of the United States."

"To coin money, regulate the value thereof, and of foreign coin, and fix the standards of weights and measures."

"To provide for the punishment of counterfeiting the securities and current coin of the United States."

And it was further charged that:

"No money shall be drawn from the Treasury, but in consequence of appropriations made by law, and a regular statement and account of the receipts and expenditures of all public monies shall be published from time to time."

Under the mandate of the Constitution, and with the help and guidance of our first Secretary of the Treasury, Alexander Hamilton, Congress passed the First U.S. Coinage Act on April 2, 1792. This act called for a bimetallic currency with a silver "dollar" of 371.25 grains pure as the monetary unit. Gold coins of $2.50 *(quarter eagle)*, $5.00 *(half eagle)* and $10 (the *eagle*) were created, and fractional silver coins and copper cents were also provided for. The first U.S. mint was established at Philadelphia and commenced operation in July of 1792.

But again, the best intentions of Congress were soon frustrated, this time by the vagaries of bimetallism and the ratio. The First Coinage Act had called for free coinage at the rate of 15 to 1, and although this had been close to the world ratio at the time it was first proposed by Hamilton, it soon became unrealistic. By 1799, the ratio in European financial centers had advanced to 15¾ to 1, and at this rate our undervalued gold coins were exported or melted for bullion almost as fast as they left the mint. And, of course, much of our domestically produced gold never got to the mint but was exported directly as bullion.

Our silver coins fared little better; speculators exchanged our new silver dollars for worn Spanish dollars (which were still legal tender in the United States) and turned a small profit by selling the shiny new American coins in the West Indies and elsewhere, where the natives found them highly attractive and preferred them to Spanish silver.[11]

In 1830, a Senate committee sadly concluded that United States coins were regarded as little more than bullion by speculators and were, therefore, "lost to the community as coins." From 1794 to 1834, U.S. coins achieved only negligible circulation despite the best efforts of the minting authorities. Our currency during this period was made up primarily of a nondescript collection of underweight foreign silver and gold coins, including the ubiquitous Spanish dollar, and a great variety of paper bank notes issued by the so-called "wildcat" private banks of the time. The latter, in particular, were a constant distress to the economy. Bank failures and defaults resulting from the overissue of private bank notes were chronic. It was the era of the *shinplaster*, the *stumptail* and the *red dog*, as these notes were derisively labelled.

The situation was partially corrected in 1834 by the Second U.S. Coinage Act, which slightly reduced the weights of U.S. gold coins and altered the ratio to 16 to 1. This placed the country on a *de facto* gold standard, but it was not until 1865 that the activities of private banks were curbed by taxing their notes out of existence. So for more than fifty years the country had to suffer from these wildcat-bank paper money issues that became worthless, on the average, every 20 years.[12] Following the

Panic of 1837, a Third U.S. Coinage Act established both gold and silver coins at .900 fine and fixed the weights for coinage that were to prevail until the respective ends of gold coinage in 1933 and intrinsic-value silver in 1965.

Before 1837, silver had been overvalued in the United States, thus establishing a *de facto* silver standard (although it did not function effectively as such because of the activities of silver-coin speculators). But after 1837, silver was undervalued, leaving the nation on a gold basis—where it has tried to remain ever since despite repeated and numerous attempts to return to silver, to reestablish bimetallism, to reintroduce fiat paper currency and to demolish the gold standard altogether.

However, the discovery of gold in California in 1848 made it possible for the United States to have an ample supply of gold coin, and contributed greatly to a further decline in the role of silver as money. The introduction of a standard gold dollar coin, as well as a $20 *double eagle,* in 1849, was an additional indication that Americans preferred gold for their standard monetary unit as well as for a *de facto* standard of value. But despite this obvious preference, we were soon to experiment with fiat paper currency again, this time as the result of a Civil War.

THE CIVIL WAR AND THE GREENBACKS

Prior to the Civil War, the courts of the United States rebuffed all efforts to challenge the exclusiveness and permanence of the metallic currency brought into being by the Constitution. The decision of the U.S. Supreme Court that introduces this chapter is typical, and it affirmed, without equivocation, that the only legal currency of the United States was intrinsic-value coin; and further, that once having established such a currency, Congress was also entrusted by the Constitution with the responsibility for maintaining its purity and value. The power to "regulate" the value of money (coin) was consistently interpreted as being, in effect, a charge to maintain such value, once established, without significant alteration. This view was upheld in all cases regarding the legitimate currency of the United States (intrinsic-value coin) until 1933.[13]

But the Constitution is silent on the subject of bank-note currency, for the simple and obvious reason that *bank notes are not money;* a bank note is only a *receipt for money.* The founding Fathers apparently could not conceive of a time when either their successors or the public at large could be led to confuse one with the other. Such an assumption was eminently reasonable, for it was openly acknowledged by all succeeding administrations (until 1963) that bank notes, including those of the Federal Reserve System, were not money, but only *promises to pay money.*

Even after our internal demonetization of gold in 1933, Federal Reserve notes continued to bear an inscription that they were not only legal tender but "REDEEMABLE IN LAWFUL MONEY AT THE UNITED STATES TREASURY OR AT ANY FEDERAL RESERVE BANK." But, beginning with series 1963, that part of the inscription was quietly dropped, leaving the public with only the dubious comfort of knowing that these notes were just "LEGAL TENDER FOR ALL DEBTS PUBLIC AND PRIVATE." The development of the silver crisis of 1963–65 and the subsequent elimination of intrinsic-value silver coinage and redeemable silver-certificate currency by the Coinage Act of 1965 had left the U.S. Government *without any lawful money* with which to redeem its internal obligations, since gold had already been demonetized (internally) in 1933.[14]

The currency of the United States today is pure fiat paper. Our Federal Reserve notes are no longer bank notes in the normal sense, because they are no longer redeemable in money. A bank note, being a promise to pay in money, cannot possibly be redeemed by itself. There is, in fact, no difference whatever between the Federal Reserve currency of today and the German Reichsbank currency of 1914–23. Both currencies were deprived of any legitimate identity as bank notes when their redeemability was denied; they then became *de facto,* pure fiat, currencies, because their value depended *solely* upon a government-decreed "legal tender" status.

In the case of the United States, the road that led to the present cynical disregard of the Constitution began in 1862, when the precedent was established that the debts of the United States could be given legal-tender status and made to circulate as currency. During the Civil War, Congress, relying on the sanction of the national emergency that then existed, provided for the issue of $450 million in non-interest-bearing, non-redeemable United States (legal tender) notes, the so-called "greenbacks."[15] The Lincoln administration agreed to the issue of this fiat paper currency with the understanding that it would be retired immediately after the war and the emergency conditions had passed.

However, the United States did not abandon metallic currency at this time, as is commonly supposed, for the minting of gold and silver continued as usual on a free coinage basis. But the Government did suspend redemption of its bonds and notes in coin, and the introduction of such a large amount (relatively) of nonredeemable currency into the monetary system, in the form of the greenbacks, did have the effect of placing the country on a pure fiat-money basis, due to the usual operation of Gresham's Law.[16] All coin rapidly disappeared in the North, including even minor coin, and the U.S. Government was soon forced to issue paper currency in fractional denominations. The public was obliged to use these fractional notes and even postage stamps for small change. By July of 1864, the greenbacks had depreciated to where $100 brought only $35 in gold, and in out-of-the-way places the decline was even more pronounced. In gold-rich California, greenbacks were refused altogether.

In the Southern Confederacy the situation was similar but far more drastic. The Confederate currency was issued in the form of interest-bearing notes that promised the bearer a yield of 8 percent from date of issue, whenever these notes were to become redeemable after the war. But the South had very little coin and absolutely no bullion in its possession. Consequently, its paper currency was regarded as pure fiat money from the beginning and depreciated accordingly. By the end of 1864, Confederate paper notes were generally not worth one percent of their face value, in terms of purchasing power, and with the defeat of the South they became utterly worthless.

At the close of the war, in 1865, the Secretary of the Treasury recommended that the greenbacks be gradually withdrawn from circulation and retired, and an act to that effect was passed by Congress. But the greenback retirement program lasted a mere 21 months before it was repealed. During the next ten years, the monetary conservatives in Congress, and President Grant in the White House, were not only frustrated in all attempts to retire the greenbacks, but had all they could do to prevent further large issues of unsupported government paper money from being created. The West had borrowed large sums of money to finance its rapid development and the South was heavily in debt due to the war and the costs of reconstruction. Both of these areas seized upon the idea of the greenbacks as a way out of their predicaments; the rural Western and Southern political leaders wanted cheap money to stimulate business, raise agricultural prices and rescue their debtors.

But, in 1875, Congress finally passed a "Resumption Act" that provided for the redemption in gold of all greenbacks presented to the Treasury on or after January 1, 1879, and for their subsequent withdrawal from circulation. The inflationists were furious and met in Indianapolis in 1876 to organize the "Greenback Party." They advocated a policy of pure government fiat money, opposed the Resumption Act and condemned the sale of gold-backed government bonds. This party elected fifteen members to the House in 1878, and, although they were unable to secure the issue of more greenbacks, they did obtain two unfortunate compromises: (a) that the value of greenbacks extant (as of May 3, 1878) would be permitted to remain in circulation, and (b) that any greenbacks presented for redemption were to be immediately reissued to maintain the status quo. Therefore, we have, to this day, $346,681,016 worth of United States legal tender notes, or greenbacks, still in circulation.[17]

Compared to the debasements of the United States monetary system that have occurred since 1933, or even since 1965, the episode of the greenbacks seems minor indeed, but its importance goes far beyond the small (in terms of current values) dollar amounts involved. It permanently damaged the integrity of the monetary provisions of the Constitution; it accustomed the public to the use of paper currency in the form of monetized government debt; and it established precedents for the far greater abuses that were to follow. But on January 1, 1879, however, the difficult greenback era seemed to have ended satisfactorily, as the (amended) Resumption Act went into effect and the United States returned once again to a full specie basis, with all its currency and obligations fully redeemable in gold.

BIMETALLISM AND THE GOLD STANDARD ACT OF 1900

But the inflationist forces, although a definite minority, were not yet contained. Having failed to obtain their objectives through the greenbacks, they next turned their attention to bimetallism as a means of expanding the currency. In this effort they had no difficulty finding ready allies among the silver mining interests of the West. During the seventies, vast new deposits of silver were discovered in several western states, and the miners were, understandably, looking for a guaranteed market for their product. But, to their chagrin, not only were the European nations suspending free coinage of silver and turning to the full gold standard, but the United States itself, by a little-noticed Coinage Act of 1873 (later regarded by the silverites as, *the Crime of '73!*), had discontinued the minting of standard silver dollars, abolished free coinage of silver and reduced silver to subsidiary status for small change only.

Once the greenback issue was out of the way, the silverites and their inflationist allies retaliated vigorously and secured the passage of the Bland-Allison Act in 1878, which required the government to purchase not less than two, or more than four, million dollars worth of silver each month at the world market price, and coin it into standard silver dollars. The actual amount to be purchased was supposed to equal the output of American mines, but, in practice, the Secretaries of the Treasury refused to purchase more than the minimum required by law.

But the silver mining industry was ably represented in the Senate, even though the industry itself was relatively unimportant at the time and located in states of sparse population. Furthermore, the silver bloc drew support not only from the greenback-inflationists, but from agrarian and populist interests as well. And while they were never able to achieve the legal return of bimetallism, they did secure direct subsidies for silver until 1893. A program of silver subsidy was also revived by the New Deal administration during the depression of the 1930's.

The Bland-Allison Act did not restore free coinage of silver, but only provided an outlet for the world's growing surplus of the unwanted white metal. Under this program some 378 million silver dollars were coined between 1873 and 1890, and this represented more than 50 times the amount coined in all prior years of the nation's existence.

Still the inflationists and silver interests were dissatisfied, and in 1890 forced the passage of the *Sherman Silver Purchase Act.* This law obliged the Treasury to increase its purchases of silver bullion to 4.5 million ounces per month. Over 187 million more silver dollars were added to the Treasury's hoard as a result of the Sherman Act. The net effect of all this addition of silver to the monetary stocks of the United States was to create distrust and misgiving abroad regarding our ability to remain on a gold standard. Increasing withdrawals of U.S. gold by foreign interests, combined with the growing instability of our domestic currency, culminated in a severe business panic in 1893.

Congress hurriedly repealed the Sherman Act, but it was too late; the damage had been done and confidence was not restored until 1896, when the "free silver" cause then being championed by Democratic presidential candidate William Jennings Bryan was decisively defeated. New discoveries of gold in Alaska and in the Canadian Yukon in that year also helped to relieve the situation and restore the Treasury's depleted gold reserves.

During the years of the great silver controversy, the silver dollar, which is now so prized by collectors and speculators alike, was a despised and unwanted coin. The Treasury was unable to put any appreciable quantity into circulation, and so they were monetized in the more acceptable form of silver certificates and Treasury notes. The coins themselves reposed in the vaults of the Treasury and remained there, largely undisturbed, until speculators and collectors happily carted them off during the silver-crisis years of the 1960's, when the price of the white metal finally rose above its par value ($1.29 per ounce) due to increasing industrial demand.[18]

The foregoing explains why silver dollars are so readily available today in uncirculated mint condition.[19] In these inflationary times, silver does have a superficial attractiveness; compared to fiat paper, silver is indeed precious. But compared to gold, silver has fared poorly in modern times. If the "silver bugs" knew something of monetary history, they would temper their enthusiasm for the white metal. Silver has not legally been a standard monetary metal since 1873, and not an effective one since 1834. For more than a century, the whole world has been turning away from silver and toward gold as the sole monetary standard. The holders of silver bullion and silver shares could be disappointed if they expect that any future monetary crisis and devaluation (rise in the price of gold) will lead to a corresponding increase in the price of silver.

The price of silver may certainly rise in the future, but it would be from other causes; such a move would have very little to do with devaluation of the dollar in terms of *gold*. There is no mystic ratio in operation today, any more than there was in 1890. The only difference is that *then* the silver lobby was powerful enough to get the government to support the price of silver. The same condition prevailed, to a degree, during the depression of the 1930's. But I do not think this will be continued in the future. Silver, as a monetary metal, is a dead issue. The price of silver as a commodity* will continue to depend on complex commercial supply-demand factors, and while continued inflation and industrial boom would undoubtedly exert an upward pressure, a major depression would seriously diminish demand and depress the price of silver.

The Gold Standard Act of 1900. This law made official what had been a *de facto* condition since 1834, as Congress formally adopted, in 1900, the "full" or gold-coin standard, the type that had been in effect in Great Britain since 1816. This meant that *all* U.S. currency and coin would be kept equal to gold at all times and redeemable in all amounts down to and including the smallest ($1) gold coin available. The dollar price of gold had been set at $20.67 per ounce in 1837, and under the terms

---

*Silver in the form of coins is a different proposition, as I said before, and I will explain why, presently.

of the Gold Standard Act that rate of exchange would remain fixed and inviolable. The gold coins of the United States, authorized under various coinage acts since 1837 and in circulation during the life of the Gold Standard Act (1900–33) were as shown in *Fig. 2*. The intrinsic values (by weight) of these coins are shown in the table, *Fig. 3*.

Fig. 2

THE GOLD COINS OF THE UNITED STATES
1838–1933

Denomination		Type	Mint Dates
$20	Double Eagle	Liberty Head	1849–1907
$20	Double Eagle	St. Gaudens	1907–1932
$10	Eagle	Liberty Head	1838–1907
$10	Eagle	Indian Head	1907–1933
$ 5	Half Eagle	Liberty Head	1839–1908
$ 5	Half Eagle	Indian Head	1908–1929
$ 3	Three Dollars	Indian Princess	1854–1889
$ 2½	Quarter Eagle	Liberty Head	1840–1907
$ 2½	Quarter Eagle	Indian Head	1908–1929
$ 1	Gold Dollar	Liberty Head	1849–1854
$ 1	Gold Dollar	Indian Head	1854–1889

Notes:
1. Gold coins minted from 1907 to 1933 were designed by the noted American sculptor Augustus St. Gaudens.
2. The three-dollar gold piece was never a popular coin and was minted and circulated only in very limited quantities.
3. A $4 gold coin was struck as a "proof" or pattern, but was never authorized for general issue.
4. Although produced in quantity, the gold dollar was actually too small to serve as a practical coin, and its minting was consequently discontinued in 1889.
5. Gold coins minted before 1837 were slightly heavier and of different fineness but, because of the ratio problem, very few of them ever got into circulation.
6. *Fig. 2* shows only the regular U.S. coinage. Private, or "territorial," issues struck during the gold-rush era and the few U.S. commemorative gold pieces minted for special occasions are not included.
7. All U.S. gold coins struck between 1837 and 1933 were .900 fine, or 90 percent gold and 10 percent copper alloy. It is necessary to

add a small amount of copper to gold coins in order to increase
their hardness and wearing ability.

Fig. 3

WEIGHTS OF U.S. GOLD COINS, 1838–1933

Coin	Grains Standard	Grams Standard	Grains Pure	Troy oz. Pure	Troy oz. Nominal
$20	516	33.4370	464.4	.9675	1.00
$10	258	16.7185	232.2	.48375	.50
$ 5	129	8.3592	116.1	.241875	.25
$ 3	77.4	5.0154	69.66	.14511	.15
$ 2½	64.5	4.1796	58.05	.1209375	.125
$ 1	25.8	1.6718	23.22	.04837	.05

Notes:
1. All coins .900 fine
2. Pure means unalloyed gold.
3. Standard is total weight of coin.
4. Difference between nominal value of gold dollar and actual gold
   content by weight is due to the original seigniorage granted the
   Treasury by the law of 1837, under which the statutory troy ounce
   worth $20.67 in bullion was exchanged for $20 in coin. This small
   "profit" was allowed to offset minting expenses.

THE GOLDEN AGE, 1900–1933

The struggle of the United States for monetary stability and
integrity had been a long and difficult one, beginning as it did
in the earliest colonial years of the young nation. But the ultimate triumph of gold and common sense was, most unfortunately, very short lived. Only 32 years after the formal adoption
of the full gold-coin standard, America was to turn back the
clock and enter upon yet another era of monetary experiment
and confusion, first making a dismal attempt to restore silver
as a monetary medium, and then slipping deeper into the
morass of debt monetization and fiat money. We have not yet
emerged from this last wilderness.

The total web of circumstance leading to our present tragedy
of fiat-money inflation is too complex for a single volume, let
alone a single chapter in this one; it involves political and economic developments on a worldwide basis, as well as those in

the U.S. In fact, the exact causes of the great world economic debacle which began in the 1930's will probably continue to be the subject of acrimonious debate between economists, financial analysts and historians for decades to come. Nevertheless, I am inclined to take a historian's point of view, that the outstanding events of an era tend to speak for themselves.

The Federal Reserve System. In 1907, a brief but rather severe business and stock-market panic struck the country, causing a wave of bank failures and suspensions. Some of the largest banks in the nation were forced to close their doors. The immediate cause of the Panic of 1907 is generally presumed to have been a sharp break in the price of copper that bankrupted a number of important commodity speculators and some of their brokerage and banking connections. But, as with all such events, the stage for the collapse was set by a prior period of excessive speculation and careless banking in many areas. Whatever the cause, the event itself pointed out rather dramatically that the banking arrangements of the United States were still woefully inadequate, despite the improvement in its monetary system brought about by the Gold Standard Act.

A Congressional Commission was appointed to study the problem, and in 1913 it recommended the establishment of a central banking system similar to those already in use in England and on the Continent.[20] The final bill passed by Congress, however, was a compromise worked out by the House Banking and Currency Committee, under the chairmanship of Carter Glass of Virginia. Because of the distinctive geographic and psychological divisions of the United States, it was decided that the establishment of twelve regional Federal Reserve banks would be more advantageous than a single central bank on the European model. The system was officially put into operation on November 16, 1914.

The Federal Reserve banks are not government banks (at least they were never intended to be!). The twelve regional banks are privately owned by the private banks that elect to belong to the Federal Reserve System.[21] Each member bank is required to purchase stock in its district Reserve bank in an amount equal to 6 percent of its own paid-up capital and surplus. The member banks elect six of the nine directors of each

Federal Reserve bank, while the remaining three are appointed by the governing board of the Federal Reserve System. One of the latter is always designated chairman by the same board. Dividends are paid on Federal Reserve capital stock held by member banks at a rate not to exceed 6 percent per annum; earnings in excess of this amount are paid into the Reserve bank's surplus fund.

But although the Federal Reserve System is privately owned, it is not privately controlled. It is subject to the overall supervision of a seven-member board of governors. Vacancies on the Federal Reserve Board of Governors are filled by presidential appointment for terms of 14 years, and one of their number is designated chairman (also by the President of the U.S.) for a period of four years. The Chairman of the Federal Reserve Board, who is also its chief executive officer, is obviously one of the key figures in the American financial and banking system.

The prime purpose of the Federal Reserve System was to increase the liquidity and flexibility of our currency and banking systems. Prior to 1920, most panics had been aggravated, if not caused, by the inability of private banks to lend money at critical moments. By tying together the member banks in a unified system and providing a central source of emergency funds and credit, it was assumed that future panics could be avoided, or at least greatly alleviated. Furthermore, the designers of the system apparently believed it could operate within the discipline of the gold standard. Each Federal Reserve Bank was required to keep a reserve of 35 percent in "lawful money" against deposits of member banks and 40 percent in gold against Federal Reserve notes outstanding. Prior to World War II, the gold "cover" on Federal Reserve notes frequently approached 100 percent.

Originally there were two types of Federal Reserve currency authorized: Federal Reserve *bank* notes and Federal Reserve notes. The former were issued only by individual regional Reserve Banks, and were the same in format and monetary status as the "National Currency" or national bank notes issued by the chartered National Banks and provided for under the Banking Act of 1865. The latter, however, are the notes of the Federal Reserve System itself and are issued as direct obligations or "promises to pay" of the United States Government itself. They were secured (originally) by gold (40 percent) and discounted commercial paper.

In actual practice, very little use was made of Federal Reserve bank notes, and their issue was suspended entirely after 1935.[22] But Federal Reserve note currency soon became an important part of our monetary system. Unfortunately, the "elasticity" provided by the use of such currency proved to be, more and more, a one-way stretch. Expanding the money supply via the magic of Federal Reserve currency and credit proved to be politically more palatable than contracting it when the economic emergency had passed. And from the beginning, the Federal Reserve Governing Board has shown a disturbing tendency to acquiesce readily in whatever is asked of it by the Treasury and the national administration.

Nevertheless, there is little basis for any assumption that the creators of the system ever intended it to become a vehicle for an evasion of the Constitution through the issuance of government-fiat currency. The 40 percent reserve requirement and the complex regulations for the selection of regional board members and officers from the ranks of private nonpolitical interests suggest the opposite. Furthermore, each Federal Reserve note, issued prior to 1934, bore the following legend, which made it, in effect, a gold certificate itself:

"REDEEMABLE IN GOLD ON DEMAND AT THE UNITED STATES TREASURY OR IN GOLD OR LAWFUL MONEY AT ANY FEDERAL RESERVE BANK"

The major flaw in the Federal Reserve System, as originally constituted, was its virtually unlimited ability to create excessive bank credit through its powers to discount commercial bills of credit or "paper," and lower bank reserve requirements. In the area of regulating credit, its policies were eventually to prove disastrous, but it cannot be denied that the "Fed" at least respected the integrity of the monetary system of the United States prior to 1933. Since then, however, both the role and the position of the Federal Reserve System have been drastically altered by subsequent Acts of Congress.

The powers of the Fed have been vastly increased, giving it, for better or for worse, absolute authority to regulate virtually every area of financial activity in the United States, including banking, the stock market, the bond market, the supply of currency and commercial credit. At the same time, however, the "independent" status of the Fed has become more and more ambiguous. By allowing its currency to become the *de facto* money of the United States, the ability of the Fed to resist unwise or obviously inflationary policies on the part of an administration has been seriously compromised. It would hardly be realistic to assume that the Fed would ever refuse to discount and monetize the fiat credit of the U.S. Government. Therefore the charge that the Federal Reserve System has been subverted into an engine of inflation is not without substance.

Few economists or bankers, and least of all this writer, will deny the need for a central banking system in the United States, but overall the Federal Reserve System has been a disappointment. It did not prevent or alleviate the depression of 1920–21, or the worst depression in our history, that of 1929–33. In fact, by its unwise credit policies during the twenties, it may have itself been a leading cause of the Great Depression.[23] Furthermore, although the lending power of member banks was made abundant during that depression, through their ability to borrow freely from the Federal Reserve, most individual banks had become so alarmed by the numerous bank failures of the time; by the drastic declines in their own portfolio holdings of stocks, bonds and notes; and by the huge amount of "frozen" receivables, in the form of defaulted and uncollectible loans already accumulated, that they saw no point in making further loans unless the collateral was of the very highest quality.

Those who hold it as an article of faith today that the government can prevent any future depression by flooding the economy with "liquidity" should remember that liquidity and solvency are not necessarily synonymous. Virtually every depression in our history, or in world history for that matter, was preceded by a period of creation of excessive credit. Trying to cure or head off a depression by creating additional credit can only intensify the debacle when it inevitably comes.

Europe and the Gold Exchange Standard.   The financial state of Europe after World War I was appalling. National gold reserves had been drastically depleted, with most of the metal going to the United States to pay for war materials and food. The financial structures of the Allied nations were left grossly inflated with fiat currency and unsupported credit; those of the former Central Powers and Russia appeared almost hopeless. Every nation carried a staggering burden of debt, both internal and external. In 1922, the monetary experts of the Allied countries met at Genoa, Italy, to seek ways to restore an effective international monetary system to replace the full gold standard destroyed so completely in 1914.

Out of this conference came the "Genoa Agreement," which created the so-called *gold exchange standard.* Under this agreement, nations were permitted and encouraged to count holdings of foreign currencies and foreign credits (obtained from countries still on some form of gold standard) as part of their own monetary reserves. Such holdings of gold-based foreign "exchange" were to be regarded as being equal to gold itself. The purpose of this system, it was said, was to "economize" in the use of gold. The value of domestic currencies could thus be kept (theoretically) equal to gold, without the necessity of maintaining large gold reserves or of providing for the internal circulation of gold coin or bullion.

Foreign exchange or credits against the currencies of other nations were to be used in lieu of gold whenever possible, which in practice meant most of the time. The gold exchange standard resulted in a sort of international version of Gresham's Law, under which the various nations jealously hoarded gold in the vaults of their central banks and passed on notes of exchange to their foreign creditors and nonredeemable paper currency to their citizens. The inflationary potential of such an arrangement as the gold exchange standard is obvious.

There were only three choices facing the world's statesmen and money managers after World War I (1914–18):

1. Devalue all monetary units as required, to restore a more realistic relationship between national currencies and gold.
2. Deflate, or remove from circulation, the excessive and unsupported currency and credit created by the distortions of wartime finance.

3. Invent some new form of credit to fill temporarily the gap between the enormous amount of fiat money and debt outstanding and the lack of sufficient gold (at then current prices) to restore liquidity.

Unhappily, they chose the third course, and through the gold exchange standard attempted to create what we would now call "paper gold." They arbitrarily assumed certain foreign exchange and credit to be "as good as gold" when such was hardly the case. Actually, the monetary systems of countries still claiming to maintain gold parity were almost as badly overextended as of those that had left gold entirely—and there was nothing to prevent them from becoming even more abused.

It was, therefore, the worst possible choice and one that led straight to the inflationary and unsound boom of the twenties and the great "bust" of the thirties. It cured nothing, but only masked for a time the poisonous evils of fiat currency and untenable credit that had corrupted the world monetary system. The first option, worldwide devaluation, would have been far better; increasing the price of gold would not only have helped to restore liquidity, but it would have greatly stimulated gold production, enabling governments to rebuild gold reserves, not only faster, but to a greater extent than ever before. Such effects did indeed come about after the wholesale devaluations of the 1930's were *forced* upon the world.

The second option, internal deflation, was used by Germany after the World War II, with outstanding success, as part of the Bonn government's monetary "reform" of 1948. Actually, a combination of steps 1 and 2 would probably be the most practical solution for today's conditions.

But, in 1922, the gold exchange standard seemed the easiest way out, and so it was adopted as the basis for the international monetary system. The United States elected to remain on a full gold standard domestically, but agreed to support an international gold exchange standard by making the gold-backed dollar less competitive through a Federal Reserve policy of low interest rates and easy credit—thus inadvertently providing the fuel for the great speculative stock market and real estate boom of the twenties. Meanwhile, Britain searched for a way to restore the pound to its former position of respect and dominance. *Great Britain Returns to Gold.*   In 1925, Winston Churchill, then Chancellor of the British Exchequer,* took advantage of a momentary calm in the world monetary scene, brought about by Germany's resumption of gold payments in 1924 and by the illusory initial success of the Genoa Agreement, and announced to a startled world that Britain was returning to the prewar gold parity of $4.86 pcr pound sterling. It was a spectacular gesture, and one that could be expected from an old warrior like Churchill (who knew virtually nothing of economics)** but it was little else. The pound should have been devalued by perhaps as much as 50 percent before a gold parity was restored, in order to make up for the inflationary inroads of wartime finance that had greatly reduced the liquidity of British currency and credit. But given Churchill's temperament and Britain's pride and sense of honor, such a realistic step was hardly possible.

The only concession made was that a "gold bullion standard" was adopted, in order to reduce domestic pressure on the pound. Under this type of standard, the monetary unit is not redeemable in small amounts through the use of gold coin, but only in large amounts and only in bullion. In Britain's case, the minimum amount of currency redeemable was limited to the value (in pounds) of 400 ounces of gold.[24] It was, perhaps, as some put it, "a rich man's standard," but it was also a tacit admission that the pound was too weak and too overvalued to stand the test of a full gold standard.

The problem was not that England had returned to gold, but that it had stubbornly, for reasons of politics and pride, refused first to devalue the pound (exactly as the United States, in the sixties, just as stubbornly and for reasons just as inconsequential, refused to devalue a grossly overvalued dollar). By 1926, Britain was already sinking into a depression, with her export goods priced completely out of the world's markets, and her imports, and the resulting balance-of-payments deficits, eating away at her inadequate gold reserves.

*Equivalent to the U.S. Secretary of the Treasury.
**He cheerfully admitted his total inability to comprehend anything connected with mathematics.

Montagu Norman of the Bank of England, Hjalmar Schacht of the Reichsbank, and Charles Rist, Governor of the Bank of France, all pleaded with Benjamin Strong, then Governor of the Federal Reserve Bank of New York,* to pursue further "easy money" policies in the U.S. to reduce pressure on the pound and help protect the gold exchange standard. Strong willingly complied, and in the spring of 1927 lowered the New York rediscount rate to 3½ percent and began to flood the system with credit. Other Federal Reserve Banks quickly followed Strong's lead. Only one member of the the Federal Reserve Board itself, Adolph C. Miller, had the courage and foresight to protest, calling the Federal Reserve's action, "the most costly error committed by it or any other banking system in the last 75 years."[25]

The "Black October" of 1929 was less than three years away, but all difficulties seemed resolved early in 1927, and the post-World War I world went blindly on its way with a patchwork financial structure that saw all three of the basic types of gold standard in use simultaneously:

1. *The Gold Coin Standard*
    Under the gold coin standard, all currency is convertible into gold on demand of the holder, in quantities as small as the smallest gold coin available.
    (This was the standard of the United States from 1900 to 1933.)

2. *The Gold Bullion Standard*
    Under the gold bullion standard, currency is convertible into gold bullion only, and this privilege is limited to some substantial minimum amount, as set by the monetary authorities.
    (This was the standard in Great Britain from 1925 to 1931.)

3. *The Gold Exchange Standard*
    The gold exchange standard is an arrangement whereby the currency of a country is convertible into drafts payable

*Before 1933, the Federal Reserve Bank of New York, because of its dominant position on Wall Street and in international finance, was looked upon as the leader in the formation of the System's policies. The Board itself had not been granted the awesome powers it has today to interfere in virtually every phase of economic activity.

in the currency of some other country that is on a gold coin or gold bullion standard. Because this arrangement can be assumed to provide equality between the domestic currency and a specific weight of gold, the gold exchange standard must be regarded as a true form of gold standard.

(This was the international standard from 1922 to 1931.)

There are only two basic principles to a gold standard: (a) that a specific weight of gold be acknowledged as the exclusive lawful money of a nation, and (b) that the domestic currency be kept equal, at all times, to this specific weight of gold. Thus, although a gold standard may take any one of the forms previously listed, or be a combination of any of these forms, it is a true gold standard as long as the two basic criteria are met.

But any system invented by men can also be distorted, evaded or corrupted by men, and the gold "standards" of the twenties were but flimsy facades behind which lay endless webs of empty promises, worthless securities and unpayable debt. By October of 1929, this burden of deceit had become too great for the existing gold standards to bear.

Notes:

CHAPTER III

1. The word "dollar" is derived from *Joachimsthaler*. In 1519, the minting of a large silver coin was begun at Joachimsthal (Joachim's dale) in the valley of St. Joachim, a silver mining district of Bohemia. This coin, stamped with the head of St. Joachim, consequently became popularly known as the *Joachimsthaler* and it circulated widely throughout Europe. Later the term was shortened to *thaler* in Germany, and corrupted in other languages to *taler, taeler, toler,* etc., and finally to the English "dollar." Hence any large silver coin was, to the English, a dollar. The expression "two-bits," which still survives to this day, became the idiom for the quarter-dollar.

2. According to Spanish records, 68,778,411 gold coins and 2,082,260,637 silver coins were struck at the Mexico City mint between 1537 and 1821.

3. There were also some locally produced coinages, but these were generally limited to small-denomination copper pieces.

4. The Spanish silver dollar was also known as the "pillar dollar" because the obverse design featured the Pillars of Hercules (symbolizing the Strait of Gibraltar). The first design showed two hemispheres, or globes, between the pillars, and 441 million of these pieces were struck until 1772. Then the design was altered to feature a Spanish-shield coat-of-arms between the pillars, and 880 million of this latter type were minted up to 1814. The shield design was also known as the "Carolus dollar" because the reverse featured a portrait of Carolus (Charles) III. Both types were also commonly referred to as *piastres.*

5. The notes of the Continental Congress were denominated in "Spanish dollars," but as the Congress had no coin or bullion in its possession the notes were considered unredeemable.

6. Charles L. Prather, *Money and Banking* (Chicago: Irwin, 1941) p. 204.

7. And French manpower as well. There were as many French troops in the trenches at Yorktown as Americans; French artillery joined in the siege, and Admiral Count de Grasse's French fleet blockaded the coast to prevent British reinforcement or escape.

8. Article I, Section 10.

9. Prather, *op. cit.*, p. 205.

10. There were fourteen states at the time; they were, in order of ratification: Delaware, Pennsylvania, New Jersey, Georgia, Connecticut, Massachusetts, Maryland, South Carolina, New Hampshire, Virginia, New York, North Carolina, Rhode Island and Vermont. The powers were granted under Article I, Section 8.

11. Spanish silver dollars remained legal tender in the United States until 1857, and at that time there were an estimated $2 million worth still in circulation.

12. Prather, *op. cit.*, p. 299.

13. See Paul Bakewell Jr., *Thirteen Curious Errors About Money* (Caldwell, Idaho: Caxton Press, 1962), for a brief but thorough review of the key legislative and judicial actions regarding money in the U.S. from 1792 to 1960.

14. Actually, it is open to question whether even silver coin, as it existed in 1963, was "lawful money," since all silver, including the silver dollar, had been subsidiary coinage since 1873. In fact, as early as 1947 a citizen who had demanded "five dollars" (in lawful money) for a Federal Reserve note of that amount was informed by the Treasury Department that "the term 'lawful money' has not been defined in federal legislation." (Bakewell, *op. cit.*, p. 89.)

15. Gold certificates were often called "yellowbacks" (for obvious reasons), but greenbacks were just that—green.

16. But they did continue to pay the interest due on the bonds of the United States in coin, on demand.

17. Perhaps the best-known United States note or greenback was the $2 bill, which in the post-1933 era existed in no other form. Since 1966, however, all $2 notes have been withdrawn and their total has been replaced by $100 denominations. Five-dollar notes of this type also continue in circulation.

18. See Rickenbacker, *Wooden Nickels.*

19. Uncirculated silver dollars are so common that they are now traded on some of the major commodity exchanges in $1,000 sealed mint bags.

20. The Aldrich Commission, under the chairmanship of Senator Nelson W. Aldrich (R) of Vermont.

21. Membership in the Federal Reserve System is not entirely voluntary. All nationally chartered banks (under the Banking Act of 1865) are *required* to become members. Only state banks and trust companies do so on a voluntary basis.

22. Prather, *op. cit.,* p. 618.

23. See Groseclose, *Money and Man* (New York: Frederick Ungar, 1961), p. 221–236.

24. At the 1925 price for gold this would equal £1701 or $8,268.

25. Robert Sobel, *The Great Bull Market* (New York: Norton, 1968), p. 57.

IV

THE FALL OF GOLD
AND THE RISE OF TYRANNY

"An almost hysterical antagonism toward the gold standard is one issue that unites statists of all persuasions. They seem to sense ... that gold and economic freedom are inseparable."

—ALLEN GREENSPAN

"Gold is not necessary. I have no interest in gold. We'll build a solid state, without an ounce of gold behind it. Anyone who sells above the set prices, let him be marched off to a concentration camp! That's the bastion of money."[1]

—ADOLF HITLER

THE stock market crash of October, 1929, is one of those unique dramatic landmarks, such as the assassination of Julius Caesar, the landing of Columbus or the Battle of Waterloo, that historians find so convenient for marking the major turning points in the destiny of man. But it would be inaccurate to assume, as so many have, that the "Great Crash" was, in itself, the primary cause of the further disasters that were soon to follow. The stock market collapse was but another symptom of the financial and monetary rot that had been accumulating, with increasing intensity, ever since the bonds to gold were loosened, or cast off altogether, in 1914.

The early thirties saw an unparalleled failure of not one, but all three of the main financial props supporting the world's economy:

1. The securities markets.
2. The banking systems.
3. The international monetary arrangements.

The general acceptance of the gold exchange standard had brought about a situation in which each nation's troubles could very quickly become the burden of all nations. When one man's debt is another man's asset, a threat to the debtor becomes a calamity for the creditor as well. Not only was this true internationally, but it was also the case within the individual countries. The great abuse of credit made possible by the new "freedom" of the gold exchange standard had turned every creditor into someone else's debtor. Debt had replaced gold as the common currency of the world.

Thus, the world of 1929 was bound together, not for the better, but for worse; prosperity could only be enjoyed alone, and at the expense of others, but financial disaster had to be shared.

At the time, however, most responsible people viewed the crash as little more than an isolated event, brought about by just another one of those recurring episodes of uninformed public speculation—a little sharper than most, perhaps, but certainly no more significant than what had occurred in 1907 or 1901. And in the latter cases, recovery was rapid and complete within a matter of months. President Hoover reflected the generally undaunted optimism of the nation, in his address of March 7, 1930, when he gave assurances that the overall economic picture was bright. "All the evidence," he concluded, "indicates that the worst effects of the crash will have passed within sixty days."

The stock market itself seemed to indicate that the nation's confidence was not misplaced. After falling from its 1929 high of 381.17, in terms of the popular Dow Jones Industrial Index, to a postcrash low of 198.69, the market rallied and, by June of 1930, had reached 294.07 on the Dow, thereby recovering more than half of its previous loss. But unemployment stubbornly persisted, despite the Federal Reserve's hasty return to a policy of monetary ease (which they had abandoned briefly in 1929, in order to curb the wild speculation on Wall Street), and the frantic slashing of the discount rate failed to produce the old magic.

By the summer of 1930, it was clear that both the United States and the world were in deep trouble and that something more than a mere stock-market panic had taken place. As unemployment soared throughout the remaining months of 1930, the stock market suddenly reversed its upward trend and by August was in a state of obvious disintegration. The extent of this disintegration, which wiped out 88 percent of the values represented by the Dow Jones Industrial Average and more than 90 percent of the Rail Average, during the 2½ years following the 1929 high, can be seen in *Fig. 4*. And the Dow Jones Averages, of course, represent only the "cream" of America's industry; thousands of corporations of lesser stature were completely destroyed.

Next to suffer was the banking system. Although it had weathered the crash itself without apparent injury, it could not withstand the growing tidal wave of liquidations and bank-

Fig. 4

DOW JONES STOCK MARKET INDEX
1922–1932

	INDUSTRIALS		RAILS	
Year	*High*	*Low*	*High*	*Low*
1922	103.43	78.59	93.99	74.43
1923	105.38	85.76	90.63	76.78
1924	120.51	88.33	99.50	80.23
1925	159.30	115.00	112.93	92.82
1926	166.64	135.20	123.23	102.41
1927	202.40	152.73	144.82	119.92
1928	300.00	191.23	152.70	132.60
1929	381.17	198.69	189.11	128.07
1930	294.07	151.71	157.94	91.65
1931	194.36	73.79	111.58	31.42
1932	88.78	41.22	41.30	13.23

Source: *Dow Jones Investor's Handbook*

ruptcies. The "call money" loaned to finance stock market speculation could be and was recovered (at the expense of the margin speculators!), but there was no way to recover more than a fraction of the billions so casually loaned in Europe and South America under the temptation of high interest rates. Nor were the portfolios of domestic bonds, municipal and corporate, much comfort. An asset that cannot be redeemed in money is, in the final analysis, no asset at all. The only lawful money of the United States was gold. The only valid international money was gold. The problem was that there was no longer enough gold, at then current valuations, to redeem any significant amount of the enormous burden of debt and money substitutes previously accumulated.

Many volumes have been written concerning the great world financial collapse and economic depression of the 1930's, but the great majority of them have surprisingly little to say on the subject of gold, except to note the passing of the gold standard and usually as a matter of no great importance. But gold played a central role in the crisis of the 1930's, just as it does in the economic and monetary crisis of the 1970's.

I do not mean to oversimplify such a complex event as the Great Depression, but the fact remains that the relationship between money substitutes, monetized debt and gold, both domestically and internationally, had deteriorated to the point of total illiquidity by 1930. At this point, further injections of fiat credit or fiat currency are no longer able to stimulate an economy but only add to the growing paralysis. Regardless of the contributing elements, the basic cause of almost all recessions and depressions is a "liquidity crisis," that is, an acute insufficiency of *sound money* (gold-based money) with which to retire or reduce a burden of debt that has become dangerous or unbearable.

At this point, the question obviously arises as to whether the repeated monetary crises of the last few years are the result of a debt burden which is merely dangerous or already unbearable. The only answer I can give is that dangerous conditions, if not corrected, eventually become unbearable anyway, and the only way to correct a condition of fundamental illiquidity is to devalue the monetary unit (increase the price of gold) to a level where a fixed gold parity becomes credible and workable again.

In order to restore order to the world's monetary and financial systems in the 1930's, devaluations, like bankruptcies, were carried out on a wholesale basis, but the bankruptcies generally came first. The extent of this disaster can be seen from *Fig. 5,* indicating bank suspensions, and *Fig. 6,* showing business failures during these crisis years.[2]

The effect of such financial carnage upon unemployment and production was bound to be catastrophic. The statistics alone are chilling, as can be seen in the Unemployment Table, *Fig. 7,* and the Price and Production Chart, *Fig. 8.* It will be noted from *Fig. 7,* that drastic reductions of the discount rate failed to halt rapidly escalating unemployment after 1929. Following the crash, the United States was hit by a massive outflow of gold, which did not reverse until after the dollar price

Fig. 5

COMMERCIAL BANK SUSPENSIONS
1922–1933

Year	Total Bank Failures	Federal Reserve Banks	Non-Member Banks
1922	366	62	304
1923	646	122	304
1924	775	160	615
1925	618	146	472
1926	976	158	818
1927	669	122	547
1928	498	73	425
1929	659	81	578
1930	1,350	188	1,162
1931	2,293	516	1,777
1932	1,453	331	1,122
1933	4,000*	2,734	1,266

*Occurred in the first 3 months of 1933.

Source: Federal Reserve System, *Banking and Monetary Statistics, 1921–1933.*

of gold was raised. And nothing was able to halt the unprecedented disintegration of the U.S. economy from 1929 to 1933, *until the dollar was devalued by a substantial amount.* But as soon as the devaluation was accomplished, gold began returning to the United States and the unemployment and production indexes began to turn up, although complete recovery was not achieved until the outbreak of World War II.

Among the interesting things that can be noted from these figures, particularly *Fig. 8,* is that industrial wage rates in a modern commercial economy tend to become so rigid that even massive cutbacks in employment and production have only a

Fig. 6

BUSINESS FAILURES AND LIABILITIES
1922–1940

Year	No. of Failures	Total Liabilities
1922	23,676	$623,895,000
1923	18,718	539,387,000
1924	20,615	543,226,000
1925	21,214	443,744,000
1926	21,773	409,233,000
1927	23,146	520,105,000
1928	23,842	489,559,000
1929	22,909	483,252,000
1930	26,355	668,282,000
1931	28,285	736,310,000
1932	31,822	928,313,000
1933	19,859	457,520,000
1934	12,091	333,959,000
1935	12,244	310,580,000
1936	9,607	203,173,000
1937	9,490	183,253,000
1938	12,836	246,505,000
1939	14,768	182,520,000
1940	13,619	166,684,000

Source: *Encyclopaedia of Banking and Finance* (Munn's), sixth edition, 1962.

limited effect on prices. On the other hand, in areas such as agriculture and food and fibre products, where prices could be reduced, the effect on production (and consequently on employment) was much less severe. Therefore, it would only be prudent to assume that with the present high and generally inflexible union wage structures in industry and construction, any future depression could be very deep and agonizingly pro-

Fig. 7

UNEMPLOYMENT AND DISCOUNT RATE CHANGES
1922–1942

Year	Total Unemployment	Percent of Unemployment	(High–Low) Discount Rate
1922	3,220,000	7.6	4½–4
1923	1,380,000	3.2	4½–4
1924	2,440,000	5.5	4½–4
1925	1,800,000	4.0	3½–3
1926	880,000	1.9	4 –3½
1927	1,890,000	4.1	4 –3½
1928	2,080,000	4.4	4½–3½
1929	1,550,000	3.2	6 –4½
1930	4,340,000	8.7	4½–2
1931	8,020,000	15.9	2½–1½
1932	12,060,000	23.6	3½–2½
1933	12,830,000	24.9	3½–2
1934	11,340,000	21.7	2 –1½
1935	10,610,000	20.1	1½–1½
1936	9,030,000	16.9	1½–1½
1937	7,700,000	14.3	1½–1
1938	10,390,000	19.0	1 –1
1939	9,480,000	17.2	1 –1
1940	8,120,000	14.6	1 –1
1941	5,560,000	9.9	1 –1
1942	2,660,000	4.7	1 –1

Note:
Discount rate maintained at 1½ percent from February 2, 1934, to August 27, 1937. And at 1 percent from August 27, 1937, to January 12, 1948.
Source: *Encyclopaedia of Banking and Finance* (Munn's), sixth edition, 1962.

Fig. 8

PRICES AND PRODUCTION
1929 to Spring of 1933

Industry	Percent Drop in Prices	Percent Drop in Production
Agricultural Machinery	6	80
Motor Vehicles	16	80
Cement	18	65
Iron and Steel	20	83
Auto Tires	33	70
Textiles	45	30
Foodstuffs	49	14
Leather Goods	50	20
Petroleum Products	56	20
Agricultural Commodities	63	6

Source: J.A. Estey, *Business Cycles* (New York, 1941).

longed, due to this factor alone—even though the depression itself could well be brought about by an international monetary failure.

THE END OF THE GOLD EXCHANGE STANDARD

The first of the European states to feel the effects of the spreading world financial crisis were Austria and Germany. The inflation disaster of the early 1920's and the exhaustive struggle over reparations had left the former Central Powers in a state of chronic near-depression. They had been sustained primarily by the generous (although hardly prudent) loans so readily available in New York (part of which had been used by Germany to make reparations payments!). The truth was that the whole banking system of Central Europe was utterly dependent on New York and London and the recall of loans and the rapid curtailing of credit by the latter meant doom for the whole gold exchange system and almost for Europe as well. The financial collapse of Europe paved the way for Hitler and his lesser imitators and sent many of the struggling democracies of the old world straight into the madness of Fascism and militarism.

In May of 1931, the principal commercial bank of Austria, *Kredit Anstalt,* was forced to close its doors. Since Germany was closely involved in Austrian business and financial affairs, the panic generated by the Austrian collapse quickly spread to Germany. In July of 1931, U.S. President Herbert Hoover tried to relieve the situation by proposing his famous moratorium on reparations payments.[3] The Hoover Moratorium was adopted, but it was too late. Germany was already prostrate, and Adolf Hitler and his Nazis were strutting about in the ruins, swelling their ranks with the discontented, the bankrupt and the unemployed.

With the German, Austrian and Eastern European banking systems frozen, England was unable to withdraw its substantial gold credits with these nations, and consequently a fatal run began on the Bank of England itself. By September of 1931, British gold reserves had been drained to the point where she could no longer continue the pledge to redeem the pound in gold bullion. When England announced its departure from gold and allowed the pound, which had been one of the key currencies in the gold exchange system, to float, the system itself was totally destroyed. The repercussions of the British action were severe. Most of the stock exchanges and financial houses on the Continent had to be closed temporarily. In addition, the majority of the other nations of the British Empire were also compelled to abandon gold payments.

THE UNITED STATES DEFAULTS ON GOLD

Despite the enormous effect it has on economic activity, the true nature of bank credit is little understood outside of the limited circle of bankers and professional economists. Bank or deposit credit may be defined simply as an obligation on the part of a bank to pay a certain sum of money on demand, and this obligation is identified only by an entry in the books of a bank, without any currency or other transferable document involved. Although bank credit had originally been established as the result of a specific deposit of specie, the extension of such credit on the basis of exterior pledged collateral, or simply on the presumed good faith of the borrower, has been practiced since the fifteenth century. In modern times, externally secured and nonsecured bank credit has become, by far, the dominant instrument of finance. And, as a result, the reliability of modern bank credit as money rests rather heavily on the prudence and discretion of the bankers.

Most bank-credit loans are actually fictitious, in the sense that no actual money or currency is involved. So long as the borrower does not draw his "deposit" in cash, but simply transfers this credit to others by means of a check, very little actual money or "reserve" is needed by a bank to support such credit. Thus bank credit can be multiplied endlessly, as checks drawn on "created" bank credit can be deposited in other banks and become assets to create new loans and more credit. John Law tried to liquify the commercial wealth of France through the use of bank notes, and his Revolutionary successors tried to monetize the very soil of France itself through the device of the *assignats*. But these futile efforts have been magnificently eclipsed by the modern banker, who has found the way to turn debt itself into money by the magic of bank credit and the checkbook.

The use of bank credit as money is so much a part of the modern financial structure that most people are dumfounded to learn that the actual amount of currency available, both in circulation and that held by banks as reserves, would redeem only a small fraction of the so-called deposits of banking and financial institutions. And, in 1930, it came as a double shock when it was learned that there was not enough gold to redeem more than a small fraction of the currency itself.

By 1930, the excessive creation of bank credit had rendered the statutory limitations on gold "cover" for Federal Reserve notes and member bank deposits (with the Federal Reserve System) quite meaningless. In fact, the ratio between total bank deposits and gold held as bank reserves was lower in the United States than in any other major industrial nation except crisis-ridden Germany. On a comparative basis these ratios were:[4]

United Kingdom	–	11.3	percent gold	
France	–	7.4	"	"
United States	–	7.3	"	"
Germany	–	3.1	"	"

The preceding figures refer only to the ratio between bank-deposit credit and bank-held gold reserves. The relationship between all debt obligations theoretically redeemable in gold, and gold available for such redemption, was probably no more than 2 percent in the United States at the time of the crash. But the collapse of the securities markets, the failure of thousands of banks, the bankruptcy of tens of thousands of overextended businesses and, finally, the default of the Bank of England had cast doubt on all instruments of credit and evidences of debt, and there developed in the world a frantic scramble for gold as everyone sought the ultimate defense against misfortune and adversity.

By the end of 1931, the banking situation was so serious that President Hoover was informed by his Secretary of the Treasury that, "unless we could put into effect a remedy, we could not hold to the gold standard but two weeks longer, because of inability to meet the demands of foreigners and our own citizens for gold."[5] The "remedy" tried was the Glass-Steagall bill, passed early in 1932, that permitted government bonds, along with gold and commercial paper, to be used as collateral for Federal Reserve notes. However, the mere suggestion that the gold standard was in danger at this time brought indignant protests from the press and others, and vigorous denials by the government.[6]

It has become part of the mythology of the Depression that Herbert Hoover was a do-nothing president, who stood idly by while the Depression consumed the nation.[7] But President Hoover did act, and act vigorously, once the Depression was fully under way. The only valid criticism that his detractors can make is that perhaps he procrastinated during the first critical six months after the crash or that he did not recognize the seriousness of the situation soon enough. Nevertheless, what they dare not admit is that, when he did react, it was with the usual bag of government-managed easy-money and easy-credit policies—the very same type of policies that are now uncritically accepted and trusted by the proponents of the so-called Keynesian "New Economics." The following, for example, were included in the program of the Hoover administration and the Federal Reserve prior to 1933:

1. The discount rate was lowered to 1.5 percent (from 6 percent in August of 1929).
2. Banks were permitted to value investment portfolios above market value.
3. The privilege of issuing national bank notes against government securities was greatly expanded.
4. The Glass-Steagall Act permitted the use of government bonds to back Federal Reserve notes.
5. A government-sponsored "Reconstruction Finance Corporation" was set up to loan money at low interest and without significant collateral to industries in trouble or facing bankruptcy.
6. Massive "open market" purchases of government securities were undertaken by the Federal Reserve to flood the system with currency and credit.
7. A Home Loan Bank System was organized to extend more credit for home financing.
8. Federal Agricultural Loan Offices were set up to provide short-term government loans to farmers.

But as long as the gold outflow continued, these efforts proved worse than useless; they only served further to extend a gold-deposit ratio already extended beyond repair, and further reduced the credibility of the whole financial system. For example, when the list of borrowers from the Reconstruction Finance Corporation was made public in December of 1932, it completely destroyed what was left of public confidence, because a large number of supposedly "strong" corporations appeared on that list. Many individuals and corporations promptly withdrew what money they had left on deposit with these institutions, causing another wave of failures. By March 4, 1933, not a single bank in the United States was open; the governors of virtually all the states had been forced to declare banking moratoriums to prevent a total financial and monetary collapse in the United States.

The Confiscation of Gold Money in the United States. When President Franklin D. Roosevelt took office on March 5, the nation was in the midst of the worst peacetime crisis in its history. In the previous two years, over $1 billion in gold, or approximately 20 percent of total U.S. monetary gold holdings, had been lost to foreign demand; while at home, panic withdrawals of gold and currency from the Federal Reserve System had brought reserve requirements below the minimum required by law and had forced the closing of all banking institutions. It was obvious that the two most urgent tasks facing the new President were to find ways to reorganize and reopen the banking system and to restore order and confidence, both at home and abroad, in the money of the United States.

On the day after his inauguration, President Roosevelt began his administration with a series of dramatic and controversial proclamations and executive orders, which were the prelude to an undreamed of era of fiscal, monetary, economic and social experiment.

The first of these orders, the famous "Bank Holiday" proclamation of March 6, 1933, was of critical importance in that it actually ended the 141-year era of circulating gold coinage in the United States, although few people were fully aware of it at the time. Acting under the authority provided by an old wartime law of October 6, 1917, which had never been repealed, and which gave the President complete control over all currency and banking transactions in times of war or national emergency, President Roosevelt issued a proclamation declaring that a national emergency did exist, by virtue of the banking and monetary crisis itself, and therefore that the Act of October 6, 1917 was in effect.*

All banks were ordered to remain closed until March 9, 1933, the day that Congress was to resume. In the interim, squads of Federal bank examiners were dispatched to go over the books of every bank to determine which could be safely reopened, which would have to be reorganized before opening and which would have to be liquidated. The Reconstruction Finance Cor-

*Because of the historical and constitutional importance of this proclamation, it has been reprinted in full in the Appendix Section of this book. (See Appendix I.)

poration was ordered to assist in the reorganizations, and no bank could be reopened without the consent of the Secretary of the Treasury. The bank examiners worked around the clock to restore order.

During and immediately subsequent to the banking moratorium, it was ordered (under the antihoarding provisions of the 1917 Act) that all holders of gold coin and gold certificates be required to surrender them to banks of the Federal Reserve System. In addition, Treasury agents had obtained lists of all those who had previously made large withdrawals of gold coin or gold certificates, and these persons were notified individually to surrender their holdings immediately, or face prosecution on the grounds of hoarding. The gold coin and gold certificate currency surrendered was exchanged for bank-deposit credit or Federal Reserve notes.

When Congress met on March 9, its first order of business was to pass an *Emergency Banking Act,* which confirmed all of the President's prior actions and orders and empowered the President and the Treasury to remain in complete control over all transactions in gold, silver, and foreign exchange, for the time being. The banking holiday was also extended for another week.

Following the National Banking Moratorium, there was a massive return of all other types of currency, as well as gold coin and gold certificates, to the banking system, and confidence began to be restored. Pressure upon the U.S. financial system was thus relieved, the dollar began to stabilize in foreign markets and the public generally assumed that there would be an early return to the gold standard, once general economic conditions had sufficiently improved.

But on April 5, 1933, an Executive Order was issued that demanded the complete surrender of all gold—gold coin, gold bullion and gold certificates—still in the possession of individuals, to the Federal Reserve System, by May 1, 1933. Failure to comply with this order was punishable by a fine of $10,000 or ten years imprisonment, or both.* And on April 20, 1933, an-

*An extract of this order is also reprinted in the Appendix Section. (See Appendix II.)

other Executive Order placed an embargo on all exports of gold from the United States, thus making it clear beyond all doubt that the nation had gone off the gold standard entirely and that there was little possibility of an early return to gold. Throughout the remainder of 1933 there were further regulations and clarifications issued by the President and the Treasury Department regarding gold. However, the Gold Surrender Order of April 5 already included an exemption that permitted the holding of gold, under license, for customary uses in industry and the professions, and another that allowed the possession of *"rare and unusual gold coins of special value to collectors."*

It should be noted here that the gold surrender orders were not exactly received with enthusiasm. Despite the heavy penalties threatened for noncompliance, it is now quite evident that a good many Americans chose to resist what they believed to be an unjust and unconstitutional seizure of private property.[8] Large numbers of American gold coins somehow found their way to Canada and Western Europe, while others apparently went into hiding at home. At any rate, in subsequent years, there were ample quantities of U.S. gold coins for sale abroad, and after it became clear that the Treasury was taking a generous view of the numismatic exemption in its gold regulations, the more common U.S. gold coins also began to appear in increasing numbers in U.S. numismatic channels.

By 1954, the Treasury Department decided officially to recognize what had become a *de facto* situation, and it then ruled that *all* U.S. gold coins (which had survived the original confiscations, legally or otherwise!) could henceforth be presumed to be of "recognized special value to collectors" and therefore could be freely bought, sold and possessed by Americans. Since then, the numismatic market for gold coins has grown tremendously in the United States. However, the possession of gold bullion by Americans is still strongly prohibited, and it can be held only by special license from the Treasury.

Another of the occurrences of 1933 that should be of interest to today's investor is what happened to the price of gold after the United States departed completely from the gold standard and remained off gold for nine months. From April 20, 1933, when the U.S. placed its total embargo on gold exports, until

February 1, 1934, when the Gold Reserve Act took effect, the U.S. dollar "floated" freely in the world exchange markets. As soon as the embargo was announced, and the President and the Secretary of the Treasury had publicly admitted that the United States was no longer on a gold basis, the gold discount against the dollar began to rise, and reached 30 percent by July. In other words, within three months after gold was "demonetized" by the U.S., *the international price of gold had risen by 30 percent* (in terms of U.S. dollars).

Devaluation of the Dollar and the Gold Reserve Act of 1934. On January 15, 1934, President Roosevelt went before Congress and asked for, "the establishment of a permanent policy, placing all monetary gold in the ownership of the Government as a bullion base for its currency, and at the same time providing for a more definite determination of the gold value of the American dollar."[9] On January 30, the Gold Reserve Act became law, and under it all gold in the possession of the Federal Reserve System was transferred to the custody of the Treasury, in exchange for special noncirculating gold certificates issued to the Federal Reserve Banks. The President was also authorized to devalue the dollar by an amount that he deemed appropriate, but not exceeding 60 percent.[10] President Roosevelt promptly used this authority to devalue the U.S. dollar from the original $20.67 per ounce to $35 per ounce of gold. The minting of gold coins was formally prohibited and all outstanding U.S. gold coins were demonetized.*

Therefore, the title to all U.S. monetary gold rested exclusively with the Government after January 30, 1934, and the President assured the nation that, "By making it clear that we are establishing permanent metallic reserves in the possession of the Federal Government, we can organize a currency system which will be both sound and adequate."[11] Unfortunately, these idealistic hopes have not withstood the test of time. Our "reserve" of gold has not only diminished by over 50 percent in the last two decades, but the remainder has been mortgaged by nearly 400 percent of its nominal value to foreign governments

---

*The President's statement relating to the devaluation of the dollar is reprinted in Appendix III.

and banks. The gold portion of our metallic reserve, therefore, proved to be neither permanent, nor a reserve, as we have now no (free) monetary holdings or "bullion base" for our currency left.

It was also part of New Deal policy and legislation to include silver in the establishment of the national metallic reserve. It was originally hoped that at least one-quarter of this so-called reserve (in terms of dollar value) could eventually consist of silver bullion. Whatever rationalizations one can use to justify the concept of an exclusive national metallic reserve, without circulating intrinsic value coinage—and to this writer the reasons advanced in support of this concept are weak and unconvincing—the decision to include such an economically unstable metal as silver as part of the reserve (when stability was one of the chief justifications of the reserve concept) is beyond comprehension.

The only discernible results of post-1934 U.S. silver policy were that the silver mining industry was subsidized in the 1930's when the Treasury bought silver to force the price up, and the silver users were subsidized in the 1950's and '60's when the Treasury sold silver to hold the price down. In the end, our silver "reserves" vanished completely and even our intrinsic-value silver coins were lost. Once again the taxpayers had been victimized by the guile of the silver lobbyists and the economic incomprehension of most politicians.

As for our currency system, since, both legally and in fact, it no longer has any gold (or even silver) backing at all, it can hardly be considered to have remained "sound." And since it has lost nearly 70 percent of its purchasing power from the time it was created in 1934, it certainly cannot be said to have been "adequate." As for the future of the U.S. dollar—well, the evidence of *Fig. 9* is hardly encouraging.*

---

*Technically, of course, one can assume that the 1934 dollar has completely expired, either as of August 15, 1971, when its international convertibility was officially suspended, or on December 19, 1971 when it was "devalued" (in theory) from $35 to $38 per ounce of gold. In that case, *Fig. 9* is a complete record. But, in any case, one can hardly expect that the record of the "new dollar," beginning in 1972, will halt or reverse the long-term trend; particularly since, unlike the 1934 dollar, the 1972 dollar is beginning its life without any gold cover or gold-convertibility limitations.

Fig. 9

PURCHASING POWER OF THE UNITED STATES DOLLAR
1934–1971
Based on Consumer Price Index, U.S. Dept. of Labor
(Beginning January 31, 1934, effective date Gold Reserve
Act; dollar devalued from $20.67 to $35 per ounce of gold.)

DATE	*VALUE*
January 31, 1934	$1.00
Year End:	
1934	.98 1/4
1935	.95 1/2
1936	.94 1/2
1937	.91 5/8
1938	.94 1/4
1939	.94 5/8
1940	.93 5/8
1941	.85 3/8
1942	.78 1/4
1943	.75 3/4
1944	.74 1/4
1945	.72 1/2
1946	.61 5/8
1947	.56 1/4
1948	.54 5/8
1949	.55 7/8
1950	.52 3/4
1951	.49 7/8
1952	.49 1/2
1953	.49 1/8
1954	.49 3/8
1955	.49 1/4
1956	.47 3/4
1957	.46 3/8
1958	.45 5/8
1959	.45
1960	.44 1/4
1961	.44
1962	.43 1/2
1963	.42 3/4
1964	.42 1/4
1965	.41 1/2
1966	.40 1/8
1967	.39
1968	.37 1/4
1969	.35
1970	.33 1/4
1971	.32 1/8

December 19, 1971—1934 gold-exchange dollar terminated. New dollar established with a (theoretical) parity of $38 per troy ounce of gold.

GOLD IN THE POST DEVALUATION ERA, 1934–1944

The Gold Reserve Act placed the United States on an international gold bullion standard, where it has attempted to remain (at least in theory) ever since. The return to a gold basis and the accompanying devaluation of the U.S. dollar produced for a time, beneficial, and in some cases quite dramatic, changes in the financial and economic health of the nation. Most particularly favored were the gold reserves of the United States—and the fortunes of gold mining companies!

At the time of the 1934 devaluation, the U.S. gold stock (in terms of predevaluation dollars) stood at $4 billion. The devaluation itself raised the dollar value of this stock to some $7 billion, although of course no increase in the actual *quantity* of gold had taken place. But from the moment of devaluation on, the United States began to accumulate gold on an ever-increasing scale, and by 1940 our gold reserves had increased to $18 billion. There were three significant and largely unexpected factors behind this phenomenal reversal in the monetary fortunes of the United States. (a) The monetary system of the United States had been thoroughly liquified by the severe deflation of the Depression and by the devaluation, thus making the dollar again appear to be sound, stable, reasonably priced and, therefore, highly desirable. (b) The growing political instability and threats of war in both Europe and the Far East had driven much of the liquid wealth of the world to the greater safety of the United States. (c) The rise in the price of gold, resulting from the devaluation of the dollar and other currencies, brought about a rapid and unprecedented increase in world gold production. (See *Fig. 10.*)

This last effect was, as might be expected, of considerable benefit to the holders of gold mining stocks. The gold mining companies found themselves the beneficiaries of the most ideal set of circumstances that could accrue to any major industry; the guaranteed price of their product was increased by a massive 75 percent, overnight, without any increase in the cost of production. In fact, production costs per ounce of gold had actually decreased substantially below predevaluation levels, because of the depression-induced deflation in labor and material

WORLD GOLD PRODUCTION
1927 – 1940

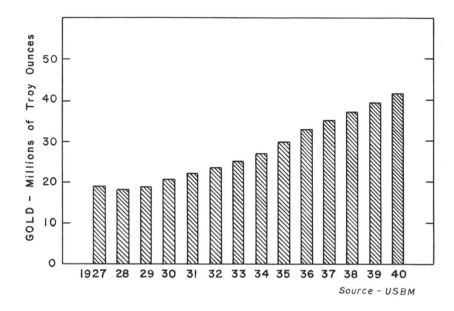

Fig. 10

The coming of the Great World Depression, which began in 1930, the ending of gold convertibility for the British pound sterling in 1931 and the devaluation of the United States dollar from \$20.67 to \$35 per ounce of gold on January 31, 1934, all combined to double world gold output from an average of 19 million ounces during the years 1927 through 1929 to a peak of 41 million ounces in 1940. But U.S. involvement in World War II brought about a drastic decline in the years 1941 through 1945. However, the development of rich new mines in South Africa during the postwar years brought about a complete recovery and the attainment of new highs in world gold production by the late 1950's. Unfortunately, both the United States and Canada failed to share in that recovery.

prices. Furthermore, the increase in the gold price made it possible to mine previously unprofitable lower-grade ore bodies. All of these factors contributed to a dramatic increase in the profits and dividends of established gold mining companies, and even made possible the opening of many new gold mining ventures.

This extraordinary situation was only temporary of course, as the relentless advance of inflation, that was to get under way after the introduction of the "new currency era" in 1934, would eventually bring the gold miners to their usual predicament of being squeezed between rising costs and a fixed selling price. But it lasted long enough to make fortunes for some. At any rate, investors in gold mining shares, unlike holders of other securities, did not have cause for complaint at any time during the Great Depression. Even those who bought gold stocks after the devaluation could have made substantial profits in the following two or three years. *Fig. 11* shows the course of the two leading gold mining shares listed on the New York Stock Exchange during these eventful years. Homestake Mining Company was the foremost American gold producer and Dome Mines was a major Canadian operation. Both of these firms are still very much in business.

Fig. 11

NEW YORK STOCK EXCHANGE PRICES:
HOMESTAKE MINING COMPANY AND DOME MINES
1929–1937

		Dome Mines	*Homestake*
Low	1929	6	65
High	1930	10-3/8	83
	1931	13-1/2	138
	1932	12-7/8	163
	1933	39-1/2	373
	1934	46-1/4	430
	1935	44-7/8	495
	1936	61-1/2	544
	1937	57-1/4	430

Production and dividend record of Homestake Mining Company:
Average yield for the quarter-century prior to

1926 was	–	$3.76 per ton of ore milled		
1927	–	4.87	" "	"
1932	–	7.07	" "	"
1935	–	13.91	" "	"
1936	–	14.10	" "	"

Homestake Dividends:

From July 1934, to May 1937, Homestake Mining Company paid
$2.00 per month extra in dividends, and on December 5, 1935, declared
an additional extra dividend of $20.00 per share. All these extras were
in addition to the regular annual rate (paid quarterly) of $7.00 per
share. The ten year record of Homestake dividends from 1928 to 1938
is as follows:

1928	–	$7.00	1933	–	$15.00
1929	–	7.00	1934	–	30.00
1930	–	8.00	1935	–	56.00
1931	–	8.45	1936	–	36.00
1932	–	10.60	1937	–	18.00

Dome Dividends:

Dome Mines dividends for the period 1928 through 1937 were:

1928	–	$1.00	1933	–	$1.80
1929	–	1.00	1934	–	3.50
1930	–	1.00	1935	–	4.00
1931	–	1.00	1936	–	4.00
1932	–	1.30	1937	–	4.50

Thus the record shows that the value of Homestake shares rose from
a low of $65 per share in 1929 to a high of $544 per share, in the midst
of a great world depression, all the while paying extraordinarily abundant dividends. And the profits of Homestake were not excessive when
compared to those of the leading foreign (South African) gold producers. Homestake stock was split 8 for 1 in 1938, increasing authorized
capital shares from 251,160 to 2,009,280. In 1957, capitalization was
further increased to 2,509,280 shares and increased again in 1966 to 3
million shares. In 1968, authorized capitalization was raised to 10
million shares and outstanding stock was split 2 for 1, resulting in a
total of 5,568,853 shares issued and outstanding.

Dome stock was split 2 for 1 in 1938, increasing authorized capitalization from 1 million shares to 2 million shares.

Note: All data compiled from Standard and Poor's Reports

THE NEW DEAL SILVER POLICY

The silver miners, however, gained very little from the devaluation bonanza. Firstly, the rapid decline in industrial activity after 1929 had brought about a severe erosion in all commodity prices. By 1932, the international price of silver had fallen to an all-time low of 25 cents per ounce. The average price for all of 1932 was 28.2 cents per ounce, giving silver a ratio of about 80 to 1 with gold. After the devaluation of 1934, the ratio approached 100 to 1 at times.

The Silver Purchase Act of 1934. This piece of New Deal legislation is virtually forgotten by the "silver bug" investment advisers of today and by the retailers of silver bullion.[12] But I feel that anyone relying on silver bullion as a hedge against monetary disruption, war, runaway inflation or depression, should be made fully aware of its contents. The laws and acts of the U.S. Government are validated or rejected in the courts, almost exclusively on the basis of established precedents. Therefore, once an action has been taken and upheld in the past, it becomes a precedent for a future similar action under similar circumstances. In 1934, the Government took complete control of the silver market in the United States and retained it, virtually without modification, until 1963.

On June 19, 1934, the President approved of an Act of Congress known as the Silver Purchase Act. Section 2 of that act read as follows:

> "It is hereby declared to be the policy of the United States that the proportion of silver to gold in the monetary stocks of the United States should be increased, with the ultimate objective of having and maintaining one-fourth of the monetary value of such stocks in silver."

To carry out the objective of the Act, the President was authorized to *seize or nationalize* all domestic silver. The price to be paid for such silver was not to exceed 50 cents per ounce (although the silver added to the monetary reserve was to be valued by the Government, for accounting and monetary purposes, at $1.29 per ounce). *All profits made from speculation in silver were subject to a special tax of 50 percent* (yes, I said

FIFTY percent). If and when the market price of silver exceeded $1.29 per ounce it could be sold by the Treasury from the national reserve. (This did not happen until 1965!) Silver accumulated in excess of the 25 percent ratio with gold could also be sold (but this ratio, the objective of the Act, was never achieved).

The Confiscation of Silver Bullion. On August 9, 1934, the President issued a proclamation requiring the surrender of all silver bullion located within the United States, to the Treasury, within 90 days. Under this proclamation, 113 million ounces of silver were seized and nationalized at a cost to the Government of 50.1 cents per ounce.

During the next 25 years, the U.S. Government purchased over 2 billion ounces of silver, from both domestic and foreign sources, at prices ranging from a low of 35 cents to a high of 90 cents per ounce. Although no further direct nationalizations were attempted after 1934, the Government maintained complete control over the domestic silver market until 1963, and all provisions of the Silver Purchase Act remained in force until that time, including the 50 percent tax on profits from the sale of silver.[13] Very little of this silver was used for coin, as the minting of silver dollars was suspended after 1935. Most of our silver "reserve" was monetized in the form of circulating silver certificate currency.

Since 1965, when the international price of silver exceeded the statutory $1.29 per ounce, the Treasury's monetary stocks of silver have been sold on the open market or used to redeem silver certificates. These reserves have now been entirely depleted. The use of silver for coinage was also terminated by the Coinage Act of 1965. Millions of ounces of former monetary silver bullion have since passed into the hands of speculators and hoarders. I cannot predict whether any future administration will ever want to establish a monetary reserve of silver again, although I am inclined to doubt it very much. But I do not doubt for a moment, if the Government becomes convinced the "national interest" requires that it have a stockpile of silver again, *for any purpose,* that it will hesitate to acquire it in the same manner used in the 1930's.

Silver is a very important strategic commodity, but silver bullion (and silver stocks) have these significant disadvantages as monetary-hedge-type investments:

1. Even though the price of gold may be raised (the dollar devalued) during a depression or money crisis, the price of silver may actually decline due to falling industrial demand and panic selling of hoarded silver bullion to get cash currency.
2. In times of severe inflation, the silver market in the U.S. will almost certainly be subject to strict government price controls and regulations. The free market in silver (and other key commodities) may be closed altogether and the 50 percent tax may be reinstated.
3. In any emergency situation, such as war or the severe threat of war, silver bullion, as an important strategic commodity, will probably be seized and nationalized. At the very least, the silver market would be returned to strict government control.

Many silver-minded investment advisers have recommended that silver bullion be bought and stored in Canada or Switzerland to avoid the possibility of confiscation by the U.S. Government. Such a suggestion, however, offers no defense against *Item 1* on the previous list.

TYRANNY AND A WAR ON GOLD IN EUROPE

It is one of the tragedies of history that the destiny of Adolf Hitler was so closely tied to the fortunes, or rather misfortunes, of German finance. It was in no small way due to the inflation trauma of 1919–23 that a nonentity like Hitler was first able to recruit the nucleus of his paranoid National Socialist party from the ranks of the hysterically frustrated, bitter and dispossessed. Hitler's first attempt to seize power, the notorious Munich "Beer Hall *Putsch*", came on November 11, 1923, less than two weeks before Stresemann and Schacht succeeded in reorganizing the currency and ending the inflation. Hitler went to prison for 18 months as a result of the Munich fiasco, but came out more determined than ever to obtain power—only this time he vowed to rely on politics and the polls.

From then on, the political fortunes of the Nazis waxed and waned with Germany's erratic and shaky economic course. Every time unemployment rose or the mark was threatened, Hitler gained new recruits and more votes. The Depression was the final crushing blow to Weimar Germany's hopes for a free and democratic future. By 1931, the two strongest political parties in Germany were the Nazis and the Communists, and they battled each other openly in the streets as Germany descended once again into political and economic anarchy. In the end, the Nazis proved to be the most ruthless.

On March 6, 1933, ironically the very same day that President Roosevelt issued his banking proclamation that ordered the surrender of the privately owned gold and gold coinage of Americans, Adolf Hitler and his Nazi party gained full control of the government of Germany, as a result of the 1933 elections. With Hitler's victory, the world lost all hope of a return to economic or political stability.

From the beginning of his administration, Hitler was a fanatic opponent of gold. Like all statists, he recognized that the right to own gold confers a degree of economic independence on the individual. If the money of the state is inferior or unreliable, the citizen who is free to keep his liquid funds in precious metals can, to a considerable extent, escape the consequences of such official incompetence or dishonesty. If a state issues intrinsic-value coin or currency, it acknowledges that the ownership and control of such money rests, where it belongs, with the people who possess it. But if the state permits nothing but its own fiat money to be used as a standard of value, then the people are at the mercy of the state. Fiat money represents only the authority of the state and, therefore, regardless of who possesses it, such money remains under the control and ownership of the state.

In reality, people are allowed only the use of fiat money—and then only to the extent and in the manner that the state permits. So the German people were put to work building *Autobahnen,* making weapons and preparing for war. But they were paid with paper marks, which were not easy to spend; everything was rationed in Hitler's Germany and strict exchange controls prevented any diversion of money abroad. When the redoubtable Dr. Schacht dared to protest Hitler's irresponsible financial policies and reckless spending for armaments, he was summarily dismissed, and his post as head of the Reichsbank was filled (literally, at any rate!) by that impossible dilettante in everything—Hermann Goering.

History is amazingly consistent on this point: the use of fiat money always leads to repression and violence by the state against the individual. In Revolutionary France, the guillotine awaited anyone caught preferring gold to the worthless *assignats* or violating the price-control "Law of the Maximum." In Bolshevik Russia, the firing squad was the chief instrument of monetary "reform." And in Hitler's Germany, the mark was "backed" by the Gestapo and the concentration camp—perhaps the cruelest monetary "stabilizing plan" of all.

Hitler wouldn't even use gold for international trade. Gold was the accepted international medium of exchange and anything requiring or promoting international cooperation or interdependence was anathema to *Der Fuehrer.* "Autarky," or economic self-sufficiency, therefore, was the order of the day for the Nazis and their imitators in Eastern Europe. Germany's foreign trade at that time was put on a pure barter basis—a special invention of Hitler's in which he took great pride. Aspirin and machinery were exchanged directly for oil, potash and other chemicals for wheat, and so forth. In theory the idea seemed workable, but in practice it was inefficient, inequitable and demoralizing. Somehow, the stronger country (Germany) always got the best of the deal.[14] Fanatical nationalism thus ended what the break-up of the gold exchange standard had begun. International understanding, as well as international trade, withered and died in those years, and the Second World War came to pass from the economic ruin of Germany and the debauching of the world's financial system.

Notes:

CHAPTER IV

1. H.R. Trevor-Roper, *Hitler's Secret Conversations* (New York: Farrar-Strauss, 1953), pp. 104–105.

2. But the Great Depression can hardly be fully appreciated from tables and charts. For those who lived through this period it was an emotional as well as a physical trauma that marked many of them for life. Caroline Bird, in *The Invisible Scar* (New York, 1966), has written movingly about this aspect of the Great Depression.

3. Although conceived of as a temporary measure, the Hoover Moratorium on Reparations became permanent by default. No subsequent action was ever taken to reopen the question.

4. According to *League of Nations Monthly Bulletin,* Special Edition, May 1933 (as quoted in Groseclose, *Money and Man*).

5. Reported by President Hoover (after the fact) in a speech at Des Moines, Iowa, Oct. 4, 1932 (cited by Prather, *Money and Banking,* p. 99).

6. Prather, *op. cit.,* p. 99.

7. A mythology understandably cultivated and encouraged by many Democrat politicians in subsequent years.

8. The U.S. Supreme Court later ruled otherwise, in a narrow (5–4) combined decision covering four related cases (the so-called Gold Clause Opinions). Basically, the majority held that since the right to own gold and to receive gold in payment for obligations previously designated in gold had been surrendered for a currency (Federal Reserve notes) of "equal value" (in terms of purchasing power at the time of exchange), no loss had been suffered, nor had anyone been deprived of property without due process or just compensation. But Justice McReynolds, summing up for the dissenting justices, had these prophetic words for posterity: "Shame and humiliation are now upon us. Moral and financial chaos may confidently be expected to follow." After January 1, 1936, Congress terminated the right to appeal to the Supreme Court in any claim arising out of the confiscation of "coins, currency, gold or silver," or any case "involving the effect or validity of any change in the me-

tallic content of the dollar or other regulation in the value of money."

9. Franklin D. Roosevelt, *On Our Way* (New York: Day & Co., 1934) p. 215.

10. The authority to devalue the dollar had also been granted under earlier legislation (Title III of the Agricultural Adjustment Act of May 13, 1933) but had not been utilized.

11. Roosevelt, *op. cit.,* p. 215.

12. Private bullion dealers often get two to three times the regular industrial-market price by selling silver in small polished bars (1 to 10 oz.) to unsophisticated speculators and hoarders.

13. In 1946, an amendment to the Silver Purchase Act altered the Treasury purchase price to a minimum of 90½ cents per ounce and the public sale price to 91⅝ cents per ounce. But in 1961, all Treasury sales below the mandatory $1.29-per-ounce level were suspended.

14. The same situation prevails today in similar trade arrangements between Russia and the East European satellites; the latter have been known to complain (but not too loudly) that the Soviets somehow always come out ahead on these schemes.

V

GOLD AND MONEY IN A
KEYNESIAN WORLD ECONOMY

"The modern mind dislikes gold because it blurts out unpleasant truths."
—JOSEPH M. SCHUMPETER

"Do not accustom yourself to consider debt only as an inconvenience: you will
one day find it a calamity."

—DR. SAMUEL JOHNSON

EVERY major war brings about a period of hypereconomic
activity, both during the war itself and, after a brief postwar
adjustment, during the years of reorganization and reconstruction that follow. The phenomenon of the inflationary postwar
"boom" has been observed and commented upon by economists
and historians for centuries. And without exception, each of
these abnormal postwar expansions has been terminated by a
serious "correction," followed by a readjustment or return to
more stable monetary and economic conditions.

We have already touched upon some of the monetary-economic events and crises that came about in the United States
as a result of major wars, and they conform very closely to the
historic pattern. The "wildcat" boom that followed the War of
1812, for example, was corrected by the Panic of 1837, and the
Coinage Act of the same year provided the necessary adjust-

ment that put the nation on a *de facto,* but workable, gold standard. After the Civil War, the monetary expansion phase was ended by the Panic of 1893 and the adjustment to a new and more stable financial era came about through the Gold Standard Act of 1900. Following World War I, the great war-inflation boom ended with the spectacular stock market crash of 1929, and the adjustment to a new monetary era was completed with the devaluation of the dollar and the Gold Reserve Act of 1934.

Since World War II was the most extensive and devastating war of modern times, it would have been logical to assume that it would be followed by an inflationary boom of extraordinary duration and intensity; yet few people were able to make such an assumption in 1945. It would be even more logical, and historically consistent, to assume now (1971) that the great post-World War II financial and economic overexpansion, like all its predecessors, will also be corrected and adjusted. It is the author's belief that this correction phase is already well under way. If I were asked arbitrarily to choose a date to mark this historic turning point, I would choose as most appropriate March 18, 1968, the day that an international gold panic ended the illusion of a fixed world gold parity of $35 per troy ounce. Furthermore, this correction could very possibly end in a world economic depression of a severity not seen since the 1930's. And to "adjust" our way out it may very well require a devaluation (or series of devaluations) that would eventually raise the price of gold to $150 per ounce.

The proponents of the postwar "New Economics" have, of course, strongly denied the possibility of either depression or devaluation. But their denials are based on little more than a cherished faith that the government now possesses the techniques and expertise (derived largely from the later theories of John Maynard Keynes) to "manage" the economy ever onward and upward, without serious interruption. Therefore, in the Keynesian view, basing money on gold is not only an anachronism, but an inhibiting nuisance that should be discarded at the earliest opportunity. But, paradoxically, the modern neo-Keynesian money managers and economists must also resist devaluation at all costs, because to permit a devaluation, or even to acknowledge the possibility of it, would be an admission that there are natural economic laws operating beyond their control.*

But there are such laws, and the events that followed World War II demonstrated rather conclusively that they have not been repealed. Two and two still equal four, paper is not gold, and debt does not make either an individual or a nation rich. But the world is filled with illusions, and the greatest and most persistent one of all is that it is possible to get something for nothing. Nowhere is this ultimate delusion more securely entrenched than in that incredible mixture of Socialism, Welfarism, Keynesianism, wishful thinking and plain nonsense that will go down in history as the New Economics. The "New Era" madness of the 1920's will one day seem innocuous by comparison.

THE AGE OF INTERNATIONAL INFLATION BEGINS

In 1944, the financial representatives of 44 Allied nations gathered at Bretton Woods, New Hampshire, to organize a new monetary system for the postwar world. The two dominant figures at this conference were John Maynard Keynes, representing Great Britain, and Harry Dexter White for the United States. The brilliant, aristocratic Keynes, an improbable but fascinating combination of scholar, connoisseur, banker, businessman and millionaire speculator, had become obsessed with the idea that the world had fallen into a state of permanent stagnation and depression. He no longer viewed economics as a descriptive science, but rather as a vehicle for social reform. In his best known work, *A General Theory of Employment, Interest and Money* (New York, 1936) he had argued that

*Officially, at any rate, U.S. resistance to devaluation was finally overcome on December 19, 1971, when Secretary Connally was forced to agree to a "token" 8 percent devaluation of the dollar, from $35 to $38 per ounce of gold. Meaningless as this so-called "devaluation" was in reality (because convertibility at the new rate could not be restored), its intent was most significant. Despite the reluctance of the U.S. to admit it, this step was actually a worldwide affirmation that gold was still the cornerstone of the international monetary system and the universal yardstick of value by which all currencies, including the dollar, would continue to be measured.

prosperity and full employment could only be achieved through government policies that provided cheap money, encouraged the production of capital goods, diverted private money to public investment and stimulated consumption through a reduction of savings. He came to Bretton Woods with the further belief that international trade and investment had to be freed by the creation of an international currency and a world central bank.[1]

Quiet, efficient and unobtrusive, Harry Dexter White was a bureaucrat's ideal of a bureaucrat. At the time he was Assistant Secretary of the Treasury and had been given full responsibility for the Treasury's foreign affairs and policies. He was to die in 1948, under mysterious circumstances, while the subject of an investigation arising out of the notorious Whittaker Chambers-Alger Hiss case concerning Soviet espionage in the United States.[2]

But there would be little point in speculating here on what devious or sinister motives might have been involved in the creation of the postwar international monetary system. It appears to me only that the system that did evolve from Bretton Woods conformed entirely to the political, intellectual and economic climate of the time. The International Monetary Fund, with its gold-dollar exchange standard, was little more than the New Deal monetary experiment extended to an international basis. It was exactly what could be expected from the improbable combination of a New Deal bureaucrat and a liberal Cambridge theoretician. Other voices among the 44 delegations present no doubt also contributed to the decisions taken, but no one now challenges the fact that Keynes and White were the chief architects of the postwar international monetary system.

Basically, the International Monetary Fund (IMF) serves as an international version of the U.S. Federal Reserve System. All member states (there are 107 at this writing) are required to deposit with the IMF a specified draft or "quota" of gold and their own currency. The size of this quota is based on the economic importance of the member state as determined by a complex formula involving the member state's total gold reserves, volume of international trade and similar items. The minimum portion of gold to currency (initially 25 percent) is also fixed by the IMF. The members may also be (and have been) called upon to increase their total deposits whenever it is deemed advisable.

The size of each nation's quota determines its voting power within the IMF and also defines the limits of assistance it can claim from the IMF. In effect, the Fund provides a pool of foreign currencies against which member states may draw whenever they encounter balance of payments difficulties. A country running a deficit may therefore settle it by paying its own currency into the fund in exchange for currency of the country it owes. Thus, if France is in debt to Germany, the Germans would receive payment in their own *Deutschmarks,* and if it were a case of Germany owing France, the payment would be in French francs. By using this facility of the IMF, the debtor country can avoid depleting its domestic gold reserve and gain more time to regain a balance of payments equilibrium.

However, these "drawing rights" with the fund were never intended to be unlimited. They were supposed to be based primarily on how much gold was included in the particular country's quota. If a member state had paid its initial quota 100 percent in gold, then its maximum drawing ability would be 200 percent of its total quota. For example, if the quota was $1 billion and it was deposited 100 percent in gold, then the nation making the deposit was permitted to draw up to the equivalent of $2 billion in foreign currencies. But if a lesser amount of the quota, say 25 percent (the minimum allowable), was pledged in gold and the total quota was still $1 billion, then the ultimate drawing power of that nation would be limited to 200 percent of the gold portion of the quota only, or $500 million.

Originally, a member state could draw the first 25 percent of its quota without hindrance, but it could not draw more than 25 percent in any one year without subjecting itself to an embarrassing investigation by the directors of the Fund to determine whether it was making a genuine effort to eliminate its excessive trade or payments deficits.

The IMF Articles include many other regulations and provisions of a technical nature, which do not require a detailed analysis here, but it should already be clear that what had been brought into being after World War II was a reincarnation of the old gold exchange standard that had failed so drastically in the 1930's. It must be admitted, however, that the formal and detailed organization of the IMF was an obvious improvement over the informal agreements of the 1920's. Nevertheless, the Fund was to demonstrate profound weaknesses within five years of its creation.

First of all, an arrangement such as the IMF requires at least a modest degree of discipline, both by its members individually and by the directors of the organization itself, if it is to have any hope of operating successfully. That is, if it is to remain solvent. A nation chronically in debt to its neighbors and trading partners must have the courage and self-discipline to put its house in order, to practice internal economy and prevent inflation, and to reduce its foreign expenditures and commitments until equilibrium is restored. But how many nations, in the course of modern history, have heroically and consistently placed international honor ahead of domestic expediency? Not too many to be sure; one thinks only of brave little Finland, or perhaps Switzerland and a few other small countries. It seems to be almost a law of history that the larger and more powerful the nation, the more irresponsible its regard for financial integrity. The United States, for example, has had 20 years of international deficits since World War II and Great Britain has been in deficit virtually the whole time.

But if the members of the Fund cannot be counted on to discipline themselves, then the responsibility for maintaining equilibrium obviously has to rest with the fund itself. Unfortunately the Fund proved to have neither the will nor the power to enforce the required discipline. Like the Federal Reserve, the "independence" of the Fund has been largely theoretical. How, for example, was the Fund to discipline the United States, that is force the United States to correct its chronic balance of payments deficit, when the United States was not only the dominant voting member of the Fund, under the organizational rules, but the largest and by far the most powerful economic, political and military entity among the member states? The answer, of course, is that it could not. So the International Monetary Fund became, in effect, an international engine of inflation, monetizing U.S. debt on a world-wide basis, just as the Federal Reserve System had been transformed into a vehicle for performing that same function domestically.

Whenever the drawing rights of the United States or its partner in monetary delinquency, Great Britain, were utilized up to their maximum permissible limits, a way was hastily found to extend the limits. Quotas were repeatedly expanded, "stand by" credits were established, currency "swaps" were arranged, extra drawing rights were granted and, finally, the "Special Drawing Rights" were created and approved in 1970. The Special Drawing Rights are special indeed; they can be created out of thin air, and in unlimited amounts, as long as the United States can pressure or bribe the IMF membership into voting them into effect.

Although they are "defined" in gold, SDR credits are non-redeemable.[3] Therefore they are, in reality, the fiat international currency that Keynes had envisioned in 1944. The SDR's now have equal status with gold, dollars and foreign currency drawings in settling international payments balances and, under the rules of the IMF, must be accepted by a creditor nation when offered in payment for an international debt. They are, in other words, international legal tender. And you can be sure that when the present issue or authorization of SDR credits is exhausted, the United States will clamor for more. Whether it will get them or not is quite another matter. Even if the IMF is to survive in something like its present form, the dominant position of the United States within the fund has been ended. It was ended beyond all doubt on August 15, 1971, when the United States was forced to admit that the dollar was no longer even theoretically "good as gold" and the promise of international convertibility had to be officially suspended by President Nixon.

THE RISE AND FALL OF THE DOLLAR

The IMF was designed to start off the postwar world with a monetary system that supposedly would provide a greater degree of flexibility and liquidity than a regular gold standard. The full gold standard had become thoroughly discredited, largely through the works of Keynes and other liberal economists, and as a result of depression-induced New Deal and Socialist theory and propaganda. But the international gold standard *had never failed in operation*; it had been deliberately abandoned because of the breakdown of international *political* conditions in 1914, which had nothing whatever to do with the world's financial system; the latter was functioning very well at the time. Nevertheless, we have already noted that the IMF was really a reversion to the discredited gold exchange concept of the 1920's which collapsed in the end because it had provided a greater quantity of reserves only by debasing their quality or convertibility. The gold exchange standard turned out to be an international confidence game, which presented the appearance of a gold standard without the reality. When put to a serious test, the confidence evaporated—and there was nothing else left.

Yet the hunger for sound monetary assets was never greater than after World War II. The industrial nations of Europe, formerly a source of international financial assets, had been left bankrupt themselves and were desperately in need of both economic and military aid. Those were the days of the "dollar shortage," the Marshall Plan and Point Four. Reconstruction and rehabilitation were then primary tasks facing the world, but, before any effective progress could be made, international monetary assets and credits had to be reestablished and redistributed. The burden of providing these monetary assets fell, naturally, to the United States, the only major nation to survive the conflict reasonably intact and relatively rich.

The U.S. dollar, therefore, became the most desired and sought-after currency in the early postwar years and Uncle Sam dispensed them with a generous hand. Later, to Americans of the 1960's, it was to appear literally unbelievable that the "almighty dollar," which had been welcomed so eagerly in Europe between 1945 and 1950, could have become, as it did, a mistrusted and unwanted currency. Some were inclined to view this turn of events as just another example of European ingratitude and perfidy. But what actually was demonstrated was only the age-old story that the laws of economics still inexorably apply to all nations, rich or poor, generous or mercenary.

But the possibility of a "fall of the dollar" was impossible to visualize or comprehend in 1944 (as was the eventuality of complete and dynamic recovery for both Europe and Japan). Behind the dollar in those days stood a "reserve" of more than $20 billion in gold, and potential foreign claims against this hoard were insignificant. The United States monetary gold reserves were more than three times the amount held by any other nation and exceeded 60 percent of the world's total of such reserves. Even Keynes was impressed enough to regard the liquidity of the U.S. as "impregnable." Consequently, the British economist was induced to abandon his own position calling for an independent international paper currency and accept the compromise plan of the United States that the dollar become the official "reserve" currency of the IMF, on an equal basis with gold.

The result of this compromise plan was that the gold exchange concept was modified still further to become a gold-dollar exchange standard.* The rules of the IMF, therefore, required that each nation establish and maintain its currency in terms of *either dollars or gold.* The official U.S. definition of the dollar as being 1/35 of an ounce of gold was duly incorporated into the articles of the IMF and (here is the most important provision of all) dollars and dollar credits held by foreign central banks were to be counted as reserves equal to gold.

Therefore the dollar was placed in the position of becoming not only the chief currency of the world, but its principal monetary asset as well. Because the U.S. credit dollar was (theoretically) based solidly on gold, foreign governments were encouraged to base their own currencies, to a considerable extent, on the credit dollar; it was a gold exchange standard with a vengeance. But there were significant benefits to be gained by the United States from such an arrangement. The prestige factor alone was of great value, and the position of being the source of a large part of the world's liquid funds was a substantial advantage in world trade. However, there were serious responsibilities as well. The dollar could only remain "equal" to gold in reality as long as the United States could guarantee its un-

*And it was modified still further in 1969, so that it became a gold-dollar-SDR exchange standard.

limited convertibility into gold, at least on an international basis. Therefore, even though it could deny its own citizens the right to obtain gold for their credit dollars, the United States had to pledge to redeem any and all dollars held by foreign central banks upon demand.

Furthermore, there was an implied responsibility on the part of the United States to maintain the domestic purchasing power of the dollar. Gresham's Law works on an international basis as well as on a domestic one, and any weakening of the U.S. credit dollar, in terms of purchasing power, would certainly be reflected in a preference for gold and a rejection of such dollars as reserves.

The parallels and repetitions of history never cease to amaze and intrigue scholars and philosophers, but they invariably seem to be lost on the so-called practical men of affairs—like bankers and politicians. The monetary system created at Bretton Woods, with a credit dollar as its principal asset, was an experiment that called for considerable caution and constant vigilance, in view of what had happened to similar arrangements in the past. But right from the beginning, the money managers of the United States seemed unable to comprehend that the new "international dollar" created by the IMF and the domestic credit dollar brought into being by the New Deal were not separate entities, but one and the same.

Actually, both U.S. law (the Gold Reserve Act of 1934) and the articles of the IMF defined the dollar as being 1/35 of an ounce of gold. In neither case did it state that the dollar was "equal" to gold, but instead that the dollar *was* gold. Consequently, "dollars" that came into being in other forms were really dollar *claims* or dollar credits, not actual dollars.

When the United States responded to the needs of the world economic community in 1945 and became its banker, the government of the United States assumed a responsibility to prevent the possibility of a "run" on its (gold) bank by preserving confidence in its notes and credit. Therefore we had a dual obligation: (a) to maintain the purchasing power of the domestic credit dollar by avoiding inflationary acts and policies, and (b) to prevent foreign accumulations of international credit dollars from becoming excessive through chronic balance of payments deficits by the United States. That we did neither is the economic tragedy of the postwar world.

The Full Employment Act of 1946.   Basing the U.S. credit dollar, established in 1934, primarily on monetizations of government debt, was an open invitation to inflation. But the *Full Employment Act* passed by Congress in 1946 virtually guaranteed it. In effect, this act made the Keynesian and neo-Keynesian economic theories the law of the land. This law required (and still requires) direct intervention by the government to "stimulate" economic activity, whenever it is deemed necessary in order to provide conditions favorable to maximum employment. The Act specifically calls for government policies that will encourage or provide easy credit, low interest rates, a high rate of consumer spending and the diversion of a substantial portion of the nation's wealth to public (government) use. It was a formula that virtually guaranteed endless inflation.

The United States was then sitting on an inflationary time bomb of an enormous public debt accumulated during the war, which would eventually become monetized. The total domestic money supply (currency and bank credit available on demand) had already skyrocketed from a mere $20 billion in 1934 to $110 billion in 1946, and a large part of the increase was in the form of idle bank deposits just waiting to be spent, as soon as housing and consumer goods were once again available. In short, there was an abundance of money and a shortage of goods; a more perfect example of a built-in potential for inflation could hardly be imagined. Yet the politicians and money managers of 1946 not only passed the inflationary Full Employment Act but they also reduced the gold "cover" requirement for both Federal Reserve notes and Federal Reserve member bank deposits to 25 percent, from 40 percent and 35 percent respectively, thus releasing still more purchasing media into the economy.

The problem was that the politicians and economists of the immediate postwar era and, it must be admitted, a large part of the public as well, had been conditioned to the Keynesian belief that the end of the war would see a return to the depressed conditions and monetary deflation of the 1930's. When this did not happen and the postwar boom arrived (on schedule), the Keynesians and their political allies became convinced that it was only the timely acceptance of their theories that had saved the day. From that time on, every U.S. administration has adopted the basic Keynesian doctrine, with its central principle that the economy must be "managed" to prosperity by government bureaucrats.[4]

But to say that Keynesianism hasn't worked would be the understatement of the decade. Let us look very briefly at what happened to the U. S. economy from 1946 to 1970.

THE NEW ECONOMICS IN THEORY AND PRACTICE

Although the postwar fiscal and monetary policies of the United States have become popularly known as the "New Economics," they contain little that is new and hardly anything that resembles economics. It would be a mistake, however, to attribute the decline and fall of the dollar, which has occurred, entirely to the Keynesian influence. Actually, at the very core of the so-called New Economics lies the ancient but naive delusion of the old Populist and Greenback parties that an abundant supply of paper currency and bank credit guarantees low interest rates, stimulates investment and promotes prosperity. The flaw in this gemlike reasoning is that paper currency and bank credit instruments are not money but only substitutes for money.

Expanding the supply of such substitute money, without a corresponding increase in the monetary base (gold), or, worse, expanding money substitutes while the monetary base is actually contracting, leads to higher interest rates, not lower, encourages reckless speculation rather than sound investment, and only guarantees inflation. The ultimate result is a vicious wage-price spiral that robs everyone of a part of his current income and confiscates an ever-increasing portion of accumulated savings. Inflation consequently accelerates bankruptcies and increases poverty and misery, especially among the millions of elderly citizens and others forced to live on a fixed income.

The Populist theory confuses the cost of money (interest) with the value of money (purchasing power). As the quantity of substitute money is increased, its value or purchasing power is decreased by whatever extent the asset base (gold, sound commercial paper, other trustworthy receivables, etc.) of such money substitutes is diluted. Therefore the lender of this so-called money is forced to demand more, not less, interest for its use to make up for the estimated loss of purchasing power he will sustain during the term of the loan.

However, when their delusion is exposed in practice by the reality of natural economic laws, the inflationists protest that it is gold that is at fault. Get rid of gold, they say, and all will be well. Again they delude themselves. Gold has evolved through the centuries as the ideal money, because it is the ideal commodity. And money, by definition, is "*merely a commodity which is used as a medium of exchange and standard of value.*"[5] Note again, that money is not something that is equal to a commodity or exchangeable for a commodity, it *is* a commodity. And by both the laws of the United States and the Articles of the IMF, that commodity is gold. Therefore, to hold as a proposition that a non-intrinsic-value currency or other money substitute need not be related to any commodity is to invite the conclusion that it is worthless! To say that such currency is based on productive capacity or total commercial and industrial wealth or faith in the government or some similar abstraction is equally absurd, because even the most unsophisticated are aware that these so-called "assets" are neither liquid, nor fixed, nor even measurable.

The refinement that the Keynesians added to the old Populist delusion was the suggestion that monetary and fiscal "stimulation" should be applied only during periods of recession or business stagnation, when such a course would be (presumably) noninflationary. And, as a corollary, whenever the economy became overactive or reached a boom stage, the money supply was to be contracted, credit was to be curtailed and government spending and the public debt were to be reduced, thus allowing for a balanced, smoothly running, depression-free yet noninflationary economy—or so it was thought. But however brilliant it might have been as an academic theory, it soon succumbed to the hard realities of life.

In the first place, it presupposed that economists and money managers could (or would) ever persuade politicians to stop spending public money once they had been sold on the idea that such policies were not only beneficial but absolutely necessary for economic salvation. It certainly should not have required genius to foresee that the Keynesian program, in the hands of politicians, would be carried to its logical conclusion, which is, that if easy money and deficit spending are the proper corrective measures to take after a recession or depression has started, then they would be the proper *preventive* measures to keep one from ever starting. And, over a period of time, this is exactly what happened; Keynesianism became, more and more, a one-way street.

By 1960, the delusion had reached the point where continuous currency and credit expansion through the monetization of public and private debt was regarded as the key to permanent prosperity. And in 1970, a Republican President, who was thought to have regarded himself as a conservative, would announce to a startled electorate that he too had become a Keynesian and, consequently, that he would relieve unemployment and insure prosperity by the simple process of allowing the Federal Government to run a series of massive deficits.[6]

This brings up another major fallacy of the Keynesian theory, which is that government deficit spending during periods of recession or business stagnation is noninflationary. This again is a confusion of ends with means. It is not *when* government borrowing and spending take place, but *how* they are done that determines whether or not they are inflationary. If the government monetizes its debt by selling bonds to the banking system, the banks can use these bonds as assets to make new loans. And this is inflationary, no matter when it is done, because additional purchasing media are both acquired by the Government and created by the banks, without any offsetting increase taking place in either the monetary base or the general wealth.

The only difference discernible in the "counter-cyclical" type of inflation is that in times of deep depression there is a time lag or delay before the usual effects of inflation are felt. Invariably, depression-induced inflation eventually surfaces during the recovery and expansion phase of the economic cycle, when it is not needed and hardly desirable. Only government bond sales directly to the public are true borrowing of assets and therefore noninflationary. But enough of theory, let's look at a few facts.

To begin with, the United States has increased its supply of purchasing media (currency, checking accounts and time deposits) by more than 100 percent since 1945. It currently stands at $210 billion. The most obvious effects of this monetary abundance have been an advance in the consumer price level by 120 percent and a rise in interest rates to the highest levels since the Civil War.[7] Well, not much accomplished there, but what about employment prosperity? Unfortunately, not a great deal of comfort in this area either. Despite the most reckless and desperate program of deficit spending ever attempted by a great nation, unemployment stubbornly persists in returning to "unacceptable" levels.[8] But, far worse than this, no less than 14 million persons are currently existing on public welfare payments and more than 30 million, by the Government's own estimate, are living at poverty levels. In fact, an ever-increasing welfare burden is the number one problem facing state and local governments in the seventies.

In our nation's largest city, New York, 1 million of its 7-million-plus population are on welfare. But despite these depressionlike conditions, New Yorkers seldom enjoy a week that is free from a strike by one or more classes of municipal, service or construction workers. Even policemen and firemen desert their posts, on occasion, in the constant clamor for higher wages to meet the unending rise in the cost of living. In many areas, garbage piles up on the streets; and the subway trains run with their windows smashed by hoodlums and their operating equipment disintegrating from lack of maintenance, simply because the city frequently cannot afford to have these conditions corrected.

New York City receives over $2 billion a year in Federal subsidies for housing, education, mass transit, youth assistance, welfare, highways, airports—you name it and they get it —but the city is still a sociologist's nightmare of poverty, crime and urban decay that grows more impossible with each passing day. And New York is just the largest and most obvious example of our expanding socio-economic crisis. The rest of our major cities are also facing disaster daily. And those who dwell in our small towns, and even in our supposedly affluent suburbs, now know that they, too, are not immune to the relentless pressure of increasing taxes and declining municipal services.

As for our farmers, they have been squeezed for so long between soaring costs and stagnating income that millions have quit the farm altogether. Some were able to sell out to the big corporations that are now moving into farming on a mass-production basis, but many were unable to salvage anything. One of the saddest sights of the time is the thousands of abandoned and decaying farm buildings that now dot the landscape in many of our once-prosperous agricultural areas.

Unfortunately, if history is any guide (and I would not have included so much historical information in this book if I did not believe that it is), it will probably take a major disaster, in the form of a runaway inflation and "blow-off" similar to the German experience of 1923, or a depression collapse and economic paralysis worse than the 1930's, to bring us to our senses and cause a universal demand for a return to honest money (based on gold) and an equitable and sensible fiscal policy. But by that time it will be far too late to take steps to protect one's individual financial assets.

GOLD AND THE DOLLAR IN THE POSTWAR WORLD

Few countries have escaped the curse of inflation in the IMF age. Some have suffered only moderately, but other nations have had their currencies virtually wiped out. Therefore, the years from 1950 to 1970 witnessed not only a flight from the dollar but a general distrust of all paper currencies.

At the time of President Nixon's surprise action of August 15, 1971, which suspended the international convertibility of the dollar, the United States had in its possession (depending on the bookkeeping system used by the Treasury!) somewhere between $7.5 and $10.5 billion in gold (at the $35 per ounce par value). In addition to the $60 billion in paper currency circulating in the United States, there has been created at least another $150 billion in domestic bank credit. Add to this the $50 to $60 billion in Euro-dollars and other foreign dollar claims and we have a grand total of at least $250 billion in dollar claims and credit dollars based, supposedly, on the $10 billion U.S. gold supply. This works out to a maximum liquidity ratio of 4 percent, or 4 cents in gold to back each outstanding credit dollar.

If we consider only international dollar claims, the figure becomes approximately 6:1, or six dollar claims outstanding for every gold dollar (at $35 per ounce) available for their redemption. If the dollar is to be restored to international credibility as a truly convertible currency, the ratio of dollar claims to gold must be reduced to no more than 3:1. This would require a devaluation of the dollar to a new fixed parity of about $105 per ounce!

But why must the dollar be convertible? Why couldn't a floating or nonconvertible dollar continue to function as a useful currency internationally, as well as domestically, even though its role as the world's key reserve currency might be ended. The answer is that it probably could, but then the United States would no longer be able to suppress the price of gold, as it has been doing since 1960. The unpleasant truth (unpleasant to the United States at any rate) is that gold has been historically, and still is, the ultimate standard of value against which all other forms of wealth are measured. We know it and everybody else knows it—and we know that they know it. Therefore, the motive for suppressing the price of gold is to make the dollar (and other paper currencies) look stronger than they actually are.

If the dollar becomes permanently nonconvertible, and gold is formally "demonetized" by the United States, that is, if all official pressures to *suppress* the price of gold were removed, the results would be most interesting to say the least. The political opponents of gold as money, the modern greenbackers, insist that without government support the price of gold, based on purely industrial demand, would drop to something like $6 per ounce. That this argument is pure fantasy will be demonstrated later, but for now let us assume that gold does become, as the neo-Keynesians and the monetarists insist that it should, just another commodity. (This of course would require a free domestic market for gold as well as unlimited international trading.) Now it would be logical to conclude that once the official pressures (including the ban on private gold holding and trading) were removed, the price of gold would adjust, not overnight to be sure, but eventually, to the price levels of other universally traded commodities. If this be so, the price of gold would have a little "catching up" to do.

Based on 1934 prices, when the fixed price of gold was established at $35 per ounce, until 1971, when the fixed convertibility of the dollar was suspended, the general level of commodity prices has risen several hundredfold. When the price of gold is freed or breaks away, at last, to adjust to the general level of commodity prices, and I believe this process has already begun, the results will surely be spectacular. *Fig. 12*, showing the overall rise in the prices of some typical commodities from 1934 to 1971, suggests that if gold is finally beginning to behave like a typical commodity, its price is overdue for an advance of some 350 percent, to a level of $157 per ounce, *merely to discount past inflation*, to say nothing of future developments!

Fig. 12

TYPICAL COMMODITY PRICES
1934–1971

Commodity	1934 Value*	1971 Value*	Percent Increase
Corn	$0.25 per bu.	$1.25 per bu.	400
Wheat	.50 per bu.	1.50 per bu.	200
Cotton	.10 per lb.	.30 per lb.	200
Sugar	.01 per lb.	.08 per lb.	700
Cocoa	.05 per lb.	.25 per lb.	400
Wool	.20 per lb.	.60 per lb.	200
Silver	.50 per oz.	1.50 per oz.	200
Copper	.08 per lb.	.56 per lb.	600
Nickel	.35 per lb.	1.40 per lb.	300
Lead	.04 per lb.	.16 per lb.	300
Average of above ten commodities			350
Gold	$35.00 per oz.	42.00 per oz.**	20

Notes:
 *Prices rounded off to nearest cent.
**London Market price.

Source: U.S. Dept. of Commerce statistics.

Of course, I believe that the U.S. Government will do its best to resist any major advance in the price of gold, even if the dollar remains completely nonconvertible. But, as events since 1965 have demonstrated, its ability to do so effectively is constantly diminishing. A permanently floating dollar and the formal demonetization of gold in the United States would, in the author's opinion, lead to a gradual but, in the long run, irresistable move in the price of gold to parity with the general level of prices in the United States as reflected by the Consumer Price Index and the Wholesale Commodity Average.

THEREFORE, A FLOATING DOLLAR WOULD BE VERY BULLISH FOR GOLD, ALTHOUGH IT IS NOT ONLY POSSIBLE BUT PROBABLE THAT SUCH AN EVENT WOULD BE INITIALLY MISINTERPRETED BY THE MAJORITY OF AMERICAN INVESTORS, BROKERS AND ADVISERS, CAUSING A SHARP BUT TEMPORARY DECLINE IN GOLD SHARES. THE WELL-INFORMED MINORITY, HOWEVER, WILL BUY THESE SHARES AT DEPRESSED PRICES AND LAY THE FOUNDATION FOR EXTRAORDINARY PROFITS LATER ON.

But what would happen, the reader may ask, if the United States were to allow the dollar to float permanently, that is, refuse to redeem foreign-held dollars for gold, and, at the same time, maintain that the price of gold, in terms of dollars, is still $35 per ounce—or some figure close to it?* Well, we would probably fare no better than the Russians, and deservedly so. The Soviet Union claims that its monetary unit, the ruble, is worth $1.12 in gold or Western currencies. But international banks, such as the Swiss Credit Bank in Zurich, exchange stray rubles for only 19.5 cents. Why? Because the Soviet Union will not redeem foreign-held rubles in gold or gold-backed Western currencies, and, in a free market, the ruble, or any other nonconvertible currency, will automatically find its *true* value, based on its purchasing power in the home country and on the demand for its country's products abroad.

What about SDR's? Can't the SDR's become an acceptable substitute for gold? It must be granted that the SDR's are more trusted abroad than dollars, because at least they are under

*Such as the (fictitious) $38 per ounce parity agreed upon by the "group of ten" major trading nations on December 19, 1971!

international control. But for the IMF to provide the United States with enough SDR credits to enable it to redeem outstanding dollars for SDR's, as well as cover future payment's deficits, would make no sense at all; it would just be substituting one type of paper for another. In that case, the world might just as well continue to accept and hold nonconvertible dollars.

The SDR's will retain some degree of value and acceptance only as long as their issue is strictly limited and controlled. Consequently they will be of little use in shoring up the dollar. Gresham's Law will function with the SDR's just as it does with any other currency, and, if they are debased by overissue, they too will be devalued and ultimately repudiated.

It has also been suggested that the world could continue to function economically with a system under which all currencies would float and be traded simply on the basis of supply and demand, without any reference to gold. But we have been down that road before and it proved to be disastrous. In the early 1920's, the currencies of the Scandinavian countries and most of Central and Eastern Europe were put on a floating basis and the result was a long period of rampant exchange speculation, economic stagnation, inflation and declining external trade. During the crisis of the 1930's, much of the world was forced on a floating currency basis. Again, it only increased the existing economic chaos and reduced international trade to the vanishing point. In the end, realistic and workable fixed gold parities had to be restored. They will have to be restored again and the price of gold will have to be raised by whatever amount is necessary to accomplish this.

The uniqueness of gold as the ultimate monetary asset will never be seriously challenged, because *gold is the only monetary asset that is not someone else's liability.*

EUROPE IN THE POSTWAR ERA

The IMF was never intended to carry the entire burden of providing international monetary assets, but was only to act as a bank of discount or lender of last resort, that could temporarily help a member state maintain liquidity during an adverse balance of payments period. The thought was that the nation concerned would then be free to take the necessary steps to correct its difficulty in a calm and deliberate manner, without being forced into hasty or detrimental actions. After the emergency had passed, the Fund was to be repaid. The Fund, therefore, was only supposed to be the balancing wheel of the international monetary system. The U.S. credit dollar and, to a lesser extent, the British pound sterling were to continue to be the basic currencies of international trade. Unfortunately, however, the Britain of 1945 was no longer the undisputed head of the greatest world empire ever conceived, but a battered and weary nation of very modest resources, no longer equal to the great burdens and responsibilities still expected of her.

Great Britain and the Pound Sterling.   The decline of Great Britain from its imperial glory to the role of a small industrial nation struggling for survival, in just 25 years, will surely be regarded by historians of the distant future as one of the most incredible events of the twentieth century; that is, if we are to have a distant future. But it is only the economic aspects of this event that concern us here.

The first surprise came in 1945, when the British Labor party won a decisive victory over the Conservatives led by wartime Prime Minister Winston Churchill. It was all the more unexpected because the militant Labor party had been only a vociferous minority before the war; the chief opposition in the prewar era had been the Liberals. Nevertheless, the Labor party, under the leadership of Mr. Clement Atlee, had won on a pledge to bring socialism to Great Britain, and immediately upon assuming office they proceeded with a grandiose plan to nationalize all major industries. But despite the fact that Britain received over $5 billion in economic aid from the United States between 1945 and 1951, the socialist Labor Party was unable to bring about prosperity or even a convincing economic recovery. In fact, Great Britain rapidly became an economic liability to the rest of the world.

The arrival of socialism in the former citadel of international finance, together with growing political disintegration of the Empire obviously did nothing to enhance world confidence in the pound sterling. Subsequent to the devaluation of 1931, the pound had been allowed to float until 1939, when a new fixed parity of $4.03 per pound was established.[9] After the war, the Labor Government announced that it would maintain the pound at its prewar (1939) parity. But, like all governments operating under the gold exchange principle, Great Britain had issued notes far in excess of its ability to redeem them. Consequently, when the faltering socialist economy of Britain itself and growing political dissension within the Empire-turned-Commonwealth began to cast doubts upon the integrity and strength of British finance, a run against the Bank of England developed, which neither massive dollar aid nor repeated emergency drawings from the IMF could stem.

After Chancellor of the Exchequer Sir Stafford Cripps had publicly denied no less than 13 times that Britain would ever again devalue the pound, the British Government, in 1949, was forced to devalue the pound from $4.03 to $2.80. The shock of that act very nearly broke up the Bretton Woods-IMF monetary system then and there. Altogether, 49 other nations were forced into parallel devaluations of their own currencies. It was only the nearly universal faith in the immutability of the dollar and in the enormous liquidity of the United States that saved the day.

Although for a time it eased pressures on the pound, the devaluation of 1949 proved to be only the beginning of Britain's economic troubles, rather than the end. Even after the Conservatives were returned to power for a time, after 1951, they were unable to reduce significantly the inflationary pressures brought about by the delayed action effect of war finance and by the disastrous cheap-money policies pursued by the Bank of England under the Labor administration. Nor were they able more than temporarily to arrest the leftward drift of British society. And neither the Conservatives nor even their own Labor Party were able to halt the growing inefficiency of the British workmen or restrain the increasingly irresponsible behavior of their powerful trade unions.

The most obvious effect of socialism in Britain has been the development of what has become known worldwide as the "English disease," an economic malady in which the public is conditioned constantly to expect more and more money and ever-increasing government benefits for less and less work. Unfortunately, the English disease has proven to be their most exportable commodity, and virtually every Western nation has now contracted this virus to one degree or another.

From 1945 on, Great Britain, which had been expected to provide part of the world's desperately needed new monetary assets, became instead the number-one customer at the IMF credit window and, in addition, periodically had to be rescued by huge loans from the United States and consortiums of other IMF nations. Nevertheless, the pound had to be devalued again from $2.80 to $2.40 in 1967. During 1970, a newly elected Conservative Government succeeded in restoring some semblance of order to the British economy after a previous decade of socialist mismanagement, but first it had to cope with the worst outbreak of labor difficulties since the great general strike of 1926. The United Kingdom now appears to be at the crossroads; one more serious outbreak of the "English disease" will surely result in another crisis for the pound, perhaps the most serious to date, and this in turn would put great pressure on the London gold price.

British citizens have been the principal investors in South African gold shares during the past two decades, which indicates, at least, that not all of them have been deluded by Labor's fantasies and that there are ways to escape the monetary perils of a socialist democracy. With two devaluations of the pound during this period, and a third perhaps imminent, gold stocks should have been a most rewarding investment for the beleaguered Briton. Furthermore, if a gold-oriented British investor had concentrated on the newer mines developed in South Africa during the fifties, he would not only have protected his capital, but would have enjoyed a truly spectacular increase in both capital asset value and dividend income over the past two decades.

France and the Franc.   The history of French finance since 1914 presents an appalling example of what prolonged wartime economics, combined with welfarist politics, can do to a nation's currency. Between 1914 and 1970, the franc lost approximately 99.3 percent of its value (in terms of U.S. dollars and gold). This shocking statistic is even more depressing when one considers that from the time the French monetary system had been stabilized and reorganized by Napoleon in

1803, until 1914, the gold value of the franc had been strictly maintained, despite the subsequent fall of Napoleon's empire, the post-Napoleonic occupation of France by allied troops, two more incompetent monarchies, two revolutions, another empire, two republics, several major European wars, military adventuring overseas and finally the massive defeat and invasion of 1870–71.

Through all the internal disorder and external strain that assailed France in the nineteenth century, the gold franc remained a bulwark for the French economy and provided the means for speedy recovery after each of her interminable political and military disasters. But after 1914, the one remaining element of continuity and stability in the administration of France, the gold standard, was abandoned. The franc was cut loose to float but, as is usual in such cases, it began to sink at once. In 1914, the franc had been valued at 20 U.S. cents, but by the time the "Great War" that was to end wars was over, the franc had declined to little more than 6 cents in terms of foreign (dollar) exchange.

France, like the rest of the world at the time, was also swept by a primary postwar inflation, and it was not until 1927 that a firm gold parity could be restored to the franc at 3.92 U.S. cents. However, the French did not devalue immediately after the U.S. devaluation of the dollar in 1934, so for a time the position of the franc was strengthened. But the renewed threat of war and the leftward drift of French politics in the late 1930's revived inflationary pressures and forced a new series of devaluations on the franc. The last official quote for the pre-World War II franc was 2.51 U.S. cents in 1939.

By the end of the Second World War, the gold (and dollar) value of the franc was still more drastically reduced; the December 1946 foreign-exchange quotation was only .84 cent. The British devaluation of 1949 forced a parallel devaluation of the franc, which further reduced it to .30 cent or 333 francs per dollar (versus a 1914 ratio of 4 francs per dollar).

From the Liberation in 1944 to the return of De Gaulle in 1958, the government of France was again dominated by Socialist and Communist elements. Immediately after the war, this left coalition nationalized the principal banks and insurance companies, the railroads, airlines, merchant marine, utilities, coal mines, and most of the munitions, aviation and automotive industries. It also voted in a broad program of increased socialist-welfare services, subsidies and benefits. But far from being pacified by these moves, the French trade unions, particularly those dominated by Communist and Socialist leadership, embarked on a perpetual round of strikes and riots to demand ever higher wages and still greater welfare benefits and payments.

To complicate matters further, France became involved in two disastrous and unpopular colonial wars during this period, one in Indo-China and another, later, in Algeria.[10] The total result of all this was continued inflation and constant economic and political chaos. Under the Fourth Republic (1944–1958), no less than 26 successive governments attempted and failed to cope with conditions that often bordered on anarchy. At last, after 14 years of such turmoil, and with the nation facing open civil war, the people of France turned to their wartime leader, General Charles de Gaulle, and he accepted the presidency on terms that made him a virtual dictator.[11]

The transformation of France under De Gaulle was extraordinary, to say the least. *Le Grand Charles* may have had his faults, but it cannot be denied that under his firm leadership the French nation was restored to a position of significance and respect among the great powers of the world. But, more importantly, economic order, domestic prosperity and national pride and dignity were reestablished within France itself. It is most significant that De Gaulle's first efforts upon assuming office were directed toward securing a sound and respected currency for France, and to help achieve this goal he demanded balanced budgets and an end to deficit spending at all levels of government.

The franc itself, which had fallen to a record low of .204 U.S. cent per franc, was exchanged for Gaullist "New Francs" at the rate of 100 to 1 (100 francs = 1 NF). Thus the parity of 1914 was reestablished by making the New Franc worth 20.4 U.S. cents. When it became generally recognized that France had indeed stopped creating printing press money, by way of monetizing government debt, the French franc, formerly one of the weakest of world currencies, became one of the strongest. The French trade balance, which had been in constant deficit under the inflation-plagued rule of the Socialists, began to show such heavy surpluses that De Gaulle was accused of trying to sabotage the Keynesian world monetary system. After all, it was this system that had already begun to foster a nearly universal belief that inflation and debt were the preferred ways of life.

Furthermore, when the volume of dollars in the French treasury began to exceed what De Gaulle and his financial adviser, Jacques Rueff, considered to be a prudent level, they were returned to the United States for redemption in gold, as provided for under IMF rules.[12] This really brought howls of anguish from the Keynesian-oriented money managers in the U.S. Treasury Department. France was hardly the only nation cashing in dollars for gold at this time, but De Gaulle, never a popular figure in the United States because of his unyielding attitude on any point he considered vital to the interests of France, took the brunt of U.S. official criticism. But blaming De Gaulle, or any other individual or nation, for the U.S. balance of payments predicament was hardly constructive. It was equivalent to accusing the creditors of the Penn-Central Railroad of causing its bankruptcy because they had the audacity to try to cash Penn-Central checks made out to them.

At any rate, De Gaulle believed (quite correctly as it turned out) that his major problem was not the health of the dollar, but that of the franc. The worldwide inflation constantly being fed by the U.S. deficit and by the tenacity of neo-Keynesian and Socialist economic thinking and expectations, continuously threatened all nations in the postwar world. Nevertheless, by 1965, De Gaulle felt that French gold reserves had recovered to the point where he could issue a public appeal for a worldwide return to the discipline of a full gold standard. This suggestion, not unexpectedly, was greeted with intense and open hostility in both Washington and London. In 1967, however, the French franc itself was finally reestablished on a full gold basis and all exchange controls and restrictions were lifted.

But the work of a decade was destroyed in a single week in May of 1968. Virtually without warning, a near revolution broke out in Paris and other major French cities while De

Gaulle was away on a state visit to Roumania. Behind the May riots were long-smoldering resentments by students and certain segments of the working population against insufficient opportunities in education and employment, inadequate housing, and inequalities in wages brought about by the past decades of inflation.

To quell the May riots, general wage increases averaging more than 15 percent had to be granted, and the result was a renewal of the wage-price spiral that sent confidence in the franc plummeting once again and caused massive losses to France's hard-won gold reserves. An even greater blow to confidence in the franc, perhaps, was the fact that De Gaulle's prestige, upon which so much of his personal style of government depended, had been seriously damaged. Early in 1969, the aging hero of Free France asked the French people for a new vote of confidence, in the form of a referendum on certain government reforms. That confidence was not granted. Therefore, having done all that he could for France, Charles de Gaulle chose to retire. He did so with dignity and honor.

Only three months after De Gaulle's retirement, his successor, M. Pompidou, was forced to devalue the franc by 12½ percent, to 18 U.S. cents per New Franc (.18 cent in terms of old francs). For years Charles de Gaulle had been accused of sabotaging the dollar—but it appears that someone had sabotaged the franc also. The incredible collapse of the French franc from its position of seemingly impregnable strength in 1967 to one of the weakest links in the world monetary system just one year later, shows how political and social instability and a failure to cope with excessive domestic demand can fatally undermine even an essentially strong and sound monetary structure. One can only wonder at this point what a similar domestic upheaval in the United States would do to our overextended dollar.

The German Miracle. The recovery of Western Germany from the appalling ruin of World War II to its present position as one of the richest and most productive nations on earth is surely one of the most astounding and unprecedented events of economic history. The case of Japan is similarly spectacular. What has happened in these countries is of special interest to

American investors, because our defeated enemies of 1945, by hard work and a dedication to economic freedom, have transformed themselves into the leading creditors of their former conquerors. West Germany and Japan together hold dollar claims that exceed by more than 50 percent the entire gold "reserves" of the United States.

Conditions in the Western Occupation Zone of Germany at the end of the war were as bad as could be imagined. More than 40 percent of all the buildings in Germany were either totally destroyed or heavily damaged. The once mighty Ruhr industrial district was a silent rubble heap. What remained of other German heavy industry was being dismantled and removed by the Allied occupation authorities, as part of a misguided policy of demilitarizing Germany by permanently crippling its industrial base.[13] Consequently, from 1946 to 1949, the principal problem of the occupying powers was to prevent mass starvation in Germany. The United States alone provided more than $3 billion in aid to the Western Zone, but very little of the total Allied assistance to Germany could be applied to reconstruction, as it had to be used almost entirely merely to sustain life and health.

In the spring of 1948, the Western occupying powers concluded that there was no hope of obtaining Russian cooperation in the administration of all Germany; they therefore decided to permit the establishment of a self-governing republic in the Western Zone. The Germans themselves took the first step toward recovery and solvency through the famous economic "reform" of June 1948, which wiped out more than 90 percent of the face value of the inflation-ruined *Reichsmarks* of the Hitler era. What remained could then be exchanged for the new *Deutschmarks* of the West German Federal Republic. Thus, Germany chose the painful but highly effective method of drastic internal deflation to restore monetary integrity and liquidity.

Monetary reform and the ending of Allied military government freed the Germans from rationing, wage and price controls, and all the other trappings of authoritarian economics that had held them in bondage since the beginning of the Hitler regime. The Germans had experienced socialism in its most virulent form, and they wanted no more of that! The Germans were unique in the early postwar years in that they openly declared themselves in favor of a free-market economy. What was later described as "the German Miracle" by amazed on-lookers was miraculous only to the extent that the Germans were able to maintain a sound currency, a price structure based primarily on the market mechanism, and a deficit-free government in a world dominated by and obsessed with socialism, Keynesianism and welfarism.

So, despite the fact that West Germany had suffered ten times the property damage of her European neighbors France and Britain, and had to absorb 10 million refugees from the Eastern Zone besides, the German Federal Republic soon left the "victors" far behind. While France and Britain struggled ineffectually with socialism, West Germany embarked on a fantastic economic boom that not only rebuilt the devastated areas in record time, but made West Germany by far the most prosperous nation in Europe and the third-ranking industrial power in the world in just two decades. The German Federal Republic's gold and foreign exchange reserves now exceed those of the United States. Such reserves totalled $15 billion for West Germany versus $14.7 billion for the United States as of April 1971. And at least $7 billion of the German reserves were in the form of dollars, mostly unwanted and unneeded, that are a potential claim on the U.S. gold reserve.

To a considerable extent, West Germany's economic success has made it a model for all of Europe. By following the German example, the smaller Continental nations have also enjoyed phenomenal economic and financial success in the last two decades. As a result, socialism is gradually being moderated in Western Europe, although government ownership of railroads, utilities and certain defense-oriented industries persists. But the nationalization of such public services is part of a socio-economic pattern that was begun decades ago and it will no doubt remain unchallenged. However, industry in general enjoys a high degree of freedom from government interference, regulation and coercion.

Private entrepreneurs in Germany also have confidence that their government will not engage in irresponsible deficit spending or monetary debasement, and this releases enormous creative and productive energies. Only when capital is freed from the fear of government penalties and confiscations can it properly do its work of providing the fuel for the economic engine. In countries with weak and mistrusted monetary systems, the energies and capital of citizens are dissipated in endless and nonproductive speculations, maneuvers and evasions required merely to protect hard-earned wealth from government confiscation through inflation and excessive taxation. When private capital has to struggle for its very existence against rapacious, corrupt or incompetent government, it can hardly be expected to assume the additional risks of financing private economic development.

THE EUROPEAN ECONOMIC COMMUNITY
The recovery of Europe from the devastation of World War II to its present position of economic and financial superiority was also aided by the unprecedented degree of intra-European cooperation that followed the conflict. The so-called Common Market or European Economic Community (EEC) is another of the miracles of the postwar world. It began in 1948 as a movement toward a federal union or "United States" of Europe, but, in the beginning, it was supported mainly by small groups of intellectuals, businessmen and other private persons in the various countries. However, the severity of their internal economic problems, combined with the threat of a renewed Soviet imperialism, soon brought the governments of Western Europe to a serious consideration of the ideas advanced by the federalists.

The first significant step was the Schuman Plan, which welded the coal, iron and steel industries of Western Europe into a single economic unit through joint production and marketing arrangements.[14] Other negotiations brought about intra-European cooperation in several additional important economic and cultural areas, such as rail, water and air transportation, electric power production, nuclear research and development, tourism and education.

However, the movement for a full political union of the European States has met, not unexpectedly, with some setbacks.

Although a "Council of Europe" was created in 1948, and still meets periodically in Strasbourg to promote the idea of a federal Europe, the political problems involved appear to be insurmountable at this time. Nationalism is still a potent force in Europe, and the political affairs of the Continent are still too involved in the complexities and entanglements of the Cold War to permit significant progress in the political area. Therefore the leaders of the European movement have concentrated on achieving economic unity first. They are wise in so doing; once a full economic union is completed, political federation will inevitably follow in time as a natural development.

By 1959, the earlier economic associations had proven so successful that the original six nations of the European Coal and Steel Community—France, West Germany, Italy, Belgium, Holland and Luxembourg—felt that the time had come to unite formally in an unrestricted customs union. Therefore, through the Treaty of Rome, they moved still closer together to promote the economic and social development of their peoples. The EEC, or Common Market, became the second-largest free trade area in the Western world, exceeded only by the United States.

There are no trade or tariff barriers between the member states and steps are taken to place EEC trade with the rest of the world on a coordinated and noncompetitive basis. The Common Market lacks only a unified currency and banking system and a common tax structure to make it the full equal of the United States as an economic entity, and plans have already been made to attain these ends. As a beginning, two of the largest banks of Europe have already agreed to coordinate their operating and lending policies on a world basis, although a full unification of the Common Market's banking system (which would severely challenge the present world domination of the Anglo-American banking houses) will have to await the creation of a common European currency.[15]

The so-called Werner Plan, prepared by a committee headed by Premier Pierre Werner of Luxembourg, sets up a program through which a Common Market "Eurocurrency" would be achieved by 1980. Such a currency would rival, if not supersede, the dollar as an international reserve currency. In addition, any currency acceptable to the inflation-scarred Europeans would surely have to be based on and fully convertible into gold. The Eurocurrency therefore would be, in effect, an international gold certificate.[16] The Werner Plan also calls for a supranational decision center or economic parliament to control and coordinate Common Market trade policies and a European central bank to oversee its monetary affairs. At present, the EEC is managed solely by a six-nation Council of Ministers.

By 1971, four more nations, Great Britain, Ireland, Denmark and Norway, were seriously negotiating for membership in the EEC.* If Great Britain gains admission, Ireland is bound to join as well, for her economy is deeply involved with the U.K. And if any one of the Scandinavian States is accepted into the Common Market, the others will surely follow. Spain has also expressed an interest in the EEC, although no actual negotiations with Spain are yet in progress. However, both Spain and Israel have concluded preferential trade agreements with the Market. Portugal has also asked for such a pact.

In addition, nearly all of the former African colonies (now 18 independent states) of Market members enjoy an "associate" membership, which grants them duty-free status for their exports to the Market in exchange for preferential treatment of imports from the EEC. Six other African states, all members of the British Commonwealth, have also been granted associate membership. Greece, Turkey and Malta are associate members scheduled to obtain full membership as soon as their economies are more fully developed. Austria would love to become at least an associate member and would apply at once if she could escape from the restrictions of the 1955 Austro-Russian Treaty that binds Austria to strict neutrality between East and West.

The potential of the Common Market, with its 320 million very advanced people and its enormous industrial base is staggering, particularly if the EEC is able to make Africa its backyard and source of raw materials. South Africa could actually become the southern outpost of this new Roman empire. But, in any case, South Africa's gold resources will help back the coming Eurocurrency.

*These negotiations were successfully completed in 1972, and Great Britain, Ireland, Denmark and Norway are scheduled to become full partners in the EEC on January 1, 1973.

I simply cannot accept that anyone in the U.S. Treasury or the IMF bureaucracy is really so stupid as actually to believe that, in the long run, the Europeans (or the Japanese for that matter) are going to be content to let the golden riches of South Africa rest peacefully beneath the earth, while their marvelous industrial machine becomes completely and helplessly dependent on a financial system composed mainly of paper, promises and debt. The EEC and the new Japanese (commercial) empire may play along with the idea of a reconstructed gold-dollar-SDR exchange standard for the time being—at least until they can figure out a way to unload their excess dollar holdings without too big a loss—but you can be sure that they will never let themselves be trapped into permanently financing someone else's debts again.

Do not be misled by any short-term arrangement that appears to take the world further away from gold and toward a greater reliance on paper. The world's central bankers are stuck with a lot of paper and they dare not admit to their depositors (their citizens) that this paper is tremendously overvalued. Therefore, they will publicly continue to profess their faith in paper, while secretly converting as much as possible to gold. The monetary crisis of our time and the "Age of Inflation" will not be ended until a new international gold standard is established and, whatever specific form it takes, the EEC will be its principal architect.

The arrangement of December 19, 1971, "devaluing" the U.S. dollar from $35 to $38 per ounce of gold and setting up a new system of international currency parities (without dollar to gold convertibility!) will survive only as long as the Japanese and our European trading partners allow it to survive. It is the author's belief that they agreed to accept such an obvious fraud only to buy time to maneuver.

Notes:

CHAPTER V

1. Basically a sound idea. World trade was free when it *had* an international currency (gold) prior to 1914. But Keynes wanted an international *paper* currency this time because his theories required a currency that could be "managed" by international bankers.

2. Assistant Secretary White denied that he was in any way involved with Soviet espionage or the Communist Party and repudiated the testimony of two witnesses against him at Senate hearings. However, after he died, notes in his handwriting were found among the Chambers' documents, and the Senate Internal Security Subcommittee, at least, regarded them as incriminating.

3. An SDR credit has been defined very precisely as being equal to .888671 grams of fine gold. The definition may seem academic, as the SDR's are nonredeemable, but without a specified measurement for accounting purposes, the whole concept of the SDR would be meaningless. Thus, there is no escape in the long run from the ultimate rule of gold.

4. Or what they thought were Keynesian doctrines. Lord Keynes himself took considerable delight in denying that he was a Keynesian, as the term was popularly understood.

5. Prather, *Money and Banking,* p. 6.

6. President Nixon's unexpected public declaration of conversion to the Keynesian dogma prompted ABC correspondent Howard K. Smith to remark that it was, "a little like a Christian Crusader saying, 'all things considered, I think Mohammed was right.' "

7. The monetary restraint of 1969–70 has brought about a reduction in the much advertised "prime rate" of interest, but the Keynesian dilemma remains and any future attempt to "restimulate" the economy through monetary expansion will drive all interest rates to new highs again.

8. Any level over 4 percent is considered unacceptable by current economic and sociological theories.

9. The 1939 ratio was, of course, in terms of devalued U.S. dollars.

Therefore the actual devaluation of the pound in terms of gold from 1931 to 1939 was considerably greater than the dollar parity would indicate. In 1930, the pound brought .235 troy ounces of gold, but in 1939 it was worth only .127 ounces. Therefore, the actual 1931–39 devaluation of the pound, in terms of gold, approached 50 percent. The profits made in South African gold stocks by British investors during this period were enormous.

10.   The United States inherited the Indo China War with equally disastrous results.

11.   The new constitution of the Gaullists provided for a strong executive, and De Gaulle's great personal prestige and authority gave it added effect; it was a potent combination.

12.   And the IMF rules were, as has been noted, primarily the work of the U.S. and British delegations to Bretton Woods. De Gaulle did not personally approve of the system, but he always scrupulously respected its rules and considered them binding on France as an IMF member.

13.   Another example of the fallacy of attempting to obtain political ends through economic means. After the passions of war had cooled, it was recognized that the great productive capacity of Germany was indispensable to the economic health of all of Europe.

14.   French Foreign Minister Robert Schuman was the chief architect of the European Coal and Steel Community, the predecessor of the Common Market, but the economics expert Jean Monnet is regarded as the originator of the initial concept of European economic union.

15.   Crédit Lyonnais, the second largest bank in France, and the third largest bank in Germany, the Commerzbank, have entered such a combined operations agreement and have invited Dutch, Belgian and Italian banks to join them. Dominant Anglo-American banking houses, such as the Bank of America, First National City Bank of New York, Britain's Barclay's Bank Ltd., and the Chase Manhattan, may soon have strong competition.

16.   Exactly as the dollar was supposed to have been, according to the IMF agreement.

VI

THE GREAT GOLD WAR: 1960–1971

"There isn't a chance in the world that central banks are going to be willing to get rid of their gold and replace it by either U.S. dollars or a new international (paper) money in order to keep the price of gold from rising above $35 per ounce."

—MILTON FRIEDMAN

"The world not only expects but the world requires that the dollar be as good as gold."

—LYNDON B. JOHNSON

AT the beginning of the past decade it became the popular cliché of economists and financial journalists to announce to the world that it was about to enter the "golden sixties." Aside from the fact that the intervening years were tarnished by war, assassinations, public rioting, the drug culture and other grave problems, they turned out to be the goldless sixties as far as the U.S. Treasury was concerned. During this period we lost more than half of our so-called gold reserve and, at the same time, monetized more debt than had existed in all of our previous 184 years as a nation.

When the assault on Fort Knox began in earnest in 1958, the money managers of the United States adopted a disastrous policy of seeking to discredit gold as money instead of strengthening the credit dollar through prudent fiscal and monetary programs. This policy, which has persisted ever since, has served only to weaken the international monetary system and the gold-dollar exchange standard beyond repair, and has split the economic world into two factions: those who have learned from bitter experience to respect gold as the bulwark of monetary integrity and those who have succumbed to what is just another recurrence of the ancient delusion of unlimited prosperity through the magic of fiat money and fiat credit.

I believe history will deal harshly with those who allowed the assault on Fort Knox to degenerate into an economic and financial Pearl Harbor. The U.S. decision to retreat from gold was more than an economic tragedy; it has led to political and social anarchy as well as financial disaster. It is the author's view, and I believe history will overwhelmingly sustain it, that, next to war, irredeemable paper currency is the worst evil that can befall a nation. A government that institutes such a currency system is bankrupt morally as well as financially. When a government establishes an irredeemable paper currency as the sole monetary medium, it gives itself an uncontrollable power over its citizens, and the opportunities for the misuse of such power are practically unlimited.

By allowing the credit dollar to become, in effect, an international as well as a domestic fiat currency during the 1960's, the United States managed to maintain much of its postwar financial superiority, even though its economic strength sharply declined relative to the rest of the world. But in doing so, we gratuitously provoked, literally, a worldwide gold war, and although we may appear to have won some of the preliminary battles, there is no doubt in the author's mind as to what the final outcome will be. Gold will have to be reestablished as the world's basic currency, or Western civilization and freedom will not survive.

Without an effective discipline, the inevitable course of any monetary system is runaway inflation and financial collapse, accompanied by social and political dissolution. The discipline of gold is nonpolitical, impersonal and automatic. The alternative, as Adolf Hitler so lucidly pointed out, is the coercive power of the state—the national police and the concentration camp. If we are to have an international fiat currency, divorced entirely from the discipline of gold, it would require a world dictatorship and an international police to force its acceptance. It would also have to include a worldwide system of wage and price controls, exchange restrictions and rationing. Therefore, an international fiat currency cannot possibly come about without the destruction of freedom, and with it Western civilization as we know it.

If, on the other hand, an international fiat currency is put into general use without a worldwide dictatorship and a complete and effective suppression of the use of gold for monetary purposes, Gresham's Law will inexorably determine the outcome. The bad money (fiat currency or credit) will gradually be depreciated, rejected and eventually destroyed, while the good money (gold) will be hoarded and retained as a safe store of value. This latter condition is exactly the one that prevails in the world today. During the 1960's, the IMF-U.S. international credit dollar was overissued to the point where it became, for all practical purposes, an international fiat currency. Since then, we have tried desperately, but obviously not too successfully, to suppress the use of gold as money internationally, as we have domestically. But the coercive power of the U.S. Government is, understandably, not as potent abroad as it is at home.

Nevertheless, it would be a mistake to underestimate the powers of "persuasion" still possessed by the United States concerning international finance. Therefore, the great gold war may continue for months or even years into the 1970's, but it is, as it has been, essentially an unnecessary and self-defeating struggle. Gresham's Law is not merely a theory, it is an inflexible rule of economics that has been tested and proved over and over again in the cauldron of history. Gold, or, more accurately, an international gold standard, will ultimately prevail. The gold exchange standard of the post-World War II era has failed, just as its predecessor did in the 1930's. We can only hope that the results will not be equally tragic, or worse.

The outlines of this tragedy rival any of the great financial follies of past history, from ancient to modern times. We have already traced the preliminary steps, which include the introduction of the gold exchange concept in the 1920's, the great international monetary collapse of the thirties, the ending of gold coinage in the United States through the Gold Reserve Act of 1934 and the sharp reduction of U.S. gold-reserve requirements in 1946. Nevertheless, the dollar was essentially a strong and highly liquid currency when it undertook its role as the world's principal reserve medium under the IMF, despite the prior two decades of intrinsic value erosion.[1]

Although the roots of the present dollar crisis can be traced back at least three full decades, it is only during the last one that the situation became irretrievable. The decade of the 1960's was really a momentous one in world history. Among other events, it saw the Common Market become a powerful economic force, it saw the dramatic recovery of Japan, it witnessed the second rise and fall of Charles de Gaulle, it brought the longest and most controversial war in U.S. history and it marked the ruin of the "almighty dollar."[2]

It has been suggested that the United States engaged in a "deliberate" policy of international deficits in the early postwar years, in order to encourage the creation of international dollar balances and help redistribute the world's gold reserves.[3] But, while international dollar balances grew rapidly during the fifties, the U.S. portion of the world's monetary gold reserves remained relatively static until 1958. (See *Fig. 13* at end of chapter). In 1958, however, a sizable gold loss ($2.5 billion) was sustained. Strangely enough, this evidence that a "redistribution" of the world's gold reserves had indeed begun was greeted not with joy but with considerable alarm in Washington.

Although it seems incredible now, in 1971, after having endured a dozen years of virtually continuous monetary crisis, the events of 1958 created a near panic. Emergency Cabinet meetings were held and the lights burned late in the Treasury Department. Secretary of the Treasury Robert B. Anderson was called to testify before a special meeting of the House Finance Committee. According to reporters Robert S. Allen and Paul J. Scott, who were present, the conversation went something like this:

> *Secretary Anderson:* "Liquid dollar balances of foreign countries are now $17,632 million, as against $12,000 million in 1952. In addition, these foreign interests now have $1.5 billion in short-

term U.S. securities. Meanwhile, the gold reserves of the United States have dropped to $20,582 million as compared to $23 billion in 1952."

Rep. Frank Karsten (D., Mo.): "Just how serious is this $2.5 billion loss of gold? We hear conflicting reports about this."

Anderson: "It could give us a great deal of trouble, if foreign countries and investors lose confidence in the dollar and demand their holdings in gold."

Karsten: "You mean there could be a big run on our gold?"

Anderson: "Exactly, that is a very real danger."

Rep. Lee Metcalf (D., Mont.): "You mean right now?"

Anderson: "Right now! In fact, the situation is steadily getting worse the longer it takes Congress to act on this problem. It's a very sensitive one and does not brook trifling with. When you are dealing with the confidence of a nation's currency, you are dealing with highly explosive dynamite.

And the preceding took place in 1958! Compare that particular reaction to the attitude of the Nixon administration, which viewed with "complete calm" and "amazing coolness" the disastrous $10.7 billion balance-of-payments deficit of 1970, the $5 billion first-quarter 1971 deficit and the European dollar crisis of the same year.[4] It reminds the author, at any rate, of the bovine complacency that inevitably precedes major socio-economic or military disasters. Such a mood of eerie optimism prevailed in the summer of 1929 and in the fall of 1941. Familiarity, it is said, breeds contempt. We have lived with the dollar crisis for so long that we have begun to doubt its reality; that is the most dangerous sign of all.

But, in 1958, there was no show of complacency; action was demanded. However, the steps taken were hesitant, ineffective and misguided. A few government offices overseas were closed or reduced in size. Some dependents of U.S. military and civilian personnel abroad were ordered home. Foreign dollar-aid recipients were urged or required to spend more of their money on U.S. products, and our allies were urged to increase their share of aid to "underdeveloped" nations. This they did, to a considerable degree, but it offered the United States no relief because its own expenses were not reduced by an equivalent amount. In fact, our "aid" was actually increased on the theory that it would promote foreign purchases of American goods.

Such is the opacity of bureaucratic, neo-Keynesian economic thinking, that it could devise a program for reducing the deficit by stimulating exports, which in turn required increasing the deficit through foreign aid to provide the necessary stimulation.

So, despite all the hand-wringing and pious rhetoric that emanated from Washington, nothing positive was really accomplished. At no time did any one in the administration associate (publicly at least) the $94 billion Federal budget, the unprecedented* $12.5 budget deficit and the $3.5 billion balance-of-payments deficit incurred for 1958, with the $2.5 billion gold loss of that year.[5] Despite Secretary Anderson's admission that a loss of confidence in the dollar was becoming self-evident, there was little appreciation of the fact that continued monetization of U.S. debt might be involved. So the deficits continued and so did the gold losses. In 1959, the U.S. gold reserve dropped by another billion and in 1960 a $1.7 billion loss was recorded. Total for the last three years of the Eisenhower administration: over $5 billion.

THE DEATH OF THE DOLLAR; AN AMERICAN TRAGEDY

In late 1960, a new danger arose: the price of gold on the London market, which tends to set the price for all nonmonetary gold, including that acquired for speculation and hoarding, rose above par. In September of 1960, the London price went to $35.26, and in October it reached the $41 level. The U.S. reaction to this challenge seemed to set the standard for all its subsequent attacks on the gold "problem": the Treasury's money doctors chose to try to suppress the effects of the dollar imbalance, rather than recognize and deal with its cause. The tragedy was, and is, that successive U.S. administrations, Republican and Democrat alike, have persisted in viewing the price of gold as a political problem rather than an economic one.

It has been pointed out over and over again by U.S. spokesmen that raising the price of gold (devaluing the dollar) would

*For a peacetime year.

provide an undeserved windfall profit for Russia and South Africa, governments with which we have ideological differences. It is also said that such an action would reward those who have mistrusted the dollar and held their assets mainly in gold, and penalize those who have kept the faith and retained large dollar balances. Furthermore, it is claimed that devaluation would be a serious blow to the international prestige of the United States. Many adjustments would also have to be made within the IMF. All the foregoing may be true, but it is irrelevant. If the alternative to devaluation is to permit the dollar deficit to continue, and that is what was allowed to happen, then the rewards to the holders of gold, the losses to the holders of dollars, and the damage to the prestige of the United States will be far greater in the long run, when the dollar is devalued not by deliberate choice, but during some great international money panic when it is forced upon us.

The free-market gold price rise of 1960 made it plain that the dollar was overvalued, and that it had become overvalued because it had become overissued. The United States was therefore presented with only two alternatives that made sense economically: devalue the dollar or stop the international dollar deficit. We elected instead the typical political expedient of suppressing the free-market price. Under U.S. leadership, a "gold pool" was formed by the United States, Canada and the industrial nations of Western Europe, and under this informal arrangement the members agreed to sell gold from their own monetary stocks (in proportion to their assets) to the London market, whenever the price of gold threatened to go above $35 per ounce and, conversely, to buy gold whenever it went below the IMF price. Although they were seldom obliged to buy gold under this arrangement, the $35 price was effectively maintained until the gold crisis of March 1968, when the famous "two-tier" price system was established, allowing for a fixed monetary price and a floating commercial price to function simultaneously.

This writer finds it fascinating that the two-tier system was not introduced in 1960. If the two-tier, or dual price, system for gold was such a great idea in 1968, and the world's monetary authorities, central bankers and IMF economists were ecstatically sure that it was, why wasn't it tried in 1960? What was all the high-priced help doing at that time that such a simple proposition as a two-level market could be overlooked? Most curious. But perhaps we cannot expect miracles from banking experts who don't seem to grasp the difference between money and credit. When the SDR's were introduced it was widely proclaimed, by some of the world's most respected monetary experts that a new form of international "money" had been created, when, in reality, they had only concocted another fiat credit instrument.[6]

At any rate, the gold pool went into operation in 1960, determined to make the dollar look good by making it appear that gold was a poor investment and a hopeless speculation. Dollars, it was widely advertised, were better than gold because dollars bore interest (paid in more paper dollars), while gold (if the price could be held at par) was a sterile and nonproductive holding. But, as usual, the neo-Keynesian or naive school of economics was merely delivering one of its smashing non-sequiturs. Brazilian and Chilean currencies bear interest too, sometimes at 20 percent a month, but who wants them? Gold is prized above paper money, regardless of interest, because it is a trusted store of value. Dollars were gladly held abroad as long as they, too, were considered a safe store of value. But when the United States openly embarked on its program of continuous economic expansion, through the virtually unlimited use of fiat money and fiat credit, the era of dollar supremacy was over. From 1958 on, the evidence became more and more obvious that the dollar was no longer "good as gold."

To this day, I have my doubts that any real understanding of the motives and mechanics of gold buying exists in either the Treasury or the Federal Reserve.[7] The monetary experts of the United States still appear to assume, as they did in 1960, that the typical gold buyer is an international gambler of sorts, out to make a quick profit. But in truth, the average private purchaser of gold (in those more civilized parts of the world where such freedom is permitted), whether he be a rich Arab oil sheik, a moderately prosperous European businessman or a simple French peasant, is seldom, if ever, concerned directly with speculative profits or high interest rates. His primary con-

cern is simply *the safe preservation of liquid capital.* Therefore, in attempting to hold down the price of gold through the
gold pool, the United States, in effect, merely sold its gold reserves to foreigners at bargain rates, while denying its own
citizens the same right of financial self-defense.

From 1960 on, virtually every ounce of newly mined gold was
fed to the London market, which in turn supplied the Continental markets in Zurich, Frankfurt and Paris. Furthermore, the
United States alone lost $7 billion of its own monetary gold
holdings between 1960 and 1968. However, our compatriots in
the gold-pool scheme managed to maintain and even increase
their own monetary gold reserves during this period by a very
obvious expedient: when called upon to contribute their particular quotas to the pool operation, they simply cashed in an
appropriate number of their accumulated dollar reserves and
recovered the lost gold immediately from the U.S. Treasury.
Thus the gold pool, like the whole American-Keynesian approach to domestic and international finance, was just another
exercise in self-delusion. In reality, there was no "pool" at all,
it was strictly a U.S. operation.

Despite the fact that approximately $1.5 billion worth of gold
(at $35 per ounce) was mined per year during the 1960's, world
monetary reserves have remained practically unchanged.
About 30 to 40 percent of this gold was used for industrial and
commercial purposes. Less than 20 percent went to satisfy the
demands of hard-core in-and-out speculators. The rest went
into permanent or semipermanent hoarding as store-of-value
money for private individuals and corporations. One of
Keynes's favorite clichés was that nobody in his right mind
would use money as a store of value. Obviously he was referring to Keynesian fiat money, and who can argue that point?
Although there are no firm figures on the total quantity of private gold hoards, world production records, minus known official reserves and estimated industrial consumption, indicate
that there could be $15 billion or more in gold functioning as
money *outside* of the present IMF system.

Next time you hear or read that gold is gradually being
phased out or replaced in the world's monetary system, ask
yourself where that phased-out gold is going. The United States

has already phased itself out of $14 billion worth of gold in the past two decades. Who has this gold now? Perhaps it belongs to Swiss bankers, French and German businessmen, Arab potentates, South American industrialists, Oriental merchants and traders, as well as various foreign governments. The U.S. Treasury would like us to believe that it swindled all those poor, unsophisticated foreigners by dumping all that "worthless" gold on them.

In India they will gladly pay up to $80 or $90 per ounce for any gold that can be smuggled in to them, over the adamant prohibitions of their socialist government. In fact, gold smuggling from the Middle East to all soft-currency countries is a major world industry. The United States is virtually alone in its official view that money does not require intrinsic value. Will the United States change its view eventually? Or will the rest of the world, in time, adopt the U.S. attitude? It is difficult to see how any foreigner in his right mind will ever accept the present U.S. position favoring the ultimate supremacy of a fully managed non-intrinsic-value world reserve currency, in view of what has happened to the fully managed non-intrinsic-value domestic credit dollar of the United States in the last decade.

The Kennedy administration took office in 1961, with the promise of great change for the United States. But what we got, for the most part, was merely an intensification of past policy mistakes—foreign, domestic and, most assuredly, economic. One of the first acts of the newly elected government was to step up the war on gold. A new Office of Domestic Gold and Silver Operations was set up within the Treasury to regulate more closely the use and possession of precious metals, the granting of licenses and permits to industrial users, importers and exporters of gold, and to tighten generally the administration of the Treasury Department's gold and silver regulations. A loophole that had permitted U.S. citizens to purchase and hold gold bullion abroad was hastily plugged by a new executive order, which forbade any such escape thereafter and required that any existing overseas caches of gold owned by Americans be sold at once.

Numerous other steps were taken to curb the outflow of dollars, none of them very effective. The principal effort was made in the area of defense spending in Europe. A "buy American" program required U.S. civilian and military agencies overseas to fulfill their material requirements from U.S. sources, whenever possible, even though these purchases might cost up to 50 percent more. Such minor economies, however, were more than offset by the dispatch of greatly increased aid to Southeast Asia, including the expansion of our military presence in Indo-China from 772 advisers and attachés to some 23,000 soldiers and airmen.

The domestic economic program put into operation by the Kennedy administration and carried on and intensified by its successor under President Johnson, was primarily just a more uninhibited application of neo-Keynesianism, as defined by the Full Employment Act of 1946. The policies were eminently successful in stimulating an overheated and uncontrollable economic boom, but the costs to the United States, in terms of inflation, soaring interest rates, balance-of-payments deficits, gold losses, the reckless consumption and waste of resources and the enormous expansion of public and private debt are incalculable.

The unprecedented social breakdown that occurred in the United States during the 1960's, and which manifested itself in urban rioting, student unrest, soaring crime, drug abuse and racial conflict has been largely attributed to the unpopularity of the Indo-China War, dissatisfaction with the Selective Service System and the struggles of minority groups for greater opportunity. While I would not deny that these things have played a substantial role, I also believe that the effect of our fiscal and monetary policies on the social order has been largely overlooked, or at least greatly underrated. While the U.S. economy was thrust forward under forced draft during the 1960's, the U.S. credit dollar, as a trustworthy and respected currency, was ravaged.

One of the most insidious effects of currency debasement is that both citizens and foreigners alike eventually lose all confidence in and respect for the government that permits it. Once confidence in a currency is lost, it spreads rapidly to include all other acts and promises of the government concerned. Yet, throughout the 1960's, the only answer that was found for the growing economic and financial imbalances of the United States was to further debase the currency. But each debasement only served to increase the loss of public confidence and aggravate the imbalances. During the three years of the Kennedy administration, the accumulated balance of payments deficit amounted to $6 billion, while gold losses totalled $2 billion. A new American tragedy was unfolding; the dollar was dying.

SILVER IS SACRIFICED

When President Johnson took office in 1964, the attention of the financial world was diverted for a time from its preoccupation with gold and the floundering credit dollar by a sudden and surprising renewal of interest in that ancient and half-forgotten money, silver.[8] Ever since the New Deal days and the Silver Purchase Act of 1934, the white metal had been under direct control of the Treasury. Initially, the objective had been to raise its price and restore monetary credibility to silver. But, after 1950, rising industrial demand and inflation combined to drive the price of silver upward without government support. By 1963, the quotation for silver was bumping against the statutory ceiling of $1.29 per ounce.

If the price of silver rose above $1.29, the intrinsic value of our 90-percent silver dollars and subsidiary coins would exceed their face value. In the usual response to Gresham's Law, these coins would then be withdrawn from circulation and melted for their bullion content or simply hoarded. In either case, the United States would be left in the embarrassing position of not having an adequate supply of small change—a situation not unique in our history, but highly undesirable all the same.

The reaction of the Treasury to the silver crisis of 1963–68 was identical to its reflex in the face of the gold crisis of 1960. The only answer that came to mind was to saturate the market by dumping the Treasury's monetary reserves. In 1963, the silver bullion market was reopened to public participation after 29 years of strict government control. The 50 percent surtax on silver profits was ended. It was thought that by allowing the public to speculate or invest in silver bullion, they could be dissuaded from hoarding silver coins. Such an expectation, however, was optimistic, to say the least. Having begun really to lose confidence in the paper currency of the United States, people became anxious to possess at least some money of intrinsic value. For residents of the United States, silver dollars and subsidiary silver coins were the only intrinsic-value money still available, and Gresham's Law inevitably drove them into hiding.

At first, the Treasury Department, with inexcusable ineptness, sought to blame the growing scarcity of silver coins on the activities of numismatic coin collectors.[9] Their remedy for this strange conclusion was to work the mints around the clock and flood the nation with silver coins, thus making them, supposedly, of less value to those imagined hoards of coin collectors. But despite this unprecedented "crash" program of silver-coin production, the amount of silver coinage in circulation relentlessly continued to decline. In 1965, the Government was forced to admit defeat. A new coinage act was therefore passed, which ended the minting of silver coins in the United States for the first time since 1792, and called for their replacement with cupro-nickel "sandwich" coins for the quarters and dimes and a debased 40-percent silver mixture for the half-dollar. Silver dollars were not affected by the new law, since they had not been minted since 1935. At any rate, the silver-dollar question had already been decided by a financially astute segment of the population, which had gradually withdrawn them all from the banks and from circulation before the Treasury even knew what had happened.

Provisions were also made for the redemption and withdrawal of all silver-certificate currency, so that, by the end of 1968, the United States was left, officially and in fact, without any intrinsic-value money in domestic circulation, except the debased 40-percent Kennedy halves. But even the latter failed to circulate adequately and, in 1969, they too were replaced with a nonsilver cupro-nickel sandwich type.

During the transition period from intrinsic value to non-intrinsic-value coinage, the Treasury Department vowed to maintain the $1.29 ceiling on silver by continuing to supply the market from government stocks. The Treasury boasted that it could hold the line on the price of silver until 1980, if necessary, but speculators and investors alike rushed to exchange their depreciating Federal Reserve notes for silver bullion in such quantities at the "bargain" $1.29 price, that direct Treasury sales had to be suspended by the summer of 1967. The price of silver immediately soared above $2 per ounce.

In August of 1967, the Government tried once more to get the price of silver under control.[10] It was feared that an uninhibited rise in the price of silver would cast further doubt on the integrity of the credit dollar and encourage additional withdrawals of gold by foreign dollar holders. As it turned out, it was a needless worry; our gold stock kept right on declining according to its own apparently inflexible schedule. At any rate, a weekly auction was established by Washington, in which its remaining stocks of silver bullion, including .900 fine silver then being recovered from melted coins, could be sold by sealed bids to industrial users through the General Services Administration, rather than the Treasury. This program remained in effect until November of 1970, when the Government announced triumphantly that it had no more silver to sell. The latest, and hopefully the last, great cycle of government intervention in the silver market, which had begun in 1933, was finally ended.

The silver experience, particularly in its terminal stages, was hardly one to inspire confidence in either the credit dollar or the Treasury Department. The U.S. Government's handling of the great coin scramble was a classic example of bureaucratic inefficiency, incompetence and even outright dishonesty.[11]

All through the silver crisis, the Treasury consistently underestimated the seriousness of the situation and overestimated its ability to cope with it. Instead of controlling events it was content merely to react to them, and invariably its reactions were inadequate and misdirected. It is an ill omen for the future, when one considers that the U.S. Government will surely have to cope with coming internal monetary crises far more serious than the disappearance of silver coins. The only bright side of the entire episode was the revelation that even governments must sometimes bow to reality. In the battle for possession of his silver coins, the citizen was clearly the victor; the Treasury admitted, in 1970, that it had been able to recover and melt only

200 million of the estimated 700 million ounces of silver coinage in circulation as of 1966.[12]

Silver was certainly not vital to our currency system, but its sudden demise was a frightening indication of just how far the debauch of the dollar had proceeded. The fact that even the debased 40-percent silver halves failed to circulate adequately (and there were some 760 million minted!) is surely an indication that the fiat dollar is seriously, if not mortally, afflicted. And, as was noted, the silver fiasco gave us no respite from the gold drain, which was rapidly becoming a hemorrhage. Gold losses for 1964 and 1965 depleted the U.S. reserve by another $2 billion.

FEDERAL RESERVE LOSES LAST TIES TO GOLD

The debasement of U.S. coinage in 1965 was accompanied by the first official debasement of Federal Reserve paper currency since 1946. The problem was that U.S. gold reserve had dwindled to the point where the legal requirement for a minimum 25 percent gold "cover" on both Federal Reserve Bank deposit liabilities and Federal Reserve note currency in circulation could no longer be met. The solution advanced by the Johnson administration was hardly a surprise; it voted to repeal that part of the 1946 law requiring a 25 percent gold backing or "cover" for Federal Reserve Bank deposits. This action, President Johnson assured the nation, would allow the dollar to remain "as good as gold," by making more gold available to back foreign-held U.S. currency (and consequently less to restrain domestic inflation).

Secretary of the Treasury Henry Fowler, in turn, promised that the government would make every effort to eliminate its chronic balance-of-payments deficit, although no specific target date was established for this laudable goal. The steps taken to achieve it, however, were, as usual, aimed at effects rather than causes. A 15-percent "Interest Equalization Tax" was levied against the purchase of foreign securities by U.S. citizens, and strong pressures were exerted on American businessmen to encourage them "voluntarily" to curtail other types of foreign investment. Domestic interest rates were raised to the highest levels in 40 years and Treasury officials were hastily dispatched abroad to persuade, implore and, if necessary, coerce creditor nations to hold on to their surplus dollars, rather than cash them in for U.S. gold. Canada was persuaded to sell some of its newly mined gold to the United States in exchange for high-interest-rate Treasury securities. West Germany was induced to accept similar bonds in lieu of gold for some of her excess dollar holdings.[13]

Despite these maneuvers, both the gold outflow and the dollar deficit continued, so that, by 1967, the dollar problem had reached the crisis stage. Furthermore, the devaluation of the British pound in December of that year sent additional shock waves through the international monetary community and set off a new wave of private gold buying on the European markets. By March of 1968, the crisis had grown to panic proportions. The United States had lost nearly $2 billion more in gold during the previous 15 months, and almost one-half billion of that total had occurred in the first two months of 1968. Much of this gold had been poured into the London market to support the gold-pool operation.

On March 11, in the face of a gold-buying fever that had absorbed $300 million in gold from the London market alone in the previous ten days, the central bankers of the gold-pool nations, meeting in Basle, Switzerland, vowed to the world that the price of gold would continue to be pegged at $35 per troy ounce. But the cause was already beyond hope. In the United States, on the 15th, Congress hurriedly passed a law cutting the last remaining link between U.S. domestic currency and gold; the 25-percent gold cover requirement on Federal Reserve currency in circulation was eliminated. This move, it was said, would "free" our entire remaining gold reserve, some $11 billion worth, so that it could be used to defend the dollar abroad.

But this last and final debasement was too late to save the gold pool and its sacrosanct $35 gold price. Gold trading had to be halted in London, and British banks and stock exchanges were ordered closed on the same day to avert the threat of a total collapse of orderly trading. A hurried weekend meeting of the gold-pool bankers was reconvened, and on Monday, March 18, 1968, the London gold market, banks and exchanges were reopened with the announcement that the gold pool was dissolved and that henceforth the private gold market would be free to find its own level, while all official transactions between central banks would continue at the fixed $35 rate.

Thus the two-tier gold-price system was born, almost by accident. Chairman of the U.S. Federal Reserve Board William McChesney Martin, however, was not unduly impressed by such "monetary gimmickry and gadgetry," as he called it, which would only "buy a little more time" for the U.S. In essence, Chairman Martin had characterized the entire monetary policy of the United States in the postwar years, which had been, and no doubt still is, just a constant and futile search for yet another "gimmick" to buy a little more time. The price of gold in London quickly soared above $44 per ounce, but then, just as quickly and unexpectedly, subsided under speculative profit taking. Once again, the central bankers of the West congratulated themselves on having solved the gold and dollar problem.

THE SDR'S AND THE LIQUIDITY MYTH

Immediately following the great March gold panic, President Johnson made a speech at Minneapolis in which he urged Americans to "join in a program of national austerity" to help protect the dollar. He emphasized the need for higher taxes and the postponement of nondefense Federal spending. Real austerity, however, would obviously have been a distasteful and embarrassing experience for the "Great (guns and butter) Society." Furthermore, there were by then some 500,000 American troops in Indo-China, which made any hope for meaningful economy in government an even more dubious proposition. Consequently, the search for another monetary "solution" was given the highest priority.

Both administration spokesmen and U.S. Treasury and banking officials turned their full attention to the promotion of a plan long favored by Treasury Secretary Fowler, the deliberate creation of a new international reserve currency or asset to supplement dollars in international trade. This particular scheme, hailed as the "paper gold" plan by both the general and financial press, called for the use of special "drawing rights" from the IMF as a form of international fiat currency. Now there was nothing unique about the concept of drawings or borrowings from the IMF; such drawing privileges were an integral part of the IMF system and had been used repeatedly in the past. What was "special" about these proposed new drawing rights was that, once having been granted, they would never have to be paid back, but could be passed on from one central bank to another, in lieu of gold or regular IMF drawings, whenever a nation acquired a payments deficit or had to redeem a quantity of its outstanding currency.

The late Dr. Melchior Palyi, an internationally renowned banking expert and economist, had some harsh words for the idea of paper gold. "The new SDR reserve currency," he wrote, "will serve only to encourage a more reckless financial expansion and inflation on a worldwide basis. The adoption of the SDR's will be the triumph of the inflationists. It will remove the last obstacle on the road to a fully managed* world currency— one that presumably will never be allowed to become in short supply. It is literally the old 'greenback' policy on a global basis."[14]

Such pointed warnings by Dr. Palyi and others were, not unexpectedly, ignored, and the United States was able to pressure the IMF membership into accepting the SDR scheme at the October 1969 meeting of the IMF delegations. And "pressure" is the proper word to use; the American representatives openly threatened the world with financial catastrophe if the plan was not adopted. The United States, it was hinted darkly, would refuse to redeem any more of its foreign-held dollars for gold if the SDR's were not accepted. The Europeans and the Japanese, as well as all our other creditors, would then be faced with the possibility of disastrous losses in the value of their monetary reserves, which were, to a large extent, made up of U.S. dollars.

American bankers and Treasurymen publicly congratulated themselves upon thus having created a "monetary nuclear de-

*Dr. Palyi did not indicate just who would do the managing. Presumably it would be the IMF directorate.

terrent" in the form of those $40 billion outstanding credit dollars. The Europeans, it was said, would have no other choice but to support the credit dollar or ruin themselves. Furthermore, there was always the question of the American military umbrella which could and, it was rumored, would be withdrawn from those who gave less than wholehearted cooperation on the monetary front. At any rate, the SDR scheme was eventually ratified by the required 75 percent of the (104 nation) IMF membership. The plan went into effect in January of 1970, when $3.4 billion of the first 3-year allotment of $9.5 billion in SDR credits were distributed. The U.S. share came to a paltry $866.9 million—hardly enough to cover our usual balance of payments deficit for much more than three or four months.

American monetary authorities were, nonetheless, positively ecstatic. "U.S. SCORES PAPER GOLD TRIUMPH" headlined the *Wall Street Journal,* and under-Secretary of the Treasury Paul A. Volcker told newsmen with a broad smile, "Well, we got this thing launched."[15] Although the SDR accord fell far short of the original U.S. demand for an initial injection of $10 billion and a three-year total of $25 billion for the first drawing, it was still welcomed by the *Journal* as a "major success for the American school of economic thought, since it dealt a blow to old-style backers of gold as the sole yardstick for monetary value and an economic cure-all."[16]

The author is convinced that the SDR plan is one of the greatest financial swindles ever perpetrated, and that it will one day be ranked by historians along with such other gems of human opacity as John Law's Mississippi Scheme, the *assignat* madness and the South Seas Bubble. Somehow, defining the SDR unit as being "equal" to gold (see note 16) and then just as solemnly declaring that it is not redeemable in gold (or anything else) strikes one as a patent absurdity. An ounce of gold can be "equal" only to an ounce of gold and it is *worth,* in currency, whatever the law of supply and demand determines that it is worth. A paper currency or unit of credit can be regarded as "equal" to gold only if it is in fact convertible into gold at a fixed price or rate, without restriction. The "price" of gold always floats in relation to all other commodities (and nonconvertible currencies) according to the law of supply and demand. Therefore equality between a unit of currency or credit, whether the dollar or an SDR, and a specific amount of gold, cannot be arbitrarily decreed, but can only be the result of a fact. The stated amount of gold must be actually available on demand.

Arbitrarily increasing the supply of nonconvertible currencies or credits creates demand for which there is no corresponding supply. The holders of such currency, therefore, can only use them to try to outbid each other for the limited amount of things (including gold as the prime store of value) that are actually available. Even though SDR units are not directly convertible into gold, they are, in their function as "reserve assets," convertible into other currencies, which in turn can, and will, be used to buy gold, both at the official rate (as long as possible) and on the private markets. Therefore, the continuous creation of SDR's will not only be ineffective as a replacement for gold, but will guarantee an even higher price for it in the long run.

Nevertheless, the view was widely accepted at the time that the creation of SDR "money out of thin air" spelled the end of gold as a monetary metal. The price of gold even plunged below $35 for a time on the London market, and in London, New York and Johannesburg, speculators and investors fell over one another trying to get out of their gold stocks. A genuine "crash" in gold shares occurred, with prices falling by one-half to two-thirds for listed and nonlisted golds alike. The real irony was that, within 18 months, many of these same speculators and investors were frantically trying to buy some of those same shares back at twice the price that they had sold them for. This, quite obviously, is not the best way to speculate in gold stocks, or in any other type of gold investment for that matter. But, as the reader shall see in subsequent chapters, such a pattern is all too common. Gold, gold stocks and gold coins are invariably bought and sold on an emotional rather than a rational basis. But there is very little hope for success in investing in any sort of venture unless it is done intelligently and unemotionally.

However, before we proceed with the remainder of this treatise, which will deal with the planning and operation of a successful gold-oriented investment program, let us examine (and dispose of) one of the more persistent rationalizations of the antigold forces, and that is the "need for liquidity" argument. This proposition, which will no doubt continue to be used to justify the creation of still more SDR's, and perhaps other international fiat credit instruments,* maintains that there is, and probably always will be, a "shortage" of gold for monetary purposes. The proponents of this view believe that world trade has expanded so fast in the postwar years, that the production of newly mined gold has not been (and cannot ever be) sufficient to provide the necessary currency to finance this trade. Therefore, according to the gold-shortage argument, new international monetary instruments, such as SDR's, must be periodically created to provide the necessary liquidity to finance continuously expanding world trade. Unfortunately, this rationalization has been accepted by a great many otherwise sensible bankers and statesmen.

The gold-shortage argument has a certain superficial plausibility, but only because it is based on the (untenable) assumption of immutably fixed gold parities for paper currencies. It totally ignores the fact that there is not, or at least there has not been since the demise of the gold standard, any real restraint on the creation of such currencies. Obviously one cannot keep printing and issuing paper currencies, supposedly redeemable in gold at a fixed parity, without regard for the amount of gold on hand or being acquired, without sooner or later developing a condition in which the amount of gold available is insufficient to redeem the outstanding currencies at the original fixed parities. But, in reality, it would be much more accurate to identify the problem as that of a surplus of fiat currencies, rather than a shortage of gold. Consequently, far from solving any liquidity problem, the creation of fictitious assets like the SDR's only aggravates it.

If there was truly a gold shortage, the obvious answer would be to permit the price to rise so as to encourage production and also to provide the holders of bullion with an incentive to sell it to the monetary authorities at a profit. But the gold shortage is just one of those monetary myths that are used to disguise the

---

*Until the whole delusion ultimately runs its course.

fact that what all too many of us want is a something-for-nothing system, without any discipline at all. Actually, there is more gold per capita now than ever before. The greatest era of gold production in history has occurred thus far in the twentieth century. There are untold billions in gold-ore reserves waiting to be mined, as soon as it becomes profitable to do so. There is more than enough gold to reestablish a full international gold standard, *if it were properly used,* as a balancing wheel for international trade. There is, and always has been, enough gold to finance balanced international trade. There will never be enough gold—or anything else—to finance policies of unrestrained deficits.

What our present-day neo-Keynesian economists and bankers give lip service to, but apparently no longer really want to believe, is that international trade is supposed to balance. Nations are supposed to live honorably and within their means. If the Western world could agree to do just that, there would be no dollar problem and no gold problem. Gold is not the problem; it is the solution. Only when the Western world returns to a full international gold standard will we see the end of the present cycle of continuous inflation and repeated crises. Unfortunately, our politico-monetary managers will probably not reach that conclusion until the world has descended into virtual anarchy—financial, economic, social and political. And by that time, the dollar price of gold could be unbelievably high by today's standards.

At any rate, Gresham's Law rather than Keynesian theory will determine the future, as it has the past. It is significant to note that in the fall of 1970, the IMF, in order to replenish its stock of currencies, approached 12 leading member nations with the request for $400 million of their money. It offered in exchange, a choice of either gold or SDR's. But only $68 million of this $400 million transfer was covered with SDR's; the rest had to be settled in gold. Even the United States, the great champion of the SDR plan, took only $30 million in "paper gold," but demanded to be paid for the remaining $102 million of its quota in the real article.

THE END OF THE GOLD-DOLLAR EXCHANGE STANDARD

The international gold dollar created at Bretton Woods in 1944 was formally buried on August 15, 1971, although it had been obvious for several years prior that it was a very sick, if not a dying, currency. Despite the repeated ministrations of the New Economics money doctors (or perhaps because of them) the illness became terminal in 1971. In that year, the U.S. balance-of-payments deficit reached $11.5 billion for the first half alone, this disaster coming on top of the staggering $10.7 billion deficit for all of 1970. Furthermore, the hopelessness of the situation was underscored when the U.S. Department of Commerce was forced to concede that it would record a deficit in U.S. trade for the 1971 period, which would be the first such deficit since 1893.

These events, coming after a decade of monetary crises, resulted in a renewed rush by foreigners to convert dollar holdings to gold or stable, gold-backed currencies. The first wave, occurring in May, was checked with the help of the European central banks that were forced to cut loose their currencies to float against the dollar. But despite the floating of the *Deutschmark* (for the second time) and most other European currencies, the flight from the dollar soon resumed in earnest, and this time it was clear that the dam had broken beyond repair.

On August 15, President Nixon, in a manner reminiscent of President Roosevelt's action thirty-eight years earlier, was forced officially to suspend the international convertibility of the dollar.* President Nixon's action, exactly like that of his predecessor, was (legally) based on an almost forgotten wartime enactment that had never been repealed. In Mr. Nixon's case, however, it was not the law of 1917, but a State of National Emergency declaration made at the beginning of the Korean War, in June of 1950, that was utilized. (The Attorney General hastily ruled that the Korean Emergency was still in effect.) Furthermore, the President's decision was reinforced by powers delegated to him by the Wage and Price Stabilization Act

---

*An extract of President Nixon's declaration of August 15, 1971, concerning the suspension of convertibility is included in the Appendix Section. (See Appendix IV.)

passed by Congress in 1970 (supposedly based on that same Korean Emergency).[17]

So once again the old truism about those not learning from history having to repeat it proved to be more than just a cliché. The gold-dollar exchange standard of the 1950's and '60's proved to be just as inadequate as was its predecessor, the gold exchange standard of the 1920's. Both failed in the end because they were based on a fundamental delusion, and that is that a managed monetary system (paper) is more reliable and more efficient than an automatic one (the gold standard). But if there is one lesson that stands out in economic history it is that politicians (and bankers and economists for that matter) cannot be trusted with the management of money.

While it is true that any standard, even a full gold standard, can be (and was) manipulated by devious men and nations, the possibility for doing great harm is far more limited under a strict gold standard than under any paper "exchange" standard. Historically, all fiat paper systems have ended in runaway inflation and misery. In order to have a workable international paper exchange standard, that is one that would remain reasonably stable, it would require either a host of angels or a world dictatorship to manage it. Since the former are not yet available and only a few crackpots would like to see the latter, exchange standards sooner or later collapse, causing great damage to the world's economic system.

The breakdown of the prewar gold exchange standard was followed by a long period of economic stagnation and political chaos, that finally ended in a world war. The breakdown of the postwar gold-dollar exchange standard ushers in another extremely dangerous era for the world. Make no mistake, August 15, 1971, marks a major turning point in world history every bit as significant as September 21, 1931, when the Bank of England was forced to abandon the convertibility of the pound sterling, the international reserve currency of its day. What may happen next is the subject of Chapter VII, but before this one is ended I must note, with some sadness, that the President's August 15th statement appears to be a presentation of the time-hallowed "devil theory" of economics.

In the brief (350 word) portion of his message that deals directly with the suspension of dollar convertibility, the President, no less than four times (See Appendix IV), placed the blame for the default of the dollar on the machinations of "international money speculators." There was no mention of the 20 years of U.S. balance-of-payments deficits ending in the horrendous back-to-back loss of some $20 billion for 1970–71. Not one word about the failure of the New Economics which, after 25 years of ever-expanding debt, had managed to saddle the United States with the "impossible" combination of chronic inflation and chronic unemployment at the same time. No, according to the President, a handful of international money speculators (the fabled gnomes of Zurich perhaps?) had brought the giant U.S. economy to its knees and "held the dollar hostage" with their devilish trickery.[18]

Not since Franklin Roosevelt proscribed the "Wall Street bankers" has the devil theory of economics been so endearingly presented. Of course there are international money speculators. And of course they take advantage of any opportunity or crisis that comes along. But could they *cause* an international crisis serious enough to threaten, let along topple, the U.S. dollar? No way. If the Nixon administration had been able to bring our international payments into balance, or even near balance, during 1970 and '71 *there would not have been any crisis.* It is as simple as that. Nearly all foreign holders of dollars *want desperately to believe in the dollar*—after all, they are stuck with 50 billion of them. The truth is that there is only one force powerful enough to discredit the dollar and that force is, and always has been, the United States itself.

A Fiat Dollar is (Theoretically!) Devalued. The last act of the great international monetary crisis of 1971 occurred on December 18th and 19th of that fateful year, when delegates from Japan and the major trading nations of Europe met with Treasury Secretary John B. Connally and other top U.S. negotiators to find a way out of their mutual dilemma. This meeting, which took place in the conference rooms of the historic Smithsonian Institution at Washington, D.C., continued the tradition established by the Group of Ten since 1960, by arriving at another smashing nonsolution to the perennial problem of the gold-dollar exchange standard.

Although the United States made it plain that the right of foreign holders to convert dollar claims into gold could not be restored, the assembled delegates, nevertheless, solemnly proclaimed that the U.S. dollar, by mutual agreement, was being "devalued" from $35 to $38 per ounce of gold. In the circumstances, it was equivalent to the United States announcing that instead of not redeeming its dollars at the old parity of $35 per ounce of gold, it would henceforth not redeem them at $38 per ounce.

Since the United States cannot possibly restore gold convertibility at the $38 rate (or any figure remotely close to it) this so-called "devaluation" was merely an accounting trick—another juggling of the books—designed to relieve the symptoms of a fundamental imbalance, without exposing the cause. It will, at best, only buy a little more time before a real devaluation—a *de facto* devaluation in the market place—exposes the artificiality of the latest currency "adjustments."

The truth is that the dollar is now a floating currency, and if all foreign currencies are to remain fixed to the dollar, in accordance with the Smithsonian agreement, then the entire world is on a floating currency basis, except, of course, for those nations that will continue to redeem their currencies in gold on demand.[19] I very much doubt, however, that there will be many of the latter, as an international manifestation of Gresham's Law will encourage all countries to pass the dollars and keep the gold. The future price of gold, therefore, will be decided in the market place rather than by international political fiat.

Already, in the United States, the sale of gold coins has reached a billion-dollar annual rate and this market continues to expand vigorously. Americans buying common date, legal (pre-1933) gold coins, which they are permitted to hold, willingly pay from $60 to $70 per ounce for the gold they obtain in this form—and the author, among others, thinks they are not unwise in so doing. The price of gold in London and on the private Continental markets remained close to its all-time high of $44 per ounce in the closing weeks of 1971. The author believes that a breakthrough to new high ground is quite imminent and this in turn will result in a rapid advance to the $50 level. In time, still higher levels will be achieved.*

*The London gold price reached $65 in May, 1972.

Once again, I state my belief that the open-market price of gold will exceed $100 per ounce before the present decade is ended and, as current indications suggest, may even approach the $150 level. However, the absurdity of the so-called 8.6 percent "devaluation" and the "official" $38 price established in 1971 will become so obvious by the time the $70 level is reached on the London market, that the United States will then be forced once again to return the dollar officially to a floating status. After this step, and a period of consolidation around the $70 level, the final phase of this historic gold price adjustment should take place. I look for a very rapid advance in the second half of the decade, leading to the $100 to $150 level at the very minimum.

The only benefit the author can find in the pseudo-devaluation of 1971 is the entertainment value it afforded through the spectacle of so many prominent Keynesian-oriented economists and politicians frantically back-pedaling from their previous years of implacable opposition in a desperate attempt to get aboard the devaluation bandwagon. What they had scathingly denounced for a decade or more as being unthinkable, impossible, barbaric and absurd, overnight became a masterstroke of economic management, a triumph of international monetary cooperation and a victory for the U.S. position. Devaluation was suddenly the cure-all, not only for our balance-of-payments predicament, but for a vast array of other economic ills as well.

President Nixon, with his usual penchant for overstatement, hailed the new arrangement as "the most significant monetary agreement in the history of the world," and he promised it would create more jobs, restore stability to world finance, benefit farmers, stimulate exports, end the U.S. balance-of-payments drain and generally bring prosperity to all. My only question is, that if the token devaluation of approximately 8.6 percent was such a brilliant stratagem in 1971, how come devaluation *per se* was so adamantly resisted by the great majority of Treasury officials, monetary experts and government economic advisers for so many years past?

Let us be forewarned; the record of those entrusted with the financial and monetary arrangements of the United States in recent years is hardly a good omen for the future. Do not, therefore, expect miracles from Washington. Trust only in realities, and be skeptical of political and academic rhetoric about the imminent demise of gold as money and of the great wonders soon to be achieved in a coming age of fully managed fiat currency and endless computerized credit.

Actually, the adjustment of foreign-currency parities in relation to the dollar was the only significant part of the Smithsonian agreement.* In a sense, the United States dealt out an immediate punishment to its strongest economic competitors; these nations not only had to reduce the value of their gold reserves, in terms of their own currencies, but were forced to accept an outright loss of many millions in exchange value on the billions of dollars they had to buy up during the prior weeks of crisis, while dutifully (under IMF rules) trying to protect the old parity system and the $35 gold price.

Furthermore, since the Smithsonian agreement is obviously designed to redress the U.S. balance of trade and payments deficits solely at the expense of Japan and the major trading nations of Europe, the probability is very great that it will eventually provoke a major recession or depression in those countries. The truth is, that as long as 50 to 60 billion, or more, nonconvertible "Eurodollars," created almost accidentally (out of nothing) by the idiotic gold-dollar exchange standard, remain in existence, there can be no effective long-term solution to the world's monetary and financial ills. If world economic stability is to be regained, these outstanding foreign dollar balances, which, incidentally, exceed the amount of currency in circulation within the United States itself, must be liquidated or written down to the point where the world can be returned to an honest and effective gold standard.

Therefore, more world-wide monetary-economic crises and further devaluations of the dollar (both official and *de facto*) are absolutely inevitable.

---

*For the specific parity adjustments agreed upon by the Group of Ten at the Smithsonian meeting, see Appendix V. (I include this information for historic as well as current interest, despite its temporary [in the author's opinion] nature.)

Fig. 13

U.S. AND WORLD MONETARY GOLD RESERVES
1913–1971
(In millions of dollars)

Year Ending	U.S. Treasury Gold Reserves	All Other Countries	Total World Central Bank Gold Reserves	U.S. Percent of World Total
1913	1,290	3,569	4,859	26.5
1920	2,451	4,804	7,255	33.8
1922	3,506	4,912	8,418	41.6
1925	3,985	5,013	8,998	44.3
1926	4,083	5,151	9,234	44.2
1927	3,977	5,616	9,593	41.5
1928	3,746	6,312	10,058	37.2
1929	3,900	6,436	10,336	37.7
1930	4,225	6,719	10,945	38.6
1931	4,052	7,272	11,324	35.8
1932	4,045	7,889	11,934	33.9
1933	4,012	7,993	12,005	33.4
1934	4,033	7,996	12,029	33.5
1935	10,125			
1936	11,258	International reporting of gold		
1937	12,760	reserves suspended from 1935 to		
1938	14,512	1945 due to government policies		
1939	17,644	of secrecy.		
1940	21,995			
1941	22,737			
1942	22,739			
1943	21,981			
1944	20,631			
1945	20,083	13,687	33,770	59.5
1946	20,706	13,414	34,120	60.7
1947	22,868	11,682	34,550	66.2
1948	24,399	10,531	34,930	66.9
1949	24,563	10,817	35,380	69.4
1950	22,820	12,990	35,810	63.7
1951	22,873	13,087	35,960	63.6
1952	23,252	13,008	36,260	64.1
1953	22,091	14,589	36,680	60.2
1954	21,793	15,547	37,340	58.4
1955	21,753	15,867	37,620	57.8
1956	22,058	16,057	38,115	57.9
1957	22,857	15,963	38,820	58.8
1958	20,582	18,908	39,490	52.1

1959	19,507	20,683	40,190	48.5
1960	17,804	22,721	40,525	43.9
1961	16,947	23,981	40,928	41.4
1962	16,057	25,418	41,475	38.7
1963	15,596	26,709	42,305	36.8
1964	15,471	27,544	43,015	35.9
1965	13,806	29,424	43,230	31.9
1966	13,235	29,950	43,185	30.6
1967	12,065	29,535	41,600	29.0
1968	10,892	30,013	40,905	26.6
1969	11,859	29,156	41,015	28.9
1970	11,072	30,208	41,280	26.8
1971	10,206	31,004	41,210	24.8

Notes:

1. Official gold reserves prior to 1934 do not include gold coins in circulation.
2. Figures for U.S. and total world gold reserves subsequent to 1933 reflect increase due to nationalization of privately owned gold and gold coins in the U.S. and devaluation of U.S. dollar, which changed basic world gold price from $20.67 to $35 per troy ounce.
3. After 1941, U.S. total includes gold in Exchange Stabilization Fund.
4. As of February 1934, estimates of world total suspended because of government policies of secrecy on gold reserves in force outside the U.S.
5. Estimates of world total resumed as of 1945 exclude U.S.S.R., other Soviet bloc countries and Mainland China.
6. Totals for all other countries after 1944 include holdings of International Monetary Fund, European Payments Union and Bank for International Settlements.

Source: Board of Governors, Federal Reserve System, Banking and Monetary Statistics.

Notes:

CHAPTER VI

1. Although it is possible that the dollar may have appeared stronger than it actually was, when compared to the economic and financial shambles of the rest of the world.

2. And perhaps, when the verdict of history is finally brought in, the Indo-China War will also prove to have been one of the most damaging and costly to the U.S., not only financially, but socially and politically as well.

3. By former Federal Reserve Board Chairman, William McChesney Martin. Re: "The Price of Gold is not the Problem," *Federal Reserve Bulletin,* February, 1968.

4. At least that is the way the press reported the atmosphere in Washington at the time.

5. The $12.5 billion budget deficit was a Keynesian-oriented maneuver designed to offset the effects of the 1958 business recession.

6. The popular press hailed the SDR's as "paper gold" or "money created out of thin air;" perhaps the Vatican authorities charged with the responsibility for investigating reported miracles should check on this. The U.S. Federal Reserve Board, with a little more delicacy, refers to the SDR's as "International Reserve Assets," but keeps them on its books as if they were really money; that is, assets not dependent on a specific offsetting foreign liability. They are included under total monetary reserves, along with gold, convertible foreign exchange and the current IMF reserve position.

7. At least one gets that feeling from reading their official publications and pronouncements.

8. Surprising to the Treasury and the Federal Reserve at least, although private commodity experts had been warning of a coming silver crisis for 10 years prior to its appearance.

9. To assume that the disappearance of the Federal Reserve's entire stocks of silver dollars (some $350 million worth) plus nearly the entire circulating supply of half-dollars was the work of the nation's "coin collectors" requires a rather broad definition of what constitutes a coin collector. Certainly the

hoarding of common coins has nothing to do with traditional numismatics.

10.   The GSA sales policy apparently did help to contain the price of silver for the time being. Prices paid at the weekly auctions ranged from a high of $2.43 per ounce to a low of $1.62 for .999 fine silver.

11.   The deluge of false and misleading statements which accompanied every Treasury maneuver regarding silver is detailed in Rickenbacker's *Wooden Nickels.* Although the period covered in this book is prior to 1967, the Treasury's heavy-handed attempts to confuse and distract the public continued unabated in subsequent years.

12.   Until mid-1969, the Treasury prohibited the melting or export of silver coins by private citizens, hoping, as a result, to have a better chance itself of recovering and melting coins for the GSA auctions. The scheme failed, of course, because the motives of the typical coin hoarder were not to make a small profit by selling his coins for bullion, but to preserve them as an emergency source of intrinsic-value money.

13.   Neither nation, however, would accept such bonds without a "gold clause" guaranteeing their eventual redemption in gold or equivalent payment in gold exchange in the event of a prior devaluation of the dollar.

14.   Melchior Palyi, "A Point of View," *Commerical and Financial Chronicle,* July 24, 1969.

15.   *Wall Street Journal,* July 25, 1969. (After initial approval of the plan by the major industrial nations meeting in Paris.)

16.   *Ibid.* The *Journal's* estimate of the situation, however, overlooked the fact that the SDR's had to be denominated or defined as being "equal" to a precise amount of gold (.888671 grams, .999 fine per SDR unit). Therefore, gold was still the undisputed "yardstick" of monetary value. Furthermore, it was specifically noted that the SDR could never be "devalued."

17.   Ironically, the Wage and Price Stabilization Act had been publicly opposed by President Nixon because of its Democratic sponsorship.

18.   It is interesting to note that President Franklin Roosevelt similarly attributed the gold crisis of 1933 to "increasingly extensive speculative activity abroad" (see Appendix I). When history repeats, so do politicians.

19. The *de facto* floating of the entire world monetary system came about exactly as I predicted it would in my book *How to Invest in Gold Coins* (Arlington House, 1970). See Chapter XIV, pp. 271–272.

VII

THE FUTURE AND
WHAT TO DO ABOUT IT

"I know of no way of judging the future but by the past."

———PATRICK HENRY

"Wisdom consists not so much in knowing what to do, as in knowing what to do *next*."

—ANON.

ALTHOUGH we have examined something of monetary history and theory thus far in this essay, the limitations of a single volume of this type have actually permitted only a very brief excursion into this fascinating and vital subject. All gold-oriented investors and potential investors should, therefore, continue to improve and expand their knowledge of these subjects through supplementary reading and study. The bibliography included with this book provides suggestions that will help the beginner as well as the seasoned trader. A grasp of financial history equips the investor with a certain intellectual detachment that allows him to view current developments as a recognizable continuation of a historical process, rather than as isolated, unique and, consequently, incomprehensible events.

History may not always repeat itself exactly, but it certainly has a notable tendency to resemble itself. The actors and the scenery change, but the play, or at least the plot, remains all too familiar. Perhaps it is because human behavior and psychology have changed so little, if at all, over the centuries, that history is able to provide us with its insights to the future. There is an ancient proverb that holds that in the kingdom of the blind, the one-eyed are giants. Knowledge of the past gives us at least a one-eyed vision of the future. We need not recognize the exact details, but only the general shape of things to come, in order to have a reasonable chance of economic survival.

A new international monetary system is now evolving in the world; the old one, jerry-built at Bretton Woods in 1944, collapsed ingloriously on August 15, 1971. Yet the gold-dollar exchange standard did have a rather remarkable life, being patched, plugged and somehow held together for a full decade longer than seemed possible. But, historically, the longer an unstable condition is artificially maintained, the more severe the inevitable adjustment becomes. The price of gold has been artificially suppressed for two, if not three, decades. Perhaps it can be suppressed a while longer. However, the longer it is suppressed, the more dramatic, I believe, will be the eventual upward adjustment.

Nevertheless, it must be recognized that the major trading nations of the world will first make every effort to "save the dollar" as an international reserve currency. Regardless of their frequently acknowledged preference for gold, they will be forced, for a time at least, (reluctantly or not) to rally to the defense of the dollar at every crisis, because nearly all of them have been trapped by the gold-dollar exchange standard into holding large percentages of their monetary reserves in the form of U.S.-IMF credit dollars.

Consequently, there may be further attempts (assuming the inevitable failure of the Smithsonian agreement) to restore at least the ghost of the old gold-dollar exchange standard, by more juggling of exchange rates and additional (but meaningless) minor adjustments in (nonconvertible) gold parities. But all arrangements to maintain the dollar as an international reserve currency (including the Smithsonian agreement) that do not provide for restoring its liquidity (international gold convertibility) are bound to fail, because it was the lack of liquidity that brought on the seemingly endless series of dollar crises in the first place.

It will take at least a 100-percent increase in the official price of gold, *plus* a major realignment of world currencies to restore liquidity to the dollar and bring about a satisfactory degree of international monetary stability. Sooner or later, such a devaluation will have to be acknowledged by the United States, or else billions of dollars will be thrown on the open market for whatever they will bring in terms of gold, thus forcing a *de facto* devaluation of that amount or more. Eventually, the cost (in terms of inflation, unemployment and world economic stagnation) of trying to maintain a completely artificial gold parity for the dollar will become so obviously unbearable that the unavoidable loss of monetary reserve values that would accompany a massive devaluation (or repudiation) of the dollar will seem like the lesser of evils. *Exactly* when that point will arrive is, of course, impossible to predict, but assume it will come sooner rather than later.

We know, of course, that many, if not most, of the economists and banking experts employed by the IMF and the U.S. Treasury would prefer a system of exchange rates, whether flexible or fixed, in which gold would have no significant role. But this is a utopian dream. We would all prefer a world without war, without crime, without crooked politicians and dishonest bankers; a world where all men are honorable, just, of blessed intelligence and without the false pride of opinion; a world where nations as well as men unfailingly place principle ahead of profit or power. But until that great day dawns, and it is, sadly, nowhere in sight, the financially astute among nations and invividuals alike will continue to trust in the reality of gold rather than depend on the frailties of men.

Gold did not become money through legislation, but through historical evolution. Gold is the supreme money, as the result of man's total experience to date. To assume that such experience can merely be legislated away is just another example of the blindness that makes history the record of misfortunes and calamities that it has been.

In the 1970's, the United States will be faced with awesome

social and economic problems. Every major problem we have experienced during the sixties (except, hopefully, the Indo-China War) will still be with us in the 1970's, but on an even greater scale. I think it is a foregone conclusion that one of the principal attempts to cope with these difficulties will be through the creation of additional fiat money and fiat credit.

There is no private gold to confiscate this time, to create a new pool of liquidity. Nor can we expect that the threat of another world war will again drive the liquid wealth of the world to the greater safety of the United States, as it did in the 1930's. In fact, the opposite may well prevail and, as in the 1960's, the liquid wealth of the United States will continue to seek the greater relative safety of certain foreign lands, in the face of continuing financial, economic and social upheaval at home. This is a grim forecast, but it must be faced realistically. The United States is, and will continue to be, challenged with very difficult problems at a time when its liquidity is at an unprecedented low point.

When the United States faced the Great Depression, the credit of the Federal Government was unquestioned, either at home or abroad. Today, that Government has borrowed to the hilt. Then, we were able to build a *free* gold reserve greater than the triple-mortgaged stockpile we have today. When the United States entered World War II it had the greatest liquidity ever enjoyed by its monetary and banking system. It ended that war with 70 percent of all the monetary gold in the world in Fort Knox. Even after three and a half years of global war, overall U.S. liquidity was still great enough to impress even John Maynard Keynes. But now, we face the crisis decade of the 1970's with empty coffers. Public and private liquidity alike were never lower. We have no free gold, nor even silver, and our credit position has already been extended to the breaking point.

To avert a renewal of the general liquidity shortage that periodically threatened to bring down the American economy throughout the 1960's, the Fed will have to provide a constantly increasing supply of money and credit to the domestic economy. We will have to run faster and faster just to stay in the same place. But it will have to be more fiat money and fiat credit; we now have no other kind available.

Prolonged inflation of a nation's currency and credit, however, eventually reaches a point of no return. From that point on, the final destruction of that currency is certain, and neither common stocks, nor real estate nor any of the usual "growth" investments can provide adequate protection for the individual. In the terminal phase of a major inflation cycle, gold-oriented investments offer the best hope of financial survival. This has been historically demonstrated many times.

I believe that the American credit dollar has already passed the point of no return in the inflationary process—where there is no longer any possibility of a return to conditions of relative stability without a major monetary-financial crisis and adjustment. The future is both perilous and, for the United States at least, unprecedented. But it is not hopeless, either for the individual U.S. citizen or his government. There are defensive measures that each can take, but my remarks are directed primarily to individuals. My advice to governments would be, of course, to begin at once to reconstruct a meaningful international gold standard, to plan to extend it eventually to domestic monetary systems, and then to resolve to live by the discipline it requires. But this will, unfortunately, not come about until after the crisis and adjustment phase has been (involuntarily) completed. Therefore, each of us must take the entire responsibility for the protection and preservation of individual monetary and financial assets until the crisis has passed.

By historic standards, the terminal phase of a major fiat money inflation cycle takes from four to ten years to complete, but the fact that the dollar is a world reserve currency may considerably shorten the process. Attempting specifically to "time" the exact course of future events, however, would not be realistic. There are actually several major alternatives that could develop during the decade of the seventies, and we shall review them presently. But regardless of the exact sequence of events that does develop, the ultimate result, based on the preconditions already established, is both inevitable and predictable.

At this point, the reader should come to a decision as to whether I have proved my case, and that case is, of course, that gold will not in the foreseeable future be replaced as the world's most effective and trusted store of value, unit of account and medium of exchange or, in other words, as the ideal money. And if gold remains the indispensable world money, then an explosive rise in its dollar price is inevitable. Furthermore, a drastic change in the price of gold is bound to have far-reaching effects, social and political, as well as financial and economic. Aside from the psychological and emotional factors, the following points have been advanced in defense of this thesis:

1. An ending of the abnormal post-World War II boom in crisis and major readjustment is inevitable according to historic patterns.
2. Currency and credit inflation now prolonged past the point of no return in the United States and most of the rest of the world.
3. Social, political and economic conditions in the United States leading to a general failure of confidence.
4. International position of the U.S. credit dollar greatly weakened and undermined through chronic deficits and overissue.
5. U.S. gold reserves drastically depleted. No free reserves left. All remaining gold in possession of U.S. Government mortgaged by 300 percent to foreign creditors. (Although it is now obvious that we are going to default either partially or entirely on that mortgage!)
6. Growing mistrust abroad of present international monetary arrangements and the IMF.
7. Relationship between the price of gold and general price levels at cyclical low point. Gold now greatly undervalued in historic terms.
8. Era of postwar monetary cooperation ending. International trade wars and protectionism increasing everywhere.
9. Overall liquidity of U.S. economy at historic low levels.
10. Growing shift of industrial and commercial power from the United States to Western Europe and Japan.

It should also be clear that the United States lost the gold war of the 1960's, despite the illusory "victory" of the SDR's. The old Washington-London alliance that had dominated the IMF since its inception was thoroughly discredited as a result of the pound devaluation of 1967, the gold-pool fiasco of 1968 and the dollar default of 1971. The SDR plan itself actually reduced rather than enhanced the power and prestige of the United States within the IMF. To get the SDR's accepted, the United States was forced to agree to an amendment of the IMF charter that changed the voting requirements for approval of major policy decisions (such as the creation of additional "drawing rights") from a 75 percent to an 85 percent majority of the IMF membership. This gives the Common Market, which now controls almost 20 percent of the voting strength, an absolute veto over all IMF policy.

Since the SDR's were activated in 1970, Great Britain has quietly, but undeniably, begun to disassociate herself from the American position on gold and is apparently in the process of abandoning altogether the historic monetary alliance with Washington. On March 31, 1971, for example, all gold coin and medal restrictions in the United Kingdom were lifted. These restrictions, which were far more severe than those in force in the United States, were imposed by the Labor Government in April of 1966, and they prohibited, among other things, the holding of more than four gold coins (minted after 1837) by any British collector.[1] Also, in early 1971, the United Kingdom began negotiating in earnest to become a member of the Common Market, and has already agreed, as a precondition, to begin phasing out the pound sterling's role as a reserve currency.

Even as early as 1969, the Governor of the Bank of England was of the opinion that, "the tendency to attack the role of gold in the system is somewhat ironic, when it is not gold which is the root cause of the present uneasiness, but doubts about the alternative reserve assets. The enthusiasm for getting rid of gold owes much to the fact that in this inflationary age, currencies cannot stand comparison with it."[2]

Still the United States clings to its official view that it is paper currencies that give value to gold, rather than gold which gives value to (convertible) paper currencies. Since this opinion is also still widely held privately in the United States (and apparently remains unshaken by the disasters of the 1960's), we will examine it here, despite the rather obvious evidence that if paper dollars were really better than gold we wouldn't have lost $14 billion worth of gold in the last two decades and there would not now be any dollar "problem." Nevertheless, the antigold economists and their naive followers were elated, early in 1970, when, following the SDR accord, the price of gold on the so-called "free" market in London "crashed" from the crisis level of $44 per ounce and actually fell below the "official" $35 monetary price.

This unexpected reaction was hailed by the U.S. Treasury and by banking spokesmen, and widely proclaimed in the popular press as providing positive proof that the use of gold as an international currency was redundant and that the price of gold could not even maintain itself without central-bank support. Typically, a major Wall Street brokerage firm released an advisory letter in December of 1969 proclaiming "King Gold is dead," and warning that gold's role in monetary affairs had been so diminished by the SDR's that investment in gold-mining shares was no longer worth the risk. As it turned out, that very month would have been an excellent time to buy gold shares; within 18 months, the listed golds alone would have yielded a capital gains profit of 100 to 150 percent.

It is almost axiomatic, that when Wall Street is uniformly bearish on golds, it is time to buy them. But when the majority of brokerage houses and investment advisers have finally climbed on the bandwagon and are feverishly recommending gold stocks, it is a good time to think about taking profits. In any case, the vast majority of the public, the press and the financial community were completely taken in by the implications (encouraged by Washington) that some sort of a "test" had taken place between the dollar and gold, based on the (temporary) retreat in the price of gold on the London market. But there was no test, because *there is no truly "free" gold market anywhere in the world*, except perhaps in the back alleys of Bombay and other Oriental cities, where it regularly fetches a black-market price of 80 to 90 dollars per ounce. The private market in London is carefully controlled; one must have a special license to buy gold in this market, and such licenses are very difficult to obtain.

Since nearly all of the 250 million private citizens, as well as the great majority of business establishments in both Britain and the United States, are forbidden to buy or own gold under penalty of heavy fine and imprisonment, one can hardly consider the private market as being "free," that is, free to operate under the natural laws of supply and demand. To imply, therefore, as the opponents of gold have repeatedly implied, that the private markets now operating in London and through certain licensed metal dealers in the United States are "free" markets is a complete misrepresentation.

THE GOLD WAR MOVES TO THE PRIVATE MARKET

What happened in 1969 was only another skirmish in the long-standing secret war between the antigold forces in Washington and the Continental believers in gold who rally behind a Zurich-Johannesburg gold "axis." The conservative Continental bankers and the South African producers are united in defense of their common interest, and they are methodically and purposefully assuming control of the world's monetary and financial affairs, as it is being forfeited by the crumbling Washington-London monetary alliance. Nevertheless, one cannot say that the Zurich-Johannesburg interests are directly responsible for the U.S. predicament. In fact, all the Continental powers have been scrupulously careful to avoid any deliberate injury to the dollar, for they recognize, as European economist Leo Brawand puts it, that "the Western world's sensitive currency system could not stand the shock of a sudden disruptive revolt against the dollar."[3]

Even South Africa, which produces more than 70 percent of the Free World's gold, has attempted nothing more than to assure an orderly market for its primary export and (before the Smithsonian agreement) never challenged the $35 fixed official price either in word or deed. The gold axis will vigorously and understandably continue to resist all attacks on the principle of gold supremacy within the international monetary system but, contrary to popular opinion (as encouraged by the U.S. Treasury), neither the Europeans nor the South African mining interests have ever tried to "ruin" the dollar or wreck the U.S. economy. A strong dollar and a healthy American economy were (and are) vital to the rest of the world and it was, and still is, well aware of that fact. If the U.S. economy collapses or we endure a financial debacle of major proportions, the repercussions will be worldwide and every nation will suffer, not only through the loss of value in their dollar holdings, but in the loss of essential needs for trade with the United States.

When the two-tier marketing arrangement was established in March of 1968, the United States secured a "gentlemen's agreement" from the Continental nations that they would not buy gold for their monetary reserves from private markets. This move was intended to seal off South Africa's enormous production from the world monetary system and force her to sell it all on the so-called free market, which was supported only by industrial users, Continental speculators and private European banks. It was presumed (correctly) that the private market alone could not absorb the entire world production without supply eventually overcoming demand (as long as demand could be restricted by eliminating monetary purchases) and forcing the free market price to retreat, thus making it appear that the paper dollar and the SDR's had triumphed.

The Zurich-Johannesburg interests, however, were less concerned with making immediate profits than in reestablishing the principle that gold was still the basis of the existing international monetary system. Therefore, rather than seriously attempting to support the price of gold on the private market (and ultimately failing) as the United States assumed or hoped they would, they deliberately sold gold in heavy quantities, both from South African stocks and from private bank holdings on the Continent. By unexpectedly "cooperating," and actually driving the free market price of gold back to par, the gold axis not only eliminated a dangerous $3 billion "overhang" of marginally held speculative positions that threatened future market stability, but also brought accumulated South African bullion stocks down to manageable levels. It was, in essence, a healthy purging of the market that forced a temporary overaccumulation of gold out of weak speculative positions and into the strong hands of permanent long-term investors.

The real payoff, however, was that forcing the private market price of gold below par provided the IMF with the necessary excuse to "come to the rescue" and purchase gold at par (despite the "gentlemen's agreement" to keep newly mined gold out of the the monetary system), in order to "protect" the currency value of existing central-bank gold reserves. Over initial U.S. protests, the IMF concluded an agreement to buy South African gold directly, whenever the private market price fell to par ($35 per troy ounce). Furthermore, the IMF also agreed to accept South African gold, regardless of the open market price, "to the extent that South Africa has a need for foreign exchange over a semi-annual period beyond the need that can be satisfied by the sale of all current new gold production in the private market."[4]

The gold acquired by the IMF under the South African Marketing Agreement could later be sold to IMF member nations, whenever a need arose for their currencies. Thus the "gold axis" was able to evade the restrictions of the "gentlemen's agreement" with the United States, without directly challenging it. At the same time, the IMF directorate blandly announced that it would be a good idea to increase IMF gold and currency quotas by an additional 35 percent. The United States could only glumly agree, as it no longer had the voting power to do otherwise.

The IMF-South African marketing accord accomplished two basic things, neither of which helped the cause of the antigold forces:

1. It reaffirmed the principle that gold was the basis of the IMF system.
2. It established a permanent "floor" for the price of South African gold at $34.91 ($35 less an 0.25 percent IMF service charge).

At the time of this writing it is an open question whether the South African-IMF agreement will be renegotiated, in the light of the Smithsonian arrangements and/or subsequent "devaluations," in order to raise the "floor" or basic sales price of new South African gold to an equal parity with the "official" IMF-U.S. price. But whether this is accomplished or not, it should be remembered that neither the IMF nor anyone else has specifically guaranteed to maintain any kind of a floor under the so-called free market or London price for gold. It is therefore still possible, under certain conditions, for the private market price of gold, not only to move down as well as up, in periodic technical corrections, but, under certain conditions, actually to fall (temporarily) below the "official" parity, whatever it may be.

In this regard, it should be noted that ever since the establishment of the two-tier marketing arrangement, the prices of gold stocks and gold coins have shown a strong tendency to move in sympathy with the so-called free market price in London, except that a $5 or $10 variation in the London bullion price can mean as much as a 100 to 200 percent change in the prices of listed gold stocks and a 20 to 40 percent variation in the price levels of common gold coins.

As an example, let us take the case of Campbell Red Lake Mines (ticker symbol CRK), one of the senior golds listed on the New York Stock Exchange. During the peak of the March 1968 crisis, the price of gold on the London market reached $44 per ounce. From December of 1966 to March 1968, CRK rose from its previous low of $16 per share to a high of $47 per share, a capital gain of 160 percent. But following the crisis high, the London gold price was, as we noted, forced back to par ($35) and it reached that level in December of 1969. During this identical period, CRK fell from its all-time high of $47 per share to a low of $15, reached also in December of 1969, for a loss of 68 percent. However, as soon as the IMF-South African accord was approved, the London market began a slow but persistent rise, and the price of bullion crossed $41 per ounce in May of 1971. During this identical time, CRK moved from its $15 low to a May 1971 high of $35 per share—a gain of 133 percent.

I have used CRK as a typical example, but Homestake, Dome Mines and American-South African, among the listed golds, made moves of equivalent scope and duration. The unlisted South African stocks and other gold equities made identical moves in time, although they were, typically, of less intensity. The prices of common gold coins followed exactly the same sequence.

There may well be more opportunities of this type to come. When to sell gold investments is a problem we shall take up later, but one of the most opportune times to buy them would appear to be whenever the London price of bullion retreats to par.

CAN GOLD FALL BELOW PAR?

We must now deal with one of the most intriguing questions of the entire gold problem, and that is can the so-called free market price for gold ever drop to, or even fall substantially below, the "official" level. However remote this possibility may appear at times, it must be considered, because such an occurrence would undoubtedly terrify large numbers of unsophisticated and unprepared gold investors, and it would very probably trigger a gold panic during which gold, gold coins and gold-mining equities would be frantically dumped on the market in large amounts, depressing prices for these articles, temporarily at least, to absurdly low levels. That is precisely why major declines in the private market price of gold are always possible, and why retreats that could take the private price even below the official parity cannot be dismissed altogether. After all, it already happened once, when the London price of gold fell below the $35 par in late 1969.

Obviously, the profit potential in arranging or provoking a "crash" in the private gold market, to a point where gold and gold stocks could be picked up in huge quantities at superbargain levels, would be simply enormous, particularly if it could be accomplished just prior to a massive devaluation of the dollar and the coming markup of gold to the $140–150 per ounce level.

But in view of the present extremely tight supply-demand situation, who or what could be powerful enough to bring about such a totally unexpected (and dangerous for the unprepared) event as a supercrash in gold? The answer is obvious: the United States and/or the Zurich-Johannesburg gold axis itself.

It is certainly conceivable that the U.S. Treasury and its Keynesian political and banking allies, in their zeal to "defend the dollar" would dearly love to discredit gold in any way possible, even if only for a short time. A crash in the private market gold price would serve the aims of the U.S. believers in totalitarian economics in at least three ways: (a) it would act as a trap to deprive those who had the foresight to try to defend themselves against the neo-Keynesians' economic war against them, not only of their potential profits, but even of their remaining financial assets as well, (b) it would make the inevitable massive devaluation of the dollar more palatable to the U.S. public and to the rest of the world, on the grounds that the gold parity of a currency didn't really matter anyway, since gold could fall below par as well as rise above it and (c) it would enable the U.S. Treasury and other central banks to acquire as much gold as possible for their official reserves, at low prices, *before* a major devaluation of the dollar was announced.

In many ways this (hypothetical) situation is analogous to what happened in 1934, when the U.S. Government attempted to remonetize silver. After allowing the world price for silver to fall to a Depression low of 25 cents per ounce,* the Roosevelt administration nationalized silver and ordered the surrender of all domestic silver bullion to the Treasury. The owners of such bullion were compensated at the rate of 50 cents per ounce, thus depriving them of the grounds (or desire) for legal action, since they had received payment well above the prevailing private market rate. The United States then "officially" revalued the nationalized silver at $1.29 per ounce. Thus the Government was able to acquire an enormous hoard of silver very cheaply, by paying only 50 cents per ounce for it, and using for that very purpose silver certificates and Federal Reserve notes valued at $1.29 per ounce! From a monetary point of view, however, the scheme was a failure, as the rest of the world refused to have anything to do with U.S. attempts to resurrect bimetallism, and elected to remain firmly committed to gold.

Given the right combination of circumstances, the United States *could* probably engineer a gold crash. If the immense balance-of-payments deficits of the United States can be refinanced by further credit or additional creations of Special or Regular Drawing Rights from the IMF, the remaining U.S. gold supply could remain intact and available to be used in a secret maneuver to smash the London gold price. A U.S. administration, if it were desperate enough and unscrupulous enough,

---

*At the time of the Executive Order of August 8, 1934, however, the world price for silver had risen to 33 cents per troy ounce.

could announce a total demonetization of gold, embargo all payments in gold for dollars, and at the same time begin secretly dumping gold on the London market, hoping to provoke a panic. Such a move would be a wild gamble to be sure, but it just might succeed—it only has to work for a short time in order to be effective.

If the price of gold could be substantially forced below par, the Treasury could then announce that it was willing to buy gold again (at prices under $38 per ounce) in order to "save" the value of gold for monetary purposes. But after this (hypothetical) adminstration had bought as much gold as possible under these conditions, it would then proclaim that it was revaluing gold to $150 per ounce in order to restore "sound money" and "prevent" further gold panics and monetary crises. Of course it may be argued that the European governments (that now control the IMF) would not let the United States get away with such trickery, that they would unite to defend the $35 price in order to preserve the value of their monetary reserves. Perhaps this is so, but there is now no floor under the London market (contrary to popular opinion) and the $35 gold price would only have to be smashed once to bring about the possibility of a panic, which would keep the market down long enough for the Treasury to make its grab. Before the European central banks could unite to come to the rescue, the game might well be over.

The foregoing is, of course, entirely hypothetical, but, as long as we are hypothesizing, let us also include the possibility that the Zurich-Johannesburg gold alliance might decide either to help the United States arrange a crash, so they could also be in on the grab, or they might even try to stage such a maneuver without us. The South African mining interests are already protected by the IMF purchasing agreement, so they would not risk anything. Switzerland is not a member of either the IMF or the Common Market. The fabled Swiss banks are probably the most completely independent financial institutions in the world. These large private banks are estimated to be holding at least $1 billion in gold, which would be more than enough to bring about a "crash" situation if it were fed rapidly to the private markets.

Zurich is the gold capital of the world. The so-called Zurich "gold pool," made up of private dealers and their banking connections, is a major world marketing agency. It has been rumored that this gold pool has been secretly buying far more gold from South Africa than it has been selling or publicly adding to bank holdings. Therefore, the existence of a secret hoard of one-half to one billion dollars worth of gold, that could be employed at a critical time to depress the market, must also be considered.

Furthermore, recent legislation passed in Switzerland during 1970, which removed legal-tender status from gold, adds to the mystery. One purpose of such legislation could be to prevent Swiss banks from using gold as part of their official reserves, so that if the price of gold *did* go below par, bank reserve ratios would not be legally impaired. There is no question but that the private interests headquartered in Zurich could also profit immensely from arranging a crash in the private price of gold, just prior to its being officially marked up to a new high par value.

I want to emphasize again that all of the foregoing is pure speculation. I frankly do not think that it will happen. The odds at this point strongly favor a buying panic and breakout on the upside, rather than any dramatic sell-off first. But the coming major adjustments in money and gold are of the type and intensity seen only once every half-century or so. Therefore, we can take nothing for granted. The fireworks marking the end of the present gold-dollar standard will undoubtedly be spectacular, and anything can happen. To the author, few things are more certain in this life than the price of gold going higher. But the forces involved in the gold war are both powerful and devious, and we can be sure that they will make every effort to secure the maximum profits, from monetary-gold adjustments, for themselves.

For years, the U.S. Government has made every attempt (officially and nonofficially) to keep its citizens from converting their paper money into gold or gold-oriented investments. From now on, you can be sure that U.S. officialdom will not only intensify its antigold bias, but will try to get holders of gold, gold coin and gold stocks, on a worldwide basis, to sell these holdings prematurely or at the wrong time. You can also be sure that other parties, both official and private, in other countries, will also be trying to get anyone with a gold investment to part with it as cheaply as possible.

Consequently, if you have or are building a portfolio of gold stocks and gold coins, and the price of gold in London is forced below par, DON'T PANIC AND SELL ANY OF YOUR GOLD INVESTMENTS. If anything, use the opportunity to acquire more, if it is financially possible. A sharp break in the private market gold price or a (temporary) gold panic, if it occurs, would only be the preliminary phase of a major upward adjustment in the world monetary price of gold. Even if they manage to hold the private price of gold down for some weeks, or even months, don't weaken. *If they can't scare you out, they might try to wear you out,* as an old Wall Street proverb puts it. But don't fall into such a trap.

Other sound Wall Street advice holds that one should follow the major trend and ignore the minor ones. The major trend for the price of gold is going to be up. The minor trends are, I concede, unpredictable. The major trend for U.S. paper currency, however, is not only down, but so hopelessly so that it has become accepted as one of the inevitabilities of life, like death and (ever-rising) taxes.

THE DESTINY OF THE DOLLAR
What will happen to the U.S. credit dollar in the next decade is obviously of vital concern to every American, investor or not. The future of the dollar and the destiny of the United States as a nation are insolubly linked. The dollar is also the key element in the gold situation, and the ultimate reliability of the dollar, as a measure and store of value, is inversely related to the price of gold; the weaker the dollar, the higher the price for gold. Unfortunately, there is no longer any point in discussing whether or not the dollar will continue to weaken. The evidence so far indicates that the only remaining questions are: (a) to what level will the dollar eventually fall before it is finally stabilized, and (b) how long will it take for it to get there.

A well-known professor of economics (who has advised U.S. Presidents) was asked, in the fall of 1969, to forecast the course of the U.S. economy during the seventies. He outlined a deeply pessimistic scenario. There will be more bouts of inflation, he said, followed by half-hearted attempts to restrain inflation, followed by worse inflation, followed by more half-hearted attempts at restraint, which, in turn, would be followed by still worse inflation and so on. But, asked the interviewer in despair, where will it all end? It will end, replied the professor, when the inflation becomes so painful that the country will be willing to endure a severe recession or even a depression, in order to stop it.

Grim as our anonymous professor's estimate is, I believe he is basically correct.[5] Nevertheless, there is considerable latitude for variations on this theme. The professor made no reference to gold in his forecast, yet we cannot construct a reasonable hypothesis without considering it. The United States cannot continue to debase the credit dollar indefinitely through inflation without drastically affecting the price of gold sooner or later. The unknown question is whether the price of gold will rise gradually or explosively.

Reaction to a Permanently Floating Dollar.   If the U.S. dollar and other major currencies are allowed, either by default or by design, to float more or less permanently, that is to have no fixed relationship with each other or with a given weight of gold, the international monetary system will gradually descend into chaos. We have, as I said earlier, been down that road before and the effects on international trade were appalling. Engaging in forward exchange operations, offset transactions and various other currency hedges necessary under such a system may sound plausible enough in theory, but in practice it becomes so complex and full of uncertainty that the average exporter or importer soon gives up in despair.

Nevertheless, we cannot say it will not happen; each generation seems determined to learn every lesson the hard way. The adoption of a system (or nonsystem actually) under which all major currencies float would leave gold floating as well. While there would undoubtedly be wild gyrations in the price of gold under such conditions, the long-term trend would surely be up, because there would then be no restraint whatever on inflation in floating-currency countries. The domestic pressures (and temptations) to create unlimited currency and bank credit would be enormous and, I believe, the world would embark on an orgy of inflation that would make the present era seem innocuous by comparison.

However, I am inclined to doubt that the Europeans would let their currencies float for very long before getting together, either to establish a Common Market currency with a fixed gold parity or to restore their individual currencies to a gold basis and reestablish mutual convertibility. But the dollar could very possibly be allowed to float against foreign gold-based currencies for some time. In that case, the situation would be analogous to what happened to the British pound sterling when it was allowed to float from 1931 until 1939. *Fig. 14,* showing both gold and dollar exchange values of the pound from 1930 to 1941, tells the story. The obvious lesson is that in the nine years after the pound was allowed to float, the price of gold increased by slightly over 100 percent, despite the operation of an exchange stabilization program by the Bank of England.

Fig. 14

GOLD AND EXCHANGE VALUE OF
THE BRITISH POUND STERLING
1930–1941

Year	Gold Value in Troy Ounces	Exchange Value in U.S. Dollars
1930	.2354	$4.86
1931	.2191	4.53
1932	.1698	3.51
1933	.1211	4.24
1934	.1437	5.03
1935	.1400	4.90
1936	.1420	4.97
1937	.1412	4.94
1938	.1394	4.88
1939	.1266	4.43
1940	.1094	3.83
1941	.1151	4.03

Notes:
1. The Bank of England, using an "Exchange Equalization Account," attempted to stabilize the pound after 1932 by buying and selling gold and foreign exchange for pounds in the open market.

2. Floating of the U.S. dollar in 1933 and devaluation of the dollar in 1934 account for increased exchange value of the pound subsequent to 1932.
3. Pound returned to official exchange rate of $4.03 in 1939 but was not completely stabilized (with U.S. help) until 1941. Fixed exchange rate of $4.03 and (assumed) gold value of .1151 maintained until devaluation of 1949.
4. Total (gold) devaluation of pound from 1930 to 1941 equal to 51.6 percent.
5. Total rise in the (pound) price of gold from 1930 to 1941 equal to 104 percent.

Another point to observe is that during this long bull market in gold, there was one moderate correction or reversal and there was a four-year period of relative stability. According to the London *Financial Times* Gold Stock Index, January of 1937 saw the peak price for gold stocks on the London Market (corresponding closely to the pattern established by U.S. and Canadian gold stocks). In 1930, the *F.T.* Gold Index had bottomed out at 80, after a long decline from the 1927 high of 140. Isn't it fascinating how the price of gold shares always seems to make new lows just prior to major changes in international monetary conditions that are extremely bullish for gold? If I were a bit cynical, I would be inclined to think that they were (and are) deliberately maneuvered there by the "smart money" boys hoping to fatten up their own portfolios first and at bargain levels.

At any rate, after making its low of 80 in 1930, the *F.T.* Gold Index advanced to exceed 250 by January of 1937. After a profit-taking decline that took the index back to the 200 level, a rally ensued that returned it to 230 in 1938. But, after the secondary high, a long decline began that lasted into the 1950's, due in part to the depletion and exhaustion of many of the older mines that made up the *F.T.* index. It is interesting to note the leverage demonstrated here; while the price of gold went up a little over 100 percent, the *Financial Times* Gold Stock Index (composed mainly of South African stocks) recorded a maximum gain of 200 per cent—a good reason why every devaluation-inflation hedge plan should include some gold-mining shares.

A Two-Tier Market for the Dollar? Another suggestion, having at least some support, is that the rest of the world will (or should) establish a two-tier market for dollars, just as it has for gold. Under this scheme, "official dollars," that is, those dollars used for regular payments between governments and central banks, would remain pegged at a fixed par value (in terms of gold and other currencies) established by the IMF. But all "private" dollar transactions, that is, dollars intended for private investment abroad and even (presumably) dollars spent by U.S. tourists, businessmen or corporations overseas, would not be pegged to any parity (gold or otherwise), but would have to be traded or "float" in the foreign exchange markets for whatever rate they would bring (in competition with other currencies) on a pure supply-demand basis.

Such systems are already in use by many unstable or "soft"-currency countries, and some of them have had both an official rate and a free rate for their currencies for years. It should be noted here, however, that the establishment of two-tier currency markets has not prevented any of these soft currency countries from periodically being forced to devalue their "official" rates anyway.

A two-tier dollar market on a world basis would present some serious problems, the principal one being how to keep the "free" dollar isolated from the "official" one. The temptation for foreign bankers and others to find ways of surreptitiously transferring free dollars, bought at a lower rate, to the official market, where they could be exchanged at a higher rate, would be overwhelming. Nevertheless, even assuming that the bureaucrats of the world could provide enough red tape reasonably to separate the two markets (even if they had to strangle world trade to do so), the system would eventually collapse because the gap between the free dollar and the official dollar would continue to grow, as a result of inflation, until the obvious disparity between the two rates would cause the official rate to be seriously questioned.

Any substantial decline in the free dollar rate would inevitably bring about distrust and finally repudiation of the official dollar in favor of gold. Just as a rising free market price for gold will eventually make a low official gold parity of the dollar unrealistic and untenable, a falling free market price for the dollar would inevitably pull down the official rate.

When a two-tier market is established for a currency, it is an infallible sign that the inflationary illness of the country concerned has reached a final stage. Because the real reason for such an arrangement is obvious to the bankers and money changers of the world, it only serves to hasten the end. In the case of the United States, it would also mean the absolute finish of our role as the world's banker.

THE UNITED STATES ENTERS A CONTROLLED ECONOMY

The collapse of the gold-dollar exchange standard has, as I long ago forecast, ushered in an era of quasi-totalitarian control by government over the economic life of every citizen. The follow-up programs prepared by the administration after the floating of the dollar and the 90-day wage-price "freeze," as well as statements subsequently made by Government spokesmen and economists, make it clear that we are headed toward a fully managed economy with an ever-growing maze of wage, price and exchange regulations, restrictions and prohibitions smothering and stagnating the United States.

But the American public has become desperately sick of the endless round of strikes and protests, and the high and often unjustified wage and fee increases granted to any group strong enough or in a position sensitive enough to paralyze the whole economy or cause massive public inconvenience. People are increasingly bitter about soaring living costs and spiraling taxation robbing them of the fruits of their labor and reducing their standards of living. It is understandable, therefore, that many U.S. citizens, in their frustration, now express a willingness to accept total government control over their economic life, in order to get some relief from the intolerable burden of constant inflation.

Unfortunately, such controls don't work well even in wartime, let alone in a nominal peacetime setting. If we could not make economic controls work effectively at the height of World War II (and we could not), when patriotic spirit was at its peak, we could hardly expect miracles from such efforts at this time.[6]

Furthermore, a controlled economy is basically incompatible with a free society. Evasions, resistance and black markets would inevitably develop, causing still further social, economic and moral disintegration.

Economic controls would only buy a little more time for the dollar, at best. They may delay the ultimate move in the price of gold, but will not prevent it. France had complete wage, price and exchange controls prior to De Gaulle, but still experienced a constant succession of strikes and riots that perpetuated a ruinous inflation anyway. Forbidding unions to strike for higher wages or greater benefits is one thing, but preventing them from doing so is quite something else. Municipal workers, for example, are forbidden to strike now, in most cities, but they strike or "get sick" at will and the cities are at their mercy. Even policemen feel entitled to strike in this new era. In addition, wage, price and exchange controls do nothing to halt or control profligate spending by politicians at all levels of government, and actually may encourage it.

There is one other alternative that must also be examined at this point, and that is the possibility of a major depression occurring *before* monetary and credit inflation gets completely out of hand. We know from our review of the mechanism of bank credit, and from what actually occurred in the 1920's and '30's, that the excessive creation of such credit sets the stage for cyclical depressions in business.[7] A few major business failures (such as Penn Central, Rolls Royce and Lockheed?) or a handful of large defaults on bank loans not only cause a crisis of confidence in business, but result in an actual shrinkage (many times magnified) of the so-called money supply, because bank credit, as we have seen, constitutes the largest single element in the monetary system of any modern industrial nation.

In the 1930's, bank loans were defaulted with such rapidity, in a chain reaction of bankruptcies and panic, that even the most determined efforts of both the Hoover and Roosevelt administrations to create additional currency and credit were inadequate to offset the massive deflation of the economy that took place. The wholesale destruction of bank credit through default brought about the collapse of collateral values in stocks, bonds, real estate and business inventories. There is no question but that the amount of bank credit outstanding (on a per capita basis) as we enter the decade of the seventies, dwarfs all preceding periods in American economic history—a history, incidentally, that is replete with similar, although not quite so drastic excesses—all corrected with panics and depressions.

We are, in the author's analysis, now (1972) in a state of precarious balance between a full-fledged depression and an inflation crisis of the type that affected France after World War II; Brazil, Argentina and Chile in the 1960's; or possibly even Germany in the 1920's. In my personal judgment, given the social, economic and historical evidence available at this time, an inflation "blow-off" lasting from four to ten years appears to be the most probable future course.

Nevertheless, I would not rule out the possibility of the "depression solution" to the liquidity problem being applied at any time. There is even a school of economic thought that holds that anything—even a depression—is preferable to runaway inflation, which completely destroys not only economic but political and social values as well. According to this group (which is admittedly a small minority, but includes some very learned and respected economists, bankers and scholars), there inevitably comes a time, in a free-enterprise economy, when the central bank has no other choice but to break the chain reaction of inflation and curb the monopoly power of certain labor unions and other such associations by a forced liquidation of the whole financial structure—in other words by deliberately bringing about a depression through stringent monetary and credit restraint. Furthermore, at the depth of a depression, a substantial devaluation of the dollar and an overall readjustment of world gold parities could be accomplished without creating undue inflationary pressures.

Exchange Controls. The imposition of severe exchange controls is a virtual certainty, as the bureaucrats and politicians will try to blame the American citizen and his fondness for travel for the balance-of-payments and trade deficits that they, the so-called money managers, have created by inflating our currency and stripping it of its gold backing. Tight border controls, including the personal search of travelers by Customs officials, will be instituted. The American citizen will lose the freedom to travel anywhere, at any time, and take whatever amount of money he pleases with him. The issuance of passports and permits for pleasure travel may be restricted to specific destinations or denied altogether. Persons desiring to travel abroad may be required to "prove" that they have urgent business or family matters to attend to before being allowed to proceed, and then the amount of money they would be permitted to take with them would be strictly limited to the estimated travel expenses.

Under full exchange controls, all transfers or remittances of money abroad would have to be approved by the Treasury Department or one of its agencies. The transfer of funds out of the country for investment or safekeeping would be prohibited and only essential commercial transactions would be allowed. If the economic and financial situation of the United States becomes really desperate, internal as well as external exchange controls may be invoked. In that case, banks and other savings institutions would be required to report all cash withdrawals (of perhaps $1,000 or more in any thirty-day period) to some Federal agency, and the person making the withdrawal, even from his own account, would be obliged to declare for what purpose the withdrawal was being made. Persons making large withdrawals, for nonapproved or unspecified purposes, would be subject to prosecution on the grounds of "currency hoarding."

All of the foregoing, of course, is hardly pleasant to contemplate, but, until a much greater degree of monetary power and freedom is returned to the individual than exists at present, there can be no effective solution to the problem of inflation.[8] As long as the long-entrenched neo-Keynesian politico-economic philosophy and our fiat monetary-credit system prevail, we can be sure that, come what may, recession, depression or further expansion—boom or bust, war or peace—printing press "money" will continue to debase our financial, economic and social structures. As long as a government has complete control of money, its citizens will not escape from inflation, recurrent financial crises and a continuous erosion of personal freedom.

I am not an alarmist, nor am I trying for sensationalism. I am not out to condemn any particular segment of the American economy. What I am in complete opposition to is the old greenback philosophy that has taken over the United States in its modern neo-Keynesian disguise. I certainly would not argue that the pressing social and economic problems of crime, poverty, pollution, inadequate housing, drugs, mass transportation, soaring medical costs, etc., can be ignored. Far from it; we must positively come up with imaginative and honest solutions for these problems. But little will be accomplished if we continue to rely on the disastrous delusion that more fiat money or credit is the answer to such national dilemmas. Regardless of how well it is intended, no one benefits from receiving more paper dollars, when those dollars continue to lose their purchasing power.

In fact, the use of nonredeemable, and consequently inflationary, currency is actually one of the curses that keeps the poor in the chains of poverty and eventually incites them to conflict and revolution. A "modest" 5 percent inflation per year, for example, takes about $45 to $50 billion out of the stream of purchasing power, and most of it comes from the pockets of the poor and lower-middle-income citizens who have neither the resources nor the financial acumen to "hedge" against this calamity. This amount of loss, incidentally, is twice what the Indo-China War cost per year at its peak.

Tariffs, Trade and Taxes.   In addition to internal and external controls on capital movements, wages, prices, dividends and profits, we can expect that more direct attempts will be made to restore a favorable trade and payments balance, by means of high tariffs, border taxes and similar charges on imported goods, and special subsidies for exports. No doubt there will be interminable and often acrimonious dispute over import and export quotas and "stabilization" programs. But every step we might take to protect our high-cost industries against foreign competition and every move the United States makes to block imports and stimulate exports will be met with strong countermeasures by our trading partners. There is no doubt about this; we have been assured repeatedly by European and Japanese businessmen, bankers and officials, that a vehement return to protectionism on the part of the United States would be regarded as a declaration of economic war by the rest of the world, and they would then have no choice but to retaliate in kind.

Notes:

Chapter VII

1. The 1966 gold coin and medal restrictions imposed in the United Kingdom also required that all British coin collectors register with the Bank of England and furnish inventories of their collections to the Exchequer authorities. Those who possessed what the Exchequer considered to be an "excessive" amount of gold coins were required to surrender them. The importation, manufacture, sale and possession of gold medals was also prohibited, except by special permit.

2. *Indicator Digest,* April 3, 1969.

3. From *Vision,* a European business magazine, as reported in *Chicago Daily News,* March 21, 1971.

4. This particular provision means that whenever South Africa has an international payments deficit (which is usually all the time) she can sell gold directly from her own monetary stocks, provided all newly mined gold for that year is sold on the open market.

5. And being still associated with government from time to time, he prefers to remain anonymous, as far as this opinion is concerned.

6. From December of 1941 to December of 1945, the dollar lost 15 percent of its purchasing power, despite the strictest wage and price controls and rationing. During this period there were also several major strikes that required military intervention. The reality that wage and price controls only temporarily suppress inflation, rather than actually prevent it, can be seen from the fact that in the two years following the removal of controls in 1946, the cost of living soared by an additional 27 percent.

7. For a fascinating (although highly technical) study of the depression alternative see *Financial Instability Revisited: the Economics of Disaster,* by Professor Hyman P. Minsky, 1966; Rev. 1970 (a research paper prepared for the Board of Governors of the Federal Reserve System, available from Publication Services, Board of Governors, Federal Reserve System, Washington, D.C. 20551).

8. The only effective guarantee of monetary freedom for the

United States would be a Constitutional Amendment, specifically granting all citizens the unlimited and unqualified right to own gold and silver. Furthermore, this same amendment must safeguard the personal control of government-issued currencies and other monetary assets legitimately in the possession of individuals.

VIII

A BASIC MONETARY-HEDGE
INVESTMENT STRATEGY

"While prosperous you can number many friends, but when the storm comes you are left alone."

—OVID

THE first criterion for any investment portfolio should be safety. Avoiding or minimizing the chances for loss of invested capital is far more important to the average individual than seeking large capital gains at the cost of taking dangerous risks. A missed opportunity will do the investor no harm, because there will always be others. But a substantial capital loss can be a crippling setback, or even an irreparable disaster. Consequently, this book is not primarily concerned with speculation, or the short term buying and selling for capital gains (usually with borrowed money for greater leverage), but with *investment,* which is the conversion of legal-tender money into some other form of asset, in the belief that such an asset will either preserve its value or increase it over a period of time.

Successful speculation requires a talent and temperament that few individuals possess. That is why the vast majority of amateur speculators, whether in stocks, commodities or coins, consistently lose more than they make. The typical technique of the amateur trader is to take large risks for relatively small gains. We must avoid this type of emotional nonthinking at all costs. By making the preservation of capital our number one investment objective, we can avoid those twin spectres of *greed* and *fear* that are the undoing of nearly all nonprofessional speculators. The more perilous the times, the more attention must be devoted to the protection of capital. It is the author's belief that the financial situation of the United States is indeed perilous, and that we face a period of difficulty equal to, if not worse than, the 1860's or 1930's.

Since we cannot determine in advance the exact course, duration or outcome of coming events, we must concentrate on preparing a basic "survival kit" that will be adaptable to all types of monetary danger. This means having actual possession of precious metals, as well as an interest or part ownership in the sources of (gold) production. It means owning these things outright, free and clear of attachments or indebtedness, so they cannot be taken away or forfeited at a critical time. There are cases when it may be appropriate to employ a part of investment capital in a trading program utilizing gold stocks, but it must be done within the basic context of the investment program, which is to avoid danger and high risk to capital at all costs. We will examine the possibilities for trading shortly, but first we must build the basis for survival itself. The first law of nature, after all, is survival—otherwise the rest of them don't count.

However, there is a ray of sunshine in all this gloom, and that is that our program to preserve capital assets through precious-metals acquisition carries with it factors that may very well yield substantial, and possibly quite outstanding, capital gains in the long run. But first we must get down to the fundamentals. *Houses and Other Real Estate.* Although it is generally true that eras of serious monetary or economic disturbance do not offer an appropriate climate for real estate investments, there are exceptions that can and probably should be incorporated into a monetary-hedge investment program. One's own home, providing it is not overfinanced, is certainly among them. We do not need to get involved in that old argument over whether it is actually cheaper, in the long run, to rent dwelling space than to own it in order to note that owning the roof over one's head, in times of severe economic trouble, is certainly a great comfort as well as a real safety factor. And houses in stable residential neighborhoods have certainly been sound investments up to the present time, even though they may not have been the most lucrative.

The same thing can be said for owning one's place of business. For most people, I would say that owning a home and, if they are so situated, their own place of business should be priority items in their investment program.

For those who prefer, or by necessity must have, the convenience of apartment dwelling, there are, of course, the options of cooperative or condominium ownership. Having an equity in real estate that is of direct use can be a highly satisfactory hedge against long-term inflation, even in the case of an inflation of the Brazilian intensity. And, if it is not overfinanced, owner-occupied real estate can also offer a high degree of personal security against other forms of economic peril.

Another attractive option for the apartment dweller or urban resident is to have an alternate dwelling or place of retreat in the country or in a small town. Cabins, cottages and country places are not always spectacular investments, but, if one does not own any other real estate, they can be a satisfactory inflation hedge and perhaps add to one's sense of personal security. An acre or two of good camping land can even serve as the retreat alternative, if no other choice is possible or practical.

Investment in rental or lease properties is not advised, however, because the owners of such equities run the risk of being squeezed between rising costs and rent controls during inflation cycles, and of being forced into loss positions by declining occupancy, falling rents and resale prices, and nondeclining taxes during a depression period.

Although I would not hesitate to buy property or dwellings for personal use, I would definitely avoid crowded urban or suburban areas. And, contrary to popular opinion, I would not borrow heavily, if at all, to finance such purchases at this time. As for suburban homes, most of them today are poorly built, outrageously priced and grossly overtaxed. The suburbs are sometimes worse off than the cities, as far as social problems and economic imbalances are concerned. I would give priority to areas at least 100 miles, and preferably further, from any major metropolitan area, such as New York, Chicago, Cleveland, Detroit, Dallas, Los Angeles, etc. Don't misunderstand me; I am certainly not advocating indiscriminate flight. I love the vitality of a great city and would rather be on La Salle Street or Wall Street than in Podunk, Idaho. But, as I said, survival is the first law, and if a time comes when the very place you live is a source of danger, then it will obviously be better to leave. Only, by that time it may be too late to start looking for an alternative—so start thinking about it now.

Your Livelihood. In both hyperinflations and depressions alike, physical survival itself can become a desperate affair. In either case, one still has to provide for the necessities of life: food, clothing, shelter, heat, light, medical and other health care, etc. Therefore, in addition to having a supply of gold and silver coins to use as money, in the event that paper currencies lose all recognizable value, one should also make plans for an alternate way of employing oneself, particularly if entirely dependent on some large corporation or enterprise for income. Physicians, nurses, dentists, and others in fields that provide essential personal services will no doubt have the least difficulty. After all, when a person has an ache or pain or illness, he will want it relieved, whether he has to pay for the service received in food, bars of soap, cigarettes, or silver or gold coins.

Public employees in vital services, such as policemen, firemen, teachers, sanitation workers, etc., may also be in a relatively more secure position, in that they probably won't lose their jobs and also can be paid in part with food or merchandise certificates, or given special consideration in housing, transportation, health care, etc. But if you are presently engaged in sales, marketing, industrial production, engineering, design, construction, or any other activity that is primarily dependent on a healthy, booming economy, it would be wise to have at least a tentative plan as to what else you could do if you suddenly lost your job—permanently. In the depths of the Great Depression, many men and women were able to launch new and successful second careers, after finding themselves more or less permanently cut off from the career or enterprise to which they had already committed sometimes decades of their lives.

If you are now in a vulnerable position, as far as employment is concerned, try to plan some alternative that you could turn to during such events as a prolonged depression, a stagnant or inflation-riddled totalitarian economy or a Brazilian, French or even German-type hyperinflation. Don't think in terms of maintaining your present standard of living. Try to think of activities and situations that would provide at least food, clothing and shelter for yourself and your dependents, if you were suddenly thrown entirely on your own. Don't make grandiose, superficial or unrealistic plans. Aim to *insure* the basic essentials of physical survival. Hope for the best, but be prepared for the worst. If one can't think of anything else, having a small house in the country to go to, with a bit of land to garden or farm on a modest basis for a year or two is not the worst idea.

Cash and Equivalent.   Believe it or not, every successful investment program requires the maintenance of sufficient reserves of ready cash, in the form of bank accounts and short term, 100-percent-liquid, bills or notes. Perhaps the most significant single mistake made by nonprofessional investors is to neglect cash positions and become overinvested in things. This tendency is, of course, quite understandable in view of the typical investor's anxiety to protect monetary assets from losses through inflation, and the all-too-human desire to maximize the profit potential of an investment portfolio. But while a fully invested position may seem to be the most advantageous theoretically, it nearly always results in unnecessary capital losses when put into practice.

The problem is that we all need not only an adequate supply of working capital to meet day-to-day expenses, but also an emergency reserve so that unexpected and higher-than-usual demands for legal-tender cash can be met without the necessity of having to liquidate part of one's investment position. It invariably happens that whenever a larger than usual demand for cash is sustained, the long-term investment portfolio is in a short-term-negative or outright-loss position. The investor is then forced to accept an unnecessary capital loss, not to mention the penalty of a round-trip commission in the case of a stock. Maintaining a suitable cash balance, sufficient to cope with unexpected demands and minor emergencies eliminates

the unwise and always unprofitable "churning" of the investment account.

Another function of the liquid balance is to act as a reservoir
of funds that can be used to take advantage of unexpected *opportunities* as well. Regardless of the fact that the long-term
trend of gold coins and gold stocks may be up, there will also
be many short-term and intermediate-term reversals of the primary trend, some of them quite sharp. The wise investor will
always have some capital available for these (expected) periodic setbacks as well as for any unpredictable windfall opportunities.

If the author may be permitted a personal example at this
point, a classic case of how one can profit from the unexpected
occurred in the fall of 1966, when the Premier of South Africa,
Dr. H.F. Verwoerd, was assassinated by a deranged fanatic. As
soon as the news was flashed over the Dow Jones news tickers,
a wave, a panic selling, struck South African gold shares (considerably encouraged, without much doubt, by the initial selling and short selling of OTC traders and specialists, hoping to
drive down the market to bargain levels and get themselves
some cheap stock!). On the following two days, heavy selling
continued, as the public was hit by the double bad news of (a)
the assassination itself and (b) the "crash" in South African
gold shares. But on the fourth day I sensed (correctly) that
rationality was about to return and put in buy orders for some
of my favorites.

Never was the advantage of having a liquid reserve more
clearly demonstrated, as I was able to get sound high-yielding
gold stocks at 25 to 30 percent discounts from their already-low
cyclical levels. Within a month, all losses sustained during the
Verwoerd "crash" were made up and, within eighteen months,
all stocks could be (and were) sold at capital gains of from 100
to 200 percent. Reason told me that one isolated tragedy, such
as the assassination of a high public official, could have no
possible effect on the coming worldwide demand for gold investments or on the earnings and dividends of sound mining
operations. If the public wanted to act irrationally and emotionally (as it usually does), there was nothing that I or any
rational person could do but graciously accept the opportunity
being offered.

The same thing happened after the flooding of the West Drie-fontein mine, which caused a 50-percent decline in its stock. Nearly all other South African golds promptly sold off by 20 percent or more in "sympathy." Why an accident in one mine should affect the valuation of other mines not even located in the same general area was incomprehensible to me, so I did the obvious and bought a few shares of some of the nonaffected mines at a nice discount. In either case, had I been "fully invested," I could have done nothing but watch the value of my portfolio decline and then wait in suspense for weeks just to get "even" again.

How much cash one should keep in the reserve fund must, of course, be determined by the individual investor, based on his or her specific conditions and requirements. All I can say is better too much than too little. So be generous when estimating your liquidity requirements and possibilities; never get greedy; never become fearful that you might miss out on some important market action by not being fully invested; be patient. And don't commit any significant part of the reserve fund until you really are presented with an unmistakable bargain.

Precious Metals and Mining Stocks.   The main part of the monetary-economic hedge program will consist of a portfolio of precious-metals investments. The assets specifically set aside for survival in a monetary-financial crisis of prolonged and intense duration should definitely not be in ordinary common stocks or other securities. They should not be in real estate (except for your own dwellings and places of business). They should not be in paper currencies or bank accounts, beyond a reasonable legal-tender cash liquidity for current use. Generally, enough cash or assets quickly convertible and equivalent to cash should be retained to provide a minimum subsistence level for at least one year. Beyond that, investment funds may be divided between:

> Common silver coins
> Common gold Coins
> Numismatic and seminumismatic gold coins
> Gold mining stocks

Common Silver Coins.   As we discussed earlier, the pre-1965, .900 fine (90 percent) silver coins of the United States were driven into hiding or into the free silver market, where they now trade at premiums over their face values. Common silver coins are available through coin dealers in the major cities and are also available by mail order.* Approximately $2.2 billion worth of U.S. silver coins have been removed from circulation in response to one of the most ancient phenomenons of economics, Gresham's Law, which holds that "bad money drives out good money." *Fig. 15* shows the common silver coins of the United States currently available for purchase with the premiums charged by dealers noted.

As the reader will note from *Fig. 15,* there appears to be very little that is "common" about silver dollars, circulated or uncirculated, judging by the premiums they sell for. They are common only in the sense that some 350 million or more are in existence, mostly in uncirculated condition. But these once-despised coins are now treasured as both collectors' items and as an ideal hedge against runaway inflation. Personally, I would not buy them at these levels, as I think that common gold coins offer better values at this time. Nonetheless, I must admit that uncirculated silver dollars have had a phenomenal and almost continuous increase in price since they were first "discovered" in 1964. They will no doubt continue to outpace future inflation, but might suffer considerably in any depression.

However, buying a supply of common circulated silver coins (they are generally sold in $500 or $1,000 face value lots), even at 20 to 30 percent premium over face value, would appear to be a prudent thing to do. They not only can serve as an additional inflation hedge, but will provide the investor with a supply of intrinsic-value change that would be honored during any crisis. They also can be counted as part of the total cash reserve and, finally, they have a built-in potential for capital gain in the event of a substantial rise in the price of silver. In the case of a depression or drastic fall in the price of silver, however, the most that can be lost is the premium. These coins, unlike bullion, have a face value as money that will probably always be maintained. Therefore, if one pays $1250 for a $1000 bag of

*For current information on the purchase and current market values of common silver and gold coins, I highly recommend the weekly tabloid newspaper *Coin World,* available at coin stores, at some of the larger news dealers, or directly from its publisher at P.O. Box 150, Sidney, Ohio.

common U.S. silver coins, the most that can be lost, no matter what happens, is the $250 premium, while the potential gain is virtually unlimited. Common silver coins, therefore, are surely the best silver investment around.

Canadian citizens may buy common Canadian silver coins for the same purpose, but U.S. residents should avoid bulk purchases of either Canadian or Mexican silver coins (because they cannot be used as money in the United States) and concentrate on U.S. common silver coins and common gold coins of all types. Uncirculated .900 fine (1964) Kennedy halves can be bought on any significant reaction or concession in price, but the debased 40-percent silver Kennedys (1965–70) should be ignored, unless they can be obtained at par or for a very minor premium.

As for the new 40-percent silver Eisenhower dollars, which were sold directly by the mint (at $3 per coin for uncirculated and $10 for proof condition), they too should be ignored as they are grossly overpriced. I would rather spend that kind of money on uncirculated .900 fine Morgan dollars. The Eisenhower dollars that will be released for general circulation will of course be cupro-nickel slugs of no intrinsic value whatever. What a tragedy that our great nation can no longer afford to honor its heroes with even a sound silver coin, let alone one of gold.

Common Gold Coins.   Although many U.S. citizens are not aware of the fact, they are permitted to own gold coins "of special value to collectors." The U.S. Treasury has established by repeated rulings since 1934, that *all* gold coins minted prior to 1933 are considered to have this special numismatic value. Consequently, there are sufficient supplies of U.S. and foreign gold coins available from coin dealers to establish a very liquid market. Common gold coins, therefore, should form a part of every portfolio and should be bought on every significant reaction in the gold market. *Fig. 16* shows typical premiums over intrinsic value (based on the $35 per ounce minimum gold price) being paid for some of the most commonly traded gold coins during June of 1971.

Despite the substantial premiums being asked for common gold coins, I believe that every monetary-hedge portfolio should include them, *because they are a reality.* A stock certificate after all is only a piece of paper—a legal document to be sure, but it represents an intangible claim on a future, rather than a direct tangible possession of a monetary asset. And even though I believe gold stocks have great merit as investments for the decade of the 1970's, I must caution the reader that situations could develop during critical periods of monetary and financial upheaval in which the repatriation of dividends, on both foreign and domestic shares, could be suspended or delayed by the imposition of special monetary and exchange controls. Furthermore, even the recovery of capital from the sale of such shares could be temporarily blocked by exchange restrictions and banking controls. Gold stocks may be the best securities around in times of monetary and financial crisis, but they still carry the basic risks inherent in any industrial enterprise, and particularly in a mining venture, plus, in most cases, the added complications of investing in foreign countries.

Therefore, in line with our primary objective, which is the *preservation* of capital, we should include a quantity of gold and silver coins in the investment portfolio. The question of proportions, or the proper ratios between coins and stocks will be discussed in the *Model Portfolios* section (Part IV).

Numismatic and Seminumismatic Gold Coins. Another area that is attracting greater and greater interest among sophisticated investors is the collection of gold coins, both for their intrinsic gold content and for their value as rare coins of special interest and attractiveness to collectors. Numismatics, or coin collecting, is one of the fastest-growing collector interests in the United States and Canada, and perhaps even in Europe as well. Serious collectors of gold coins as numismatic treasures are invariably people in the higher income brackets, such as physicians, dentists, corporate executives, bankers, etc. Consequently, there is not only an excellent market for such items, but there is also the promise of a continuing increase in demand (and therefore value) for this type of coin, even though they have already enjoyed phenomenal price increases over the last three decades. In fact, rare coins of all types, and especially U.S. coins of the eighteenth and nineteenth centuries, have proved to be extraordinary investments during the entire 30-year period.

Antiquities and collector's items of all types, but particularly rare coins, are ideal investments for periods of "suppressed" or controlled inflation. In a totalitarian or quasi-totalitarian economy, with its stifling maze of wage, price and exchange controls, inflation more or less goes underground. In this type of economy, the excess purchasing media (which always continues to be created) tends to flow to noncontrolled areas in a kind of a parallel to Gresham's Law. It has been historically demonstrated in many countries and during many inflations that the antique, coin and stamp markets are uniquely immune from the attentions of government price fixers and economic bureaucrats. During the long debacle of the Third and Fourth Republics of France (1914–58) in which "controlled" inflation continuously ravaged the franc, the art, antique, coin and stamp markets far outperformed other supposed inflation hedges, such as common stocks, real estate and commodities.

I personally like numismatic investment of all types, but because the 1970's are going to be, in my opinion, the "age of gold," I feel that gold coins will be the stars. Consequently, any investor so inclined may consider building a collection of numismatic-type gold coins, in addition to acquiring a store of the more common gold coins for their intrinsic value.*

Gold Bullion. Although American investors are now forbidden under the threat of heavy fine and imprisonment, to purchase or retain gold bullion, there have been several bills introduced in Congress over the last few years to repeal this odious and discriminatory law. Thus far, all of these bills have been killed in committee. Actually, I don't think there is much chance that this provision of the Gold Reserve Act will be repealed in the foreseeable future, but it is remotely possible that it could be tried as a last desperate bluff to accompany the "demonetization" of gold in the United States and the permanent floating of the dollar.

If this is ever tried, I strongly suspect that the price of gold would immediately be chased sky-high by eager speculators and investors. Nevertheless, I would go easy on the purchase of

*As a guide to the acquisition of both common gold coins of high intrinsic value and rare gold coins of special numismatic value, modesty does not forbid me to recommend my previous work: *How to Invest in Gold Coins,* by Donald J. Hoppe (New Rochelle, N.Y.: Arlington House, 1970).

gold bullion, even if it were suddenly made legal, for the simple reason that it could easily be confiscated again by another government edict. What Congress and the Executive give, they can also take away. Only if it were guaranteed by Constitutional Amendment would it be entirely safe to own bullion, and there is hardly any chance that the latter will occur. Even if given the right to own bullion, I would rather buy more gold coins, knowing that any rise in the price of bullion would correspondingly increase the intrinsic value of gold coins and that gold coins are a safer and more negotiable holding.

But we cannot keep all of our capital assets in the form of "hard" money. The storage problem alone would prohibit it.[1] Furthermore, the best leverage or opportunity for profits will come from having an interest in the actual production of gold. If the price of gold increases by 100 percent, for example, the earnings of selected gold mining companies could rise by 300 or 400 percent, and the capital valuations of these companies, as reflected in their share prices, could increase by even greater percentages. Therefore, we must take a close look at gold mining stocks.

Fig. 15

U.S. COMMON SILVER COINAGE
WITH MID-1971 PREMIUMS*

Type	Fineness	Condition	Percent Premium
Dimes	.900	circulated	20–30
Quarters	.900	circulated	20–30
All half-dollars	.900	circulated	30–40
1964 Kennedy half-dollars	.900	uncirculated	40–50
1965–70 Kennedy half-dollars	.400	uncirculated	10–20
All silver dollars	.900	circulated	175–200
Morgan silver dollars (1878–1921)	.900	uncirculated	250–300

"Peace" silver
dollars
(1921–35)   .900   uncirculated   225–275

*Compiled from typical dealer offering prices as of June 1971. Morgan
silver dollars, for example sold readily at $67 per roll (twenty coins per
roll), while circulated dimes and quarters brought about $1250 per
($1,000 face value) bag.

Fig. 16

COMMON GOLD COINS OF THE WORLD
WITH MID-1971 PREMIUMS
(Over Intrinsic Value at $35 Par)

Type	Troy Oz. Pure Gold	Intrinsic Value at $35 Par	Average Retail Price	Percent Premium
U.S. 20 Dollars (Double Eagle)	.9675	$33.86	$69	104
U.S. 10 Dollars (Eagle)	.48375	16.93	38	124
U.S. 5 Dollars (Half Eagle)	.241875	8.47	35	313
Mexican 50 Pesos (Centenario)	1.2056	42.20	65	54
Mexican 20 Pesos (Azteca)	.4823	16.88	27	60
Mexican 10 Pesos (Hidalgo)	.24115	8.44	14	66
British Gold Pound (Sovereign)	.2354	8.24	12	46
Austrian 20 Corona	.1960	6.86	14	104
Belgian 20 Francs	.1867	6.53	13	99
French 20 Francs	.1867	6.53	13	99
Hungary 20 Korona	.1960	6.86	12	75
Italian 20 Lire	.1867	6.53	13	99
Colombian 5 Pesos	.2354	8.24	12	46
Russian 10 Roubles	.2489	8.71	17	95
Russian 5 Roubles	.12446	4.36	7	60
Swiss 20 Francs	.1867	6.53	14	114

Notes:
1. Retail prices based on dealer advertising in *Coin World* and at other retail levels for the month of June 1971, averaged and rounded off for convenience.
2. All U.S. gold coins are of limited availability and are considered to have significant numismatic as well as intrinsic value.
3. London-market gold price averaged $40 for month of June, so that actual premium would be somewhat less than the maximum indicated.
4. Retail prices noted are for coins in uncirculated condition for U.S., Mexican and British coins, and for extremely fine to uncirculated for other foreign coins.

WORLD POWER REALITIES OF THE FUTURE

Prior to World War II, the United States was just one of several so-called "great powers" competing with others, politically, militarily and, above all, economically, for the fortunes and favors of the world. The war itself eliminated the majority of these competitors and left the world, for a time, in the unusual position of being dominated by only two surviving "superpowers," the United States and the Soviet Union. But while these two giants recklessly spent their wealth and energies in the intense and often vicious competition of the so-called Cold War (which all too often got hot for the U.S.!), new world power realities inevitably developed. The long twilight of the Cold War is over. It is no longer simply a question of East versus West, or the United States and its satellites on one side and Russia and her captives on the other. The satellite nations themselves were the first to sense that the "postwar era" was finally ending, and have been going, or attempting to go, their independent ways for several years.

In the final quarter of this century, the United States will have to adjust to the reality that there are not just *two* superpowers contending for politico-economic domination or survival, but *five*. These five superpowers will be: the United States, the Soviet Union, the European Economic (and political?) Community, Japan and China.

Each of these superpowers will, of course, gather its quota of captives, satellites and allies from among the smaller nations, but all of the giants will have to accept and adjust to the presence of the others, on a political, military and economic basis, if the world is to survive. Neither the United States nor the Soviets, however, will be able unilaterally to "manage" their "halves" of the world to suit their specific interests, as they have been accustomed to doing in the past two decades. What this means for the citizen of the United States (and for the rest of the peoples of the world as well) is that nations will have to depend more and more on socio-economic *performance* than on military or political prestige to survive and prosper. Economic competition, in the remainder of this century, will be the most intense the world has ever experienced.

Unfortunately, the United States has become a "have-not" nation in recent years, as far as many essential minerals and raw materials are concerned.[2] We *must* continually import these items to keep our industrial machine operating. However, when the dollar is no longer *the* official reserve unit of the IMF, but just another competing currency (and such a development is inevitable) the United States will have to do just what Russia and China, or any "soft"-currency country is required to do today: we will have to cover our foreign deficits with gold or hard (gold-backed) currencies.

There are only three ways a nation can obtain gold: (a) mine it, (b) earn it through balance-of-payments surpluses or (c) bid for it on the open market. The first option, even if we bring all marginal U.S. deposits into production, through subsidies or a higher gold price, would barely satisfy our commercial-industrial requirements. Even if the manufacture of jewelry and luxury items was totally prohibited and present U.S. output doubled (very doubtful) we would still not make available more than $100 million per year (at $38 par) for Treasury use. If the price of gold were raised to $100 per ounce, the United States could produce internally probably no more than $300 to $350 million per year in gold—hardly an impressive figure, when the U.S. deficit has been running into the billions for a decade or more.

If the United States is forced to bid for gold on the open market with its "soft" dollars, the $150 per ounce figure could be achieved long before 1980. At any rate, we will surely have great difficulty generating trade and payments surpluses during the fiercely competitive decade of the seventies. And if we can't mine enough or earn enough to get gold to cover our external monetary needs, we will have to buy it. And if the United States needs gold for internal monetary stabilization, we will have no choice but to try to buy it for that purpose as well.

A United States of Europe? In our review of the Common Market (Chapter VI), it was suggested that a full political union of (ten) European states would be a logical and inevitable development. The first step, the economic union of the six, will soon be expanded to include ten or more nations. The second major step, monetary union, will, I believe, be accomplished during the decade of the seventies. Negotiations on monetary union have already begun, as we noted, but have made little progress. However, the approaching collapse of the U.S. dollar will soon bring greater urgency to these negotiations and force the EEC to accept (probably on an emergency basis) a unified monetary and banking system.

One of the more intriguing ideas that has been proposed for an EEC federal currency is to have it based on the ancient *florin** (ducat) gold coinage of the thirteenth century. Europeans are very conscious of history and tradition, and restoring the first successful "gold standard" coinage of all Europe, as the basis for a new European federal currency, would have very positive psychological effects. Several government and private mints in Europe are still striking commemorative coins and medals in ducat/florin denominations, on occasion, so the tradition, at least, has remained intact from A.D. 1252 to the present. Any official move to make the gold florin/ducat the standard gold coin of the EEC would attract much popular support in Europe.[3]

Another suggestion that has aroused widespread interest in Europe is that the gold franc of the nineteenth-century Latin Monetary Union be revived and made the standard gold coin of the EEC. Under the leadership of France, in 1865, an attempt was made to standardize the minting of gold coins by international treaty. The .900-fine gold 20-franc coin established by

---

*Also *floren.*

Napoleon in 1803 was generally accepted as the model unit, and all signatories to the treaty agreed to mint their individual gold coins at a uniform weight, fineness and value, thus making them interchangeable. Although only five countries formally adhered to the Union, no less than 26 nations, around the world, eventually struck gold coins according to Latin Monetary Union Standards. They were:

Albania	Peru
Argentina	Philippines
Belgium*	Poland
Bulgaria	Roumania
Colombia	Russia
Finland	Salvador
France*	San Marino
Greece*	Serbia
Guatemala	Spain
Honduras	Switzerland*
Italy*	Tunisia
Monaco	Venezuela
Montenegro	Yugoslavia

The Union was formally dissolved in 1926, due to the general suspension of gold coinage during and after World War I, but great quantities of Latin Standard coins are still privately traded and held as a store of value in Europe today. Therefore, a revival of the Latin Monetary Union gold standard, as the basis for a new gold-denominated Common Market currency, would also appear to be a sound and popular choice.

In any case, I believe there is an excellent chance that the introduction of a new standard gold coinage will accompany the creation of a European federal currency. Such a move would naturally be of considerable benefit to the gold-mining industry. But, far more importantly, the reintroduction of circulating gold coinage would have very positive social, psychological and political effects, as well as financial advantages. A worldwide return to sound money is absolutely essential if Western civilization is to be saved. It would be most appropri-

*Indicates Latin Monetary Union member.

ate if an international gold currency and coinage is first created in Europe, the cradle of that civilization.

Monetary union is, of course, a necessary condition or precondition for the full political federation of Western Europe. And political federation, in the author's view, is inevitable, because the United States will soon be so occupied with its own internal problems, that it will no longer be interested in maintaining a strong military presence in Europe. Furthermore, the attention of Russia will be drawn more and more to the Far East, by the expanding economic, political and military power of both China and Japan, which the Russians regard (no doubt with some justification) as a threat to the vast Soviet Siberian and Mongolian provinces. Consequently, the European states, both East and West, could enjoy an unprecedented freedom from Soviet threats and harassments during the seventies.

With the U.S.-Soviet Cold War subsiding and with the attention of the two giants increasingly diverted from European affairs, both the opportunity and the incentive for a federal union of the EEC countries may prove irresistable. Sometimes, the only way small companies can survive in economic situations dominated by corporate giants, is for them to merge and become a giant themselves. This, I believe, is the obvious path that the European states are now taking, and will continue to take in the future.

As the dollar weakens, and the U.S. trade position becomes even more precarious, we can expect to see an even greater expansion of the already growing trade between the EEC and the East European states and between Western Europe and the Soviet Union itself. Russia still needs Western technology, production equipment and consumer goods, and Western Europe must have many of the raw materials and fuel supplies available in Russia and the Eastern states. None of this, of course, will be good for the U.S. economy. Restoring faith in the dollar, therefore, will, sooner or later, have to become one of the major objectives of the United States, and a sound dollar means a noninflationary gold-backed dollar.

Japan and the Far East. The fantastic economic strength developed by Japan in the past decade is now one of the accepted facts of life, but what is still not generally realized is that Japan is also on its way to becoming a major world financial power. Whether Japan's goal of becoming the world's leading economic, industrial and exporting nation by 1975 is achieved or not, it is certain that she will economically dominate the whole Western Pacific. Since further expansion of Japanese exports to the United States will, no doubt, be strongly resisted by Washington, and since the earning of increasingly "soft" dollars will become less and less attractive to Japan, one can expect that she will concentrate, in the future, on developing stronger economic and financial ties with other nations. The most logical choices for such endeavors are Canada, Australia and South Africa.

Japan has already made significant moves aimed to developing and improving economic relations with these three key areas. Although the Japanese, by nearly miraculous effort, have transformed their small and almost barren homeland into an economic colossus, they are still precariously deficient in three vital areas: raw materials and commodities, living space and sound money.[4] Japanese businessmen have already been quite active, in recent years, developing sources of supply for their vitally needed minerals, fuel supplies and raw commodities, *other than from the United States*. Japan has recently concluded several important agreements with both Canada and Australia for the joint development of specific mineral resources within those nations.

Japan has, or soon will have, a level of industrial and scientific technology second to none. But is is also clear that Japan cannot succeed in her goals, or even continue to maintain her present dynamic society, without strong "junior partners" to help supply the three missing ingredients. Therefore we can expect some startling changes in the relationships between Japan and the United States, Canada, Australia and South Africa.

As U.S.-Japanese trade is gradually frozen or even reduced by the weakening dollar and rising U.S. protectionism, Japan will come to depend more and more on Canada, Australia and South Africa to provide raw materials essential to her industrial machine, and also to become markets for the finished products.

Consequently, more direct penetration by Japanese businesses and corporations, in the area of cooperative and joint-development ventures, is to be expected. But, most unusual of all, an unprecedented wave of Japanese *emigration* to these areas may well develop.

Japan is virtually at the point of explosion, as far as population is concerned, while the potential "junior partners" are not only sparsely populated but actually in desperate need of educated manpower from advanced nations to further their economic development. All three countries, Canada, Australia and South Africa, for years have had programs to encourage the immigration of Caucasians. However, I believe that the realities of the future will force all three nations, and particularly Australia and South Africa, into a drastic reappraisal of their present policies and attitudes.

Japan is one of the world's great reservoirs of educated, industrious and creative manpower. Consequently, I feel that one of the more surprising developments of the future will be the emigration of substantial numbers of Japanese to Australia, *and even to South Africa.* It will begin with relatively small groups of businessmen and technicians entering as "temporary" residents and they, in turn, will furnish the basis and the excuse for large-scale permanent immigration later on. The present and future relationship between Japan and South Africa is, and will be, particularly intriguing.

It may seem peculiar to refer to South Africa as an underdeveloped and underpopulated country, in view of the extraordinary rate of economic growth it has achieved in recent years, but such is actually the case. South Africa has mineral wealth and other resources in abundance, but is far short of the trained and capable manpower required to develop them fully. The programs for encouraging European immigration have been helpful, but they have not brought in adequate numbers of new residents to fill the demand. Time is against South Africa in this effort.

It is no secret that the main reason for South Africa's much criticized *apartheid* policy of racial segregation is the overpowering concern of white South Africans that their hard-won civilization might be submerged in a tide of black nationalism if they were to adopt more liberal political and social attitudes. But if the South African government fails to attract European immigrants in sufficient numbers, in their understandable desire to achieve a better racial balance within the Republic, they may, incongruous as it sounds now, see the merit of opening their doors to Japanese immigration.

The South Africans have already decided that the irksome *apartheid* laws do not apply to Japanese businessmen or travelers in South Africa.[5] Let me clear up one thing at this point: the author is not in favor of or in sympathy with *any* form of racial chauvinism. I agree that many of the *apartheid* provisions are arbitrary and unjust, even though I can understand the political and psychological reasons that are behind the whole program. But I have not the time to moralize on any nonmonetary questions in this particular book. The most important thing is that we face realistically what I believe are the realities of the future; and one of those realities is that South Africa, Australia and Japan may form a new economic, financial and, perhaps, even military partnership.

The economic and political influence of Great Britain, which once dominated the Far East, is virtually dead. The influence and prestige of the United States in this area was dealt a severe blow by the disaster of the Indo-China War, and tarnished even further by the 1971 default of the dollar. Therefore, two of the five giants will remain in serious contention for domination of the Far East, the Western Pacific and Southern and Eastern Africa—Japan and China. With that choice, the smaller nations (at least those that are geographically free to do so) will obviously choose Japan for a friend and ally. In any case, even though China will probably double her gross national product from 1970 to 1980, she will remain, economically at least, far behind Japan. China's influence and prestige will be mostly political and military, and this can be balanced by the political and military power of the United States and the Soviets. Japan's great power, however, will be economic and financial.

The final ingredient necessary to make Japan a superpower will be sound money; the yen will have to become a respected and sought-after "hard" currency. Up to the present, Japan has scrupulously played the game according to IMF rules and, as a result, has a smaller percentage of gold in her official monetary reserves than any other industrial nation. Most of Japan's reserves are in the form of U.S. credit dollars, and a collapse of the dollar will certainly be a bitter pill for the Japanese. But any major devaluation or default of the dollar, I believe, will be an invitation and excuse for Japan to abandon the rules of the IMF and purchase gold, in large quantities, directly from South Africa. There have already been persistent rumors that Japan will soon legalize the private holding of gold bullion by Japanese citizens, as well as greatly increase the amount of gold held as official reserves.

The inauguration of a gold-backed European Common Market currency would very probably encourage Japan to try to establish a fully convertible "gold yen" of equal prestige and value. A coordinated move in this direction by both the EEC and Japan would, in effect, return a large part of the world to a meaningful gold standard, and increase the division between the hard-currency and soft-currency countries. Unfortunately, the United States would then be left with the soft-currency group. And if a free and open private gold market is established in Tokyo, with official sanction, it would also help make Japan the acknowledged financial center of Asia and the Western Pacific.

But South Africa also has another metal, produced mainly as a by-product of its gold mines, that the Japanese will no doubt be interested in, and that metal is uranium. If Japan becomes determined to have a significant nuclear industry or, unhappily, nuclear weapons, she will require South African uranium in substantial quantities. It is also possible that a Japanese nuclear-development program might be carried out as a joint venture with South Africa, and perhaps Australia, utilizing the remote desert regions of those countries for research and manufacture.

GOLD STOCKS DURING HYPERINFLATION

The question of what happens to gold mining companies and to the value of their securities during periods of hyper- or runaway inflation is very difficult to answer satisfactorily. True hyperinflations, where the currency of a nation is virtually destroyed within a matter of months or a very few years, are relatively rare, and there is no record of one having occurred in a major gold-producing nation. We do know that the position of gold itself, as the ultimate standard of value, is always strongly reasserted during periods of extreme inflation. But regarding the price action and value of gold mining stocks during such a period, we have no adequate precedents.

The experience of twentieth-century hyperinflations in Europe and elsewhere indicates beyond doubt that the general run of common stocks, including utility and transportation issues, are very poor holdings at such times. Under the chaotic financial conditions that result from runaway inflation, nearly all industrial enterprises have great difficulty, and many are actually forced into bankruptcy. Others more or less voluntarily curtail or abandon operations completely, pending a return to more normal times. During the French inflation of the 1920's, bankruptcies, strange as it may seem, ran far above the normal rate. Certain industries, such as railroads and utilities, were caught between fixed rates, frozen by government edict, and rising labor and other costs that defied effective government control. Immediately following the great German inflation of 1919–23, a severe wave of bankruptcies and reorganizations struck Germany as business after business found that the inflation had so disorganized their financial structures as to make it impossible to return to normal operations without major adjustments.

Gold mining companies, however, are quite unique in that they could pay their employees and pay for their supplies in gold itself. During the great nineteenth-century bonanza years of gold mining in the United States, Australia, Canada and Alaska, it was not uncommon for the miners to receive their wages in gold dust. Today, mining companies would easily establish their own mints and strike private gold coinage if necessary. However, I doubt very much that they would be allowed to do so, and they surely would not be permitted to pay their stockholders' dividends in gold!

The real question, therefore, would be whether or not a gold mine, operating in a country undergoing a severe inflation, would be able to, or even want to, market its product. I'm sure that the management and stockholders would see little benefit in exchanging their primary asset, the gold itself, for rapidly depreciating or virtually worthless paper currency. Consequently, most of the mines in affected countries would prefer simply to suspend operations until the crisis had passed and stable monetary conditions had been reestablished. Probably the biggest danger such mines would face would be the threat of direct government intervention or nationalization.

Of the three basic areas we are concerned with, the United States, Canada and South Africa, the United States is by far the only real candidate for a hyperinflation of at least the South American type. We have reviewed the monetary-financial situation of the United States in some detail and there should be no illusions on this point; an inflation blow-off of historic magnitude is a very real possibility for the United States.

Canada, with its economy and financial structure tied so closely to that of the United States, is also in a very difficult position. She, too, has had her share of neo-Keynesian financial mismanagement in the postwar years, and will pay a heavy price for it. But Canada's biggest problem is that she is holding some $2.6 billion U.S. credit dollars, which make up more than 70 percent of her official monetary reserves. Under previous agreements, Canada has been steadily selling gold to the United States in exchange for U.S. dollar credits and Treasury bonds. If the U.S. dollar is sharply devalued, or if it is allowed to float (permanently) and falls victim to uncontrolled inflation, Canada will be dealt a severe financial blow.

Nevertheless, the Canadian monetary experience could be less severe than that of the United States as a result of an international collapse of the dollar. Canada's gold production is still high, in relation to her population and economy, even though it has been in a steady decline for many years. By diverting most of her gold production into official monetary channels (at a higher price) in support of the domestic currency, Canada at least has the means to prevent inflation from reaching the runaway stage. Whether she has the will to do so is another matter.

Canada presently permits the free and unlimited holding of gold by private citizens. Canadian mines are free to sell all their gold on the private markets (if they are not receiving government subsidy). Therefore, inflation in Canada almost automatically guarantees a higher gold price, in terms of Canadian dollars, unless the Canadian government (a) prohibits the private ownership of gold and (b) nationalizes or takes over the mines. I do not think, however, that the Canadian government will take either of these two steps, or be permitted to do so by the Canadians themselves. Canada cannot avoid considerable hardship, arising out of the failure of the U.S. dollar and the coming international monetary shakeup, but I believe that the Canadians will rise to the occasion and eventually return their great nation to a sound, gold-backed currency basis. However, since a substantial writing down (or writing off) of Canada's internal and external debts and her U.S. dollar holdings is inevitable, a higher Canadian dollar price for gold is assured. During the final reorganization, a "new" Canadian dollar may be tied to an emerging gold-denominated Common Market currency, instead of the U.S. dollar.

At the present time, South Africa is, and has been, a fellow victim of the worldwide inflation malaise, because her monetary unit, the *rand,* is tied to the IMF-dollar international monetary system. As long as the present system prevails, South Africa, like all the other "members," will continue to be affected by the operation of an international engine of inflation. Furthermore, aside from her gold sales, South Africa has been consistently incurring balance-of-payments and trade deficits that add to her internal inflationary pressures. However, South Africa is singularly free from the danger of any extreme or runaway inflation situation.

In the case of a dollar or IMF collapse, South Africa could, and probably would, adopt a full internal gold standard. She already has minted a well-known gold coin in substantial quantities, the "Krueger rand," containing a full troy ounce of pure gold, that could easily be made the standard gold coin.[6] However, living costs in South Africa might continue to rise somewhat, even under a full gold standard, because of the sheer abundance of the metal, particularly if gold exports were temporarily blocked and gold production was not consequently limited or stockpiled pending resumption of exports. But, at any rate, South Africa's paper currency would certainly remain "good as gold."

In the event of a world financial disruption due to the collapse of the dollar or a break-up of the IMF, one can assume that South African gold production would be quickly diverted to the EEC and Japan. The Republic's usual payments and trade deficits will facilitate the use of gold for direct payments to her creditors. In any case, one can be sure that South Africa's surplus gold will flow, in response to universal economic laws, to whatever areas of power and financial safety remain, or are reestablished in the world.

South African gold stocks, therefore, would appear to be a safe and ultimately rewarding holding for citizens of countries liable to be affected by conditions of extreme inflation. Canadian gold stocks, however, would be somewhat less attractive as a hedge against such conditions. But although Canadian mines might be forced to close for a time, during the course of any really severe inflation in Canada, they would, if they were sound properties, eventually resume production and their shares would undoubtedly attain much higher values after stabilization.

The major problem faced by investors in foreign gold stocks during any period of domestic hyperinflation would be that the repatriation of dividends and transfers of capital resulting from the sale of such shares abroad might become extremely difficult, due to the rapid fall of foreign-exchange rates. I would hope that, under such conditions, the directors of South African and Canadian mines would see the wisdom of placing dividends due U.S. stockholders in escrow, pending the restoration of stable exchange rates.

As far as selling foreign gold stocks in domestic markets or for domestic currency during periods of extreme inflation, it should be avoided at all costs. Unless one really needs legal-tender cash to pay debts or current obligations, one should not sell *any* sound assets during periods of runaway inflation; the last thing one wants to have at such times is depreciating paper currency. There is an old story, probably apocryphal, concerning a German farmer that dramatically illustrates the problem. This farmer paid 10,000 marks for his farm in 1914. When the postwar inflation was running wild, he was offered 1 billion marks for the same property. The thought of becoming a "billionaire" was irresistible, and our farmer sold. Three weeks later he could not have bought a single cow for the amount previously received for his entire farm, and a week after that —not even a chicken. An extreme example, of course, but the principle remains.

The big profits in gold mining stocks will come *after* a runaway inflation has ended and a new monetary system, based on gold, has been created to restore stability. Historically, that is the way nearly all previous hyperinflations have ended. Ideally, of course, one should acquire a gold portfolio *before* inflation reaches the more painful stages, although there may at least be opportunities to acquire gold stocks during true hyperinflations, because all noncommodity assets, even gold stocks, may become suspect during extreme inflation conditions. But I wouldn't count on it.

Actually, the best asset to hold during true hyperinflations would be gold (and silver) coins. They could be sold in small quantities or, in the case of gold coins, even one at a time, whenever it was necessary to raise legal-tender cash. However, if one could do so, it would be better to continue to hold gold coins, as well as gold stocks, until *after* the inevitable reorganization, for there is no way of judging just how long a runaway inflation will last, or what extremes will be reached, before sanity returns.

Under conditions of more or less continuous inflation, which does not get completely out of hand, foreign gold stocks, as well as gold coins should prove to be sound investments, because of the inevitability of repeated devaluations.[7] The repatriation of dividends and profits from foreign sales may be hampered by exchange controls and erratic exchange rates, but there are ways to minimize these problems, and they will be discussed in Parts 2 and 3 of this book.

GOLD STOCKS AND WAR

So-called "limited" war situations, such as the Vietnam conflict, tend to have a bullish effect on gold investments, because all wars and threats of war intensify inflation, encourage hoarding and increase feelings of uncertainty and apprehension. But there is little I can say about the merits of gold stocks if the United States becomes involved in a major war with another superpower. Conditions will then be so bad that to worry about one's stock holdings would be superfluous. Anyway, the beginning of another world war, or even the serious threat of one, with its potential for atomic holocaust, would probably cause the entire stock market, including gold issues, to collapse in a panic of unprecedented proportions unless, of course, all markets were ordered to be closed at once and trading was suspended indefinitely.[8] In any case, about the only thing a holder of gold stocks could do, under such circumstances, would be to put his certificates in a (presumably) safe place and then (a) hope to survive and (b) wait for the crisis to pass or peace to return.

However, if one could sell gold stocks during or just prior to a major war situation or threat, without taking unacceptable losses, it would probably be advantageous to do so, if the money regained were used to buy gold coins. Gold coins, in the author's opinion, would be the safest and best asset to have under full wartime conditions or during an all-out war economy.

Both the calamities of the past and the uncertainties of the future, therefore, indicate the desirability of including gold coins in the gold-investment portfolio. As for gold stocks themselves, the safety-of-capital principle would indicate that we select our shares from at least two, if not all three, of the principal gold-producing areas. But in any case, I believe that every portfolio should have *some* South African shares, regardless of which North American companies are represented.

Notes:

CHAPTER VIII

1. Medium- and large-size bank safe deposit boxes can be rented for a modest annual cost, and they provide the best answer to the coin storage problem. You must insure the contents of the box yourself, however, through your own agent. But the premium for such insurance is very modest. It is too dangerous to keep coins at home, even in a home safe.

2. Though once mineral rich, the United States is now mineral poor. Some 60 vital commodities must now be imported in major quantities. The U.S. is almost totally dependent on foreign sources for chrome, nickel, tin, manganese, cobalt and bauxite. It is substantially deficient in lead, zinc and tungsten. Over half of the present U.S. consumption of even such basics as iron ore and petroleum is presently being imported.

3. Because the ducat/florin is .986 fine, it would be somewhat soft for modern circulating coinage use. Any "New Floren" would probably be struck at .900 fine, with the same intrinsic gold content, thus making for a slightly larger coin than the original. It can also be assumed that coins in denominations higher than 1 floren would be provided for.

4. Only 16 percent of the Japanese home islands is suitable for cultivation. Japan is extremely deficient in most industrial raw materials and completely without a national source of oil.

5. The Japanese are simply classified as "white," whereas Chinese, Indian and other Orientals are held to be "colored"!

6. *Krueger rands* are also available in Canada and Western Europe at a price slightly above the going rate for gold bullion. (The one-troy-ounce *Krueger rand* should not be confused with the smaller 1-rand and 2-rand commemorative gold coins previously minted by South Africa).

7. As examples of continuous long-term inflation, one could take the French experience from 1914 to the present, or the now chronic inflationary conditions of Brazil, Chile and Uruguay.

8. Almost immediately after the outbreak of World War I, all U.S. stock exchanges were ordered closed (on July 31, 1914) to

avert a threatening panic. They remained closed until December 12, 1914, at which time they were gradually reopened for limited trading. All restrictions were finally lifted on April 1, 1915.

SMELTING AND WORKING GOLD IN ANCIENT EGYPT. The Egyptians were the first people to mine and utilize gold on a large scale. Between 4000 and 2000 B.C., the Egyptians may have produced as much as 1,500,000 lbs. of gold. Most of this vast treasure became the property of the Pharaohs and a great part of it was used for the elaborate decoration of royal tombs. The illustration shown is from an Egyptian wall painting which depicts the technical level of gold metallurgy achieved by 2000 B.C. Note the foot-operated bellows.

Historical Pictures Service, Chicago

GOLD PANNING IN CALIFORNIA, 1849. Few episodes in American history caused such a world-wide sensation as did the discovery of rich deposits of placer gold in California during the middle of the 19th century. The initial strike was made by James Marshall on January 24, 1848 at Sutter's Creek in what is now El Dorado County. Although Marshall and his employer, John Sutter, tried to keep their discovery secret, word soon leaked out and within a year tens of thousands of gold-hungry adventurers were converging on California, not only from all parts of the United States, but from many foreign lands, including Australia, South America and China. The first arrivals often needed no more than a metal pan to try for a fortune.

Historical Pictures Service, Chicago

THE RUSH TO CALIFORNIA, 1849. This satiric cartoon of 1849 lampoons the frenzy of gold-crazed fortune seekers to get to California. The artist exhibited a prophetic sense of humor in showing imaginary transportation by airships and rockets. In real life the trip was not so humorous. Many who went overland by horseback and wagon train perished along the way from hunger, exposure and Indian attacks. Others died in the malaria and yellow-fever infested swamps of Panama, attempting to take this short-cut on the sea route. Even those who took passage on ships sailing around the Horn risked death by storm and shipwreck in those treacherous waters.

Historical Pictures Service, Chicago

CALIFORNIA PLACER MINING, 1850. The simple panning operations typical of the initial phase of the California gold rush soon gave way to more ambitious enterprises, such as this elaborate placer works.

Historical Pictures Service, Chicago

EL DORADO GAMBLING SALOON, SACRAMENTO, CALIFORNIA, 1850. The gold rush brought a roaring boom to California, with all the raucous, uninhibited and sometimes violent enthusiasm that inevitably accompanies such times. But only a small portion of the thousands of would-be miners and prospectors actually struck it rich. Others lost their hard-earned gold dust to cold-eyed gamblers in places such as the El Dorado. Nevertheless, despite the hardships, sufferings and bad luck, most of the "Forty Niners" were inclined in later years to look back and see this period of their lives as a happy and exciting time.

Historical Pictures Service, Chicago

GOLD PROSPECTORS IN AUSTRALIA, 1852. Close on the heels of the California strike, a major discovery was also made in southern Australia. Many of the California gold seekers who had not yet found their fortune promptly reembarked for Australia, to try their luck in this new promised land. Others came from Europe and the British Isles. In this contemporary illustration, two English seamen set out for the interior with a minimum of equipment.

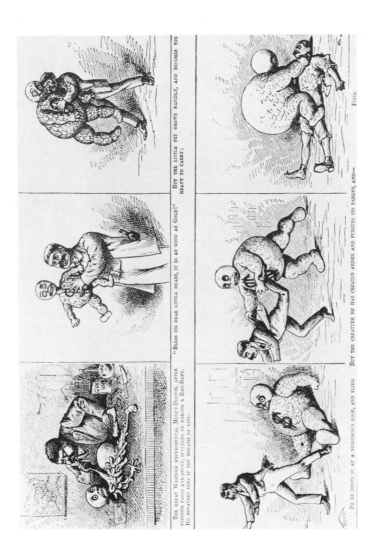

THE GREAT GREENBACK CONTROVERSY, 1862–1879. During the Civil War, the Lincoln administration issued non-redeemable paper currency with the understanding that such notes would be withdrawn from circulation after the war emergency had ended. However, when the time came to withdraw these so-called "greenbacks," agrarian and populist interests, who thought they would benefit from more inflation, not only resisted redemption but demanded further issues of fiat paper money. This 1876 cartoon by Frank Bellew shows that the monetary conservatives of that day were well aware of the danger brought about by the introduction of the greenbacks, derisively called "rags" by their opponents.

Historical Pictures Service, Chicago

GREENBACKS DRIVE OUT GOLD AND SILVER, 1862–1879. This contemporary cartoon shows one of the effects of the fiat money standard endured by the U.S. from 1862 to 1879. American citizens were then forced to accept non-redeemable, inflationary greenbacks, while foreigners were free to demand and get gold and silver. After 1933, the clock was turned back and Americans were once again forced to accept non-redeemable fiat currency,

Historical Pictures Service, Chicago

GOLD MINING IN COLORADO, 1880. From 1870 to 1890, the promise of finding gold lured tens of thousands of settlers to the American West. Notable gold booms occurred in Arizona, Nevada, Idaho, Colorado and South Dakota. By the turn of the century, however, most of these areas were past their peaks and well into decline, as far as gold mining was concerned. This contemporary woodcut shows Colorado miners literally honey-combing an entire mountain with their tunnels.

Historical Pictures Service, Chicago

GOLD IS DISCOVERED IN SOUTH AFRICA, 1886. The greatest and most prolific gold boom in history, and one that has not yet ended, began in South Africa in 1886, when a rich find was made at Langlaagte farm on the Witwatersrand in southern Transvaal. This contemporary illustration shows an excited crowd viewing newly discovered gold nuggets being exhibited in a store window in Durban, a port city in the Natal province of South Africa.

Historical Pictures Service, Chicago

GOING DOWN THE VICTORIA SHAFT, 1887. The early days of mining in South Africa were a far cry from the huge and technologically advanced works of the present era. This 19th century woodcut shows a mining engineer about to descend into the main shaft of the Victoria mine at Barberton, Transvaal in 1887, using a rather elementary elevator!

PROSPECTORS ASCENDING CHILCOOT PASS, ALASKA, 1897. The Alaska-Klondike gold rush of 1896–98 was perhaps the last great adventure of its kind. It was the last time, at any rate, that an ordinary individual with little more than courage and a dream could hope to strike it rich on his own. Modern gold mining and prospecting are highly technical and very expensive processes. This photo shows thousands of would-be prospectors ascending the Chilcoot pass in the winter of 1897, hoping to find their luck in the Klondike territory along the Yukon River in the Canadian northwest. Many found only a frozen grave, but some did make a fortune.

Historical Pictures Service, Chicago

FIAT MONEY INFLATION IN GERMANY, 1919–1923. Paper money without convertibility can eventually become just paper, as was tragically demonstrated in Germany during the early 1920's. This German citizen found that the only useful function possible for his paper "money" was to use it for wallpaper.

COAL USED AS MONEY—GERMANY, 1923. A powerful lesson in economics is presented by this picture. When paper money becomes completely divorced from a realistic and dependable exchange basis through the demonetization of gold, loss of convertibility and over-issue, commodities themselves begin to serve as money. In this photo, a German movie exhibitor fixes his admission price at "two lumps of pressed coal." The title of the film is, appropriately enough, *Judas*. Inflation was surely the Judas of the struggling German democracy of the 1920's.

Historical Pictures Service, Chicago

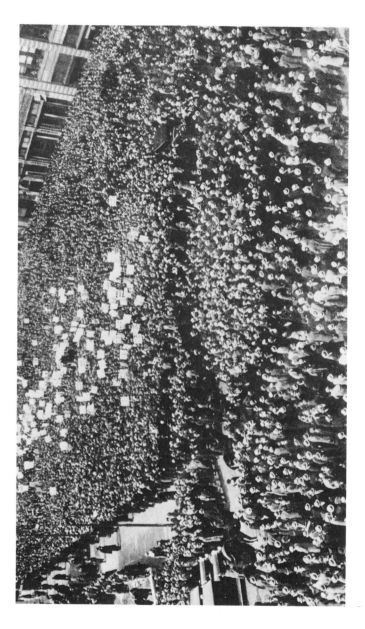

UNEMPLOYED AT MASS DEMONSTRATION—NEW YORK, 1930. The so-called gold exchange standard brought about by the Genoa agreement of 1922 encouraged a wild speculative boom in the 1920's, due to the virtually unlimited availability of credit money, supposedly "as good as gold." The collapse of this artificial prosperity in the fall of 1929 ushered in the Great World Depression. Despite this lesson, another gold exchange standard was adopted after World War II.

Historical Pictures Service, Chicago

GENERAL VIEW OF THE HOMESTAKE MINE, 1971. First opened in 1876, the Homestake Mine at Lead, South Dakota (pronounced "Leed") is the only large underground gold mining operation left in the United States. Nevertheless, it is still one of the world's major gold producers and the largest gold mine in the Western Hemisphere, milling nearly 6,000 tons of ore daily and yielding more than 500,000 ounces of gold per year.

Homestake Mining Co.

LOADING AN ORE CAR AT THE HOMESTAKE MINE. A compressed air-powered mechanical shovel is used by a miner to fill an ore car in the Homestake Mine. This mine has more than 200 miles of tunnels and is being worked to a depth of 6,800 feet below the surface. Future plans call for extending the underground works to the 8,000 foot level.

Homestake Mining Co.

BALL MILLS AT THE HOMESTAKE MINE. Each of these mills contains 80,000 pounds of steel balls, ranging from 1¼″ to 2″ in diameter. Semi-processed ore from the rod mills (in the background) is crushed into a fine powder by the action of the steel balls in rapidly rotating drums. After the finely ground ore leaves the ball mills it is subjected to further mechanical and chemical treatment to extract the gold.

Homestake Mining Co.

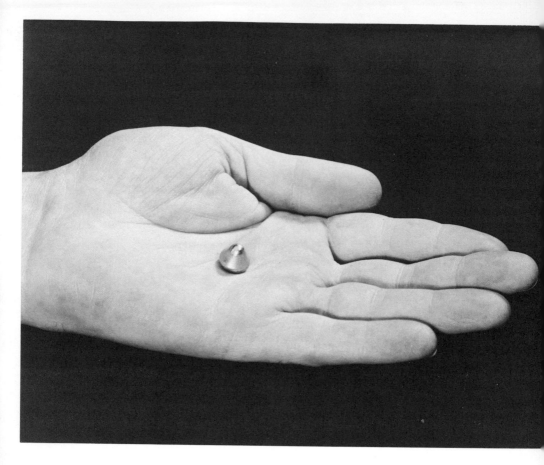

YIELD PER TON AT THE HOMESTAKE MINE. This little button of pure gold, weighing only 3/10 of a troy ounce, is the result of the mining and milling of ONE TON of ore at the Homestake Mine. In recent years, about 2,000,000 tons of ore per year have been mined and treated at Homestake.

Homestake Mining Co.

AERIAL VIEW OF DOME MINES. First opened in 1911, the Dome Mine at South Porcupine, Ontario, is still one of Canada's major producers. In addition to the Dome Mine itself, the parent company, Dome Mines Ltd., holds a controlling interest in two other prominent Canadian gold operations: Campbell Red Lake Mines and Sigma Mines. The company also has other subsidiary interests and holdings. The Dome property at South Porcupine produces about 180,000 ounces of gold per year.

Dome Mines Ltd.

UNDERGROUND DRILLING AT THE DOME MINE. A drilling crew prepares a stope for blasting at the Dome Mine, South Porcupine, Ontario.

Dome Mines Ltd.

POURING A GOLD BAR AT THE DOME MINE. Gold "sponge" recovered from the treating and refining of gold-bearing ore is melted in an oil-fired furnace and poured into molds at the Dome refinery, South Porcupine, Ontario.

Dome Mines Ltd.

THE CAMPBELL RED LAKE MINE. This relatively low-cost gold producer, located in Balmer Township, western Ontario, has long been a favorite of gold-oriented investors and traders. First opened in 1949, this mine produced 178,974 ounces of gold in 1970, from 262,021 tons of ore, with an average recovery of 0.68 ounces of gold per ton.

Campbell Red Lake Mines Ltd.

AERIAL VIEW OF MADSEN RED LAKE MINES. The Madsen Mine is one of Canada's smaller gold operations, but it is still an active producer. First opened in 1941, this mine, located in the Red Lake district of western Ontario, produced 44,497 ounces of gold from 146,162 tons of ore in 1971.

Madsen Red Lake Gold Mines Ltd.

GIANT GOLD DREDGE IN SOUTH AMERICA. Although a Canadian company, Pato Consolidated Gold Dredging Ltd. presently operates four of these huge gold dredges on the Nechi River and its tributaries in Colombia, South America. The vessel shown here, Pato No. 8, was originally built by Natomas company for use in California, but was sold to Pato in 1962 and commenced operations in Colombia in 1964. This dredge, ready for digging, is 70 feet wide, 173 feet long, has a hull depth of 11 feet and weighs 2260 tons. It is a bucket-line type machine with a theoretical maximum capacity of 624,555 cubic yards per month. However, actual production has averaged 428,000 cubic yards per month during the past few years.

Pato Consolidated Gold Dredging Ltd.

JOHANNESBURG—CITY OF GOLD. Visitors to Johannesburg, Transvaal, in the Republic of South Africa, find it hard to believe that this ultra-modern city of more than 1,200,000 inhabitants began as a raw mining camp in 1886. Johannesburg is literally built on top of the original Rand mining area and several old mine dumps can be seen in the background. The large building under construction in the middle foreground is the new Carlton Center project, scheduled to be completed in 1972, which is to become the new headquarters of the giant Anglo-American Corporation.

South African Information Service

GENERAL VIEW OF WESTERN DEEP LEVELS MINE. Western Deep Levels, one of South Africa's newest and most productive gold mines began regular milling operations in 1962. Located at Carletonville, on the mile-high grassy Veld 40 miles west of Johannesburg, the total works consists of three main shaft systems and associated structures. In the foreground can be seen an olympic-size sports stadium and company housing for both married and single Bantu workers.

South African Information Service

DRILLING AN ORE SEAM IN SOUTH AFRICA. White and Bantu mine workers, using a water-lubricated, air-operated drill prepare a seam for the placing of blasting charges.

South African Information Service

ORE REDUCTION WORKS AT THE BUFFELSFONTEIN MINE. These large settling tanks are part of the ore treatment facilities at the Buffelsfontein gold mine near Klerksdorp in the Transvaal. Such extensive works are typical of most South African mines.

South African Information Service

ATHLETIC RECREATION FOR BANTU MINEWORKERS. The South African Chamber of Mines requires that all Bantu contract mineworkers be provided with suitable opportunities for recreation as well as furnished with adequate housing and other necessities. Consequently, elaborate sports and recreational complexes are found at every mine. In this view a track meet is shown in progress at the Hartebeestfontein Gold Mine in the Klerksdorp field.

South African Information Service

SINKING A NEW SHAFT AT SOUTHVAAL. This new shaft, begun in 1970, will descend thousands of feet into the earth. South African mining engineers pioneered in the development of these large, concrete-lined, circular shafts, which are later divided into compartments and equipped with multiple elevator systems.

South African Information Service

GOLD BULLION IN THE SOUTH AFRICAN RESERVE BANK. The South African central bank at Pretoria not only maintains the country's gold reserves but serves as a marketing agency for all South African gold producers. Premiums obtained from selling gold on world markets, at prices above the fixed South African monetary price, are returned to the participating mines on a pro-rated basis.

South African Information Service

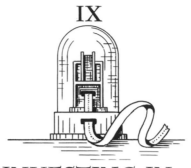

IX

INVESTING IN
GOLD MINING STOCKS

"Who says gold is dead? It was never livelier. Who tries to bury gold? The tired and frightened money men who know and fear gold's resurging strength. To all of us who know that the power of gold is great, the future of gold has never been brighter."

—PAUL C. HENSHAW,
PRESIDENT, HOMESTAKE MINING COMPANY

INVESTING in any industrial or commercial enterprise involves certain risks on the part of the investor. Buying and selling in open-auction markets involves another type of risk. When we buy common stocks, we assume a combination of the two risks: (a) the risk involved in the success or failure of the enterprise itself and (b) the risks inherent in an auction market where prices may fluctuate widely due to the technical and emotional factors inherent in such markets. The subtitle of this book implies that the careful trader or investor can avoid the pitfalls involved in buying gold mining stocks improperly. We can easily avoid the common mistakes and obvious dangers, but we cannot expect totally to avoid risk. Our aim, however, must be to reduce the risks to the minimum.

One cannot buy gold stocks at random. To minimize both types of risk, the venture risk and the market risk, one must try to buy the RIGHT STOCKS at the RIGHT TIME. Let us take up first the question of the right stocks. Mining corporations are unique among economic enterprises in that they are constantly depleting their principal capital asset, which is the reserves of payable ore in the ground. A mine, by its very nature, is a self-limiting enterprise. When the reserves of economically payable ore are exhausted, the mine has to be closed, and is usually permanently abandoned. The machinery and other salvageable assets are sold off and the corporation liquidated, with any remaining funds being distributed to the stockholders.

Therefore, one of the first factors one must know to judge the merits of a mining venture is the estimated size and grade of its unmined ore reserves (as determined by underground geologic drilling and sampling). By dividing the total estimated ore reserves by the annual processing rate at the mine, geologists can determine the estimated life of the mine itself. Most mining companies are constantly engaged in extensive exploration programs in an effort to find new ore bodies to replace depleted reserves, but the results of such explorations are highly uncertain and can never be anticipated in advance. Therefore, only proven reserves can be counted. The estimated life of a mine is generally categorized as belonging to one of the following classifications:

SHORT –   Less than 10 years
MEDIUM –   11 to 20 years
LONG –   More than 20 years

While short-life and declining mines sometimes have substantial leverage possibilities in a devaluation situation, due to the fact that relatively poor earnings can suddenly and dramatically improve, they are obviously a high-risk proposition. If a major gold-price rise could be delayed for a few more years (even though it is highly unlikely) such mines would be dangerous holdings. There may be occasional trading opportunities when a relatively short-life mine can be utilized, but I do not even advise that. For trading as well as investment purposes we should concentrate on sound medium- and long-life mines, particularly the latter.

Next to adequate ore reserves and a long-life potential, a good mining enterprise should not be overcapitalized; that is, there should not be an excessive amount of common shares issued and outstanding, and there should be few if any senior securities, such as bonds or preferred stocks, having priority over the common. Preferably, the entire capitalization should be in the common shares and any outstanding debt should be in the process of rapid retirement. Because of the ore-reserve depletion factor, the dividends paid by a mining company represent a partial return of capital as well as a distribution of profits or earnings. Consequently, any heavy or continuous draining of current earnings to pay long-term debt would be a highly negative factor, far more so than in the case of an ordinary industrial enterprise or a utility, where long-term debt, if acquired at low interest rates, may actually be an advantage. We must always remember that mining is a self-terminating enterprise, even though some mines have had remarkably long lives.[1]

Fortunately, nearly all the primary gold producers operating today are soundly capitalized and financed. My previous remarks are directed primarily toward the evaluation of new mining ventures, which will surely proliferate as soon as the dollar is devalued or the international price of gold is substantially raised. Another important factor in the evaluation of a mining enterprise is the quality of its management. If the management team of a new mine has had a record of previous successes, or has formerly been associated with a top quality mining operation, it is an excellent sign. Mining executives, managers and engineers of the first rank seldom risk their time and energies on second-rate ventures. If first-class mining people become involved in a new discovery or venture, one can be sure that it has substantial possibilities.

Another factor along this line is the quality of financial backing and investment interest attracted by the mine. Any mine in which virtually the entire capitalization in common stock is owned by the general public is probably a dubious proposition. There is an old axiom of Wall Street that holds that the way to financial success is to follow the "smart money." It is, unfortunately, all too true that the public, in general, is nearly always misinformed, if not actually misled, and tends to act emotionally rather than logically. The smart money, on the other hand, acts in quite the opposite manner. The sources of this type of money, the large corporations, banks, investment trusts and similar institutions, do not act without careful prior investigation. Unlike small investors, who are often at the mercy of rumors, tips and hearsay information, the large organizations and financial interests can afford to send their own investigators and experts directly to the mine or claim to verify the actual conditions.

Small investors can further reduce their risk conditions, therefore, by following the lead of the "smart money." In recent years an ever-increasing amount of such sophisticated capital has been going into operating gold mines, into gold mining claims and into land areas with potential gold mineralization. The multimillionaire recluse Howard Hughes, for example, has been buying up gold mining claims and abandoned gold mining properties in the western United States, particularly in Nevada, as fast as he can arrange things, without attracting undue public attention. Furthermore, many mutual funds and investment trusts are now carrying large blocks of gold mining stocks in their portfolios.

Actually, I think that such areas as new mines and mining claims are for the experts, rather than for the typical U.S. investor. Pioneers seldom get rich. Only if they are already wealthy do they generally succeed. Consequently, I am quite willing to let the big money interests do the pioneering, and prefer to follow at a respectful distance. But when I do see big money moving into either a new or established venture, I weight it very heavily on the positive side.

There will, no doubt, be fortunes made in new ventures and in situations that are relatively unknown today, but the odds against success in this area are very formidable. Consequently, we must concentrate on well-established and proven mines if we are to hold to our basic strategy, which is to ensure the safety and preservation of capital, as well as to aim for capital gains and earnings. Although this book is primarily concerned with setting forth programs for the safe employment of capital by nonprofessional investors, there are lessons we can learn from the professional trader and speculator, and even from those outcasts of society (whom I nevertheless find fascinating) the professional gamblers.

These people all have one thing in common; they never play the long shots. I have studied the operations of successful gamblers, commodity traders and stock speculators (not necessarily in that order) for years and have concluded that their success is primarily due to the fact that *they never take unnecessary risks.* They never commit money to any situation unless the odds are strongly in their favor. To a real pro, the best gamble, speculation or investment is not the one with the biggest odds or the greatest leverage, or the fattest potential payoff, *but the one that comes as close as possible to being a sure thing.*

The typical amateur, on the other hand, whether he is betting a horse or buying a stock, is emotionally attracted to the long-shots rather than the favorites, because he is always seeking the magic of the big win, the great, ego-satisfying "killing." That is why, over the long run, the amateur always loses and the professional always wins. Over the past two decades, for example, literally millions of amateur speculators and investors have continuously lost money, through the greatest bull market in history, by putting their money into low-priced cat-and-dog stocks in the vain hope of finding another Polaroid or IBM or Xerox, while the professionals became millionaires by the simple expedient of buying Polaroid, IBM, Xerox and other established quality stocks whenever the market gave them a fresh opportunity.

The great bull market of the '50's and '60's is over, but the basic lessons remain:

1. Always invest your money in things and enterprises of established and *proven* quality.
2. Don't ever try to make a killing. Look for investments that provide a reasonably safe refuge for capital as well as an opportunity for gain.
3. Have patience. Everything, even gold, will at times be overpriced. Don't chase after rapidly rising prices. Don't buy anything on an emotional basis. Fear and greed are the great enemies of investment success. Be a careful bargain hunter, not an emotional plunger.

Mining shares have always been in a special category of common stocks. Because of the ore-depletion factor and other hazards peculiar to mining, they are frequently available, or at least should be available, at a lower price in relation to their current earnings (price-to-earnings or PE ratio) and provide a higher yield in the form of dividends than the ordinary run of industrial enterprises. Actually, many mining corporations have had far longer and more profitable lives than the majority of industrial concerns, and it sometimes proves easier to extend an ore body than to find new markets or products for a dying corporation or industry.

Nevertheless, we must pay close attention to the price-to-earnings ratio in the case of gold stocks, because the most common mistake made in the purchase of such shares is to pay too high a price for them, in relation to their earnings or potential earnings and dividends. All too often the public is induced by mass hysteria and market manipulation to buy gold shares at their peak PE ratios, only to see them suddenly fall to much lower levels as soon as the emotion accompanying some monetary crisis subsides. As I said earlier, gold stocks have been selling on a highly emotional basis in recent years, due to the underlying world monetary crisis. But the real money has been made by those who kept their heads and shopped for bargains on a fundamental basis, whenever the opportunity was offered.

Although few gold stocks conform exactly, at any time, to what might be considered as the ideal gold stock investment, there are a few basic rules that can be used to judge the merits of a prospective gold stock purchase, both as to fundamentals and timing:

BASIC RULES FOR BUYING A GOLD MINING STOCK
1. It must be a good current producer or have property or claims in a rich producing area.
2. It must have competent and experienced management.
3. It must have adequate financial backing.
4. It must have attracted professional financial interests.
5. It must not be overcapitalized or burdened with excessive debt.
6. It should be available on a reasonable price-to-earnings or price-to-assets basis.

7. It should pay a generous dividend or have the promise of a generous dividend, in order to compensate for gradual capital depletion.
8. It must have sufficient proven ore reserves or have had enough geologic investigation to indicate a reasonably long life.

As the reader will soon note, very few if any gold stocks currently available will adequately fulfill *all* of the given criteria. For one thing, there are so few really sound gold mining operations in the world, and there is so great a demand for them, that they are far more apt to be overpriced at any given time than reasonably priced or underpriced. Nevertheless, these criteria are a good rough guide, and those whose resources are limited and who cannot afford more than a very moderate risk should adhere to them as closely as possible and should not make a commitment until the given conditions are at least 70 percent fulfilled.

Another of the difficulties involved is that the typical listed gold mining corporation, when compared to ordinary industrial enterprises, is thinly capitalized; that is, the basic financial structure of a gold mine usually consists of a relatively small number of common shares. Such "thin" markets often make for extremely volatile price movements. With fewer shares available for purchase or trading (and with an ever-increasing number of those shares going into "permanent" investment accounts), a relatively limited amount of buying or selling pressure can cause wide fluctuations in share prices. This is the case with all of the listed North American gold stocks.

The South African corporations are far more generously capitalized, but, because they are not listed on the major American exchanges, they are less frequently the object of professional attention for trading purposes. Nevertheless, the price trend of the unlisted South African shares tends to follow rather closely the precedent set by the action of gold stocks on the "Big Board."* Therefore, even if one is primarily interested in acquiring a portfolio of South African gold stocks which are

*The New York Stock Exchange

admittedly of much higher quality *as mines* than the North American companies one should still follow the action of the popular listed golds for clues regarding the proper timing of purchases and sales for all types of gold shares. But whether buying listed or unlisted golds, especially if acquiring them for long-term investment holdings, one must avoid the following principal dangers:

1. Buying at too high a PE ratio or price level.
2. Buying a dead or dying mine.
3. Buying a high-cost producer.
4. Buying in a foreign country subject to political dangers and nationalizations.

In addition to the pressures of monetary developments and the emotional and technical factors inherent in all securities markets, gold mining companies are also subject to the following negative factors: excessive taxation, labor difficulties and escalating costs of production. Rising labor and material costs have been particularly hard on the earnings of established mines in recent years. The picture in general has been one of declining profits, despite increased production. Only a very few of the strongest South African mines have been able to counter the trend and show a generally rising level of profits and dividends over the past decade. There is no question but that the great majority of operating gold mines today are in a critical condition, as far as hope for continued profitable operations is concerned.

It is a virtual certainty that much higher prices for gold during the 1970's will relieve the gold mining industry of its present marginal operating situation, but there still looms the specter of excessive taxation. The reality must be faced that governments will undoubtedly attempt to seize some part of the windfall profits resulting from a higher gold price. We need be concerned with the tax policies of only three countries in this regard: the United States, Canada and South Africa. Unfortunately, residents of the United States who invest in foreign enterprises are, and will continue to be, subject to a heavy burden of taxation. First, we pay an income tax on the money we earn before we can invest, then we must pay an "interest equal-ization tax" on the purchase of foreign securities. And finally we are taxed *twice* on the dividends received, first by the for-eign country concerned and then by our own government via the income tax.

This tax problem is one of the reasons I favor keeping part of the monetary hedge portfolio in the form of gold and silver coins. The only conceivable tax liability on coins would be the capital gains levy, if and when they are sold. An inheritance tax might also become involved at times, but your lawyer or ac-countant can advise you on the ways to minimize this particu-lar hazard. Although the tax policies of the three major produc-ing countries will vary somewhat (and will be discussed more fully in Parts 2 and 3), I believe they will generally follow traditional patterns. We can expect, after devaluation:

1. A higher rate of tax on the purchase of foreign securities abroad (if indeed such purchases are permitted at all).
2. A higher tax on dividends by foreign governments them-selves.
3. A special U.S. tax on dividends received by Americans from overseas investments (over and above the regular income tax).
4. A special U.S. tax on legitimate industrial users of gold bul-lion to confiscate any windfall or speculative profits re-ceived in the course of their regular business.

Despite the tax handicaps, I still recommend the purchase and retention of gold shares because (a) they have paid off so handsomely in past periods of monetary upheaval and (b) there simply are no other equivalent areas in which to risk a part of capital under the present highly uncertain circum-stances. Furthermore, I don't believe that under our constitu-tional form of government a specific industry, even gold mining, can be singled out and subjected to any special, and therefore discriminatory, tax on its income or profits. I also do not believe that the governments of Canada or South Africa, which are dedicated to the free enterprise system, will act differently; they surely would not want to penalize a major export industry.

Actually, it will be so much in the interest of all countries to do their utmost to *encourage* gold production in the next decade, that they may even pay subsidies or bonuses to the mining companies, as well as give them special tax consideration.[2] Consequiently, it is the author's opinion that the major thrust of any special gold taxation will be directed against the individual rather than the mining companies themselves. A special excise tax might be placed on gold itself, but such a tax would be paid by industrial users rather than the producers. It must be remembered that, in the coming era of international currency and financial disintegration, all governments will be desperate to get gold.

Perhaps the greatest danger the gold mining industry itself will face will be the threat of nationalization, although I personally believe that the odds are against it in all three of the major gold-producing countries. In the United States, there are not enough operating mines left to make such an action rewarding enough.[3] In addition, it would be strongly resisted by both the courts and the public as opening the door to the socialization of other industries.

Canada produces more than enough gold for both its industrial and monetary needs and has been a net exporter of gold. Although the Canadian economy is closely tied to, if not actually dependent on, that of the United States, and Canada would suffer seriously from any U.S. monetary or economic collapse, the Canadian government does not have the kind of international-payments difficulty that burdens the United States. Nationalization of the Canadian mines would hardly yield significant benefits to justify such a drastic step.

The situation in South Africa is quite unique. The major financial problem of nearly all other nations is how to maintain adequate gold reserves, but the South African Government has to struggle to keep its gold reserves from becoming too large! Gold is South Africa's principal asset and export, and keeping the export market open and free has been its main concern. Therefore, nationalizing the gold mines of South Africa would make no sense at all, either economically or politically. Furthermore, whatever else are its faults, the government of South Africa has always pledged and maintained its staunch support of the free-enterprise concept.[4]

But while nationalization may be impractical and economically unrewarding for the governments concerned, one never knows for sure what rash and foolish moves politicians will make during periods of national hysteria and crisis. Nevertheless, I believe that this risk is marginal, and definitely should not deter one from investing in gold stocks for the seventies. In any case, one must assume that the owners of property subject to nationalization would receive compensation at least equal to the market value of their shares at the time of seizure.

Although heavier taxes may be incurred on dividends received from foreign gold mining enterprises, profits from the sale of gold stocks should remain relatively undisturbed, except for the usual capital gains tax. I do not see how the United States could devise a special capital gains surtax on the sale of gold mining shares without it being discriminatory and therefore unconstitutional. All in all, I feel that the risks involved in owning sound gold mining stocks, bought at reasonable prices, are certainly no worse, and conceivably a great deal more favorable, than any other group of stocks available at this time.

THE WORLD GOLD MINING SCENE

Perhaps one of the most startling discoveries for the investor who approaches the gold group for the first time is how few really sound gold mining properties there are to choose from. Another surprise is that they are nearly all concentrated in only three countries: the United States, Canada and South Africa, with the last-named having by far the dominant position. Nature was originally more generous in the distribution of gold-bearing ores, but these were mostly close to the surface or in the form of wet and dry placer-type sands and gravels. Since no other mineral has been sought so intensely and continuously since the dawn of history, it is understandable that the rich surface ores and placer deposits are virtually exhausted.

What remains are a relatively few deeply buried quartzite and old alluvial deposits concentrated in a very few select areas. Because of the extraordinary depth of these deposits, they are accessible only through the use of the most modern mining and engineering techniques and, because of their relatively low grade, they require very complex and expensive extraction and refining processes.[5] Despite these handicaps, world gold production in the past decade has broken all previous records, due largely to the rapid advance of mining and metallurgical technology and the opening of several new and highly productive mines in South Africa. *Fig. 17,* showing world gold production from 1934 to 1970, clearly indicates how South Africa, with more than 70 percent of the West's production, has been responsible for the gain.

The picture for Canada, the world's second-ranked producer, has been one of steady decline, while the United States, in a poor third position, has barely managed to stay even (at a greatly reduced level from prior years).

Production figures for Russia, China and other Communist-bloc nations are not included in the table, *Fig. 17,* because statistics on gold production (and monetary gold reserves) are closely guarded state secrets in these countries. Despite Lenin's boast that gold (as money) was a capitalist snare and delusion, and that in the "workers' paradise" it would serve only to decorate public lavatories, his successors have found more effective uses for it. In fact, it is the opinion of some mining experts and economists that the Russians are forced to pay production costs (in terms of labor and materials expended) equivalent to $100 per ounce to get the yellow metal from their difficult Siberian mines. But without gold, with which to purchase vitally needed manufactured goods, production equipment and even basic foodstuffs from the West, the Soviet economy would have collapsed long ago.

Fig. 17

WORLD GOLD PRODUCTION
1934–1970
(In millions of U.S. dollars at $35 per troy ounce)

Year	Estimated World Total	South Africa	Canada	United States	All Others
1934	$ 958.0	$ 366.8	$ 104.4	$ 108.2	$ 378.6
1935	1,049.9	377.1	115.4	126.3	431.1
1936	1,152.6	396.8	131.7	152.5	471.6
1937	1,229.1	410.7	144.1	168.2	506.1
1938	1,319.6	425.6	165.9	178.1	550.5
1939	1,383.7	448.8	179.0	196.4	559.5
1940	1,437.3	491.6	186.7	210.1	548.9
1941	1,265.6	504.3	187.1	209.2	365.0
1942	1,125.7	494.4	169.4	125.4	336.5

1943	871.5	448.2	127.8	48.3	247.2
1944	777.0	429.8	102.3	35.8	209.1
1945	738.5	427.9	94.4	32.0	184.2
1946	756.0	417.6	99.1	51.2	188.1
1947	766.5	392.0	107.5	75.8	191.2
1948	805.0	405.5	123.5	70.9	205.1
1949	840.0	409.7	144.2	67.3	218.8
1950	864.5	408.2	155.4	80.1	270.8
1951	840.0	403.1	153.7	66.3	216.9
1952	868.0	413.7	156.5	67.4	230.4
1953	845.0	417.9	142.4	69.0	215.7
1954	895.0	462.4	152.8	65.1	214.7
1955	940.0	510.7	159.1	65.7	204.5
1956	975.0	556.2	153.4	65.3	200.1
1957	1,015.0	596.2	155.2	63.0	200.6
1958	1,050.0	618.0	158.8	61.6	211.6
1959	1,125.0	702.2	159.6	57.2	206.0
1960	1,175.0	748.4	162.0	58.8	206.6
1961	1,215.0	803.0	156.6	54.8	200.6
1962	1,290.0	892.2	146.2	54.5	197.1
1963	1,355.0	960.1	139.0	51.4	204.5
1964	1,405.0	1,018.9	133.0	51.4	201.7
1965	1,440.0	1,069.4	125.6	58.6	186.4
1966	1,445.0	1,080.8	114.6	63.1	186.5
1967	1,410.0	1,068.7	103.7	53.4	184.2
1968	1,420.0	1,088.0	94.1	53.9	184.0
1969	1,420.0	1,090.7	85.2	60.1	184.0
1970	1,450.0	1,125.7	81.8	61.0	180.7

Notes:
  1. Does not include U.S.S.R., Soviet-bloc nations and Mainland China.
  2. U.S. totals include production received from Philippines prior to 1945. (After 1945, Philippine production included under "All Others.")
  3. Sources: Board of Governors, Federal Reserve System, *Banking and Monetary Statistics* bulletins, and *World Almanacs.*

The volume of Russian gold sales to the West over the past two decades indicates not only that they have indispensable needs for trade with the capitalists, but that the Soviet Union is very probably the actual third-, if not the second-, ranking gold producer in the world. The Communists are as hungry for gold as any Western nation because they know that it is the world's *only* universal and acceptable currency. They are hardly so naïve as to believe the fantasies of their own propaganda and they appreciate the reality that no foreigner in his right mind is going to accept Russian paper rubles or ruble credits in payment. The dollar may be a weak and shaky currency at present, but compared to any Communist paper it is a veritable mountain of strength and integrity.

The dreary fact is that Soviet-bloc currencies are so unreliable and inflation-ridden that they are even despised by their own citizens. The Socialist and Keynesian dreamers in the West should take note that despite the most monolithically planned and controlled economic systems, the Communist nations have been unable to defeat Gresham's Law and maintain sound, inflation-free fiat currencies. Consequently, gold smuggling has become almost an established industry behind the Iron Curtain.

For years Western journalists have been observing and reporting (with unconcealed merriment) the scene at the Bratislava, Czechoslovakia, railway station, where every morning the "smuggler's express" arrives from Vienna, just 35 miles away, bearing its usual quota of smugglers and police agents trying their best to look like carefree tourists. The smugglers themselves, mostly adventurous young Czechs and Yugoslavs, combine methods as old as the Hapsburg Empire with innovations peculiar to the crazy world of Communist finance. Their pockets bulge with gold coin on the way in and are stuffed with East European paper currency on the way out. For a small cut, the border guards and police can be induced to be neither thorough nor inquisitive.

The smugglers exchange the Eastern currencies for hard money at black-market rates in Vienna and then use the Western currencies obtained to buy gold coins, which are freely sold by both Austrian banks and the Vienna State Mint. The coins are ultimately delivered to their customers in little second-floor coffee shops in various Eastern cities, where the smugglers are known to meet. This is a business much in demand by East Europeans, who willingly pay five or six times official rates to convert their liquid assets into something of lasting value. The

East-bloc governments themselves not only tend to ignore this gold-coin socialism, but in some ways actually support it. Gold coins, for example, can be freely exchanged for the government *tuzek* coupons that are the official Communist currency for making purchases abroad or for obtaining hard currencies for travel in the West. As was noted earlier, the Communist governments are as eager for gold as their citizens.

GOLD HOARDING A WORLDWIDE PHENOMENON

But the smuggling and hoarding of gold is hardly unique to the Communist nations. It is endemic in every country attempting to maintain or impose pure fiat-currency systems, including the United States. Even in the face of such awesome penalties as a 10-year jail term, plus $10,000 fine and confiscation of the gold, American citizens, according to world currency expert Dr. Franz Pick, have already stashed away some 4,000 tons of gold—half in the bank vaults of foreign nations and half in their own homes or elsewhere in the U.S. Dr. Pick believes that U.S. citizens are hoarding (illegally) about $2 billion of the estimated $25 billion total of privately owned gold held around the world.[6]

I am definitely not advising any American to violate the law in this regard. As was pointed out in the previous chapter gold coins offer a satisfactory and legal alternative for Americans. But I think it is self-evident that no government will ever be able completely to prevent the holding of gold as a store of value. Even Hitler and Stalin couldn't prevent it. In fact, it is quite obvious that the worldwide demand for gold as a private store of value will continue to increase in the seventies in the face of unstable and further deteriorating international currency conditions.

INDUSTRIAL DEMAND FOR GOLD TO CONTINUE

One of the unique aspects of the present high-technology era has been the enormous increase in demand for precious metals for industrial, technical and scientific purposes. It was soaring industrial consumption, as well as hoarding demand, that brought about the great silver crisis of the mid-1960's. And while gold does not have as many industrial and technical uses as silver, commercial demand for the yellow metal has been increasing at a phenomenal rate in recent years. The gold plating of delicate electrical circuits and components, as an anticorrosion measure is now commonplace in the electronics, computer and aerospace industries. Other technical and scientific uses for gold are multiplying almost daily, while the traditional dental, jewelry and artistic usage continues to expand with world population growth.

Paul Jeanty, a director of Sammuel Montagu and Co., the famous London bullion dealers, recently predicted that the free-market price for gold would reach $100 per ounce by 1980, *through private industrial and hoarding demand alone*, regardless of any official action by either the IMF or the U.S. Treasury.

"Barring world political or economic disasters," said Mr. Jeanty, "it can be safely assumed that both industrial and jewelry consumption of gold will grow at an accelerated pace. Moreover, should hoarding in all its forms continue, even at present levels, it will represent a considerable shortfall of production, which can only be met from sales of existing monetary stocks or by sales from the Soviet Union."

However, Mr. Jeanty was also convinced that the world's central bankers, "have drawn the right conclusion from the experience of the ill-fated gold pool, and that no disinvestment from monetary stocks will actually take place." Mr. Jeanty's prediction also suggests that the $75 level will be reached by 1975.[7]

The overall consumption of gold falls into the following categories:

1. Dental, industrial and scientific.
2. Regular jewelry and the arts, gold coins and medals and jewelry made for hoarding.
3. Gold bars for private investment and speculation.
4. Gold bars for official monetary reserves.

The first two categories, covering all industrial and commercial uses, have shown the most consistent increase over the past decade and now account for nearly 70 percent of total annual production. If the present trend continues, and there is ample evidence that it will, industrial and commercial consumption alone will exceed new production by 1975. Hoarding demand is more erratic, but it too has been constantly expanding and every indication points to continued heavy demand from this area as well. *Fig. 18,* Availability and Distribution of Gold, 1956–1971, shows that private demand alone is rapidly overtaking supply, even at higher free-market prices for gold. At present, only the availability of gold from speculative holdings prevents an explosive shortage situation from developing.

Fig. 18

AVAILABILITY AND DISTRIBUTION OF GOLD
1956–1971
(In millions of dollars at $35 per troy ounce)

Year	Newly Available Gold (A)	Additions to World Monetary Reserves (B)	Estimated Industrial And Artistic Use (C)	Estimated Private Hoarding Demand (D)
1956	1,130	490	310	330
1957	1,279	690	320	269
1958	1,261	680	360	221
1959	1,382	750	380	252
1960	1,378	280	430	668
1961	1,490	605	470	415
1962	1,500	370	510	620
1963	1,906	820	540	546
1964	1,856	710	600	546
1965	1,840	220	690	930
1966	1,371	−45	745	671
1967	1,401	−1,580	815	2,166
1968	1,388	−700	890	1,198
1969	1,408	110	930	368
1970	1,412	275	990	225
1971	1,450	−75	1,060	438

Notes:
(A) New production, plus sales by Soviet Union, minus purchases by Mainland China.
(B) From IMF statistics.
(C) IMF staff estimate.

(D)   Residual amount: Columns A − (B + C) = D.

Because gold is such an expensive metal, great care is taken to recover and recycle the gold scrap generated by jewelers, industrial users and dental laboratories. As much as 30 percent of the gold used for industrial and commercial purposes may eventually be recovered as scrap and recycled or resold as new gold. However, the Table does not indicate in-house recovery and direct reuse by industry, but only external demand (Column C). Available supply (Column A) may include small amounts of recycled gold offered for sale as new bullion.

By the end of 1972 or '73, at the latest, the world will be in a net deficit position and the London gold price should be at $50 or more per troy ounce. This projection does not include or require any significant monetary demand or changes in monetary stocks. But *Fig. 19*, World Monetary Reserves, 1960–1970, indicates that the rapid downward trend in the gold percentage of such reserves may soon bring strong psychological and emotional demands for further monetary additions. Combining all present and potential demands, plus the great probability of continued deterioration of the dollar and other fiat currencies, leads to the conclusion that Mr. Jeanty's projection is actually a very conservative one. My own estimate would be closer to $150, and this of course is based, as is Mr. Jeanty's, only on projecting current trends and does not consider the very real possibility of a major world monetary collapse or the complete ruin of the dollar. Also, *Fig. 20* shows that many of the major trading nations, on an individual basis, are already seriously deficient in gold reserves. They will be active buyers in the future.

Fig. 19

WORLD MONETARY RESERVES
1960–1970
Showing Ratio of Gold to Exchange Assets

	1960	1964	1968	1969	1970
Gold	61.4	58.5	53.1	52.8	49.8
SDR's	—	—	—	—	4.2
Reserve Positions in IMF	5.8	6.0	8.9	9.0	9.1
Foreign Exchange	32.8	35.5	38.0	38.2	36.9
Total (Percent)	100.0	100.0	100.0	100.0	100.0

Notes:
1. Does not include Soviet-bloc nations or Mainland China.
2. Gold valued at $35 U.S. per troy ounce.
3. Source: IMF statistics.

Fig. 20

DISTRIBUTION OF WORLD GOLD AND EXCHANGE RESERVES
AUGUST 15, 1971

IMF Member Nation	Monetary Gold Reserve	SDR's & IMF Res. Position	Dollars & Other Exchange	Total Monetary Reserve	Percent Gold in Reserve
United States	10.2	1.6	0.3	12.1	84.3
West Germany	4.4	1.7	12.0	18.1	23.8
France	3.5	0.7	3.4	7.6	46.1
Switzerland*	3.0	—	3.4	6.8	44.1
Italy	2.9	0.5	3.2	6.6	43.9
Netherlands	2.0	0.8	0.5	3.3	60.6
Belgium	1.7	0.9	0.8	3.4	50.0
Great Britain	1.2	0.5	3.3	5.0	24.0
Portugal	1.0	0.1	0.7	1.8	55.0
Canada	0.8	0.7	3.5	5.0	16.0
Austria	0.7	0.2	1.3	2.2	32.0
Japan	0.7	0.8	11.9	13.4	5.2
South Africa	0.6	0.1	0.1	0.8	75.0
All others	4.2	0.6	8.2	12.6	33.0
Totals	36.9	9.2	52.6	98.7	37.0

*Non-IMF member nation

Notes:
1. Figures for gold reserves (column A) are in billions of dollars at $35 per troy ounce of gold.
2. Total monetary reserves (Column D), in billions of dollars at $35 per ounce of gold, includes gold, SDR's, IMF reserve positions and foreign exchange holdings of central banks (Columns A + B + C).
3. "All Others" includes balance of IMF membership, but does not include the U.S.S.R., Mainland China, or other Communist-bloc nations.
4. Source: IMF statistics.

GOLD STOCKS IN BEAR MARKETS

One of the more interesting features of the gold group is its pronounced countercyclical tendency. In other words, under more or less normal conditions, gold stocks are strongly inclined to move *against* the prevailing stock market trend. When the trend of the market as a whole is definitely up, that is, when there is a "bull" market, gold stocks generally are weak and declining. But during rapidly falling, or "bear," market conditions, the gold group usually makes strong gains.

This phenomenon is, understandably, due to the fact that gold is considered to be the ultimate hedge against financial adversity. Gold mining companies, therefore, are expected to thrive during periods of deep recession or depression. Furthermore, such conditions, or even the threat of such conditions, usually bring renewed anticipation of devaluations. Since major bear markets often precede (and forecast) periods of financial and economic adversity, one can expect a strong rally in the gold group when such markets are running their course.

Now it must be admitted that current monetary developments and problems have tended to distort the usual countercyclical pattern of the gold-stock group, but it has not been altogether eliminated. At any rate, we can assume that after a major gold-price adjustment has been accomplished and the threat of world monetary collapse relieved, the countercyclical pattern will again dominate the gold group. I am referring primarily to those gold stocks that are listed for trading on the major exchanges. These stocks demonstrate the most pronounced price movements in response to general market conditions. The South African stocks, which are traded in the "Over-the-Counter" or OTC market, however, follow the lead of the listed golds, except that their price movements are seldom as extreme as the listed stocks.

Many successful market traders and speculators make excellent use of the countercyclical action of gold stocks. In the author's opinion, it is far safer and generally more profitable to "go long," or buy gold stocks, when anticipating a significant bear market, than to make short sales of stocks from the general list. Since most people are uncomfortable in a short* posi-

*Short selling is the practice of selling stocks one does not yet own in the hope of covering or buying for delivery at a lower price, subsequent to the sale.

tion, gold stocks furnish an ideal way to trade a bear market from the long side.

The action of gold stocks may also furnish significant clues as to the future course of the general market. A sudden strengthening of the gold group on significantly increased volume of trading, in the absence of important monetary news, may actually be a warning of an impending bear market. On the other hand, bear-market bottoms are often preceded by an unexpected "falling out of bed," or sharp drop, in the gold group after a previous substantial rise in these stocks.

The beginning and end of the 1966 bear market, for example, were perfectly forecast by the action of gold stocks. In the late fall of 1965, a substantial increase in trading volume throughout the gold group could be observed by astute tape watchers, chartists and technically oriented traders.[8] This action was, in the author's opinion, accurately forecasting the general market break that began so suddenly in January 1966, and which led to a 25-percent decline in the Dow Jones Industrial Average. But, as the general market skidded and tumbled day after day, the gold stocks methodically advanced. By August 1966, with the general list off by more than 20 percent, gold stocks were making new highs, with gains of from 70 to 100 percent over their 1965 levels.

In September of 1966, however, the gold group succumbed to a wave of profit-taking and embarked on a rather precipitous decline. A month later the Dow Jones Industrial Index had recorded its low for the year and, as we see now in retrospect, the 1966 bear market was over. Gold stocks continued to decline and recorded their lows in December of 1966, having returned, at this time, to the price levels of late 1965. However, the December lows proved to be an ideal buying point again for gold stocks, as they began a slow rise from that point which led, eventually, to the gold-panic highs of March 1968.

The action of gold stocks, as a group, can thus serve as a rather unique timing device for the trader or speculator, particularly when used to verify other indicators. A sudden reversal in the gold group after a long rise and during a major decline in the general market, is apparently one of the significant indications that the bear market may be approaching its end.

Since 1967, however, the market actions of gold stocks have been, understandably, far more influenced by international monetary developments than by the usual cyclical trends. But it should always be remembered that the underlying cyclical pattern remains and will reassert itself in the absence of monetary pressures. The unusual behavior of gold stocks during the 1969–70 bear market, in which they *did not* perform countercyclically for the first time since the 1930's, but followed the general list down and then up again, is just another indication to this writer that the market break of 1969–70 was unique.[9] It was not merely a repeat of the usual type of correction and recovery that has occurred at approximately four-year intervals since World War II, but a historic turning point foreshadowing major changes and adjustments in both U.S. and world economic and financial structures.

SEASONAL PATTERN OF GOLD STOCK PRICES

Ever since the U.S. balance-of-payments deficit became an international problem, beginning in 1958, the market performance of gold stocks has also been noticeably influenced by a seasonal pattern that appears to be based on the annual meeting of the International Monetary Fund, normally held in September. Prior to the IMF meeting, gold stocks tend to rise in price. But after this annual get-together (which seldom results in any constructive actions) gold stocks often experience a sizable retreat. When this seasonal pattern is superimposed on a bear-market year, as it was in 1966, the total yearly cycle can be quite pronounced—and profitable for the trader who understands and anticipates it.

A hypothetical market year for gold stocks, based on seasonal patterns observed in the past decade or so, would go something like this: moderate rise in January and February; small correction or sideways movement through March and into April; further gains in May; intermediate correction in June, erasing from one-third to one-half of the total January-through-May move; final upthrust and "blowoff" in July and August, with yearly high prices recorded in late August or first week in September. In the declining phase, which becomes progressively more severe in the fall months, yearly lows are recorded in late December.

There is of course no way of knowing how long the present seasonal pattern will endure. The coming major international gold and currency adjustments may impose an entirely different set of conditions on the securities markets and on gold stocks in particular. But whatever these conditions are, if they allow professional traders and speculators to bid gold stocks up to mid-summer or late summer highs, you can be sure that the lows will be seen in late December.

Don't be shocked by this suggestion that the listed golds are subject to such manipulation by market professionals; all other stocks are the object of similar attentions, particularly those with small capitalizations and their resulting "thin" trading markets. Such stocks can be moved quite easily by astute professional traders. The big-money operators are always quick to sense the natural rhythms and cycles of any given stock situation and they then give added momentum and weight to those movements by carefully timed buying and selling operations. Virtually every stock and every market has a periodic cycle of accumulation by insiders and professional traders, when prices are at low bargain levels, and distribution to the unsophisticated general public when the same stock is highly priced or overpriced.

The typical nonprofessional investor or speculator is invariably attracted to stocks that are either advancing rapidly under heavy volume, or "churning," that is, trading very actively and prominently without further advance. Unfortunately, such actions are typical of stocks in the "blowoff" phase about to make a cyclical or seasonal top. Consequently, the great majority of investors, including those who are attracted to gold stocks, too often find themselves saddled with a loss almost immediately after making their purchase. And, in such cases, the great majority, again, do nothing until December, at which time they are reminded by their brokers or accountants of the advantages of establishing their losses for tax purposes. As a result, a period of distress tax-selling begins the week before Christmas and reaches its climax during the brief trading period between Christmas and New Year's Day.

If gold stocks have made a summer high on good volume, and have sold off thereafter into the fall, it will be virtually guaranteed that bargains will be available in late December. Now I do not advocate a general or full-trading approach to gold stocks for the seventies. I believe that the average investor will be better off building a long-term portfolio of sound gold mining equities over a period of time. However, if one is in the fortunate position of having enough liquid capital to build and maintain both a long-term "insurance" portfolio of gold and silver coins and gold equities, *and* a speculation or trading account, the listed golds, in the author's opinion, will serve as excellent trading vehicles. They frequently make substantial price moves in relatively short periods of time.

But remember, the long-term trend for sound gold stocks has got to be up. So unless you are an experienced trader (or even if you are), don't take unnecessary risks. Never use more than one-third of your capital for trading purposes. Keep the rest in permanent long-term positions. Otherwise you may get caught in the unhappy circumstance of being completely sold out, during what appeared to be a cyclical top, only to see the gold group explode into a new and permanently higher trading range as the result of a major dollar devaluation or some other world-shaking monetary news. The best advice I can give regarding gold stocks (or any other investment for that matter) is: BUY RIGHT AND SIT TIGHT.

"Buying right," however, takes some sophistication, and that is where a knowledge of the cyclical and seasonal nature of gold stocks is most helpful, whether you are working a trading account or building a long-term portfolio. As a general rule, do not chase after stocks that are rising rapidly on heavy volume, especially if they have already made substantial gains during the prior six months or year. There are times when patience is a supreme virtue. After an obvious summer peak and early fall decline, plan to take advantage of the December tax selling. If possible, put some cash aside before Thanksgiving, for the specific purpose of adding to your portfolio after Christmas. Don't be misled by minor rallies from September to December; unless the summer highs are exceeded and held, you are bound to get the best prices in late December.

The best time to buy gold stocks is when everyone else appears to have lost interest in them. After a 30 to 50 percent cyclical or seasonal decline, the unsophisticated small-time speculators will be washed out, and the stocks concerned will turn dull, trading in very low volume without making new lows in price. This is usually the time to begin buying such stocks. A good trading rule, and one that works very well with gold stocks, is that if, after a substantial decline (30 to 50 percent), a stock does not go any lower in price for three months, the next significant move for such a stock will be higher, not lower.

THE STOCK TRADING CYCLE

One of the oldest aphorisms of Wall Street is that the most important thing to know about a given stock is *when* to buy it and when to sell it. A trader or investor can make money buying even a weak or questionable stock at the right time, but he will surely lose by buying even the best stock at the wrong time. Despite this rather obvious fact, nothing is more difficult for the average nonprofessional investor than developing an effective sense of timing. It is far easier to determine what issues to buy than when to buy (or sell) them. Fundamental statistics on the progress (or lack of it) of any corporate enterprise can be found in every broker's office. But timing is an art, not a science, and it can only be developed by the individual trader through careful observation and study.

Information concerning price changes and trading volumes of listed common stocks can be found in most metropolitan newspapers and in daily business papers such as the *Wall Street Journal.* These papers print a daily summary of all New York and American Stock Exchange transactions, including the high, low and closing prices and the total daily trading volume (in 100's of shares) of each issue traded. While such summarized data may not be quite as helpful in getting the "feel" of a market situation as actually watching the ticker tape or electronic board in your broker's office, it will be more than adequate if properly understood.

Simply keeping a daily ledger or record, in which the closing price and total trading volume of each stock under consideration is noted, can be very useful in sizing up a particular market situation. At least it will show which way a stock is moving, how long the trend has been in force and whether or not the stock concerned could be nearing the top of a trading cycle or the bottom. If you prefer to "chart" or record such information in graphic form, fine, but be sure that the type of chart or method of charting selected includes provisions for showing the daily volume of trading.

For some reason, the much favored "point-and-figure" chart (which does not consider volume, but only price changes) is not very reliable when used with gold stocks. It has been the author's experience that such charts, when used for gold stocks, are prone to give false signals. They will show very definite "buy" or "sell" formations on occasion, only to have the stock itself do just the opposite of what the chart suggests it should do.

It is very important therefore to observe trading volume, as well as price movements, when dealing with gold stocks. The two most important points to remember are: (1) that very heavy volume invariably occurs at the *end* of a major upward move and (2) a period of sluggish or dull trading on low volume, after a substantial downward correction, is a strong indication that the decline is over.

As was noted earlier in this chapter, nearly all stocks go through a cycle of accumulation, at bargain prices, by insiders and astute professional and semiprofessional traders, and distribution to the general public at much higher prices. And after the distribution has been accomplished, prices are "marked down," with the help of judicious professional selling and short-selling. At the bottom, the disenchanted nonprofessional speculators are inclined to sell out in disgust (and at a substantial loss), while the professionals obligingly reaccumulate the same stocks and the whole process is repeated.

I realize that the preceding sounds a bit cynical, but it is a reality and it must be faced without illusions by the gold-stock investor. When one goes into the stock market, one does so in competition with some of the sharpest minds to be found anywhere. I'm not alluding to crooks or thieves; there are some in the securities business, of course, but they are a very minor element. On the whole, the securities markets are more carefully policed than most other areas of commerce. I am referring to the perfectly honest traders and money managers who just know their business. When these professionals buy a stock they must buy it from someone else, and when they sell stock they must, after all, sell it to someone else. Now if the professionals are invariably correct in their timing, and they are, then whoever is buying and selling in opposition to them has got to be wrong. Therefore, we should pay some attention to the market cycle, even when buying gold stocks for long-term investment. Buying at cyclical bottoms is obviously a better path to long-term investment success than being fooled into buying at market tops. And certainly successful trading depends almost entirely on understanding the rhythm of the stock-trading cycle.

After the accumulation phase in a stock or stock group has been completed, prices begin to move noticeably higher. This is called the "markup," and prices are methodically raised or marked up by stronger bidding and a greater urgency to acquire the stock. Following a substantial markup, however, there is usually a sizable intermediate correction, during which any remaining weak holders or nervous amateur speculators, fearful that the rally might have ended and that a new major decline could have begun, are induced to part with their stock. In some cases more than one intermediate correction is required before the markup can be completed. Intermediate corrections give the professionals further opportunities to accumulate or acquire stock at bargain prices.

After the markup (and final intermediate correction), the stage is set for the final upward move—the "blowoff" rise and distribution. During this phase, trading becomes very aggressive. Prices advance rapidly and daily volume becomes heavy, increasing from five to ten times the normal rate. Large block trades, in thousands of shares, frequently cross the tape. Rumors abound in the board rooms of brokers' offices and the financial press is full of articles and analyses attempting to "explain" the unusual activity. And plausible explanations are never hard to find, for it must be remembered that the cycle itself always has an underlying fundamental basis. In the case of gold stocks, the basis will be the constantly changing tide of monetary and economic events.

Professional traders and speculators do not create stock or

market cycles, they merely anticipate future developments well ahead of the general public and take advantage of them. Successful traders and investors use fundamental, seasonal and cyclical patterns as a guide for action, and their own trading activities become a "feedback" influence on the market itself, serving to intensify price movements in both directions. The professionals may not create market cycles, but they do know how to help them along.

At any rate, the excitement created by rapidly rising prices and heavy trading volume during the blowoff phase invites massive public participation. But when amateur traders enter the market itself or a particular stock or group of stocks, the professionals know it is time to get out. Therefore, at the top of every market or stock cycle there usually occurs what is known as a "buying climax." At this point the stock "churns" or trades in heavy volume for several days in a row (three days is usually sufficient to complete a buying climax in the case of gold stocks), without making any further or appreciable advance in price. What happens during a buying climax is that emotional and uninformed buying is balanced and eventually overpowered by informed professional selling.

Very often during the climactic buying stage, or just prior to it, some important fundamental news of an apparent bullish nature concerning the particular stock or stock group, will be released. This revelation will dramatically explain the previous rise in the stock and furnish a final invitation and excuse for the uninitiated to buy "before it's too late." But instead of going higher on the new wave of buying generated by the news, the stock will simply "churn" for a short time, sometimes only for a few hours, or at the most a day or two, and then break sharply downward in price.

The break down occurs because (a) the professionals are selling out and "shorting" the stock, instead of supporting it as they did during the markup; (b) short-term traders are taking their profits, in accordance with the time-honored trading rule of "buy on the rumor; sell on the news" and (c) amateur speculators, seeing their hopes of quick profits unexpectedly collapsing, fall over one another trying to get out of the market without further loss. The breakdown phase, however, is also of very short duration, seldom lasting more than a few days and sometimes only a matter of hours.

In the great majority of cases, the breakdown phase is quickly arrested by a sharp rally that terminates at a price level somewhat below the previous high. Support for the rally comes from short covering by traders who sold short during the climax in anticipation of the breakdown, and buying by late-coming amateur speculators who see the breakdown as a "second chance" to acquire the stock at a "bargain" price. The top of the intermediate rally may be characterized by a minor buying climax of its own, just as the bottom of the breakdown movement may see a selling climax in which stock is dumped profusely without going lower. The rally may also end on a much quieter note, with volume just gradually drying up prior to a sudden reversal of the movement.

In either case, the markdown phase inevitably follows (unless some new and totally unexpected development fundamentally alters the situation), and the stock or group begins a long and erratic decline, interrupted only by occasional brief and ineffective rallies. The bottom of the cycle may be heralded by a second selling climax, followed by dull, listless trading or, more typically, the downtrend may end with the stock just drifting sideways for many weeks on extremely light volume.

I want to emphasize here that this entire discussion of the stock-trading cycle is being presented on a purely hypothetical basis. No two stock cycles will ever behave in an identical fashion or follow an entirely predictable course. However, they do share certain common characteristics, and an awareness of the general nature of the trading cycle may save the investor some money and help the trader secure profits.

Perhaps the most difficult thing for the gold-stock investor will be to differentiate between a typical buying climax, which will be followed by a markdown to lower levels, and a potential breakout, that might catapult the stock to unprecedented higher levels. But to put this problem in its proper perspective, the reader is advised that *every* strong upward move, and even one that turns into a major breakout, is inevitably followed by a substantial correction. Therefore, it is seldom profitable to chase after any runaway situation, especially one that is obviously supported by excited and emotional public participation.

Heavy and increasing volume will eventually kill off any upward move and bring about a substantial reaction. Plan to do your buying in quiet periods, when gold stocks are (temporarily) out of style. Don't worry too much about being too late or missing a move. A missed profit doesn't hurt you financially, but an out-of-pocket loss always does. Keep calm at all times; never let emotions become a factor in decision making. Emotionalism may be useful or desirable in the arts, but it is fatal in the stock market. Greed and fear are two basic emotions that are the greatest enemies of financial success.

Whenever a stock or stock group, or the whole market itself, has had a long decline or has "fallen out of bed," and the news concerning it is uninspiring or decidedly bearish, the majority of investors will not buy because they react emotionally to such situations and become paralyzed by fear. On the other hand, after a stock or the market has had a long rise and is churning into new high ground on enormous volume and amid waves of bullish news, the majority will rush to commit every cent they possess, in the vain and greedy belief that an opportunity to make enormous profits has been offered. The "pros," however, control their emotions and use their reason. They condition themselves to "buy low and sell high."

Try to think like a professional. Be patient. Don't ever try to make a killing. Give more consideration to providing for safety of capital than to finding opportunities for large capital gains. Do not commit all of your funds to any single venture, even gold mining, or at one specific time. Don't ever put all of your investment capital into a single situation, a particular stock or limited investment area. Diversify your purchases in time as well as direction. Above all, DON'T BECOME GREEDY. Keep a liquid cash reserve, to be used only to take advantage of any unexpected setback in the gold group. Add to your portfolio in a calm and deliberate manner, particularly on weakness, and if you have depleted your cash reserve through previous purchases, sell something whenever the gold group is very strong and active.

For the convenience of the reader, I have put the typical stock-trading cycle in table form, *Fig. 21,* and in graphic form,

Fig. 22. But, let me emphasize again, don't expect your particular stocks to behave in exactly the same manner. Keep the basic idea of the trading cycle in your mind, but also keep your mind open. And remember this: when a gold stock looks like a real bargain, it probably is, and when it looks greatly overpriced, you can be sure that it is.

Fig. 21

TYPICAL TRADING CYCLE OF A LISTED STOCK: VOLUME AND PRICE ACTION

Market Phase	*Trading Volume*	*Price Action*
Accumulation	Low	Unchanged or slowly advancing
Markup	Moderate	Gradually but steadily advancing
Intermediate Correction	Moderate	One-third to one-half retreat from previous high
Blowoff	Heavy	Rapid advance
Buying Climax	Extremely heavy	No further upward progress
Breakdown	Heavy	Rapid decline
Selling Climax	Very heavy	No further downward movement
Intermediate Rally	Moderate to heavy	Advancing
Markdown	Moderate	Steady decline with occasional small rallies
Bottom	Very light	Unchanged

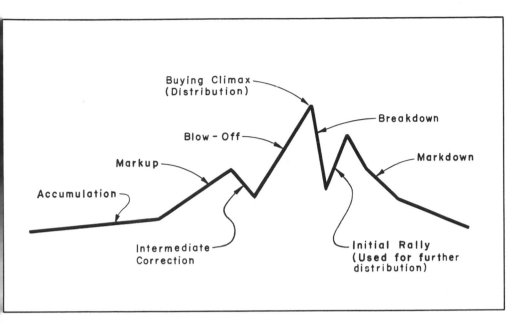

TYPICAL TRADING CYCLE OF A LISTED STOCK

PRICE MOVEMENT PATTERN

Fig. 22

Notes:

CHAPTER IX

1. The famous Homestake mine at Lead, South Dakota, for example, was opened in 1876 and is still one of the world's leading producers.

2. To a certain extent this is being done today. There are direct subsidies available to marginal mines in Canada, Australia and the Philippines, and special tax exemptions for new mine exploration and development are granted by nearly all gold-producing nations.

3. Primary gold production in the U.S. is currently insufficient to supply even domestic industrial needs, so there would be little point in nationalizing the mines for monetary purposes, only to have to import more gold for industrial use.

4. Following the European example, however, South Africa has nationalized its railways, electric utilities and even its coal and steel industry (see Part 3).

5. Most of South Africa's gold mines now operate at depths varying from 5,000 to 10,000 feet, or from one to two miles below the surface.

6. *Chicago Daily News,* May 12, 1969.

7. *Wall Street Journal,* September 22, 1970.

8. At least the author had no trouble observing this change.

9. It was also the worst bear market since that of 1937–38.

Part 2

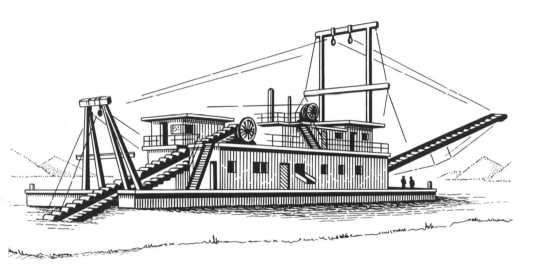

The Gold Stocks
of North America

X

GOLD MINING AND MINING
INVESTMENT IN NORTH AMERICA

"Inasmuch as the calling of the miner excels in honor and dignity that of the merchant trading for lucre, while it is not less noble though far more profitable than agriculture, who can fail to realize that mining is a calling of peculiar dignity? Certainly, though it is but one of the ten important and excellent methods of acquiring wealth in an honorable way, a careful and diligent man can attain this result in no easier way than by mining."

—AGRICOLA, 1556 (*Hoover translation*)

"The desire for gold is the most universal and deeply rooted commercial instinct of the human race."

—GERALD M. LOEB

GOLD occurs in minute quantities in almost every type of rock, but only very limited amounts and types of rock contain sufficient quantities of gold to be regarded as extractable ores or deposits. Sea water contains anywhere from .03 to 1 grain of gold per ton, but such a small amount would obviously be uneconomical to recover even if the price of gold were increased tenfold. Of the commercially extractable ores, nearly all are associated with what geologists call "acidic igneous intrusions." In laymen's terms, this means hard, volcanic or fire-formed material that originally forced its way out of the earth's interior in a molten state. The ore itself, however, may be either magmatic, metamorphic or a conglomerate derived from the original intrusion.

Gold is also frequently associated, in small amounts, with the ores of other metals, principally silver and copper, and is sometimes recovered as a by-product in silver and base-metal mining. Weathering and erosion cause some of the gold held in surface deposits or outcroppings of gold-bearing rock to be released in its natural metallic form, ranging in size from invisible sub-micron-sized particles to gold dust, grains, flakes, crystals and nuggets. The last named may weigh anywhere from one-quarter of a troy ounce to several pounds. The largest nugget ever found was the famous "Welcome Stranger," weighing 2,520 ounces or 210 (troy) pounds. It was discovered in 1869 in Victoria, Australia, just a few inches below the surface in a wagon rut. At today's prices it would be worth (allowing for assay loss) at least $100,000.

Regardless of the size of the particles, gold in its free metallic form is associated with what are called "placer" deposits. There are two basic types of placers: wet placers, consisting of gold-bearing sands or gravels found in flowing streams, rivers and other bodies of water, and dry placers, which are gold-bearing sands and gravels, crevice deposits and gold-gravel pockets not associated with water (although a "dry" placer deposit may originally have been created by water erosion).

The recovery of gold from placer deposits is accomplished by several related methods. For wet placers, the techniques range from the simple "panning" and sluicing operations of the independent prospector to the use of giant dredges that dig or suck up thousands of cubic yards of river sand and gravel per day and process it to recover the particles of gold it may contain. Around the turn of the century, gold-dredging operations were well established on the rivers and streams of both California and Alaska and continued for sixty years thereafter on a gradually declining basis, as rising costs and the exhaustion of workable deposits took their toll.

The last big gold dredge to operate in Alaskan waters was retired in 1961. A mammoth six-story-high dredge built in 1911 was also in service on Bonanza Creek in the Canadian Yukon Territory until 1958. This boat, formerly owned by the Yukon

Consolidated Gold Corporation is now on permanent display as a museum piece in the Yukon Historic Park, dedicated to exhibiting the history and artifacts of the famous Klondike Gold Rush. All other dredging operations were ended by Yukon Consolidated in November of 1966.

In the continental United States, the last big dredge to remain in operation was old No. 21 of the Yuba Consolidated Gold Fields Corporation, at Marysville, Yuba County, California. This 500-foot-long bucket-line boat, shut down in October of 1968, was the last of twenty-one such vessels built and operated by the Yuba Corporation after it began operations in 1905. At one time, ten large dredges were operating in the Hammonton area of Yuba County alone. And in 1902, fourteen dredges were working the Feather River in the Oroville region of Butte County, California. As recently as 1965, Yuba Corporation still had three boats going in the Marysville area and the company recovered some 54,000 ounces of gold, making it the sixth-largest gold-producing operation in the United States for that year.

But the old boats are undoubtedly gone for good. The economics of operating and maintaining old bucket-line dredges, built many years ago mainly of wood planks and timbers, are no longer profitable. Furthermore, not only has the availability of recoverable deposits been drastically reduced, but most counties in the affected areas have passed ordinances severely restricting the use of dredges by requiring the operators to restore the land and stream courses dredged to their original condition. Only a few gold dredges remain in operation around the world, notably the vessels of Pato Consolidated Gold Corporation, operating in Colombia, South America.

However, the recovery of gold and other minerals from the shallow coastal areas of the ocean floor, using modern, all-steel, seagoing dredging vessels is at least a possibility, and one that is currently being investigated by several major U.S. corporations, including the Tenneco Inc. conglomerate and the Shell Oil Company. But, so far, this possibility has not been carried beyond the very preliminary exploration stage. Virtually nothing has been done, as of 1971, to develop the technology that would be required for practical underwater mineral exploration, development and production. Successful mining of the ocean floor is at least a decade away—if it is to come about at all.

Dry, as well as wet, placer operations on a small scale have been practiced since the earliest days of mining. Separating the metallic occurrences of gold from dry sands or gravels by screening, "dry washing" over baffles or riffles, concentrating, shaking, vibrating and other mechanical procedures, sometimes augmented by chemical or mercury collection to recover the smaller particles, are typical. There are still dry placer operations in production in the western United States, but they are generally too limited to be of concern to the investor.

Another form of placer development is, or at least was, hydraulic mining, in which powerful jets of water are directed against exposed gold-bearing ore or gravel banks in order to release the gold particles by rapid erosion. The resulting slurry or silt-bearing water is then sluiced and processed as a conventional wet placer to recover the freed gold. Because of the environmental damage caused by this method and because of the silting and pollution of streams that often results, hydraulic mining has been outlawed in most areas of the United States and Canada. Before 1900, however, it was quite popular in the American West, particularly in California.

But the most important and most common form of gold recovery in modern times, and perhaps historically as well, is lode or vein mining. Lode mining, which dates back at least to ancient Egypt, involves extracting the mineral element directly from an undisturbed rock matrix or ore, usually from subsurface deposits. Open pit or strip mining of gold ores close to the surface is quite unusual, even though two such mines are currently operating in the United States. In the great majority of cases, lode mining requires the sinking of shafts, tunnels, galleries and compartments, etc., into the rock mass or ore body.

Any type of lode mining, however, involves the blasting or breaking of the rock mass into fragments that can be hoisted or hauled to the surface and carried to a fairly complex processing plant. To extract the gold, the mined ore must first be crushed or "stamped" into a fine conglomerate or sand, which is then treated by any one or a combination of processes including roasting, smelting, flotation, mercury amalgamation and cyanidation.

There is no need to go into the chemistry or engineering details of these processes except to note that they involve considerable expense, both in the original cost of facilities and in operating charges, All told, the initial investment in a modern lode mine, including the sinking of shafts and cross galleries, the construction of haulageways, skip hoists, ventilating systems, ore crushers, processing plants, smelters etc., may require the expenditure of many millions of dollars before a single ounce of gold is recovered. Consequently, intense geologic exploration and investigation must precede every lode development and the orebody discovered must prove out to be of sufficient size and grade to give a reasonable expectation of success to the primary investors.

But despite extensive and continuous exploration, the opening of a new gold mine is a noteworthy occurrence in our time. Although there are some 9,000 known gold mining properties in the United States and thousands more in Canada, there are, as of 1971, less than 50 operating gold mines in the whole of North America that can be considered worthwhile commercial enterprises—and many of these are in a marginal, if not a precarious, financial condition.

ECONOMIC AND POLITICAL PROBLEMS

The gold mining industry of North America has been beset by a series of extraordinarily difficult political and economic problems during the course of the twentieth century and they have taken a heavy toll, particularly in the last decade. Many of the great historic names in gold mining have been forced to abandon the enterprise in the postwar years, either ceasing operations altogether or transferring their interests to another area of mining or another industry. Among them we find such famous and well-known identities as LAKE SHORE MINES, YUBA CONSOLIDATED, NATOMAS, GOLDEN CYCLE CORP., SHATTUCK DENN, ALASKA JUNEAU, YUKON CONSOLIDATED, and MALARTIC GOLD FIELDS.

Still other firms, formerly renowned as gold mining operations, such as McINTYRE PORCUPINE and HOLLINGER

CONSOLIDATED, have been obliged by diminishing ore reserves and rising costs to engage in other mining or industrial ventures to the point where gold mining now provides only a small fraction of their income and assets.

In addition to the usual hazards of mining and the inevitability of declining ore reserves, the aforementioned mines fell victim to a political-economic system based on the phony gold-dollar exchange standard; they were forced to sell their finished product, gold, to government treasuries at a fixed price of $35 per ounce, while the politicians were free to monetize debt without limit, creating the worldwide inflation that doubled the cost of wages and mining supplies during the 1960's.

After the March 1968 gold crisis and the establishment of the two-tier system of marketing, U.S. and Canadian gold producers were allowed to market their bullion on the so-called free markets, which, as was pointed out previously, are not really free at all. At any rate, the 10 to 15 percent increase in the world gold price that resulted, on average, was insufficient or came too late to prolong the lives of many marginal mines. Even the $42-per-ounce price generally maintained by the London market during the latter half of 1971, was not enough to keep the following well-known Canadian firms in the gold mining business:

ANNCO MINES
BRALORNE CAN-FER RESOURCES
COCHENOUR WILLANS GOLD MINES
HALLNOR MINES
MARBAN GOLD MINES
UPPER CANADA MINES
WILMAR MINES
WRIGHT-HARGREAVES MINES

All of these eight companies ended gold mining operations, or were scheduled to end them, during 1971. There were many factors responsible for this heavy loss from the now very limited roster of active mines, but nearly all the mines involved were older operations that had been in production for 25 years or more—some dating back to the gold boom of the middle 1930's. Rising costs and the exhaustion of ore reserves were basic to the ending of such long and formerly profitable operations.

Some of these properties, however, still have some ore reserves, mostly of a relatively low grade, and intend to maintain their underground and surface works in a standby condition pending a higher gold price. Others have dismantled their mills and abandoned their properties altogether. If the price of gold is doubled, or more, in the next year or two, the gold properties of Wright-Hargreaves and perhaps one or two of the others may be returned to production for a time. But even then, the limited nature and generally low grade of remaining ore reserves would rank them as highly uncertain and probably short-life operations, unsuitable for general trading or investment.[1]

The high rate of attrition of gold mining enterprises during the last decade points up the dangers of investing in older mines with obviously declining ore reserves. All of the mines affected gave warning that they were heading for trouble by reporting a consistent decline in ore reserves, both in tonnage and in grade, for several years prior to their respective ends. But the closing of these mines still came as a shock to many investors (and even some investment advisers!) who did not do their homework. And the most indispensable homework for any investor is to read carefully the annual, semiannual and quarterly reports of the companies in which he has an investment position, or which he has under consideration for commitment. One should also keep closely informed about day-to-day developments by reading the financial and mining press. A suggested list of appropriate daily, weekly and monthly publications is given in the back section of this book.

Actually, the chronological age of a mine has very little direct bearing on its future. The only thing that counts is *known* ore reserves. Therefore, we must concentrate, for investment purposes, only on those mines that have proven ore reserves sufficient to maintain operations at their current rate, for another 15 to 20 years. Even when assuming strictly trading positions in the gold group, the author recommends, as a safety factor, that they be limited only to the higher grade companies—believe me they are volatile enough.

It is, of course, true that the lower-grade and marginal mines have most leverage. That is, if the price of gold is soon dramatically increased, the mines presently just getting by would show the greatest percentage of improvement in their earnings and consequently the greatest (percentage) gain in the price of their shares. But speculating in such stocks is a very risky proposition. If a mistake is made in timing the purchase, and the speculator is forced or inclined to wait for the next cyclical upswing in the gold group to bail him out, he may find instead that he has bought a ticket on a dying horse that won't make it to the quarter-post, let alone finish the race in the money.

The whole thesis of this book is that a much higher price for gold is coming and coming soon, but it is possible, I must concede, that my timing may be a year or two or even five years off schedule (although I doubt it very much). However, if I am making such an error, those with investment or even trading positions in the sound, long-life gold issues will still find ample opportunities for profit in the interim. But every year that a major increase in the price of gold is forestalled by political maneuvers or pressures will extract a further toll from among the short-life and marginal mines. On the other hand, a sky-rocketing price for gold could result in superior trading profits, at least initially, in the lower-grade issues. But don't say I didn't warn you about the risks involved.

A little more than a decade ago, a famous economist and long-established investment adviser wrote a book in which he predicted, with considerable accuracy, the sequence of events that would (and did) lead to the collapse of the postwar gold-dollar exchange standard and the fixed $35-per-ounce price for gold. But, unfortunately, many of the stocks then recommended for retention as hedges against devaluation are no longer in operation. In 1960, there were 72 operating gold mines listed on U.S. and Canadian exchanges, but by the end of 1971 only 15 remained in production.

Quite obviously, that particular investment adviser made a sizable error in timing. He underestimated the power of the political forces throughout the world constantly seeking to destroy economic and monetary freedom by first destroying the gold standard and ending completely the role of gold as money.

He also assumed that events would move much faster and gather momentum much quicker than they actually did.

I sincerely believe that I will not be similarly confounded. I did read that particular book in 1960, and, although satisfied that it was theoretically correct, was not convinced that the $35 gold price was *then* seriously or imminently threatened. But I am so convinced now. Not only has the sacrosanct $35 barrier been finally and irrevocably broken, but the antigold forces are now permanently on the defensive. They may yet delay or resist a major upward move in the currency value of gold, but they can no longer prevent it. Nevertheless, safety of capital must continue to be our primary consideration. That means buying the right stocks at the right time and avoiding all high-risk situations no matter how tempting or how urgent they may momentarily appear.

Environmental Protection a New Consideration. Although a better price structure is absolutely essential if a gold mining industry is to survive in North America, there are other problems that must also be overcome. The mining industry in general, like other ecologically hazardous occupations, will be required to bear its share of the long-term costs of protecting the environment. The Canadian mining industry as a whole (not just gold mines) is going to spend an estimated $450 to $500 million on pollution control in the next five years alone.[2] Extensive research is also being conducted to find ways of reducing or eliminating the fumes produced by smelters and other processing plants.

In the United States, the gold mining industry has already been required to meet many costly restrictions aimed at curbing or preventing environmental damage. At the Carlin open pit mine in Nevada, for example, a tailings (waste rock) disposal system had to be adopted that will eventually cost the company at least $1 million more than tailings-disposal methods formerly practiced. This was done to minimize the disturbance to existing grazing lands in the area. In another case, the famous Homestake Mine in South Dakota, the largest gold mine in the Western Hemisphere, was obliged, in 1971, to convert its extraction plant from primarily a mercury amalgamation system to an all-cyanide process. The mercury technique had to be discontinued because of the water-pollution hazard.

There is no question that pollution control will be an additional burden on the gold mining industry during the '70's, but hardly an insurmountable one, given an adequate advance in the price of gold. Obviously the marginal and smaller mines could be more adversely affected by severe antipollution laws, and this is just one more reason to have the major portion of the gold portfolio represented by the larger, stronger mines. But, on the whole, I do not believe that ecological protection requirements are a serious enough problem to deter the gold-oriented investor or trader.

Labor and Tax Problems.   One of the more persistent difficulties facing the Canadian gold mining industry, and the mining industry in general, has been a chronic shortage of skilled miners, technicians and engineers. Because most of the mines are located in relatively remote regions of the North Country, it has been hard for them to attract and retain the necessary skilled personnel. In the past, they have attempted to correct this deficiency, in part, by encouraging the immigration of experienced miners from Europe and by offering scholarships and other inducements to young Canadians interested in pursuing careers in geology or mining technology.

Their efforts, however, have not entirely relieved this particular problem, and it is interesting to note that some Canadian mining firms, having contracts for mineral deliveries to Japan and unable to meet them on time because of a shortage of skilled labor, are seriously considering the employment of Japanese miners and technicians. McIntyre Porcupine has been reported to have already begun a recruiting campaign in Japan.[3] This development, of course, is exactly in line with the forecast for Japan presented in Chapter VIII.

Labor difficulties of the more conventional kind, resulting in a continuous pressure for higher wages and greater benefits, have not been too disruptive in recent years, although this is a highly unionized industry. But the demand for annual increases regardless of the profitability of the industry, now apparently inevitable in every labor contract, has been, and will continue to be, a factor depressing earnings. Again, only a higher gold price can effectively relieve this situation. One encouraging note is that some hard-rock mines have successfully introduced an entirely new production-incentive system by placing all mine personnel on a salary-plus-profit-sharing basis instead of the conventional hourly wage arrangement.

Another very real threat to the mining industry has been the attitude of certain segments of government regarding taxes. Some local authorities, apparently not yet acquainted with the old proverb about killing geese laying golden eggs, have been pressing for higher assessments and higher taxes on mining properties in recent years. And, on the national level, there are those misguided or opportunist legislators and bureaucrats who periodically raise the cry about ending the special tax exemptions presently allowed the extractive industries. They would end or reduce the so-called "depletion allowances" that recognize and give credit for the self-consuming nature of mineral production in which part of the "income" reported by a mine actually represents a permanent depletion of a capital asset (that is, the ore body). Furthermore, they have even threatened to end the present tax exemptions on income spent on geologic exploration for new ore bodies—surely a short-sighted and self-defeating viewpoint.

However, it is the author's belief that labor and tax problems, over the long term, present no serious threat to the gold mining industry. In fact, I believe that the future will see increasing government assistance to this industry, because it will soon be demonstrated that domestic resources for gold are indispensable to the economic and financial future of both Canada and the United States. But, for the short term, periodic threats from these quarters will no doubt continue to add to the volatility of North American gold stocks. As was noted in Chapter IX, this group of stocks is subject to frequent and extreme moves from undervaluation to overvaluation and vice versa. Most people tend to buy and sell gold stocks on an emotional basis (a practice we must absolutely avoid!).

But far from being discouraged by the extreme volatility of the North American gold group, the successful gold-oriented trader or investor welcomes it for the opportunities for profit it provides. Before we review the possible trading and investing approaches to North American gold stocks, however, let us take a preliminary look at their present availability.

THE CURRENT NORTH AMERICAN GOLD SCENE

Since the world entered its new monetary era subsequent to August 15, 1971, the number of publicly owned gold mining enterprises with common stocks available for speculative holding, trading or investment purposes has dwindled to a mere handful. *Fig. 23* shows all primary gold producers listed on American and Canadian stock exchanges, with the exception of the American-South African Investment Trust, which is included in Part 3 of this book. These stocks will be reviewed individually in the next two chapters. In addition, there are several integrating mining and mining-investment combines that still have producing gold mines as subsidiaries or investment holdings. This group is presented in *Fig. 24,* in order to alert the reader to the fact that, whatever other merits these companies may have, and they may be considerable, their gold mining interests are not sufficient to consider or evaluate them as gold mining stocks.

Another important factor in total gold production in North America is by-product gold recovered in the course of copper and silver mining operations. While the percentage of gold found in these ores is small, it is often possible to recover substantial quantities during the refining stages, due to the vast amounts of ore processed to obtain copper, silver and other nonferrous metals. Actually, the giant copper complexes, such as Anaconda and Kennecot, rank among the major producers of gold in North America. But again, such companies cannot be considered as gold mining investments because their success as investments depends almost solely on the demand for copper and other metals. The price of gold would have to reach unrealistically high levels to justify mining copper and other base metal ores primarily for their very low gold content.

But although the stocks listed in *Fig. 23* are the only practical candidates for direct gold investment outside of South Africa, they are, as was noted, not completely without problems for the future, even after a substantially higher price for gold is achieved.[4] But if a major devaluation of the U.S. dollar can be postponed for a considerably longer time than now seems possible, and if, somehow, the London gold price can be held below

$45 per ounce, some of the mines listed in *Fig. 23* may be forced to close during the next few years. Therefore, investing or even speculating in North American gold shares cannot be done in a casual or off-handed manner; this is obviously no place for a "lock them in the box and forget them attitude."

Nevertheless, North American golds have made very handsome profits for many in the past and I believe they will continue to do so in the future, if they are approached with the proper investment techniques. Actually, as trading vehicles, they are much preferred over the South Africans, because of their ready marketability through the major stock exchanges. The South African stocks, while generally superior as long-term investments, are handicapped by being traded only in the Over-the-Counter (OTC) market.*

The main point to remember about the North American gold group is its volatility. Consequently, these stocks, whether acquired for investment, speculative or trading purposes, must be bought at the right time. The correct timing of both purchases and sales, but particularly the former, is probably the most important single factor in the success of a gold-stock portfolio. We have already reviewed some of the aspects of timing in Chapter X and elsewhere, but I stress it again, because correct timing is the one market technique that is vital to all three of the basic types of stock market activity: *investment, trading* and *speculation.*

At this point, perhaps we should define our terms, since all of these operations tend to overlap somewhat in practice and certainly do so in the minds of the investing public. However, I believe that the following distinctions can be made:

Investment —The purchase of stocks or other capital goods with the intention of retaining them as long-term assets, in the belief that they will increase in relative value or provide a generous income, or both. The investor seeks to attain his goals with a minimum of risk to investment capital.

Trading —The frequent buying and selling of stocks for capital gain based on the anticipation of short- and in-

*The OTC market will be reviewed in Chapter XIV.

Fig. 23

OPERATING PRIMARY GOLD MINING COMPANIES
WITH UNITED STATES AND CANADIAN EXCHANGE LISTINGS—1971

Canadian Companies	Location of Mine	Mill Capacity Tons per Day	Price per Share High	Low	Earnings Per Share	Dividends Per Share	Exchange Listing
Aunor Gold Mines Ltd.	NE Ontario	760	3	– 1-3/4	$0.09	$0.04	TSE
Camflo Mines	Quebec	1,000	4	– 2	0.20	0.10	TSE; CSE
Campbell Red Lake Mines	NW Ontario	825	35	– 18-1/4	0.48	0.45	NYSE; TSE
Dickenson Mines Ltd.	NW Ontario	480	2-1/2	– 1	0.14½	0.06	TSE
Dome Mines	NE Ontario	2,000	67-3/4	– 45	1.64	0.80	NYSE; TSE
Giant Yellow-knife Mines	NW Territory	1,200	12-5/8	– 6-1/4	0.31	0.40	ASE; TSE
Kerr Addison Mines Ltd.	NE Ontario	4,000	14-1/2	– 5-1/2	0.75	0.56	TSE
Madsen Red Lake Mines	NW Ontario	825	1-1/2	– 5/8	d0.12	0.03	TSE
Pamour Porcu-pine Mines	NE Ontario	1,800	2-5/8	– 1-3/4	0.18	0.15	TSE; CSE
Sigma Mines	Quebec	1,400	5	– 2-1/2	0.26	0.25	TSE
Pato Consoli-dated Gold	Colombia, S.A.	Dredging Operations	10-5/8	– 4-7/8	d0.04	0.20	ASE; TSE

U.S. Companies

Day Mines Inc.	Idaho & Washington	500	16-1/2 – 5-1/2	d0.03	Nil	ASE
Homestake Mining Co.	S. Dakota	6,000	31-7/8 – 16-1/8	0.61	0.40	NYSE

Notes:

1. *Earnings* and *Dividends* stated for calendar year 1970 ("d" indicates deficit).
2. *Price per Share* stated in terms of high and low price for period Dec. 31, 1969 to Dec. 31, 1971.
3. *Exchange Listings:*

   NYSE – New York Stock Exchange
   ASE – American Stock Exchange
   TSE – Toronto Stock Exchange
   CSE – Canadian Stock Exchange

Fig. 24

INTEGRATED MINING COMPANIES AND CONGLOMERATES
WITH GOLD-PRODUCING SUBSIDIARIES

Company	General Offices	Principal Interests	Percent of Income From Gold	Exchange Listings
Cominco Ltd.	Montreal, Que.	Lead, Zinc & Copper	2.5	ASE; TSE
Hollinger Mines Ltd. (Formerly Hollinger Consolidated Gold Mines Ltd.)	Toronto, Ont.	Iron Mining & General Exploration	5.0	ASE; TSE
McIntyre Porcupine Mines Ltd.	Toronto, Ont.	Coal Mining, Nickel & Copper	3.0	NYSE; TSE
Newmont Mining Corp.	New York, N.Y.	Copper, Oil & Gas (Owns Magma Copper)	3.0	NYSE
Noranda Mines Ltd.	Toronto, Ont.	Copper Mining & Misc. Mining Investment	2.0	TSE
Teck Corp. Ltd. (Formerly Teck-Hughes Gold Mines Ltd.)	Toronto, Ont.	Oil, Gas & Base Metal Mining	3.0	TSE

termediate-term movements generated primarily by *technical conditions* within the market itself or affecting certain stocks or groups of stocks.

Speculation —The purchase (or selling short) of stocks in anticipation of major movements in price due to some fundamental change in general economic conditions or in the prospects of a particular stock or stock group. Speculation generally involves the holding of "leverage" stocks having a higher-than-usual potential for capital gain, but also carrying a correspondingly greater degree of risk.

Perhaps the most common point of misunderstanding concerns the differences between a trader and a speculator. It must be conceded that all forms of stock commitment are, in the broadest sense, forms of speculation in that they all involve taking risks against an unknown future. But the true trader never deals in high risk, high leverage, "speculative"stocks, but confines his operations to the best known, most respected and, consequently, the most marketable stocks in the group he trades in. A trader is primarily attuned to the condition of the market, rather than concerned with the prospects of individual corporations. He assumes his stocks represent good, sound companies, the leaders in their field. What he tries to determine is whether they are currently being overvalued or undervalued and to what degree.

A good trading stock has a broad public and institutional following, it is listed on a major exchange and has been publicly traded for many years so as to be thoroughly "seasoned;" that is, it has established long-term patterns of behavior under varying market conditions that can be recorded, observed and studied. It has a sufficient supply of stock available to make an active market but, at the same time, is limited enough to guarantee that substantial price moves will result from significant increases in buying or selling, and, finally, it represents a fundamentally sound, stable and well-known enterprise with large capital assets that has maintained a good record of earnings and dividends for many years.

In the gold group, the following have been the favorite trading vehicles: AMERICAN SOUTH AFRICAN (NYSE), CAMP-

BELL RED LAKE MINES (NYSE), DOME MINES (NYSE), GIANT YELLOWKNIFE MINES (ASE) and HOMESTAKE MINES (NYSE). All of these will undoubtedly remain trading favorites in the future, except perhaps for Giant Yellowknife, which has been experiencing declining ore reserves and other difficulties in recent years. In my opinion, Giant is becoming more of a speculative situation rather than a trading stock. *Fig. 25* shows the twelve-year price range of the five trading favorites in the gold group.

INVESTING PRINCIPLES AND TECHNIQUES

The evidence of *Fig. 25* indicates that there was at least the *theoretical* possibility of substantial capital gains from intermediate-term (three-to-six-months) trading operations in every year since 1959, utilizing one or more of these five stocks. Since 1967, trading swings appear to be increasing in intensity. I certainly do not assume that this book will make the reader a successful stock trader. Stock trading is an art that must be learned more through actual experience than theoretical instruction, and that experience is generally acquired over a period of years rather than months. The most the author can do here is to show something of the nature of gold stocks and point out their adaptability for trading as well as investing purposes.

Actually, there are probably no more than four or five out of every hundred potential stock investors who have the personality, the type of mind and the emotional stability required to be an active and consistently successful stock trader. If you are one of those fortunate few, then no doubt you have already recognized from what you have read so far, that gold stocks offer excellent opportunities for intermediate-term trading. But even for seasoned traders, I recommend that some of the basic capital and part of trading profits be regularly committed to long-term investment-quality gold issues over the next few years, or until we return to a workable gold standard and reasonable monetary stability.

Whether to use a strictly long-term-investment approach in acquiring a gold portfolio or whether to combine investment with an active short- or intermediate-term trading plan, is of course a decision the individual investor has to make, depend-

Fig. 25

PRICE RANGE OF LEADING GOLD STOCKS
1961–1971

Stock:	American South African (ASA)		Campbell Red Lake (CRK)		Dome Mines (DM)		Giant Yellowknife (GYK)		Homestake Mines* (HM)	
Ticker Symbol:										
Year	High	Low	High	Low	High	Low	High	Low	High	Low
1961	13-5/8	9	18-3/8	11-3/8	28-1/2	20	15	9-1/2	26-1/8	20-3/8
1962	16-5/8	10-3/8	17-5/8	12-3/8	31-3/4	22-5/8	14-1/2	8-1/2	29-3/8	20-1/2
1963	19-3/4	13-1/4	17	12-3/4	33-1/8	23-1/8	12-5/8	9-5/8	26-1/4	20-1/2
1964	25-1/8	14-3/8	24-7/8	13-1/2	41-1/4	25-1/8	18-1/8	9-7/8	26-7/8	19-3/4
1965	39-1/8	20-3/4	25	17-3/4	42-7/8	32-1/4	18-5/8	12-1/2	24	19
1966	44-5/8	27-3/4	27-3/4	16-5/8	51-3/8	35-3/4	15-1/2	6-3/4	27-3/8	17-1/8
1967	58-7/8	30	28-3/4	16-3/4	58-3/4	37-5/8	11-1/2	7-1/4	33-3/4	18-7/8
1968	82	49-1/4	47-1/4	24	82-1/4	46-1/4	15-3/8	8-1/4	46-1/2	21-7/8
1969	69-7/8	26	40-3/8	14-1/2	89	42-3/4	17-1/8	7	46	16
1970	49-1/2	27-3/4	34-3/4	15-3/8	67-3/4	45	12	7	27-7/8	16-1/8
1971	53-7/8	31-3/4	35	18-1/4	73-5/8	49-1/2	12-5/8	6-1/4	31-7/8	16-5/8

*Homestake adjusted for 2 for 1 stock split.

ing on his financial and personal situation. As a general rule, the more inexperienced one is, and the more limited the investment capital, the more conservative should be the investment technique. If you are very inexperienced and have only limited capital, concentrate on buying only the best stocks—those that are designated as *INVESTMENT GRADE* in the individual stock reviews found in the remainder of this book—and plan on holding them for several years. Investment portfolios should not be completely liquidated until (a) the stocks show a long-term capital gain of at least 100 percent or more, (b) the dollar has been devalued by 50 percent or more and (c) at least two years have passed since a new fixed gold parity for the dollar was established and maintained.[5]

Stocks that are rated *FOR TRADING AND INVESTMENT* in the individual reviews can be acquired with caution but should never be chased when they are rising rapidly on heavy volume. They should be bought, whether for trading or investment, only on substantial price concessions and at low points in the trading cycle described in Chapter IX. Stocks rated *SPECULATIVE* may be included in an investment portfolio only if the investor can safely assume the higher risk. But in any case, speculative stocks should not make up more than 25 percent (in terms of currency values) of any long-term portfolio. If one can afford some risk, however, I believe that some of the speculative stocks (and they will be pointed out in the reviews) are definitely worth a modest commitment.

Probably the safest and most rewarding method of stock operations is more or less a combination investment-trading approach. This technique is basically to buy for long-term holding good quality investment issues, plus a few of the better speculations if one can afford extra risk, but to plan on taking *some* profits whenever a major opportunity presents itself. For example, if one has been able to accumulate a portfolio during quiet markets and at reasonable prices, and then experiences an occurrence of gold panic or cyclical buying that drives prices up 50 to 100 percent or more to what appears to be an emotional buying climax, by all means plan on taking at least part of the profits. Perhaps one-third of the portfolio should be liquidated under these conditions. The more emotional and

exciting the previous rise, the greater percentage of the portfolio that should be sold.

At least half of the *profits* (after taxes) from such long-term
profit taking should be retained for reinvestment when calm
returns and prices retreat to more reasonable levels. But don't
be too anxious to get back in after what appears to be a buying
climax. Gradually recommit the liquidated capital plus the
one-half share of profits during the markdown and bottom
phase of the cycle. If you don't think you can correctly feel the
actual bottom, begin reinvesting funds automatically after a
30-percent decline from the previous peak, and become fully
invested only after any decline reaches or exceeds 50 percent
from a climax or cylical top.

As an example of the "automatic" guideline, let us assume
our old favorite Campbell Red Lake (CRK) undergoes a buying
climax at a cyclical top and distribution takes place at the $40
to $42 level. And let us further assume that we correctly an-
ticipated what was occurring and sold some of our stock at the
$40 level. Using the automatic guideline, we would not begin to
reinvest in these shares until they had declined to the $28 level.
At that point we would commit 50 percent of the reinvestment
capital. At the $24 level we would commit another 25 percent
and at the $20 level or below, the final 25 percent. The prices
given in the foregoing example are, of course, purely hypothetical and designed only to illustrate the automatic reinvestment
guideline. Another factor to consider is, as was noted in Chapter IX, the time element of the cycle. If the top occurs in late
summer or early fall, and a marked decline ensues, it will probably be better to withhold *all* reinvestment funds until late
December in order to take advantage of the inevitable tax-loss
selling.

Taking profits on a single speculative stock, however, may
have little to do with general or cyclical market movements,
but may be caused by some specific development (such as a new
ore discovery) affecting only that particular stock. In the latter
case, if you develop a substantial (100 percent or more) profit
in a single stock over a relatively short period of time, don't get
greedy—*take part of it.* That way you can have your cake and
eat it too. If the stock continues to rise you will still be in for

further gains, but if the bubble should suddenly burst and the stock falls back to reality you will still have some money.

For example, if you have acquired 500 shares of a speculative stock and it doubles in price, sell two or three hundred. If it goes still higher, say by another 30 to 50 percent, sell another hundred. Save the last hundred until you feel quite sure that the party is over. If you have only 100 shares in a similar situation and it doubles or more, sell 50 shares even if you can't detect any apparent climax buying. Save the second fifty until you are convinced that the rise has ended for the time being.

Most inexperienced investors have a harder time bringing themselves to sell something now and then, than to continue buying. But every holding should be considered a candidate for sale if and when it reaches its maximum potential—just when that occurs, however, is no easy task to determine. That is why I recommend a combination *trading-investment* approach, which liquidates *part* of the portfolio, at what appear to be cyclical tops within the gold group, but almost never all of it. This does not mean that the great majority of investors should attempt to become professional traders—far from it. But we can trade or "cash in" on the obviously big moves while ignoring short-term and intermediate fluctuations.

The true trader, of course, is primarily concerned with the technical condition of the market itself or his stock groups. He tries to make sure that his stocks always represent good fundamental values so as not to have any unexpected external events interfere with his trading plan. The speculator, on the other hand, bases his judgments and evaluations primarily on factors external to the market, such as the earnings potential of a specific stock under certain conditions or the effect of changes in general economic conditions on a particular industry, etc.

The gold investor, like the speculator, is primarily interested in "fundamentals," or external factors directly affecting stock holdings, except that the investor limits his risk by concentrating on safer, less volatile issues. Among the fundamentals considered by the investor before choosing a stock are ore reserves, the estimated life of the mine, other holdings and investments of the mining company, its current financial status, its earnings and dividend record, and the quality of management. But, in addition, the investor should be aware of the market cycle and the so-called technical factors that can, in themselves, cause substantial swings in the prices of gold shares, as well as intensify movements originated by some external stimulus. Now the author admits that his *investment-trading* technique is not simply a mechanical process, but one that works best when the investor has some degree of market sophistication. However, for the inexperienced, the program can be summed up as follows:

BASIC INVESTMENT-TRADING METHOD FOR GOLD STOCKS
1. Buy on extreme weakness.
2. Sell *part* of holdings on extreme strength.
3. Convert *part* of profits from each move into permanent, long-term, nonstock investments: *gold coins, silver coins, selected real estate, art objects, antiques, rare coins, etc.*
4. Spend some of the profits on yourself (and family) for: *education, travel, vacations, entertainment, new clothes, etc.*
5. Reinvest balance of profits and liquidated funds at intervals during and after major market corrections.
6. Maintain adequate cash reserves, so that the investment program will not have to be disturbed frequently to obtain cash for noninvestment purposes.
7. Become fully invested only after major market declines. Never become completely sold out.

There are two exceptions to the seven rules of the investment-trading method. (1) During periods of hyperinflation, all attempts to take partial profits in periods of extreme strength are suspended and (2) following any *major* devaluation of the dollar to a new *fixed* gold parity, the trading part of the program is also suspended, for at least a two-year period following the devaluation.

For the purpose of definition, hyperinflation may be assumed whenever the rise in the general level of prices reaches a rate equal to 15 percent or more per year.[6]

A major devaluation would be one in which the dollar price of gold is advanced, officially, to the $70 level or higher *in a single move*, or any other official act, such as the creation of a gold-based "Eurocurrency," that, in effect, raises the international price of gold by 100 percent or more.

Under conditions of a floating dollar and other major currencies, or in the event of a series of small devaluations, the investment-trading method should yield superior results.

One of the major advantages of this method, to the author at least, is that it calls for making half of the "temporary" profits permanent, by transferring 50 percent (after taxes) of the profits from each trading move into nonstock areas (see items 3 and 4). Item 4 of the method, that which suggests using part of one's profits for strictly personal benefit and/or self-improvement, is the one that is probably the most overlooked by successful traders and investors. But to me, at any rate, it is a most important one. The tendency to try for maximum leverage and the greatest gain by continuing to reinvest 100 percent of profits (or dividends) is an all-too-frequent human failing, but one that is surely self-defeating in the end.

To my mind there is nothing more futile in this life than to amass wealth, or try to, just for the sake of having it, or in order to see just how much one can accumulate before being obliged to depart (without it) from this vale of tears. So whenever you get a nice windfall from the stock market, spend a little on yourself or your family. And if you feel that you have been especially fortunate, donate a little to your favorite charity as well. The "golden rule" of life calls for us to deal generously with others, but few of us can do this effectively unless we also make a habit of behaving generously toward ourselves.

Therefore, don't overlook item number 4 on the program; it is the only area of investment where I can absolutely guarantee that you will never experience a loss—you can't go wrong investing in yourself. But please note again that rules 3 and 4 call for withdrawing half of the *profits* from any trade, not half of the total capital recovered from a sale. And, of course, sales should not be made unless they have the promise of substantial profit. However, even if your profit from a trade is very modest, due to a limitation of basic capital or through bad timing, the method should still be followed, if only for the experience of it. If you make only $100 on a trade, take $50 and spend it for an evening's entertainment, or buy a new article of apparel, or just add a couple of books to your library or a coin or two to your collection, if you have one. You will be surprised at how "successful" you will feel, as an investor, after doing this.

However, for investors not wishing to attempt *any* trading, and this is certainly a valid option for those with limited investment capital or who simply do not feel that their judgment or emotional makeup is adaptable to the uncertainties of an active market, the model portfolios presented in Chapter XVI may be used as a guide for straight, long-term investing as well as for the investment-trading approach. But even a long-term investment-holding portfolio requires continuous supervision. There are times when a weakening or lacklustre issue should be sold and replaced by a stronger or more promising one, even if there is no other reason for action. Therefore, the general principles of portfolio management will also be reviewed in Chapter XVI.

Notes:

Chapter X

1. That is unsuitable as gold mining ventures. Most of these companies are still in business and have other profitable interests and investments. However it is not within the scope of this work to evaluate stocks involved in nongold activities.

2. *Northern Miner,* April 29, 1971.

3. *California Mining Journal,* November, 1971.

4. There are a few Australian and other mines in the Western Pacific area (such as Fiji Gold) but, in the author's opinion, they lack suitable marketability in the U.S.

5. For U.S. tax purposes, long-term capital gains are defined as profits resulting from the sale of capital assets (including stocks) held for more than six months. One-half of long-term capital gains are generally exempt from income tax. Short-term capital gains or profits obtained from the sale of assets held for less than six months, however, are fully taxable as ordinary income.

6. The U.S. Dept. of Labor Consumer Price Index has been a reasonably reliable barometer of inflation in the past, and its figures are released monthly. But there is no guarantee that in the future it won't be "doctored" to make the rate of inflation appear to be less than is actually the case. Therefore, consider private as well as official statistics in times of obvious deterioration in the value of money. Actually, the "official" statistics on such things as federal debt, balance of payments deficits, gold reserves, unemployment, housing starts and numerous other key economic indicators are already being distorted and gerrymandered to make them appear less ominous than they really are.

XI

UNITED STATES GOLD STOCKS

"In prosperity, prepare for a change; in adversity, hope for one."
—JAMES BURGH

GOLD mining in the United States has had a long and dramatic history. The Spanish, according to local tradition at least, were mining gold in Arizona during the early 1700's, but the first significant gold strike in what is now the United States occurred in Carrabus County, North Carolina. In 1799, Conrad Reed, a twelve-year-old son of one John Reed, a former Hessian soldier in the Revolutionary War, found a shiny rock while fishing in a local stream.[1] He took it home to his father, who, in turn, sold it to a local jeweler for $3.50, not realizing that he had parted with a 17-pound nugget worth more than $8,000. One account has it that Reed subsequently sued the jeweler and recovered $1,000, but there is no definite proof of this. At any rate, Reed soon rectified his initial mistake by ultimately digging some $10 million more in gold from his own and nearby Appalachian meadowlands.

In subsequent years other major finds were made in the area and the North Carolina gold fields became so productive that a branch of the U.S. Mint was opened at Charlotte in 1838, to permit the coinage of gold at its source.[2] The Charlotte Mint operated until the beginning of the Civil War in 1861, and, before gold was discovered in California, North Carolina remained the principal gold-producing state in the United States. Other states, however, notably Georgia and Alabama, shared in the Appalachian lode. In the latter two cases, gold strikes were made between 1820 and 1830 primarily on lands belonging to the Cherokee Indians, despite the fact that white men were, at that time, forbidden to enter or settle on these lands by treaty. Nevertheless, the clamor and trouble caused by prospectors and adventurers soon became so great that both state and Federal governments yielded to the pressure.

An "Indian Removal Act" was passed by Congress in 1830 and, by 1838, virtually all of the unfortunate Indians had been forced to leave their ancestral lands and walk the "Trail of Tears" to take up a new residence in the western "Indian Territory" set aside for them (which later became the state of Oklahoma). It is perhaps poetic justice that some of the descendants of these transplanted Cherokees later acquired considerable wealth as the result of the discovery, on their new land, of another form of gold—the black gold of oil.

Another U.S. Branch Mint was established at Dahlonega, Georgia, in 1836, and this too remained in operation until 1861.[3] Slightly more than $6 million worth of gold coins were struck at the Dahlonega Mint and approximately the same amount was coined at the Charlotte Mint during their relatively brief lifetimes. All told, the amount of gold taken from the Appalachian fields was small by modern standards, perhaps less than $60 million, but for its time it was considered a substantial amount.

The California Gold Rush of 1849 caused the abandonment of many of the Appalachian gold deposits, as miners and prospectors by the thousands deserted their jobs and struck out for the West, despite the pleas of local mine owners and geologists that they continue to work the gold resources at hand. This episode, it is said, gave rise to that immortal phrase, "But thar's gold in them thar hills!", supposedly the appeal of those urging the miners to stay.[4] Some of the better mines, however, did manage to remain in operation until the outbreak of the Civil War, but at that time the area was occupied by Confederate military forces and virtually all mining activity ceased for the duration.

After the Civil War, gold mining was resumed in the Southern Appalachians on a very reduced scale and continued sporadically until the 1930's. The Geologic Survey Offices of the three states continue to believe that significant quantities of gold still remain to be mined in this area. Weekend prospectors do bring in a trace now and then, but no serious geologic explorations on a commercial scale are presently in progress. Perhaps a much higher price for gold will bring about a renewed interest in the Southern Appalachian area.

From 1849 on, the story of gold in the United States is intimately involved with the opening and settlement of the Western Territories. The California strike was, of course, one of the greatest in world history, eclipsed only by the opening of the South African Rand in 1886. Adventurers from all over the world, as well as from east of the Mississippi, abandoned all other pursuits and flocked to California, where untold riches were to be had for the taking. So intense was this gold fever that the ships carrying would-be prospectors to San Francisco were unable to make their return voyages; their crews promptly deserted and took to the hills themselves to look for gold.

It was the greatest bonanza ever discovered, up to that time, and, in the century that followed, over $2 *billion* worth of the yellow metal was recovered from California alone. Almost coincidental with the California find was the Australian Gold Rush, begun in 1850, which netted the world another billion in gold from the fields of Victoria and New South Wales. As in all new gold strikes, the initial riches, found in stream beds and other placer deposits easily accessible to the hordes of small miners and prospectors, were soon depleted. By 1870, the "easy pickin" days in California were definitely over and, by 1873, deep-lode mining surpassed placer mining in total production and from then on provided an ever-increasing share of the state's gold output.

But as gold mining became more and more a large-scale industrial enterprise in California, the prospectors, gamblers, adventurers and their painted ladies and dance-hall girls moved on—to the Cripple Creek area of Colorado, to the fabled boom towns of Arizona and Nevada and to the Black Hills of South Dakota. Wherever the cry of "Gold!" was raised anew in the

West, this unlikely vanguard of the white man's civilization surged forward in wild, uncontrollable explosions of greed, ruthless energy and a thirst for adventure, which left many more Indians victims of the white man's insatiable passion for the yellow metal. In each case, nature's lavish initial bounty was quickly skimmed, often leaving only rotting ghost towns and memories after a few years. Those few enterprises, however, that did survive were invariably deep-lode mines of considerable complexity, which sometimes had remarkably long lives and produced fabulous yields.

From 1850 to 1886, the United States led the world in output, and alone produced more than one-third of the world's annual new gold supply. From 1887 until 1930, the United States remained second among the world's gold producers, but after 1930 the United States was displaced by Canada and Russia in turn, subsiding to the fourth position after World War II and remaining there to the present.

When lode or vein mining became dominant in the United States after 1870, the fabled Mother Lode and Grass Valley Lode districts in the Sierra country of central California, the Comstock, Goldfield and Tonapah Lodes of western Nevada, and the Cripple Creek Lode in central Colorado were all large producing areas, each supporting numerous rich mines, many with names famous in the history of the Old West. Among them were the Orient, Carson Hill, Utica, Argonaut, Sixteen-to-One, Central Eureka, Keystone, North Star and Empire mines of California, the Bullion Monarch, Blue Star and Manhattan mines of Nevada and the Caribou, Ajax and Carlton mines in Colorado.

THE WORLD GOLD MINING SCENE AFTER 1850

Total world gold production advanced from an annual rate of around 2.5 million ounces in 1840 to more than 6 million ounces per year in 1860, due largely to the California and Australian discoveries. From 1860 to 1890, world output remained relatively stable, averaging between 5 and 6 million ounces annually. Beginning about 1891, however, world gold production began another major period of expansion as a result of the discovery and development of the South African fields and the Alaska-Yukon Gold Rush of 1896. The latter was noted for the riches of the initial (placer) discoveries and for the hardships endured by the thousands of miners and prospectors, both professional and amateur, who flocked to the frozen North in search of fortune.

In the Yukon Territory, a single pan of river sand sometimes yielded as much as 15 ounces of gold to those fortunate few who were the first to work the virgin streams. But like all placer deposits, the fabulous initial bounty was exhausted within a very few years and the remainder had to be recovered through large-scale dredging operations, which continued at a gradually declining rate over the next half-century.

New methods of recovery and extraction, notably the cyanide process that came into general use around 1900, made possible the recovery of gold from low-grade ores and ores containing very minute particles of gold. Consequently, during the twentieth century, for the first time in history, the production of gold became largely a technical-industrial process. Annual output reached a peak level in 1915, for both the United States and the world, and then declined until 1922. Since then it has increased steadily, on a world basis, except for the major interruption caused by World War II. The newer South African mines accounted for nearly all of the increase in the postwar years and these mines have been the most prolific in history.

A new era of gold production began with the devaluation of the U.S. dollar in 1934 and the resulting increase in the basic world gold price from $20.67 to $35 per troy ounce. Annual world output soared to a new all-time high of 42,270,000 troy ounces in 1940, which was 66 percent above the predevaluation record of 25,367,000 ounces established in 1933. The coming of World War II, however, caused a temporary but severe setback in gold output, and dealt a heavy blow to the gold mining industry, particularly in the United States. After the war, a record surge in output from the South African mines lifted annual world totals to record highs, year after year, exceeding 50 million ounces per annum by 1970. *Fig. 26,* ANNUAL WORLD GOLD PRODUCTION, 1850–1970, illustrates the intensity of the wartime decline and dramatic postwar recovery.

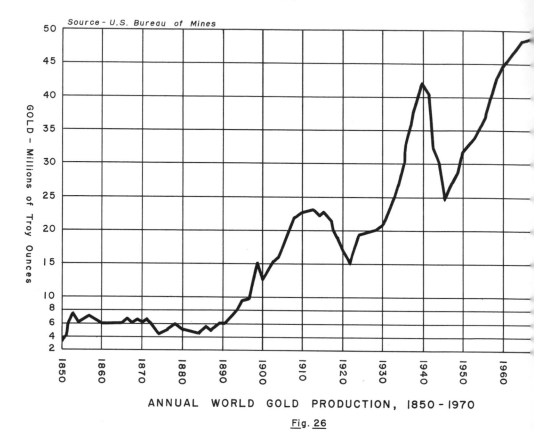

ANNUAL WORLD GOLD PRODUCTION, 1850-1970

Fig. 26

UNITED STATES GOLD PRODUCTION
1905 – 1963

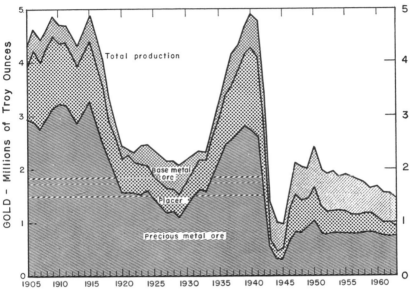

Fig. 27

Gold production in the United States reached a peak of nearly 5 million ounces per year in 1915, but was drastically reduced almost immediately thereafter by the currency inflation resulting from World War I, which made many of the older mines in the West no longer economical to operate. The Great Depression of the 1930's and the devaluation of the U.S. dollar from $20.67 to $35 per ounce of gold on January 31, 1934 brought about a sharp but very temporary revival of the U.S. gold mining industry, and the former peak of 4.9 million ounces annually was slightly bettered in 1940. However, World War II and War Production Board Order L–208, which declared gold mining a non-essential industry, sent production plummeting to a mere 20 percent of the prewar high, most of it obtained as a byproduct of base metal mining. A postwar recovery high of 2.4 million ounces per year was reached in 1950, but by the middle 1960's production had levelled off to an annual rate of about 1.7 million ounces.

U.S. GOLD PRODUCTION IN THE TWENTIETH CENTURY

Following the peak production year of 1915, which saw a yield of nearly 5 million ounces, the output from U.S. mines declined rapidly, due in no small part to the closing of marginal mines unable to operate in the inflationary climate that arose out of World War I. By 1920, annual U.S. production had been reduced to 50 percent of the 1915 level. It then continued to decline, but at a far more gradual rate, reaching a low point in that memorable year of 1929.

The Depression and the 1934 devaluation of the dollar brought about a vigorous reversal of the downtrend of the previous 14 years, and, by 1940, U.S. gold production had reached an all-time high, exceeding slightly the previous peak recorded in 1915 (See *Fig. 27,* U.S. GOLD PRODUCTION, 1905–1963). This prosperity for gold miners and investors, however, was short-lived. In that same year of 1940, the United States moved toward a war economy, and rising costs soon began to curtail domestic gold mining operations. In 1942, the bottom fell out. War Production Board Order L-208, issued that year, stopped all primary gold mining in the United States, declaring it a nonessential industry.

The avowed purpose of L-208 was to divert manpower and mining equipment into the production of minerals considered more directly essential to the war effort, such as copper, lead, zinc, iron, etc. The overall effectiveness of this action for the war effort is still the subject of dispute, but the results for the gold mining industry were catastrophic.[5] Some 9,500 gold mining operations were shut down as a result of the Board's order and the only gold produced during the war years came as a by-product of base-metal mining.

In mid-1945, Order L-208 was rescinded, but the death knell had already rung, in the form of inflation, for a vast majority of the mines closed in 1942. Most of them were unable to reopen because material and labor costs had doubled or tripled during the war years, while the price of gold remained fixed.[6] Furthermore the years of idleness had caused such deterioration in both plants and workings that, in most cases, a prohibitively large expense would have been required for rehabilitation.

Therefore, gold mining was resumed on a greatly reduced scale in the United States after the war and continued to decline slowly thereafter. (See *Fig. 28*, U.S. GOLD PRODUCTION IN MILLIONS OF FINE OUNCES, 1953–1970.) Since 1960, output has remained more or less constant, as the closing of older lode mines has been offset by the opening of two new open-pit mines in Nevada.

Fig. 28

U.S. GOLD PRODUCTION
In Millions of Fine Ounces
1953–1970

Year	Output
1953	2.0
1954	1.8
1955	1.9
1956	1.8
1957	1.8
1958	1.7
1959	1.6
1960	1.7
1961	1.5
1962	1.5
1963	1.5
1964	1.5
1965	1.7
1966	1.7
1967	1.5
1968	1.5
1969	1.7
1970	1.7

The Current Scene.   Investors hoping to include a representation of the U.S. gold mining industry in their portfolios will find (as of 1971) a drastically limited selection of such companies available. Only two U.S. companies are currently considered to be primary gold producers: HOMESTAKE MINING COMPANY, listed on the New York Stock Exchange and DAY MINES, INC., traded on the American Stock Exchange. Even in these two cases, gold mining revenues contributed only 36 percent of income to the former and 18 percent to the latter. The two other U.S. gold developments that contribute significantly to current output, the newly activated Carlin and Cortez open-pit mines in Nevada, are wholly-owned subsidiaries of large investment trusts and provide less than 5 percent of the total income earned by their parent corporations. Consequently, such trusts or hᴏlding companies can hardly be considered as gold-oriented investments.

The present attempts by the U.S. Government to "manage" the economy or, more accurately, to manage the inflation process, casts a cloud on investment in *any* U.S. corporation. If profits and dividends are to be controlled indefinitely, it becomes very difficult to estimate the investment potential of a given stock. Nevertheless, on the grounds that economic controls have never proven very effective in the long run, they will not be considered in the following reviews of operating, listed U.S. gold produers:

UNITED STATES GOLD MINING COMPANIES

HOMESTAKE MINING COMPANY (HM)

Capitalization

LONG-TERM DEBT	$19,350,126
PREFERRED STOCK	None
COMMON STOCK	Authorized: 10 million shares
	Issued: 5,568,853 shares.
EXCHANGE LISTINGS	New York Stock Exchange, Midwest Stock Exchange and Spokane Stock Exchange.
PRICE RANGE (1971)	31-7/8–16-5/8
DIVIDEND (1971)	$0.40 ($0.10 quarterly).

History.   Incorporated in 1877, Homestake is not only the largest, but by far the longest-lived, gold mining enterprise in the U.S. Located at Lead, South Dakota, the Homestake Mine itself produced 578,644 ounces of gold and 116,680 ounces of silver from 1,954,129 tons of ore in 1970. Average grade at mill-head was 0.325 ounces (gold) per ton. Gold recovered averaged 0.296 ounces per ton. Production of gold at the Homestake Mine alone amounted to 34 percent of total U.S. output for 1970. Except for the years 1943 through 1945, dividends have been paid continuously since 1878 and averaged 74 percent of earnings from 1965 through 1970.

Fundamental Position.　Homestake, while the largest U.S. gold producer, is also a major producer of uranium through subsidiary mines and holdings. The 50-percent-owned Missouri lead-zinc mine and smelter that went into production in 1969 is expected to contribute to earnings on an increasing scale in future years. The Company is also engaged in an active program of mineral exploration in the U.S., Canada and Australia. Other interests include brick manufacturing and sand and gravel production.

Operating revenues for the entire corporation in 1970 were derived 36 percent from gold, 39 percent from uranium, 16 percent from lead and zinc and 4 percent from brick and aggregate products.

Financial Position.　As of December 31, 1970, tax-loss carryforwards totaled about $6 million, available through 1974. Unused investment-tax credits amounted to $1.5 million.

Homestake holds $1 million worth of commercial paper that has been defaulted as a result of the Penn Central bankruptcy.

The Company announced on November 1, 1970, that a program for the development of the deeper levels of the Lead gold mine would cost about $8 million over the next five years.

Ore Reserves.　At the beginning of 1971, measured ore reserves at the Lead gold mine totaled 9.04 million tons with an estimated (millhead) grade of 0.325 ounces per ton.

The projected development of the mine from the present 4,850-foot level to the 7,400-foot level over the next decade is expected to encounter "better-than-average" grade ore, judging from preliminary test drilling.

INCOME STATISTICS (per share)*

Year	Earn's	Div's	Price Range High	Low	P.E. Ratio High	Low
1961	$1.25	$0.98	26-1/8 –	20-3/8	21 –	16
1962	1.36	0.78	29-3/8 –	20-1/2	22 –	15
1963	0.98	0.78	26-1/4 –	20-1/2	27 –	21
1964	1.09	0.78	26-7/8 –	19-3/4	25 –	18
1965	1.13	0.78	26-1/2 –	21-1/8	24 –	19
1966	0.83	0.78	27-3/8 –	17-1/8	33 –	20

1967	0.68	0.39**	33-3/4 – 18-7/8	51 – 28
1968	0.54	0.40	46-1/2 – 21-7/8	86 – 41
1969	0.56	0.40	46 – 16	82 – 29
1970	0.61	0.40	27-7/8 – 16-1/8	46 – 26

* Adjusted for 2 for 1 stock split in 1968 and 2 percent stock dividend in 1967.
**Plus 2 percent stock dividend.

Rating:　TRADING—INVESTMENT

Comment:　Despite the declining trend of earnings and dividends over the last decade, the ample ore reserves and future promise of HM make it quite attractive for both long-term investment and intermediate trading. Financial position of the Company appears sound (despite the Penn Central blunder), but development expenses over the next few years may continue to restrain earnings and dividends. Nevertheless, HM must be considered an excellent (long-term) devaluation-inflation hedge and investment. Purchases made at low (under 25) price-to-earnings (P.E.) ratios should provide ample margin of safety. The additional capitalization authorized in 1968 may be intended for future acquisitions.

DAY MINES, INC. (DMI)

Capitalization

LONG-TERM DEBT	None
PREFERRED STOCK	None
COMMON STOCK	2,919,536 shares.
EXCHANGE LISTING	American Stock Exchange, Spokane Stock Exchange
PRICE RANGE (1971)	13-5/8–5-3/8
DIVIDENDS (Last)	Paid $0.15 at year end 1969.

History.　Incorporated in 1947, Day Mines, together with associated companies, mines gold, silver, lead, zinc and copper in the Coeur d'Alene district of Idaho and in the State of Washington. A substantial amount of unexplored acreage is also held by Day in these areas. Cash dividends were paid from 1948 to 1951 and from 1956 to 1969. After several years of declining profits, a loss was reported for 1970 and the usual year-end dividend was omitted.

Fundamental Position. In 1970, Day Mines derived 48 percent of its operating revenues from silver, 18 percent from gold, 17 percent from lead, 11 percent from zinc and 6 percent from copper. Day's share of production from the Gold Dollar Mine amounted to 10,273 tons, averaging 1.1 ounces of gold and 4.2 ounces of silver per ton. At properties being mined as joint ventures, DMI's share of production totaled 17,108 tons, averaging 0.5 ounces of gold and 3.1 ounces of silver per ton. Other operations and joint ventures produced additional amounts of silver, lead and zinc.

Financial Position. At the end of 1970, Day Mines held shares in other mining companies having an estimated market value of $3,154,066. Net working capital was $1,915,017. Net asset value per common share was $2.33. Employees (1971): 88.

Ore Reserves: At the beginning of 1971, measured reserves of both gold-silver ore and base-metal ores were sufficient for three full years of production at current rates.

INCOME STATISTICS (per share)

Year	Earnings	Dividends*	Price Range
1963	$0.30	$0.10	6-1/4 – 5
1964	0.27	0.35	12-1/4 – 4-3/4
1965	0.11	0.20	11-3/8 – 6-3/4
1966	0.10	0.35	18-3/8 – 7-3/8
1967	0.25	0.25	18-5/8 – 12-1/2
1968	0.22	0.15	29-1/4 – 16-1/4
1969	0.17	0.15	23-7/8 – 10-3/4
1970	d0.03	Nil	16-1/2 – 7

*Dividends include special non-taxable and capital gains distributions.

Rating: SPECULATIVE

Comment: The declining percentage of income from gold production may eventually convert this company entirely into a silver-base metal operation. Future gold prospects depend on what may be found in the unexplored acreage and on a gold price high enough to warrant the reactivation of gold mining properties in the Knob Hill and Gold King areas of Washington. But for the present, DMI is unappealing as a gold speculation.

FUTURE PROBLEMS AND POSSIBILITIES

Since John Reed's first strike in 1799, gold has been mined in commercial quantities in 25 of the 50 United States. The principal states in order of total output were California, Colorado, South Dakota, Alaska, Nevada, Montana and Utah.

The present (1971) order of production places South Dakota first, with Nevada, Utah, Arizona and Washington following. Almost the entire output of Utah and Arizona, however, comes as a by-product of the mining and smelting of base-metal ores.

For the period 1968 through 1971, gold production for the United States was derived 35 percent from base-metal ores as a by-product and the remaining 65 percent from primary gold deposits. Approximately 75 percent of total output for the period came from just three mines: the Homestake lode mine in South Dakota, the Carlin open-pit mine in Nevada and the Kennecot copper mine at Bingham, Utah.

According to the U.S. Bureau of Mines, 96 percent of presently available U.S. mineral-gold reserves, amounting to some 23 million ounces, are to be found in just two states: South Dakota and Nevada. This is the total U.S. gold resource producible, according to the Bureau, at current prices ($35 to $43 per ounce), using present technology and assuming no further depreciation of the dollar (an assumption the author would not care to make!). Another 30 million ounces is presumed to be available (at 1968–71 prices) from the processing of base-metal ores. The Bureau further estimates that an additional 214 million ounces from precious-metal ores and another 30 million from base-metal ores would become available to the United States at gold prices ranging up to $145 per ounce, again assuming no offsetting inflation of the dollar.[7]

The Bureau of Mines' estimates on the demand side project an annual domestic consumption, for industrial, commercial and scientific purposes, of about 30 million ounces by the year 2000, versus 8 million for 1971. This works out to a cumulative total demand, for the period 1972 thru 1999, of about 532 million ounces. For the rest of the world, commercial demand is expected to approach 56 million ounces by 2000, versus 24 million in 1971. Total cumulative (nonmonetary) demand for the rest of the world therefore is about 1,120 million ounces. The Bureau's projection is based on an assumption that "industrial use of gold in the rest of the world will probably not expand at rates as high as those in the United States."[8] The author certainly would not rely on such an assumption, but will accept it just for the purposes of this argument.

Total supply available to the rest of the world is estimated to come to 300 million ounces producible at 1968–71 prices and an additional 600 million ounces available at higher gold prices, ranging up to $145 per ounce. Therefore, based on U.S. Bureau of Mines' statistics and projections, the world's gold supply-demand situation for the remainder of the century can be summed up as shown in *Fig. 29,* POTENTIAL WORLD SUPPLY AND DEMAND FOR GOLD, FROM 1971 TO 2000 A.D.

Now statistical projections of future conditions, such as *Fig. 29,* cannot be regarded as highly reliable. In the first place, they cannot take account of the future course or intensity of currency inflation, and secondly, they are invariably based on mathematical extensions of current trends and conditions, which can hardly be expected to remain unaltered by changes in both technology and public preference in the years ahead. But whatever happens, it appears certain that there will be a large and constantly growing gap between world supply and demand for gold between now and the end of the present century, even with the price of gold rising to much higher levels.

Fig. 29

POTENTIAL WORLD SUPPLY AND DEMAND FOR GOLD
FROM 1971 TO 2000 A.D.*
(In Millions of Fine Ounces)

	Producible at 1968–71 Price Average	*Producible at Higher Prices***	*Overall Supply Resource*	*Cumulative Overall Demand*
United States:				532
Gold Ore	23	214	237	
By-product	30	30	60	
Rest of World:	300	600	900	1,120
TOTALS:	353	844	1,197	1,652

Notes:

*For industrial, commercial and scientific uses only, based on U.S. Bureau of Mines statistics and projections.

**At prices ranging up to $145 per ounce, in terms of constant 1968–70 dollars.

The Bureau of Mines hopes that at least part of the excess of demand can be met by the future release of official monetary reserves and the dishoarding of private accumulations—neither of which appears very likely to the author in the light of the probability that unstable monetary conditions will require such reserves for the foreseeable future.[9] However, further advances in the technologies of mining, geologic exploration and ore processing may add considerably to available supply, although such advantages may well be partially, or even wholly, offset by future inflation. New sources of gold, not currently considered as being part of overall resources, may come into being as a result of higher gold prices. For example, as the Bureau notes: "The gold potential of offshore marine deposits appears to be significant, but before these deposits can be considered as a potential source of minerals, sampling problems must be resolved and marine mining technology must be developed."[10]

As for development along more conventional lines, within the United States, the Bureau of Mines is of the opinion that, "New and commercially significant primary sources of gold are likely to be low grade and would involve large-volume mining and major surface disturbance. Major land use conflicts must be expected and equitably resolved."

The USBM obviously feels that future developments are most likely to follow the pattern established by the Carlin and Cortez operations. In that case, because of the heavy initial expense required to prepare a large open-pit mine for production, one can assume that most, if not all, developments of this type will be subsidiary efforts of major mining and investment conglomerates or holding companies. Under such conditions, the opportunity for direct public participation in the gold venture itself would be extremely limited or nonexistent. However, much exploration for these types of deposits is now in progress and geologists employed by the U.S. Geodetic Survey and the

Bureau of Mines, as well as those of several large corporations, are already engaged in a quiet but urgent search for huge tonnages that will assure large scale, long-term operations. But they now calmly speak of "parts per million" in describing their prospects, rather than the historic "ounces per ton" of past eras.

The Bureau estimates that approximately two-thirds of the total gold resources available to the United States, which could eventually become producible at higher prices (ranging from $50 to $145 per ounce), will be found in just four states: Alaska, California, Nevada and Montana. The greatest potential resource is presumed to be in Alaska, and it is quite possible that advancing gold prices will eventually permit the resumption of dredging operations on some of Alaska's gold-bearing streams, using modern dredging vessels and techniques designed to minimize ecological disturbance.

It is also a very good bet that there is still a lot of gold left in the historic lode districts of California, particularly in the deeper levels that would now be accessible, for the first time, through the latest mining and engineering technology. A realistic price for gold could bring about a lot of activity in California, and new mines might be developed that would rival the great producers of the past. Both Nevada and Montana have the potential for developing new lode mines, as well as large-scale open-pit operations, and the former may provide opportunities for public participation.

After the devaluation of 1934, a gold mining boom of considerable intensity took place in the western United States, and with it came a period of hectic speculation in both new gold mining issues and in the stocks of long-dormant older mines suddenly given a new lease on life. No doubt the same thing will happen again, with the coming of another historic advance in the price of gold. The public may be frozen out of new giant open-pit operations by the big mining trusts, but there will undoubtedly be plenty of opportunities to take a chance on smaller lode and placer claims and properties, which are sure to be developed in profusion. Among them may be another Homestake or Sixteen-to-One, but for every real winner there will be literally thousands of failures. Mining is a risky business at best, but speculating on unproven and undeveloped properties is really a form of gambling, exactly in the same class as "wildcatting" for oil.

New Issues. Pioneers, it is said, seldom get rich and speculators who purchase new flotations or first issues of common stock in unseasoned and untested enterprises are essentially pioneers. Stock flotations for newly incorporated enterprises are generally not listed for trading on any exchange, but are sold "Over-the-Counter," that is, directly from a securities dealer who holds them as inventory, to the customer, through a regular broker. The public brokers who are selected by the primary broker-dealer to "handle" a new issue are usually allotted a limited block of the stock'that must be sold at a fixed "subscription" or offering price. This fixed initial offering price is set by the principals of the corporation, with the help and counsel of the broker-dealer firm selected to market the issue. This broker-dealer firm acts as a wholesaler and it distributes allotments from the initial flotation to the (public) brokerage houses it regularly does business with, and they, in turn, retail it in small lots to individual customers.

Most brokers like new issues because they usually get double or triple the normal commission for selling them. Furthermore, many brokers feel that they are doing their customers a favor by getting them into new issues, because *sometimes,* after a new issue is marketed and the fixed offering price is no longer in effect, these issues make sharp initial gains on the open market.[11] On the other hand, since initial offerings tend to be overpriced (after all, the company making the offering is trying to raise as much capital as possible), they often merely subside to a considerably lower and more realistic level quite promptly after being distributed to the public and released for unrestricted trading. Furthermore, they are then prone to stay at that low level for a very long time, until either the enterprise begins to show definite signs of profitability—or fails.

Experienced speculators who have had long and trusted associations with brokers who have done well for them in the past, by getting them into attractive new issues, will probably want to play this game again, with the waves of new gold issues sure to follow large-scale future devaluations (just as in 1934–

35). However, the "new issue" game is not only highly speculative, but seldom lasts for more than a few months. Latecomers nearly always get badly burned. So if you have not had considerable previous experience in this area and do not have a broker you can trust implicitly (by experience) in such matters, by all means *leave it alone.* Let someone else do the pioneering. There are ample opportunities for profit (and risk!) through investment and speculation in seasoned, established operations.

Speculating in Penny Mining Stocks. One of the oldest and soundest pieces of market advice is not to speculate in so-called "penny" mining stocks. A penny stock is one that habitually sells for less than $1.00 per share. In the United States there are a considerable number of penny gold mining stocks listed for trading on regional exchanges, particularly the Spokane Stock Exchange and the San Francisco Mining Exchange. Nearly all of these penny gold stocks represent dormant, defunct or bankrupt mines or nonoperating investing or prospecting companies holding patents, claims or acreages thought to have gold-bearing ores. Still other penny gold stocks are not listed on any exchange but are available Over-the-Counter, on a bid-and-asked basis, from broker-dealers who make markets in such stocks.

While it is possible that some of these penny stocks could double or triple a speculator's capital in a short time, the odds against it are phenomenal. Unless you are privy to inside information (that you can be sure is genuine!), penny stocks are another area the gold investor should avoid completely. In fact, this is not even speculation for the uninformed, it is pure gambling. The lure of the penny stock is, of course, the enormous leverage involved in the possibility of holding a large number of shares for a relatively small amount of invested capital. Furthermore, if, say, a 20¢ stock makes a move to only 80¢ per share, it represents a gain of 300 percent. And, admittedly, there are cases now and then where penny stocks advance from a few cents per share to several dollars, although the odds against this are enormous.

The principal problems and handicaps involved in the trading of so-called penny stocks are (a) commission rates on very low priced stocks are high in relation to the amount of money involved and regular brokers often charge extra fees for handling them, (b) for every one that becomes a successful speculation there are literally dozens that do nothing or sink into oblivion and (c) by the time the typical amateur speculator is "tipped" about a penny stock, it has invariably already made its move and is just ripe for distribution.

Remember this, the most important rule of speculation is: DON'T BE A SUCKER. Incidentally, that is also the most important rule of investment. Come to think of it, it's even the most important rule of trading.

U.S. GOVERNMENT ATTITUDES AND POLICIES REGARDING GOLD MINING

Perhaps the main thing that can be said, up to the present at least, regarding the attitudes and policies of the U.S. Government toward the gold mining industry is that they have been notable for their ambivalence. The Treasury has, for decades, adamantly resisted any plan or program for directly or indirectly increasing the price of gold, thus causing the ruin of many historic gold mining companies and discouraging new exploration and development. On the other hand, the Bureau of Mines and the U.S. Geologic Survey have been conducting direct explorations and maintaining programs designed to encourage gold production.

But, at present, the United States still remains one of the few countries in the world that does not directly subsidize its gold mining industry. In the past two decades, bills have been introduced in Congress, on virtually an annual basis, calling for direct subsidy payments to producing gold mines whose costs have risen beyond the point of profitability. But, just as regularly, those bills are killed or shelved. A successful subsidy program would undoubtedly be a (mildly) bullish factor for U.S. gold stocks but, judging from the experience of Canada, which has had a subsidy program since 1949, it will not, in itself, resurrect or even save the U.S. gold mining industry; only a substantial increase in the basic price of gold will do that.

In the United States, gold mines are taxed on the same basis as other industries, except for the depletion factor. The U.S.

depletion allowance for gold mining is 15 percent of gross income, with a limiting qualification that it not exceed 50 percent of net income.

To encourage private exploration, the Office of Minerals Exploration (OME) of the U.S. Geologic Survey provides direct financial assistance to firms engaged in the search for vital minerals. Government participation in gold exploration may go as high as 75 percent of total expenses. However, this generous aid is somewhat offset by reports that independent prospectors and miners sometimes meet with considerable hostility from officials of other Federal agencies, such as the Bureau of Land Management and the U.S. Forest Service, who, apparently, are not sympathetic to the needs and problems of gold miners and the gold industry.[12]

Gold Prospecting and Treasure Hunting.   If you, good reader, have or have ever had, the urge to search for gold yourself, you are certainly not alone; untold numbers (including the author) have been bitten by the same bug at one time or other. Each year, thousand of letters are received by the U.S. Geologic Survey from people who want to know where to look for gold in the United States. Although both the Geologic Survey Department and the Bureau of Mines think it highly improbable that any promising gold-bearing deposits remain that have gone undiscovered by the legions of both amateur and professional gold hunters intensely active in past years, they nevertheless will concede that there is at least some chance, however small. And as long as any chance remains, there will always be those willing to try their luck.

One obvious preparation that should considerably enhance a prospector's possibilities is to make a careful study of existing mining and geologic records of both potential and previously developed mining districts. To assist in this endeavor, the Survey Department has assembled a list of nine U.S.G.S. reports and maps on gold-producing areas that are currently available from the Survey, and this list may be obtained by writing to the U.S. Geologic Survey, Washington, D.C., 20242. Another source of preliminary information is a booklet published by the U.S. Bureau of Mines entitled *How to Mine and Prospect for Placer Gold.* It is available from the Bureau or from the U.S. Public

Documents Distribution Center, 5801 Tabor Avenue, Philadelphia, Pa. 19120 (refer to cat. no. I 28.27:8517 S/N 2404–0964—price 50¢). This 43-page report supplies basic information on areas of occurrence, equipment needed, prospecting, sampling and mining techniques and Federal regulations concerning the possession and sale of gold.

In general, the independent gold prospector must be prepared for a certain amount of hardship, possess a motor vehicle capable of traveling the roughest and steepest roads and trails, and not be discouraged by repeated disappointment. The Geologic Survey notes that "it is a conservative estimate that fewer than one in each thousand persons who have prospected in the Western part of the United States have ever made a strike." But, the Survey adds, "this does not imply a total discouragement for those who wish to prospect for gold." Actually, a prospecting trip is always an interesting and exciting experience, even though it usually proves to be profitable in ways other than the purely financial. The search itself is often the greatest reward.

Two periodicals that should be of interest to prospectors, would-be prospectors and gold bugs in general are the *California Mining Journal* (2539 Mission Street, Santa Cruz, California 95060) and the *American Gold News* (P.O. Box 427, San Andreas, California 95249). Both publications are available by subscription, or can sometimes be found at the larger newspaper or magazine outlets.

Another outdoor activity that has been growing rapidly in recent years (and which is less complex and perhaps less arduous than actual mining or prospecting) is treasure hunting, using electronic metal-detection equipment. Some of these detectors (which resemble the old mine detector of World War II) are sensitive enough to pick up not only buried gold and silver coins, but gold nuggets and even gold-bearing deposits in sands or rocks.

Although few significant strikes of natural gold have been reported by the detector method, weekend "treasure hunters," using these instruments, frequently do make substantial finds of lost and buried coins (including gold coins), rare bottles and numerous other buried artifacts and collectors items. Ocean beaches, abandoned farms and deserted western ghost towns are generally regarded as the most likely locales for successful treasure hunting. At any rate, it is a way for the complete amateur at prospecting to begin. For further information, those interested can write to *The Association,* 300 State Street, Oscoda, Michigan 48750. This organization not only sells and services metal-detecting equipment and other prospecting supplies, but publishes a fascinating monthly newspaper of great interest to detector treasure hunters and prospectors.

Notes:

CHAPTER XI

1. John Reed, like a considerable number of other German mercenaries employed by the British, deserted during the Revolutionary War and elected to settle permanently in the United States.

2. Because of the danger of attacks by bandits and stray Indians, it was considered too dangerous to ship the bullion to Philadelphia for coining. Furthermore, the road system of the time was quite primitive.

3. *Dahlonega* is the English equivalent of the Cherokee word for "yellow metal" or gold.

4. One account traces this classic line to a Dr. M.F. Stephenson who, when addressing some 200 departing miners from the Dahlonega Courthouse steps, is said to have pointed dramatically to the nearby hills and pleaded, "Why go to California? In that ridge lies more gold than man ever dreamed of. There's millions in it!" The miners, while ignoring Dr. Stephenson's advice, supposedly took their paraphrase of his remarks to California with them, where it became a byword.

5. Some contend that most of the gold miners ended up in the shipyards, where wages were double and triple that of mining employment. At any rate, whether the small gain in manpower and material provided for war industries by L-208 was worth the ruin of about 80 percent of the U.S. gold mining industry is surely debatable.

6. As noted earlier, the author's view is that the dollar should have been devalued in the early post-WWII years to compensate for the wartime inflation.

7. BUREAU OF MINES BULLETIN 650, *Mineral Facts and Problems* (Gold Section) 1970 ed., U.S. Government Printing Office.

8. *Ibid.,* p. 584.

9. It is the author's belief that any future release of (foreign) central bank reserves (excluding routine international payments) would be limited strictly to the provision of bullion for new (EEC?) coinage.

10. USBM BULLETIN 650, p. 584.

11. These initial gains are usually quite temporary, however, as profit-taking and a more sober evaluation of the company's prospects correct the initial exuberance.

12. Both the *California Mining Journal* and *American Gold News* constantly report incidents of harassment and conflict between Western miners and prospectors and (non-mining-oriented) Federal agencies.

XII

THE GOLD MINES OF CANADA

"A citizen should never hesitate to increase his property for fear it will be taken away from him, or to open a new business for fear of taxes."
— NICOLO MACHIAVELLI

ALTHOUGH Canada has produced gold in commercial quantities for more than a hundred years, its emergence as a major gold-producing nation is a fairly modern event. The first noteworthy Canadian gold rush occurred in the period 1860–65, when numerous strikes were made in the Fraser River and Cariboo districts of British Columbia, but gold production at a rate significant enough to affect the national economy did not come about until the opening of the Yukon Territory during the great Klondike gold rush of 1896–1900. The enormously rich gold-bearing gravels found in the creeks tributary to the Klondike and Yukon Rivers were instrumental in advancing Canada to third place among gold-producing nations at the beginning of the twentieth century. And even though the heavy yield of the Klondike placers was, as in all such cases, short-lived, their decline was more than offset by lode discoveries, in other areas, that were of major importance.

Between 1910 and 1920, the Kirkland Lake and Porcupine districts of Northern Ontario were opened to rail service and the famous McIntyre, Hollinger and Dome properties were put into production. In 1930, Canada displaced the United States as the world's second-ranking gold producer and, by 1931, gold had become Canada's most important mineral product (in dollar value), surpassing coal, iron, nickel and copper. The devaluation of the U.S. dollar in 1933–34, and the resulting 75-percent rise in the basic world price for gold, gave another generous lift to Canadian gold output. The 1930's saw a mini-gold rush in Canada, just as in the United States, and the increased level of exploration resulted in the opening of a considerable number of new mines.

World War II brought about a sharp curtailment of gold production in Canada; but the problem was handled more intelligently there than it was in the United States. Most Canadian mines were allowed to continue in operation on a reduced scale and, consequently, a wholesale collapse of the gold industry did not occur in Canada as it did in the United States. Nevertheless, the end of the war found most Canadian gold mines in a precarious position. The wartime and postwar inflations had tripled production costs, while the currency price of gold remained fixed by the Bretton Woods agreement.

The Canadian answer to this dilemma was a direct subsidy program. An *Emergency Gold Mining Assistance Act* (EGMA) was passed, which provides for government payments to miners whose production costs exceeded $26.50 per ounce. Payment is made at the rate of two-thirds of all costs above $26.50, with a limiting provision that total payment to any single enterprise cannot exceed $12.33 per ounce of gold produced.* Mines accepting EGMA payments are required to sell their entire production to the Canadian Treasury at the fixed ($35 U.S.) IMF price.* Those not requiring EGMA are free to sell their gold on the open market for whatever they can get.

EGMA will probably disappear, or at least be substantially redefined, with the coming of higher prices for gold. At any rate, it will then no longer be a significant factor in the prospects of Canadian gold mines. A government subsidy, of course, was no substitute for a reasonable price for gold, but it did enable a considerable number of mines that would otherwise have gone under to survive for many years in the postwar era.

In the late 1940's, the Red Lake district of Western Ontario

---

*All figures in Canadian funds, and based on pre-1972 gold parity. One can presume, however, that the EGMA will be revised to make allowance for the late 1971 devaluation of the U.S.-IMF dollar from $35 to $38 per ounce of gold.

and the Yellowknife area of the Northwest Territory added two more important producers to the Canadian roster—Campbell Red Lake and Giant Yellowknife—as well as a new group of smaller operations. Nevertheless, the postwar period was, in general, one of relentless and accelerating decline. In 1940, Canada reported 140 producing gold mines but, by 1960, their number had dropped to 68. In 1965, only 45 commercially viable gold mines were in operation, and, by the end of 1971, just 20 were left.

Overall Canadian gold output for 1971 declined for the eleventh successive year. From 1954 to 1960, production remained remarkably stable (with the help of EGMA), but since 1960 there has been steady deterioration. (See *Fig. 30,* CANADIAN GOLD PRODUCTION IN MILLIONS OF FINE OUNCES, 1953–1970.) Since gold production in Canada was first recorded, the country's gold industry has produced over 190 million ounces with a currency value of more than $6.2 billion.

Fig. 30

CANADIAN GOLD PRODUCTION
In Millions of Fine Ounces
1953–1970

Year	Output
1953	4.1
1954	4.4
1955	4.5
1956	4.4
1957	4.4
1958	4.6
1959	4.5
1960	4.6
1961	4.5
1962	4.2
1963	4.0
1964	3.8
1965	3.6
1966	3.3
1967	2.9
1968	2.7
1969	2.5
1970	2.4

Notes:
1. Total production for 1970 was 2,357,620 ounces having a value of $86,218,120 (Canadian funds).
2. Ranked according to dollar value of minerals produced by Canada, gold declined to eighth place in 1970, from seventh in 1969.

SPECIAL PROBLEMS OF CANADIAN INVESTMENT

Although we have already discussed, to some degree, tax, labor, political and ecological problems that may challenge the North American gold mining industry and try the patience of the gold investor in years to come, there are a few special situations that concern Canadian mines exclusively. Judging from Canadian and financial press reactions in recent years, the two most worrisome of these concerns (aside from the usual financial-monetary difficulties) are the so called "White Paper" report on taxation and the Quebec Separatist Movement.

Taxation and the White Paper.   In the mid-1960's, the Canadian Government set up a commission to study and report on its federal tax structure, with a view toward enacting a program of overall tax reorganization and reform. The final report of this commission (the so-called "White Paper on Taxation") struck the mining industry like a bombshell, for it recommended, among other things, that most, if not all, of the tax exemptions and allowances now granted the mining industry be eliminated. Among the benefits under attack were three items considered to be of vital importance to the gold mining industry: (a) the tax exemption for income diverted to exploration for new ore bodies, (b) the "new mines" exemption under which newly developed mines are either exempted from ordinary income tax, or pay at a reduced rate, for the first five years of production and (c) the depletion allowances granting tax credits to offset the consumption of capital assets.

Fortunately for the mining industry, the recommendations of the White Paper were advisory rather than binding, and no Canadian administration has yet taken significant actions as a result of them. However, the White Paper (or at least its basic theme) is by no means dead, but only dormant. Such ideas are bound to arise again, and will, no doubt, cause further periods of uncertainty in the market for Canadian golds. When the contents of the White Paper were first made public, a brief but sharp selloff of Canadian mining stocks occurred. But when it became obvious that the government was not going to act on the White Paper recommendations, these stocks quickly recovered their losses.

While it is possible that some of the large conglomerate corporations and mining investment trusts that now control a large share of the Canadian mining industry are so powerful as no longer to need the assistance afforded by the present tax provisions, one can hardly say that about the gold miners. Most gold mines are still relatively small and independent operations; they are already having a difficult struggle to remain profitable, even with EGMA, let alone the depletion allowance and the exploration and new-mines exemptions. Since the long-term future of the majority of the remaining Canadian gold mines is heavily dependent on their discovering new sources of ore to replace the continuous exhaustion of present bodies and to keep mills operating up to capacity, a removal or severe reduction of the present allowances for exploration, new mine development and ore depletion would be a heavy and, in many cases, fatal blow.

It is the author's belief, therefore, that any future revision of the tax laws designed to extract a larger toll from the "big boys" will contain offsetting provisions to protect the smaller mines from being squeezed out of business. Perhaps a restructuring of the EGMA could accomplish this for the gold industry. Under present conditions, however, a serious revival of the White Paper recommendations would be, psychologically at any rate, very upsetting to the market for Canadian gold stocks. But because I believe that long-term realities will always triumph over short-term expediency, I would view any future tax-scare "crash" in Canadian gold shares as just another opportunity to acquire quality issues, for trading or investment purposes, at bargain prices.

Allow sufficient time, however, for *any* emotional selloff to run its full course. The time to buy always coincides with the period when public bearishness or pessimism (regarding gold stocks) reaches its maximum intensity. Admittedly, this is a difficult thing to gauge, but the commentary of the financial press and the opinions of amateur speculators (and ordinary brokers) are a helpful guide. When *everybody* believes that gold shares have permanently lost all merit as investments, they should be bought with great confidence by the gold-oriented trader and investor. Remember that gold is not only an indispensable monetary asset but a vital industrial and scientific metal as well, and no country (outside of the United States) has ever failed to recognize this and take whatever steps found necessary to protect its resources.

Of course, a substantially higher price for gold, bringing greatly increased profits to the gold mining industry, will undoubtedly encourage all levels of government to try to cut themselves in on the bonanza by altering or increasing tax rates, but by that time Canadian gold stocks will already have advanced to new high levels, providing generous capital gains for traders and investors alike. In any case, I would never be deterred from making what otherwise appeared to be a sound committment for fear of having part of the potential profits forfeited through an increased rate of taxation. Besides, increased taxation may be more than offset by lowered production costs brought about by further and inevitable advances in the technologies of mining, ore processing and geologic exploration.

The Quebec Separatist Movement. The dual socio-political nature of the Canadian Federation, with its six million French-speaking citizens residing mainly in the Province of Quebec, has always added to the charm and vitality of this great nation. But, unfortunately, it has also been a source of recurrent political dispute throughout Canada's history. Although the Federal administration has made strenuous efforts, in recent years, to correct past injustices and assure that full economic and political equality prevails for all its citizens, regardless of their linguistic and cultural heritage or choice, it is still not certain that the Quebec "problem" can be or will be resolved without further disturbance to Canada's political and economic tranquility.

About 20 percent of Quebec's voters are members of the *Parti Québecois,* which advocates the peaceful separation of Quebec from the rest of Canada. A very small minority secretly belong to or support the so-called Quebec Liberation Front (FLQ), a fanatical terrorist organization that advocates violent revolution to establish an independent Quebec, and that already has carried out acts of sabotage, kidnapping and even political murder.

Although the situation has calmed considerably since the senseless and brutal murder of Quebec Labor Minister Pierre Laporte by FLQ terrorists in 1970, the passion of many French Canadians for a separate national identity has by no means been extinguished.[1] This issue, therefore, is sure to be the cause of further disturbance before a final settlement, agreeable to all concerned, is reached.

Speaking strictly as an outsider, and based only on a few visits to Quebec and on obviously limited conversations both with members of the *Parti Québecois* and those (of the majority) still favorably disposed toward remaining in the Canadian Confederation, I would say that, whatever periods of difficulty may still lie ahead, a solution will be found that grants the *Québecois* the separate cultural identity and recognition they desire (and are certainly entitled to), yet allows them to remain as full partners in the Canadian Union. At present, the Ottawa Government appears determined to carry out its program to make Canada a bilingual and bicultural nation in reality as well as in principal, and this should go a long way toward removing any basis for further resentment and future charges of discrimination.

On the other hand, concessions could still be made that would grant a degree of political autonomy to Quebec, although this would obviously be moving away from the concept of full and equal participation in the Federation, rather than toward it, as it ideally (in the author's opinion) should be. But complete separation and independence for Quebec would be a disaster for both Canada and Quebec, but particularly for the latter. Whatever their cultural differences, Quebec and the rest of Canada are inseparably bound together, economically as well as geographically, and to try to sever these ties at this late date would be to risk an economic setback so severe, and perhaps so permanent, that only the most unreasoning fanatics could, in the long run, continue to demand it whatever the cost.

Nevertheless, while I am confident that good will and common sense (on both sides) will eventually prevail, I would not rule out further serious disturbances due to the separatist movement, and the effect such disturbances would have on the Canadian stock markets. Undoubtedly, serious political upheavals of this nature, if they became widespread, could play havoc, at least temporarily, with Canadian stock markets. Companies located in Quebec itself would possibly suffer the most pronounced setbacks. But, in any case, *don't panic* in the face of possible political difficulties in Canada if you are caught holding Canadian stocks at the time. Such troubles are sooner or later ended, and nothing is going to happen to the mines themselves in the meantime. If you are not holding Canadian issues and their whole market breaks as the result of *political* crisis, regard it as an ideal trading opportunity, if nothing else. In the long run, there are only two things that will affect the stock of a particular mine: the price of gold and the *profits* derived therefrom, and the availability of ore reserves of adequate quantity and grade.

Where to Find Information on Canadian Stocks.   Before we begin our review of the ten active and publicly owned Canadian gold mining stocks currently available for investment or speculative commitment (plus the lone Canadian company conducting its operations in South America),[2] the reader should note that the stock reviews presented in this book will naturally become less relevant with the passage of time. Therefore, additional sources of information, on a continuing basis, will be absolutely essential to the investor, trader or speculator considering any of the stocks reviewed in this book.

For the stocks listed on the New York or American Stock Exchanges, daily quotations can be found in the *Wall Street Journal* and on the financial pages of any U.S. metropolitan newspaper carrying complete daily stock exchange transactions. Since these companies, Campbell Red Lake, Dome Mines, Giant Yellowknife Mines and Pato Consolidated, are listed on the major U.S. exchanges, their general situations and activities are followed by the Dow Jones News Service and reported over the Dow Jones teletypes (broadtapes) found in most brokerage offices, and on the pages of the *Wall Street Journal.* The weekly financial newspaper *Barron's* carries a weekly summation of all stock market transactions, including those of the Toronto and other Canadian exchanges, plus news and feature articles of interest to all investors, and frequently involving gold and international monetary developments.

For daily transaction reports on the balance of the Canadian stocks, one must refer to the metropolitan newspapers of Toronto or Montreal. Many gold-oriented investors in the United States subscribe to a Canadian paper just for that purpose, although most brokers can provide current quotations at any time through their wire services. But a subscription to a Canadian paper with a good financial section may save the investor in Canadian stocks the trouble of phoning his broker frequently. If one lives in the Northeast, or within one day's mail delivery of Toronto or Montreal, the time lapse may not be too great. During very active markets, however, one should check daily with the broker for up-to-the-minute quotations.

For general news of the Canadian gold mining scene, the weekly *Northern Miner* (Circulation Dept., 77 River Street, Toronto 247, Ontario, Canada) is invaluable. For anyone having, or planning to have, $1,000 or more invested in Canadian gold mining stocks, a subscription to the *Northern Miner* should certainly return many times its cost, in the timely and detailed information it can bring to aid vital investment decisions. The Northern Miner Press also publishes an annual *Canadian Mines Handbook,* which is available from their circulation department in July of each year. The *Handbook* is a summary of all activities of the previous calendar year concerning the Canadian mining industry, and contains annually updated reviews of every known mining company in Canada, whether active or inactive.

The quarterly reports published by Standard and Poor's Service cover the major mines but not the smaller ones. All of these publications are usually available through the larger brokerage offices. Customer's men or brokers are usually quite willing to do all they can to help clients secure accurate and up-to-date information about their stock holdings or interests, and the individual broker, working for a major house, has the research and analytical facilities of the home office to back him up. Incidentally, while we are on the subject of brokers, by all means exercise great care in choosing a broker or brokerage firm.

Make sure the brokerage house you select is a member of one or more of the major U.S. (or Canadian) stock exchanges and has an unchallengeable reputation for integrity and service. Furthermore, if your personal customer's man or account executive is *not* giving you the type of service desired, or is slow or reluctant to secure information or data that you may request, or is unsympathetic to your feelings about gold stocks, by all means request a different account executive or switch your accounts to another brokerage house. Don't string along with a broker with whom you do not feel comfortable or whose ideas are consistently incompatible with yours. Otherwise your confidence and judgment will be eroded and your ability to make profitable commitments will suffer in consequence.

In general, don't lean on your broker too much for personal help and counsel; it will be far better for you to learn to make your own investment decisions, as far as possible, even though you may make some mistakes in doing so. Painful though it may sometimes be, experience *is* one of the best teachers—at least in the stock market. In my opinion, a good broker is one who fills orders promptly and at the best possible price, but who does not offer advice or criticism unless specifically requested to do so. And of course never, but NEVER, agree to purchase stock from some unknown "boiler room" operator who calls you on the phone (usually long-distance from New York or Toronto or Johannesburg or some other impressive place) with a "hot tip" on some obscure situation that he guarantees will make you rich. Never do business with anyone who is not well known in the business and investment community and whose identity and reputation cannot be readily verified.

The U.S. Interest Equalization Tax. United States investors and speculators considering Canadian or other foreign securities must take precautions not to run afoul of the so-called *Interest Equalization Tax* (IET). This irritating and, in the author's opinion, discriminatory levy was enacted in 1963 for the avowed purpose of helping to correct the U.S. balance-of-payments deficit by discouraging the investment of U.S. funds abroad. From the course of events since then, it is obvious that this tax was not only unfair and unnecessary, but completely unsuccessful. Nevertheless it is still with us, although the original 15 percent rate was reduced to 11¼ percent by the Nixon administration. Inasmuch as "temporary" taxes have a way of becoming permanent, I doubt that we will see the end of this one for a long time to come—at least not until the world returns to a new and *effective* international gold standard.

The Interest Equalization Tax *does not* apply to foreign stocks listed for trading on American stock exchanges. Therefore, purchasers of DOME MINES, CAMPBELL RED LAKE, GIANT YELLOWKNIFE and PATO CONSOLIDATED, through U.S. brokerage houses in the normal manner, are exempted from payment of this tax.[3] However, stocks purchased *directly* from the Toronto, Montreal or other Canadian exchanges (even though the purchase is made through an American broker) are subject to this tax, which is 11¼ percent of the total actual value of the purchase. For example, if you buy 100 shares of a particular foreign stock for $2 per share, your total actual value would be $200. (The costs of the sale, such as broker's commissions, transfer fees, etc., are not considered to be part of total value.) The tax due therefore would be 11¼ percent of $200, or $22.50.

The broker does not pay this tax for you or add it on to the total amount due his firm to close the transaction. The purchaser of foreign securities through foreign sources is obliged to file an *Interest Equalization Quarterly Tax Return* (I told you it was irritating), enclosing the appropriate payment due. This return must be filed with the Internal Revenue Service (IRS) within 30 days of the end of the calendar quarter in which the stock was purchased. Failure to file, or late filing, results in penalties and interest costs being charged to the taxpayer, in addition to the tax originally due. Tax forms, general information and taxpayer assistance are available at IRS regional offices.

If you want to *avoid* the nuisance of having to file an IET return when purchasing Canadian securities not listed on American exchanges, *make sure that your broker requests AMERICAN-OWNED stock when placing your order.* If you buy foreign shares from another American (through the Over-the-Counter market), the tax does not apply because there is no transfer of U.S. funds abroad. (The fact that you purchased American-owned shares, however, must be noted on the confirmation-of-purchase statement you receive from your broker.)

Of course, if there is no American-owned stock of a particular issue you want being offered for sale at the moment, and you still want to have it, then there is obviously no other choice but to buy in Canada (or elsewhere abroad) and file the tax. You will *pay* the tax in either case, because American-owned stock will invariably be approximately 11¼ percent (or whatever else the IET rate may become) higher than its counterpart sold through a Canadian or other foreign exchange.

Consequently, on large orders one should perhaps check both the American OTC market and the appropriate foreign (Canadian) exchange. If there is too large a "spread" or difference between the U.S. and Canadian prices, it might be less expensive to buy in Canada and take the trouble to file a return and pay the tax directly. There is one advantage in buying on a foreign exchange: if, when you sell the stock, you are able to sell it abroad, you may then claim a refund of the IET previously paid on that particular stock, because an equivalent amount of dollars will be returned to the United States as a result of the sale. In conclusion, I can only say that if I felt strongly about a certain stock and it could only be obtained abroad, I would not let the prospect of filing an IET return be a deterrent.

On the other hand, I don't really know what the tax liability of an American would be who took cash, or otherwise transferred funds, to Canada personally, bought stocks from a Canadian broker using Canadian funds, and left those stocks in Canada, either in the custody of a Canadian broker or in a Canadian safe-deposit box. Since stocks bought in Canada and never transferred to the United States would eventually be sold in Canada, one might presume that there would be no IET liability to the United States. (At any rate, there would be no

U.S. record of this type of transaction!) If anyone is really concerned about this, I'm sure the IRS would be happy to advise you.[4]

Canadian Income Tax Withholding. If you haven't had enough of taxes by now, there is still one more to consider. The Canadian Government withholds 10 percent of all dividends paid by Canadian corporations to stockholders residing outside of Canadian jurisidiction. Therefore, if, say, Giant Yellowknife declares its regular quarterly dividend of $0.10 per share, an American stockholder owning 100 shares would receive $9.00 (in Canadian funds), with $1.00 being withheld for Canadian income tax. On the plus side, however, there is usually a small gain due to exchange-rate differences between U.S. and Canadian currencies, so that the actual payment might turn out to be $9.30 to $9.40 when converted to U.S. currency.[5]

If your stock is held in a street name, the broker will send you checks directly in U.S. funds for dividends accrued. However, he *may* send you the full amount of the dividend in U.S. funds ($10 in the case of Giant Yellowknife) and then deduct the Canadian tax and the exchange differences from your (margin) account. In that case, you would report the full amount received on your U.S. income tax return and then claim credit for the Canadian tax paid. Again, I'm sure the IRS will be able to advise you, should you have any further questions on this or other tax matters.

Custody of Stock Certificates. One of the recurrent questions facing investors and speculators is whether to leave stocks with their broker to be held in the "street" or brokerage firm name, or whether to request that the actual stock certificate be issued and transferred to the stockholder's personal custody. Active traders usually prefer to leave their stocks "on the street," that is, not to receive a certificate but merely to be credited with purchases and sales through entries in the broker's books and confirmation statements from the brokerage firm. The confirmation statement is usually adequate evidence of a particular purchase or sale.

There is, of course, no point in having a broker initiate the complex transfer and registration process required to obtain a stock certificate, which takes anywhere from two weeks to two months, if the trader is likely to sell the stock before the transfer can be completed. Furthermore, if stocks are held in a margin account, that is held on partial credit with the broker, there is no choice in the matter; title to such stocks cannot be transferred to the purchaser because they are not fully paid for. They must therefore be held in the broker's name, although credited to the customer's account.

But for long-term investors and speculators holding for major market cycles, there are certain advantages in having outright ownership of stocks and personal possession of the stock certificates. The use of margin, or money borrowed through your broker (or borrowed from anyone else), may very well increase your "leverage" by giving you a claim on a greater number of shares, but leverage is a two-way street. If you are on a 60 percent margin, that is you paid 60 percent of the purchase price in cash and are carrying the 40 percent balance on credit, your profits, based on the actual amount of cash committed, will obviously be 40 percent greater, providing the stocks go up. But if they should be so inconsiderate as to go down, one's losses will also be increased by 40 percent or by whatever other percentage of margin the trader is carrying.

In the author's opinion, most investors and even the majority of intermediate- and long-term speculators should avoid the use of margin. That way they will be more inclined to be calm and judicious in their market strategy and less apt to panic or be forced or frightened out of their holdings at the wrong time. Having the stock certificates in one's physical possession helps to reinforce the idea that the stock market is not, or at least was not intended to be, a gambling casino, but a place to buy and sell actual capital properties.[6] A stock certificate is a document of ownership no less tangible than a deed to a piece of real estate.

If, when one decides to sell a stock, one is obliged to go to a safe-deposit box, get the actual certificate, sign it in the presence of witnesses and deliver it to a broker, the impression is indelibly made on the mind that a transaction of substance is taking place. As a result, the investor or speculator personally handling the actual stock certificates becomes far less emotionally involved with "the market" and concentrates more on the fact that what he is trying to do is buy properties at the best possible price and sell them at a substantial profit.

Even if his concern is only to secure a safe refuge for capital, the holding or dealing in the actual certificates predisposes the investor to act only on *substantial* changes in the values of gold shares. A person who buys a stock and then waits for two to six weeks for delivery of the certificate will be reinforcing the virtue of patience, and patience is absolutely essential for success in gold investing.

Another factor, of course, is the element of financial safety inherent in the actual possession of the certificate. During the great 1969–70 bear market, the "impossible" occurred; many old-line brokerage houses failed and others narrowly missed failure or avoided it only by being hastily merged with a stronger competitor. Some of these firms had proud records going back to the nineteenth century, and many had survived the crash of 1929; nevertheless, they succumbed to the euphoria of the late sixties and overextended themselves beyond repair. Persons having stock held in the "street" name of brokerage houses going into bankruptcy may suffer anything from a total loss to a painfully long delay in recovering their capital.

Some, but far from all, of the losses sustained by the public through the brokerage house fiascos of 1969–70 were recovered (usually after considerable delay) from insurance funds set up by the major stock exchanges, notably the New York Stock Exchange. Such funds were set up to protect public accounts, managed by member firms, against such failures. But for many of the smaller houses, and for other (U.S. and Canadian) brokerage firms not adequately protected by such insurance funds or plans, the situation ranged from grim to disastrous; customers holding margined stock, stocks in street names, and even cash balances with such companies, often suffered heavy or complete losses and were left without recourse.

For the United States, new Federal legislation was hurriedly put into effect in 1971 that established a "Securities Investor Protection Corporation." This SIPC is designed to protect individual investor accounts with U.S. brokerage firms, up to a limit of $50,000 per account. It is supposed to guarantee that the investor will not lose either cash or securities held in margin accounts or street names, in the event of the bankruptcy or failure of his firm. The criterion, of course, is that the brokerage house in question be a contributing member of the Corporation.

The SIPC is perhaps a significant improvement over the generally inadequate systems of private insurance that previously existed, but it has yet to be tested in the fires of a really serious financial-economic panic. The same can be said, incidentally, of its counterparts, the Federal Deposit Insurance Corporation (FDIC), which protects depositors in commercial banks, and the Federal Savings and Loan Insurance Corporation, which performs a similar service for Savings and Loan depositors. I think some question remains, concerning the new Securities Investor Protection Corporation: whether, in the event of a severe financial panic, the investor would always be guaranteed to receive his cash or securities if they were immobilized by a default, without experiencing prolonged and costly delays; and whether there are loopholes in the Act that would exempt the corporation from the responsibility to replace certain types of foreign securities.

Therefore, despite the fact that efforts are being made to insure investors in better fashion against losses suffered as the result of brokerage-house failures, I would advise all gold investors and speculators, particularly when buying foreign securities, to pay for their stocks in full and request transfer of the stock certificates to their personal custody. The only gold stocks I would even consider holding on margin, for short- and intermediate-term trading purposes, are those listed on the New York Stock Exchange and purchased through a New York Stock Exchange member firm: These stocks arc:

AMERICAN SOUTH AFRICAN	(ASA)
CAMPBELL RED LAKE	(CRK)
DOME MINES	(DM)
HOMESTAKE MINES	(HM)

And even then I would qualify this opinion by stating again that only those with considerable experience in stock trading should even consider attempting to catch anything but the major cyclical moves. The majority of gold investors or potential gold investors would be better advised to purchase *all* of their stocks for cash, including the ones just listed, and request delivery of the certificates. Fortunately, in the case of low-priced stocks, most brokers will not even allow margin on issues selling for less than $5.00 per share.

The stock certificate is the actual legal evidence of ownership of a specific equity or property. Once you have that certificate in your possession, it can be sold and transferred anywhere— in the United States, in Canada, in Europe, in South Africa— anywhere. A broker's confirmation or your statement of account are merely acknowledgments that you have a claim on the brokerage house that issued them and have no negotiable value in themselves. An account with a broker can only be liquidated through that particular broker. If his doors are closed, *for any reason,* you obviously cannot transfer, sell or remove stock you hold on account with him.

If you did not realize it already, you are probably beginning to suspect, by now, that investing in stocks is no easy task, and you would be quite justified in drawing such a conclusion. But it is actually not as complex as it may first appear. "Nothing is really hard," said Henry Ford, "if you divide it into small parts." Let Mr. Ford's sagacious advice be the key to your strategy. Keep things as simple as possible: take things one step at a time.

1. Buy for cash only—no margin or credit. Never borrow money to buy stocks. Never use money that should be reserved for future living expenses to buy stocks.
2. Get the certificate transferred to your own name and keep it in a safe place.
3. Don't try to catch short-term movements; concentrate on the major market cycle (for gold stocks) or on long-term growth potential.
4. Keep in mind, always, that you are buying, selling and holding actual capital properties, not making bets in a casino.

I think it is time, now, to look at some specific gold stocks.

LISTED CANADIAN GOLD MINING STOCKS
(All dollar figures given in Canadian funds.)

AUNOR GOLD MINES LTD.
Capitalization

LONG-TERM DEBT	None.
PREFERRED STOCK	None.
COMMON STOCK	2,000,000 shares (Authorized & issued).
EXCHANGE LISTING	Toronto Stock Exchange.
PRICE RANGE	(1964–71) $1.75–$4.65
DIVIDENDS	1962–68, 20¢ per year. 1969, 15¢. 1970, 04¢

History. Incorporated in 1939, Aunor Gold Mines currently holds and operates 21 gold mining claims in the Porcupine area of Northern Ontario. In 1969, Aunor acquired all remaining assets of adjacent Delnite Mining Company, including eight gold claims, miscellaneous surface works and buildings, and underground developments extending to the 5,250 foot level. Delnite and Aunor shafts have since been interconnected by lateral drifts. The Aunor flotation-cyanide mill, opened in 1940 and improved in 1950 and 1963, has a current capacity of 760 tons per day. Dividends have been paid since 1941 and totaled $10,880,000 through December 31, 1970. Total gold production from 1940 through 1970 amounted to $77,169,074, from 6,408,-752 tons of ore with an average recovery of $12.04 per ton.

Fundamental Position. In 1970, Aunor milled 261,720 tons of ore with an average yield of $10.31 per ton. EGMA received totaled $765,000, and income from investments amounted to $501,807, allowing for a net profit of $184,811 or 9.2¢ per share, vs. 5.6¢ per share in 1969 and 25.3¢ per share in 1968.

Financial Position. Aunor is controlled by Noranda Mines Ltd. As of December 31, 1970, Noranda held 1,104,778 shares or 55 percent of the total Aunor shares authorized and issued. Aunor itself had outside investments with a market value of $1,060,582, and investments in associated and affiliated companies that totaled $1,300,100. Net working capital, as of December 31, 1970, was $4,794,200.

Ore Reserves.

Dec. 31, 1970   834,000 tons av. 0.33 oz. gold per ton
"   " 1969   858,000 tons av. 0.32 oz. "   "   "
"   " 1968   855,000 tons av. 0.32 oz. "   "   "

Lateral drifts are currently being extended from the former Delnite shafts into Aunor properties below the 3,000-foot level, in the belief that additional ore will become available. Previous mining and development work on the Aunor properties had been confined to the areas above the 3,000-foot level.

Rating: SPECULATIVE

Comment: Despite a setback in earnings reported for 1969 and 1970, Aunor appears to be making a comeback in 1971, with somewhat higher profits being reported for the first half. With known ore reserves adequate for more than three years production at current rates and with its sound financial position, Aunor is not without merit as a low-priced gold speculation. Success would depend largely on buying this type of stock at a good discount, perhaps during periods of obvious price weakness in the whole gold group, and holding it until a considerable advance in the price of gold has been achieved. Present dependence on EGMA is the only obvious negative factor.

CAMFLO MINES LTD.
Capitalization

LONG-TERM DEBT	None.
PREFERRED STOCK	None.
COMMON STOCK	Authorized: 5,000,000 shares. Issued: 3,411,107 (460,000 shares escrowed).
EXCHANGE LISTINGS	Toronto Stock Exchange, Canadian Stock Exchange.
PRICE RANGE	(1964–71) $0.80–$7.75
DIVIDENDS	1967, 20¢; 1968, 15¢; 1969, 10¢; 1970, 10¢ (annually).

History.   Incorporated in 1953, Camflo holds and operates 12 gold-producing claims on 683 acres in the Malartic area of northwest Quebec. Initial production began March 1965. In 1971, the main shaft was extended to 2,750 feet, adding three new production levels, for a total of 19 levels. Mill capacity 1,000 tons per day. Dividends have been paid since 1967. Total production from March 1965 to Dec. 31, 1970, was 1,925,527 tons milled, yielding 481,456 ounces of gold and 8,354 ounces of silver, having a market value of $18,754,430.

Fundamental Position. In 1970, Camflo milled 374,580 tons of ore, with a net yield of $8.89 per ton. Average monthly production rate was 30,780 tons. Total market value of output for the year was $3,331,112. EGMA received amounted to $367,000. Income from outside investments was negligible. Net profit for 1970 was $668,510 or 19.6¢ per share, vs. 23¢ per share in 1969 and 27.4¢ in 1968. No appreciable improvement in earnings is forecast for 1971. Camflo also conducts a modest exploration program in northern Quebec and Ontario and has filed several new claims that warrant further investigation.

Financial Position. United Siscoe Mines Ltd. owns 467,000 shares or 13.6 percent of (issued) Camflo stock. Camflo held (1970) investments with a market value of $162,700 (not included in 1970 assets). As of Dec. 31, 1970, declared assets totaled $864,555 and included $21,311 in cash and $277,990 in bullion. Liabilities amounted to $179,593.

Ore Reserves

Dec. 31, 1970 2,174,000 tons av. 0.241 oz. gold per ton
  "   "   1969 2,109,000 tons av. 0.224 oz. "   "   "
  "   "   1968 1,715,503 tons av. 0.249 oz. "   "   "

Rating: SPECULATIVE

Comment: Substantial ore reserves (allowing for five full years of production at current rates) make Camflo one of the better low-priced gold speculations. Speculators buying this stock on weakness could be generously rewarded for the relatively modest risk assumed. Negative factors: dependence on EGMA and relatively low grade of ore.

CAMPBELL RED LAKE MINES LTD. (CRK)

Capitalization

LONG-TERM DEBT	None
PREFERRED STOCK	None
COMMON STOCK	Authorized: 4,000,000 shares
	Issued: 3,999,500 shares.
	(2,270,105 shares owned by Dome Mines).

EXCHANGE LISTINGS: New York Stock Exchange, Toronto Stock Exchange.

PRICE RANGE (1971)   35–18-¼

DIVIDEND (1971) $0.45 (11¼¢ quarterly).

History.   Incorporated in 1944, Campbell Red Lake currently operates a large low-cost gold mine on 27 patented claims in Balmer Township in the Red Lake area of NW Ontario. The Company has been a leading Canadian gold producer since operations began in 1949. In 1970, CRK's 825-ton-capacity mill averaged 718 tons per day, vs. 717 tons per day in 1969 and 715 tons in 1968. Total production from June 1949 to December 1970 amounted to $111,338,575 from 5,053,153 tons of ore milled. Dividends have been paid continuously since 1952, and averaged 77 percent of earnings in the five years preceding 1971.

Fundamental Position.   In 1970, the Red Lake mine produced 178,974 ounces of gold from 262,021 tons of ore for an average recovery grade of 0.6831 per ton. Operating costs averaged $20.70 per ounce recovered versus $17.22 per ounce in 1969. Average price received for gold was $37.64 in 1970 against $43.45 in 1969. Profits for 1970 fell to 48¢ per share from 73¢ per share in 1970 and the all-time high of 80¢ per share in 1968. Despite increased labor and other costs, profits for 1971 and 1972 are expected to resume their previously steady long-term uptrend. Large reserves of high-grade ore indicate a long life for the Red Lake mine, and other interests and holdings of the corporation should also contribute to increased earnings and dividends over the remainder of the decade. Employees (1971): 264; shareholders: 5,701. CRK does not require EGMA and is therefore free to sell all of its gold at a premium on the private markets.

Financial Position.   Campbell Red Lake is controlled by Dome Mines Ltd., which owns 2,270,105, or 56.8 percent, of outstanding CRK shares. Campbell, in turn, has a 21-percent participating interest in all new exploration ventures and developments of its parent corporation, Dome Mines, and of Dome's other subsidiaries, Sigma Mines and Dome Petroleum. During 1968, Campbell Red Lake purchased $2,000,000 worth of 5-percent convertible (at $87.75 per common share) debentures of Dome Petroleum Ltd. CRK also holds an equity interest (through Dome) in Panartic Oils Ltd. In addition, Campbell Red Lake conducts independent outside exploration work, for gold and other minerals, on a limited scale. H.G. Young Mines (inactive since 1962), 20 percent owned by CRK, plans to sell all of its Red Lake gold properties to a new concern that will be 80 percent owned by Campbell and 20 percent by H.G. Young. Plan awaiting shareholder approval.

Ore Reserves

Dec. 31, 1970 1,376,000 tons av. 0.696 oz. gold per ton

"   "   1969 1,331,100 tons av. 0.692 oz. "   "   "

"   "   1968 1,288,400 tons av. 0.691 oz. "   "   "

Proven reserves are calculated only to the 18th level of the mine, but the 4-compartment main shaft is being extended to the 26th (4,200-ft.) level. At the end of 1970, all major operations above the 15th (2,200-ft.) level were terminated. Ore grade has tended to increase at lower levels and the ore body appears to be open for substantial additional development below the 15th level.

INCOME STATISTICS (per share)

Year	Earn's	Div's	Price Range High	Low	P.E. Ratio High	Low
1961	$0.46	0.40	18-3/4 –	11-3/8	40 –	25
1962	0.51	0.44	17-5/8 –	12-3/8	35 –	24
1963	0.59	0.45	17 –	12-1/4	29 –	22
1964	0.60	0.50	24-7/8 –	13-1/2	41 –	23
1965	0.61	0.50	25 –	17-3/4	41 –	29
1966	0.62	0.50	27-3/4 –	16-5/8	45 –	27
1967	0.63	0.50	28-3/4 –	16-3/4	46 –	27
1968	0.80	0.50	47-1/4 –	24	59 –	30
1969	0.73	0.50	40-3/8 –	14-1/2	55 –	20
1970	0.48	0.50	34-3/4 –	15-3/8	72 –	32

Rating: TRADING-INVESTMENT

Comment: Relatively low production costs, substantial reserves of high-grade gold ore and an excellent financial position make Campbell Red Lake perhaps the best North American gold commitment, despite its typical low dividend yield and relatively high average price-to-earnings (P.E.) ratio. With the price of gold continually moving toward new higher levels in the '70's, CRK should soon show a marked increase in both earnings and dividends. This stock is always a good buy on significant reactions in the gold group. Very limited amount of stock available for trading make it a highly volatile performer.

DICKENSON MINES LTD.

Capitalization

LONG-TERM DEBT	None
PREFERRED STOCK	None
COMMON STOCK	Authorized: 3,750,000
	Issued: 3,556,000
	(Kam-Kotia Mining Ltd. holds 534,409 shares, or 15 percent).
EXCHANGE LISTING	Toronto Stock Exchange
PRICE RANGE (1964–71)	$6.40–$1.00
DIVIDENDS	1961–62: 18¢; 1963: 26¢; 1964: 28¢;1965: 22¢; 1966–67: 10¢; 1968–69: 5¢; 1970: 6¢ (annually).

History.   Formed in 1960, from the merger of New Dickenson Mines (Inc. 1948) and Lake Cinch Mining Ltd., Dickenson operates a gold mine on 32 patented claims adjacent to the E. side of the Campbell Red Lake property, Balmer Township, Red Lake district, NW Ontario. In 1970, Dickenson acquired an 80-percent interest in Robin Red Lake Gold Mines Ltd., holding 12 patented claims adjacent to the Dickenson property in E. Balmer Twp. Dickenson and Robin Red Lake underground workings are currently being interconnected. Robin is expected to contribute 100 tons per day to the Dickenson mill by 1972. Current rate is 450 tons per day (from Dickenson property). Mill capacity of 480 tons per day will require upgrading. From 1948 to Dec. 31, 1970, the Dickenson mine produced 1,569,352 ounces of gold and 134,566 ounces of silver, having a total value of $56,879,000, from 3,236,272 tons of ore. Total dividends paid to December 31, 1970, amounted to $7,801,770. Dickenson also holds substantial interests in numerous other mining properties and claims, both active and inactive, and is currently engaged in further exploration and development work.

Fundamental Position.   In 1970, the Dickenson mine yielded 163,714 tons of ore, while an additional 3,949 tons were obtained from the adjacent Robin Red Lake mine. Total net from bullion sales was $2,571,000. Investment income was $305,000, while EGMA contributed $650,000. Operating expenses and other charges totaled $3 million, allowing for a net profit of $511,000 or 14.4¢ per share, down from 20.9¢ per share in 1969.

Financial Position.   As of December 31, 1970, Dickenson held investments and interests in other mining companies, active and inactive, having a market value of $2,518,000 (down from a market value of $7,680,000 in 1969). Principal holdings in producing companies were 1,800,008 shares (60.0 percent) of Kam-Kotia Mines (copper, zinc) and 2,090,108 shares (48.7 percent) of Jameland Mines Ltd. (copper, zinc). Net working capital at end of 1970 was $533,000.

Ore Reserves (Dickenson Mine).

December 31, 1970   420,769   tons av. 0.516 oz. gold per ton
   "   "   1969   474,669   tons av. 0.505 oz. "   "   "
   "   "   1968   513,281   tons av. 0.530 oz. "   "   "

The bulk of known reserves is located mainly between the 15th and 27th levels of the Dickenson mine. Present indications, however, are that additional high-grade ore will be found below the 23rd level on the Robin Red Lake property currently under development.

Rating: SPECULATIVE

Comment: Dependence on EGMA a negative factor, although rising gold prices could eliminate this problem. Known reserves are adequate for about three-years production at current rates, but proving of additional reserves on the Robin Red Lake property would greatly enhance this situation. Dickenson also has a majority interest in several dormant gold mining properties in the Red Lake area, which could become active given a substantially higher price for gold, and, in that case, Dickenson could develop into a major gold producer. A good speculation to be bought on significant price concession.

DOME MINES LTD. (DM)

Capitalization

LONG-TERM DEBT	None
PREFERRED STOCK	None
COMMON STOCK	Authorized: 2,000,000 shares.
	Issued: 1,946,000 shares.
EXCHANGE LISTINGS	New York Stock Exchange, Toronto Stock Exchange, Canadian Stock Exchange
PRICE RANGE (1971)	73⅝–49½
DIVIDEND (1971)	$.80 (20¢ quarterly)

History.   First incorporated in 1911, Dome Mines operates a large but relatively high-cost gold mine in the Porcupine district of N Ontario. In addition, Dome holds a controlling interest (57 percent) in Campbell Red Lake Mines and in the smaller Sigma Mines (36 percent). Despite the relatively large output of the parent Dome mine, most of the Company's profit from gold production was derived from its two gold mining subsidiaries and principally from Campbell Red Lake. However, Dome's large portfolio of other investments also contributed significantly to gross income. The Dome mine itself was one of the earliest operations in the Porcupine gold mining district of N. Ontario and it has been in continuous production since 1910. The property itself comprises 3,459 acres in Tisdale, Shaw and Whitney Townships and extends for 3½ miles along the Dome ore zone. Main (No.3) 5-compartment shaft extends to the 18th level and a large internal (No.6) shaft extends from the 16th (2,035-ft.) level to the 29th (4,000-ft.) level. No. 7 internal shaft was deepened to reach the 37th (5,260-ft.) level in 1965–66.

From 1911 until December 31, 1970, the Dome Mine at South Porcupine produced $298,344,851 worth of gold from 32,003,814 tons of ore. Total dividends paid during this period amounted to $98,983,900. Dividends have been paid continuously since 1920, and averaged 47 percent of consolidated net earnings in the period 1966 through 1970. Present mill capacity at the Dome mine is 2,000 tons per day.

Fundamental Position.   In 1970, the Dome Mine at South Porcupine produced 180,586 ounces of gold, valued at $6,664,437, from 690,000 tons of ore assaying 0.2616 ounces per ton.

Average milling rate was 1,945 tons per day. EGMA contributed $1,490,000, while outside income amounted to $3,434,366. Total income of $11,588,773 was offset by operating expenses and other charges of $8,405,862, allowing for a net profit of $3,-182,911 or $1.64 per share, down from $1.95 per share in 1969 and $2.00 in 1968. Earnings for 1971 and 1972 are expected to show an increase due to higher earnings of subsidiaries. Dome remains very active in exploration for gold and other minerals through its wholly owned subsidiary, Dome Exploration, and is presently engaged in a wide range of geophysical programs covering a broad area of Canada and Alaska.

Financial Position.   Dome's financial resources are exceptionally strong. In addition to the 2,270,105 shares (57 percent) of Campbell Red Lake and 625,536 shares (63 percent) of Sigma Mines, the Company owns 100 percent of both Dome Exploration Ltd. and Bluffy Lake Iron Mines. Other investments include an 18-percent interest in Dome Petroleum Ltd., plus $15 million in 5-percent convertible debentures of Dome P. (conversion of the latter would raise DM's interest in Dome Petroleum to 22 percent), 400,000 shares of Mattagami Lake Mines (zinc, copper, silver and gold), 800,000 shares of Canada Tungsten Mining Ltd. and 80,000 shares of Cities Service Corporation common stock. Total cash resources are not fully reflected in the Company's regular balance sheets, since marketable securities are carried at cost, rather than at market value.

At the beginning of 1971, Dome's investments, on a consolidated basis were listed at their book or acquisition value of $19 million, but had a market value of $74.9 million. Capital expenditures at the Dome mine itself are virtually all covered by a cash flow from depreciation.

Ore Reserves (Dome mine).

    Dec. 31, 1970 1,685,000 tons av. 0.281 oz. gold per ton
      "   " 1969 1,819,000 tons av. 0.270 oz. "   "   "
      "   " 1968 1,962,000 tons av. 0.279 oz. "   "   "

Ore reserves at the Dome mine are satisfactory and there are no present indications of exhaustion. Development below the 29th level should prove additional ore. However, the generally low grade of ore and constantly rising production costs make the future of the Dome mine critically dependent on a higher price for gold.

INCOME STATISTICS (per share)

Year	Earn's	Div's	Price Range High Low		P.E. Ratio High Low	
1961	$1.05	$0.70	28-1/2 –	20	26 –	19
1962	1.16	0.70	31-3/4 –	22-5/8	27 –	20
1963	1.46	0.80	33-1/8 –	23-1/8	23 –	16
1964	1.46	0.80	41-1/4 –	25-1/8	28 –	18
1965	1.56	0.90	42-7/8 –	32-1/4	27 –	20
1966	1.54	0.90	51-3/8 –	35-3/4	33 –	21
1967	1.64	0.80	58-3/4 –	37-5/8	36 –	23
1968	2.00	0.80	82-1/4 –	46-1/4	41 –	23
1969	1.95	0.80	89 –	42-3/4	46 –	22
1970	1.64	0.80	67-3/4 –	45	41 –	27

Rating: TRADING—INVESTMENT

Comment: Despite the marginal nature of the Dome and Sigma mines, this stock earns an INVESTMENT rating through its controlling interest in Campbell Red Lake, its aggressive exploration, development and investment programs and its very substantial investment portfolio. The small capitalization of the parent company, however, makes it an extremely volatile performer. Dome is an excellent trading vehicle, but investors and traders alike should be wary of chasing this stock during periods of rapid advance under heavy volume. It should also be remembered that Dome is vulnerable to a considerable reduction in the value of its investment portfolio during prolonged bear markets and that both Dome and Sigma mines are presently dependent on EGMA to remain in operation. All in all, Dome is a highly leveraged stock—but leverage works both ways.

GIANT YELLOWKNIFE MINES LTD. (GYK)
Captitalization

LONG TERM DEBT	None
PREFERRED STOCK	None
COMMON STOCK	Authorized: 4,500,000

Issued: 4,303,050
(824,413 shares, or 19.2 percent, owned by Falconbridge Nickel Corp. Ltd.)

EXCHANGE LISTINGS   American Stock Exchange, Toronto Stock Exchange.

PRICE RANGE (1971)   12⅝–6¼

DIVIDENDS (1971) $0.40 (10¢ quarterly.)

History.   First incorporated in 1949 and rechartered in 1960 (as the result of an amalgamation of Giant Yellowknife Gold Mines and Consolidated Sudbury Mines), Giant Yellowknife operates three adjoining gold properties, on a unified basis, located at Yellowknife, on the N shore of Great Slave Lake, Northwest Territory (NWT). The original *Giant Mine* (inc. 1949) consists of 25 leases, plus 3 claims, covering approximately 1,600 acres. *Lolar Mines* (87½ percent owned) consists of 6 contiguous claims and *Supercrest Mines* (50.01 percent owned) comprises 28 adjacent claims. Underground workings of all three properties are interconnected and total output is treated at the Giant mill (1,200-tons-per-day capacity). Main 5-compartment shaft of Giant mine extends to 11th (2,000-ft.) level. Three additional shafts are connected by 7,593-ft. main haulageway at 750-ft. level. From incorporation of the parent mine in 1949 to Dec. 31, 1970, Giant Yellowknife has produced gold valued at $156,583,680 from 6,926,642 tons of ore (including Giant's share of output from Lolar and Supercrest Mines, beginning in 1967). Total dividends paid from original incorporation to December 1970 amounted to $37,984,011.

Fundamental Position.   In 1970, GYK produced 228,000 ounces of gold and 41,269 ounces of silver from 424,774 tons of ore. Average milling rate was 1,164 tons per day. Gold output has remained fairly steady in recent years, but rising costs have eroded profit margins. Although still one of Canada's major producers, Giant has now become dependent on EGMA for survival. Gross income for 1970 was $9,624,712, including $900,000 in EGMA. Net profit was $1,348,137 or 31¢ per share, down from 44¢ in 1969 and 46¢ in 1968. As in several previous years, earnings did not cover dividend payments, the last such occurrence being in 1967.

Giant Yellowknife also carries out an extensive program of mineral exploration and development, principally on the extensive gold claims of Northbelt Yellowknife Mines (51.4 percent owned) and on wholly-owned base-metal (copper) prospects (Errington and Vermillion Lake) in the Sudbury basin area. The Company also conducts outside geophysical explorations throughout the Northwest Territory and in the Yukon. But except for proven copper deposits at Errington and Vermillion Lake (no production presently planned), results thus far have been disappointing. Employees: 400; shareholders: 12,633.

Financial Position.   The Company's financial position remained strong at the beginning of 1971, with a net working capital of $6,323,560, versus $6,989,223 and $7,382,442 in the prior two years. Market value of subsidiary and minority investments not stated or included in working capital, which consisted of $76,325 cash, $759,132 in bullion, $5,112,560 in short-term notes and securities and $917,091 in accounts receivable (including EGMA).

INCOME STATISTICS (per share)

Year	Earn's	Div's	Price Range High	Low
1961	$0.56	$0.45	15	– 9-1/2
1962	0.93	0.70	14-1/2	– 8-1/2
1963	0.93	1.00	12-5/8	– 9-5/8
1964	1.13	1.00	18-1/8	– 9-7/8
1965	0.84	1.00	18-5/8	– 12-1/2
1966	0.49	0.60	15-1/2	– 6-3/4
1967	0.33	0.40	11-1/2	– 7-1/4
1968	0.46	0.40	15-3/8	– 8-1/4
1969	0.44	0.40	17-1/8	– 7
1970	0.31	0.40	12	– 7

ORE RESERVES:

Giant Mine

Dec. 31, 1970   662,200 tons av. 0.67 oz. gold per ton
"   " 1969   1,144,500 tons av. 0.69 oz.   "   "   "
"   " 1968   1,275,450 tons av. 0.73 oz.   "   "   "
"   " 1967   1,628,500 tons av. 0.71 oz.   "   "   "
"   " 1966   2,134,000 tons av. 0.68 oz.   "   "   "

Lolar Mine

Dec. 31, 1970	265,100 tons av. 0.67 oz.	"	"	"
" " 1969	340,000 tons av. 0.66 oz.	"	"	"
" " 1968	331,000 tons av. 0.71 oz.	"	"	"
" " 1967	317,000 tons av. 0.67 oz.	"	"	"

Supercrest Mine

Dec. 31, 1970	148,200 tons av. 0.66 oz.	"	"	"
" " 1969	129,000 tons av. 0.69 oz.	"	"	"
" " 1968	81,400 tons av. 0.76 oz.	"	"	"
" " 1967	99,300 tons av. 0.65 oz.	"	"	"

Rating: SPECULATIVE

Comment: Despite its long and productive history, it now appears that the Giant mine itself is a dying enterprise. Since gold exploration on numerous other properties and interests has been unrewarding thus far, the future of GYK, as a gold operation, would seem to depend on finding large additions to ore reserves on the Lolar and Supercrest properties and/or great luck in outside exploration—two propositions I would not care to bet on. A large increase in the price of gold might give the Company a new lease on life for a few years and make substantial profits for shareholders, due to the high leverage involved, but surely there are far better and safer opportunities around.

KERR ADDISON MINES LTD.

Capitalization

LONG-TERM DEBT	None
PREFERRED STOCK	None
COMMON STOCK	Authorized: 12,500,000 shares.
	Issued: 9,534,499 shares.
	(4,144,027 shares, or 43.5 percent, owned by Noranda Mines.)
EXCHANGE LISTING	Toronto Stock Exchange
PRICE RANGE (1964–71)	19½–6⅝
DIVIDENDS	1964–67: 40¢, 1968:52¢, 1969–70: 56¢ (annually).

History. Kerr Addison owns and operates a large gold mine consisting of 34 claims on 1,193 acres in McGarry Township, Larder Lake area of N Ontario. *Normetal Mining Corp.* and *Quemont Mining* (copper-zinc producers) in Quebec are wholly-owned subsidiaries. Since 1963, the original corporation (*Kerr Addison Gold Mines Ltd.,* inc. 1937) has been engaged in an active and aggressive program of diversification, largely into base-metal mining, through acquisition, investment and outside exploration and development. Nevertheless, the original Kerr property remains one of Canada's major gold producers.

From 1938 to Dec. 31, 1970, the Kerr mine produced 8,912,340 oz. of gold, valued at $321,798,138, from 33,287,790 tons of ore. Total dividends, on a consolidated basis, to December 1970 were $92,651,654 (not including dividends paid by Normetal and Quemont subsidiaries prior to amalgamation in 1968).

Fundamental Position. In 1970, the Kerr mine produced 137,100 ounces of gold, having a value of $6,010,000 (plus $995,346 EGMA), from 341,151 tons of ore. Average milling rate was 935 tons per day, versus 1,296 tons for 1969 and 1,395 tons per day in 1968. Production has been on a decreasing scale since 1960, when average milling rate reached a peak of 4,556 tons per day.

The Normetal property added 6,072 ounces of gold, 321,583 ounces of silver, 11,553,571 lbs. of copper and 40,707,191 lbs. of zinc to total production, while the Quemont mine (scheduled to close at the end of 1971) yielded 28,534 oz. of gold, 127,850 oz. of silver, 4,153,304 lbs. of copper and 7,914,086 lbs. of zinc.

Consolidated gross revenues for 1970 (including investment income of $5,213,718) amounted to $25,640,249. Operating expenses and other charges of $18,212,762 allowed for a net profit of $7,166,502 or $0.75 per share, down from $1.01 per share in 1969, but up from $0.74 in 1969 and $0.66 in 1967.

Exploration and development work on other base-metal mining prospects and interests in Canada, the United States, the United Kingdom and Ireland is scheduled to continue on an active and aggressive basis in 1971-72, by the wholly owned

Keradamex Inc. exploration and investment subsidiary.

Financial Position.   The basic financial position of the Company (on a consolidated basis for Kerr Addison, Normetal, Quemont and Keradamex) is quite strong, with a net working capital of $15, 585, 119 and a ratio of working assets to liabilities of 8.7 to 1. Kerr's investment portfolio, consisting principally of other mining securities, had a market value of $55,271,500 as of Dec. 31, 1970, not including other sundry holdings and partially-owned investments acquired and carried at a cost of $16,-201,887.

ORE RESERVES:

Kerr Mine

> Dec. 31, 1970 2,040,025 tons av. 0.53 oz. gold per ton
>   "   "   1969 2,491,848 tons av. 0.50 oz.   "   "   "
>   "   "   1968 3,249,128 tons av. 0.46 oz.   "   "   "
>   "   "   1967 3,750,329 tons av. 0.45 oz.   "   "   "

The gold-ore body at the Kerr mine appears to be largely defined. Extensive drilling and exploration in the lower levels of the mine in recent years has failed to disclose additional ore. Although reserves appear adequate for five to six years production at current rates, a higher gold price would undoubtedly bring about increased milling and accelerate the rate of exhaustion.

Normetal Mine

> Dec. 31, 1970   760,000 tons av. 1.94 pc. copper 6.0 pc. zinc
> " " 1969   953,000 tons av. 1.95 "   "   6.38 "   "
> " " 1968 1,198,000 tons av. 2.15 "   "   6.25 "   "
> " " 1967 1,595,000 tons av. 2.11 "   "   6.47 "   "

Rating: SPECULATIVE

Comment: The future of Kerr Addison as a gold investment appears quite limited, although a substantially higher price for gold, coming soon, might provide short-term speculative leverage. Base-metal prospects depend on higher prices for copper and zinc and on developing new mines to replace the exhausted Quemont property and the declining reserves at Normetal. As a gold speculation, pass it up, even though some of its base-metal prospects appear to hold promise for the future.

MADSEN RED LAKE GOLD MINES LTD.

Capitalization

LONG-TERM DEBT	None
PREFERRED STOCK	None
COMMON STOCK	Authorized: 5,000,000 shares.
	Issued: 3,499,528 shares.
EXCHANGE LISTING	Toronto Stock Exchange
PRICE RANGE (1964–71)	$2.95–$0.67
DIVIDENDS	1958–60: 20¢; 1961–64: 15¢; 1965: 7½¢;
	1967: 10¢; 1970: 3¢.

History.	Incorporated in 1935, Madsen Red Lake Gold Mines consists of 97 patented claims in Baird and Heyson Townships, Red Lake district, NW Ontario. Main shaft to 25th (4,175-ft.) level. Current mill capacity, 825 tons per day. Total production to Dec. 31, 1970, valued at $80,098,103 from 7,639,624 tons milled. Dividends paid through December 1970 totaled $10,-444,891. Company has an active exploration program and holds numerous base-metal and gold claims and prospects.

Fundamental Position.	In 1970, Madsen Red Lake produced gold valued at $1,494,251 from 184,530 tons of ore. EGMA received amounted to $416,600, while investment and other income was $58,371. Total income of $1,969,222 was offset by operating costs of $2,283,716 and depreciation of $96,629, resulting in a *loss* of $411,123 or 11.7¢ per share vs. a profit of 8.7¢ per share in 1969 and a flat year for 1968. Company appears to be making a small profit for 1971. In mid-1970, milling rate was deliberately curtailed to reduce costs and preserve assets pending a higher price for gold.

Financial Position.	Capital assets at end of 1970 were $2,-270,039 against liabilities of $172,493, leaving a net working capital of $2,097,546. In addition to its numerous other base-metal and gold claims, interests, holdings and options, the Company held, as of December 1970, 671,459 shares, or 19.93 percent, of Baffinland Iron Mining Ltd (preliminary exploration and development completed) and 860,300 shares (48.7 percent) of Ava Gold Mining Co. (currently under exploration).

Ore Reserves

Dec. 31, 1970	245,000	tons av. 0.272 oz. gold per ton
" " 1969	328,000	tons av. 0.279 oz. " " "

" " 1968   336,700 tons av. 0.270 oz.   "   "   "
" " 1967   431,500 tons av. 0.290 oz.   "   "   "

Underground diamond drilling carried out in 1969–70 confirms continuity of ore zone below present (4,175-ft.) bottom level of mine. Higher-than-ever grade of ore being developed in No. 8 ore zone, first discovered in 1969. However, ore development temporarily curtailed to conform to reduced milling rate.

Rating: SPECULATIVE

Comment: This is a most interesting speculation. Low grade of ore and dependence on EGMA are negative factors but prospect of a substantial increase in production given an adequately higher price for gold, provides extraordinary leverage, if this stock can be purchased cheaply. Despite the fact that this stock sold as low as $0.69 per share in 1969, I would not put it down as a "penny" stock; it has far more promise than that. For those who can afford to speculate *only,* it is a situation worth watching closely.

PAMOUR PORCUPINE MINES LTD.

Capitalization

LONG-TERM DEBT	None
PREFERRED STOCK	None
COMMON STOCK	5,000,000 shares authorized and issued (2,308,239 shares or 46.16 percent held by Noranda Mines).
EXCHANGE LISTINGS	Toronto Stock Exchange, Canadian Stock Exchange.
PRICE RANGE (1964–71)	$3.50–$1.02
DIVIDENDS	1964–65: 12¢; 1966: 11¢; 1967–68: 10¢; 1969–70: 15¢ (annually).

History.   Incorporated in 1934, Pamour Porcupine operates a gold producer on 1,180 acres in Whitney Township, Porcupine area, N Ontario. Main (East) 5-compartment shaft to 3,145-ft. level. No. 4 internal (West) shaft, 4,800 ft. from main shaft, extends to 2,400-ft. level. Mill capacity 1,800 tons per day. From incorporation to Dec. 31, 1970, the Pamour mine produced gold valued at $75,454,854, from 18,395,222 tons of ore. Total dividends paid to December 1970 amounted to $10,750,000. Pamour is controlled by Noranda Mines, which held, as of December 1970, 46.16 percent of Pamour shares.

Fundamental Position.   In 1970, Pamour produced $2,924,-078 worth of gold from 633,665 tons of ore milled. Average milling rate was 1,736 tons per day. EGMA contributed $507,400 to gross earnings, while miscellaneous investment income added $506,639. After operating charges and depreciation totaling $3,036,744, a net profit of $900,373, or 18¢ per share, remained. This was less than the 22¢ per share earned in 1969, but more than the 14.7¢ recorded for 1968.

Financial Position.   At the end of 1970, the Company had a net working capital of $1,000,200, plus an investment portfolio of common shares and bonds in associated companies having a market value of $9,710,400.

Ore Reserves

Dec. 31, 1970   1,530,870 tons av. 0.124 oz. gold per ton
  "   "   1969   1,571,260 tons av. 0.126 oz.   "   "   "
  "   "   1968   1,600,700 tons av. 0.116 oz.   "   "   "

Declining ore position at main body, located in area of East shaft, currently being offset by increase in quantity and grade of newer West orebody. 1970 estimate for East orebody: 1,227,-890 tons av. 0.116 oz. per ton, while West orebody had proven reserves of 302,980 tons av. 0.158 oz. gold per ton.

Rating: SPECULATIVE

Comment: Like all low-priced stocks, this one has leverage, if nothing else. Ore is low-grade, but operating costs are not prohibitive. EGMA is obviously of considerable importance at present. Ore reserves are apparently being maintained and a three-year supply is available at present rates of production. Development of additional reserves in West orebody over the next year or two would add greatly to attractiveness of this issue. Based on recent market value of its investment portfolio, Pamour's asset value alone would be worth two to three dollars per share. This is another case, where, if one can afford the risk, the stock could be bought on weakness and held for leveraged profits during the next upswing in the gold group.

SIGMA MINES (QUEBEC) LTD.
Capitalization

LONG-TERM DEBT   None

PREFERRED STOCK	None
COMMON STOCK	1,000,000 shares authorized and issued (625,536 shares, or 63 percent held by Dome Mines Ltd.).
EXCHANGE LISTING	Toronto Stock Exchange
PRICE RANGE (1964–71)	$8.50–$2.40
DIVIDENDS	1963–69: 30¢; 1970: 25¢ (annually).

History.   Incorporated in 1937, Quebec charter, the Sigma mine consists of 21 claims on 1,150 acres in Bourlamaque Township, NW Quebec. In 1970–71, Sigma acquired adjacent Gamma Mines (Quebec) Ltd. as a wholly-owned property. Company also participates in exploration ventures with parent company and its affiliates on the following basis: Dome Mines (40 percent), Dome Petroleum (33 percent), Campbell Red Lake (21 percent) and Sigma Mines (6 percent).

Mine development consists of main shaft (no. 2) extending to 24th (3,317 ft.) level and No. 3, 5-compartment internal shaft extending from 2,700-ft. level to 5,081-ft. depth, serving 12 additional levels. Mill capacity 1,400 tons per day.

From 1937 to Dec. 31, 1970, the Sigma mine produced $87,-974,344 in gold values from 13,277,054 tons of ore. Total dividends paid during period amounted to $12,375,000. The Company has remained on a regular dividend basis since 1940.

Fundamental Position.   In 1970, the Sigma mine produced gold valued at $3,288,555 from 510,780 tons of ore milled. Average milling rate was 1,399 tons per day, up slightly from the previous two years. EGMA contributed $912,000, while investment and miscellaneous income added $122,000. Gross income of $4,322,598 was offset by operating expenses and other charges of $4,057,607, allowing for a net profit of $264,991, or 26¢ per share, vs. 33¢ in 1969 and 36¢ per share in 1968.

Financial Position.   For the year ending Dec. 31, 1970, net working capital was $1,596,669, remaining at about the same level as in prior two years. In addition, Company held $1 million in 5 percent subordinate convertible debentures of Dome Petroleum Ltd. Sigma also maintains a small participation in ventures of Panartic Oils Ltd., through its affiliation with Dome Mines.

Ore Reserves
Dec.31, 1970   1,219,300 tons av. 0.225 oz. gold per ton
"   "   1969   1,270,470 tons av. 0.225 oz. " "   "
"   "   1968   1,293,560 tons av. 0.224 oz. " "   "

Main development work at Sigma mine during 1970–71 was between 10th and 36th level, with only minor amounts of ore found in the 6 bottom levels. Work is being extended, however, to the adjacent Gamma property between the 16th and 21st levels to outline further a partially developed orebody.

Rating: SPECULATIVE

Comment: Sigma is an old and steady producer, and there is no reason to believe, as of this writing, that it will not continue to produce for some years to come. Probably a lot depends on finding additional ore on the newly acquired Gamma property. Present heavy dependence on EGMA, however, is a very negative factor. Unless I could buy this one at a very low P.E. ratio (perhaps less than 10), I don't think I would be too interested.

PATO CONSOLIDATED GOLD DREDGING LTD. (PO)

Capitalization

LONG-TERM DEBT	None
PREFERRED STOCK	None
COMMON STOCK	Authorized: 5,000,000
	Issued: 3,502,000
	(International Mining Corp. of New York owns 2,360,900 shares, or 67.5 percent).
EXCHANGE LISTINGS	American Stock Exchange, Toronto Stock Exchange, Montreal Stock Exchange and Vancouver Stock Exchange.
PRICE RANGE (1971)	10⅝–4⅝
DIVIDENDS (1971)	$0.40 (total).

History.   Incorporated in Vancouver, B.C., Canada, in 1934, Pato Consolidated mines placer gold from the Nechi River and its tributaries in the Zaragoza district, Department of Antioquia, Colombia, S.A. The Company currently operates 4 dredging vessels. Pato owns mineral rights to 75 alluvial and 45 lode claims and holds 79 additional alluvial claims under lease. All claims are contiguous and cover a total of 385 square miles. Mining area is located about 450 miles inland from the Magdalena River delta.

Gold produced is sold to the Bank of the Republic of Colombia at U.S. $35 per ounce, with bonuses paid by the Bank (on a voluntary basis) to compensate for the difference between the fixed $35 price and the higher European market price. Since beginning production in 1934, pato has recovered gold valued at $136,918,095 from 678,519,500 cubic yards of placer material dredged. Production in recent years has been as follows:

Year	Cu. Yds. Dredged	Oz. Gold Recovered
1970	19,146,000	62,085
1969	23,129,000	72,312
1968	25,616,000	76,684
1967	26,606,000	88,465
1966	28,096,000	90,628
1965	30,492,000	115,367

Pato also holds a 16.5 percent interest in *Companhia Brasileira de Metalurgia e Minearcao,* the largest columbium mine in the free world, located in Brazil. CBMM produces about 60 percent of the free world's supply of this exotic metal and contributes about one-fifth of Pato's annual income.

Fundamental Position. In 1969 and 1970, Pato suffered a reversal of its prior general uptrend in earnings and dividends. Bullion revenue for 1970 amounted to $2,736,228, while investment dividends (mainly from CBMM) contributed $889,432 and interest earned added $193,808 to overall earnings of $3,819,468. Operating costs and charges, however, were $3,961,798, resulting in a net *loss* of $142,330, or 4¢ per share, vs. a profit of 21¢ for 1969 and $1.27 in 1968. Not included in 1970 income was a $1,391,685 insurance settlement received for a dredge that sank in 1969, which would have added a gain of 40¢ per share. Operations for 1971 are expected to return to profitability, due to higher gold prices and better cost control.

Financial Position. Net working capital at the end of 1970 remained strong and steady at $6,359,345, while the Company's investment portfolio had a market value of $3,713,859.

INCOME STATISTICS (per share)

Year	Earn's	Div's	Price Range High	Low
1963	$d0.06 *	$0.10	3-3/4 – 2	
1964	0.17	0.10	4-1/4 – 2-1/4	
1965	0.27	0.20	4-1/2 – 3	
1966	0.14	0.10	5-1/8 – 3	
1967	0.36	0.30	12-1/4 – 3	
1968	1.27	0.70	20-1/4 – 8-3/4	
1969	0.21	0.20	16-7/8 – 4-1/4	
1970	d0.04 *	0.20	9-3/4 – 4-7/8	

*deficit

Rating: SPECULATIVE

Comment: Pato has both strong positive and strong negative values for speculators to consider. On the positive side, we have ore reserves adequate for 10 to 15 years operation and the possibility that, in the event of a substantially higher price for gold, additional dredging vessels could be put into service and production greatly increased. On the negative side, we have the present high operating costs and the uncertainty of any business relationship with a South American government, even though the Government of Colombia has thus far proved to be one of the most stable and honorable governments in the Americas.

Nevertheless, corporations with a major part of their assets or operations in South America are generally regarded with some suspicion by U.S. and Canadian investors and are consequently expected normally to sell at low P.E. ratios and offer generous yields.

In the case of Pato Consolidated, the leverage is invariably quite pronounced (see Income Statistics for yearly price ranges!). It seems to me, therefore, that those who can afford the risk might find unusual opportunities for trading profits in this stock. Buy on the bad news and sell on the good. (For seasoned speculators only.)

This concludes our review of the listed and active Canadian gold mining companies. But let me add here that the statistical information presented concerning these and all other stocks reviewed is derived from *public* information that is presumed to be reliable. However, there is no way that I can absolutely guarantee that it is. My conclusions and comments are, of course, based on my assumption that this statistical information, as released by the companies themselves, is both accurate and honest. Furthermore, the data presented is the latest available at the time of this writing. But any reader contemplating the purchase of *any* security mentioned or reviewed in this book, should first be sure to obtain from his broker, from other reliable sources or from the company concerned itself, the most recent report or summary of operations and financial condition available.

The investor or speculator should study the most recent data concerning his chosen stock or stocks most carefully, and then reevaluate the author's recommendations and suggestions in the light of the latest developments revealed. The basic rules outlined in previous chapters of this book are designed to assist the investor in making a final judgment as to whether to buy, sell or hold specific stocks.

Before we leave the Canadian scene, however, there are a few "special situations" that have aroused considerable interest among gold-oriented investors in recent years. These stocks are: EAGLE GOLD MINES LTD. (CSE); MENTOR EXPLORATION AND DEVELOPMENT CO. (TSE); and AGNICO MINES LTD. (TSE). *Eagle* and *Mentor* are still essentially exploration companies that have not yet been able (or willing) to bring their known gold-bearing properties into production. Consequently, the risks on these two stocks are high, although rewards could be substantial for the patient holder who buys them cheaply. *Agnico* is a potential silver-gold combination, one of the few silver properties that appears to the author to have some merit at this time. Here is a brief summary of these properties:

EAGLE GOLD MINES LTD.

This company is one of the few newcomers to the Canadian gold mining scene. Although originally incorporated in 1945, development work did not commence until 1967. Located in

Joutel Township, Quebec, the Company has established an initial ore possibility of 2,397,748 tons, averaging 0.285 ounces gold per ton. A 3-compartment shaft has been completed to a depth of 1,860 ft., with 11 stations cut for levels at 150-ft. intervals. A 1,000-ton-per-day-capacity mill was under construction in 1970, when a decision was made to defer production pending a higher price for gold. The Company holds a sizable area of 122 adjacent claims. Authorized capital shares: 8,000,000; issued: 6,555,000. Price range per share, 1967–71: $8.40–$0.72. This is a very interesting prospect for speculators, but *buy low* and don't chase it.

MENTOR EXPLORATION AND DEVELOPMENT CO.

Mentor holds 25 promising gold claims in the Red Lake area that are currently being investigated by trenching and diamond drilling. The main interest, however, is in the Company's investment portfolio, which consists of 552,996 shares of *Eagle Gold Mines,* 416,000 shares of *Agnico Mines* (silver) and 1,-235,582 shares of *Sudbury Contact Mines*, a promising copper-nickel prospect. Authorized capital shares: 5,000,000; issued: 3,455,745. Price range, 1964–71: $1.55–$0.17. A penny stock perhaps, but one with unusual possibilities.

AGNICO MINES LTD.

Silver producer, Cobalt Lake area, N Ontario. Earned 11¢ per share in 1970, up from 5¢ in 1969 and 5.2¢ in 1968. Holds $800,-000 worth of debentures of *Eagle Gold Mines,* plus warrants to purchase 800,000 shares of Eagle at $1.00 per share. Rumored as a possible merger partner for Eagle Gold Mines and/or Mentor Exploration. Authorized capital shares: 5,000,000; shares issued: 3,584,327. Price range, 1964–71: $3.65–$0.44. This stock could show a handsome capital gain on either (a) a strong rise in the price of silver or (b) an announcement of merger with Eagle and/or Mentor. But you would have to own it (cheaply) before those things happen.

Canadian Penny Mining Stocks. There are some 12,000 active, inactive, defunct, dormant, dying, developing and hopeful mining incorporations in Canada. Only a very small percentage are actual producing enterprises. Most of the remainder, generally characterized by the low price of their shares and the ambiguity of their assets, are legitimate, but the odds against their ultimate success are quite large. Some are merely schemes to sell "moose pasture" to the gullible. The market behavior of most very-low-priced stocks tends to be too erratic for routine trading techniques, and the chance of their becoming suddenly insolvent (without warning) is, unfortunately, not uncommon. Above all, never buy such stocks merely on "tips" or "hunches."

The advice given in Chapter XI, regarding U.S. penny mining stocks applies equally well to their Canadian counterparts. Believe me, there is danger enough in speculating in established and proven issues, without venturing into the untested and unknown. Again, please remember that the most important rule of speculation is: DON'T BE A SUCKER.

Notes:

CHAPTER XII

1. Like most acts of brutality and terrorism, the murder of Pierre Laporte served only to diminish the cause of its perpetrators. Many *Québecois,* once sincerely committed to separatism, were so revolted by the barbarous behavior of the terrorists that they have since adopted more moderate positions.

2. Pato Consolidated, although incorporated in Canada and having its head offices in Vancouver, does all of its mining in South America. Therefore, I guess it is not really a Canadian company —but I just didn't know where else to put it!

3. It is possible, however, to buy "foreign" (foreign-owned) shares of these companies on the New York and American Exchanges, if such stock is specifically ordered. Foreign-owned shares sell for slightly less than American-owned shares of the same company, but the purchaser of foreign-owned shares is required to pay the IET, even though the shares were obtained on an American exchange. Foreign-owned shares listed on U.S. exchanges have a lower-case "fn" following their regular ticker symbol for identification. For the private investor there is no point in buying foreign-owned shares rather than their listed American counterparts—they are strictly for the professional trader and arbitrage specialist.

4. Frankly, I'm not concerned enough myself really to want the answer to this (hypothetical) situation.

5. Based on exchange rates in effect for 1971.

6. Stock certificates, like other important legal documents, must obviously be stored in a secure place. The bank safe-deposit box is recommended.

Part 3

South Africa:
The New Eldorado

XIII

A MOST UNUSUAL NATION

"Nothing contributes so much to the prosperity and happiness of a country as high profits."

—DAVID RICARDO

THE Spanish and Portuguese explorers and adventurers who first embarked on the perilous voyages of discovery in the fifteenth and sixteenth centuries were impelled, in no small part, by the dream of finding the mythical kingdom of *El Dorado,* a land supposedly so rich in gold, diamonds and other precious minerals, that the wealth previously amassed by all the great empires of the world would seem trivial by comparison.[1] These Spanish and Portuguese *conquistadores* eventually found enough gold in the Americas to satisfy all but the most avaricious expectations, yet many of them felt that their exalted vision of El Dorado remained unfulfilled.

The initial explorations of the United States were carried out by Spanish adventurers, enduring untold hardships—and often perishing from disease or at the hands of hostile natives—as they roamed the South and Southwest unshaken in their belief that, despite the great riches seized from the Aztecs and the Incas, the land of El Dorado remained to be found. They were of course quite correct; the mineral wealth of Mexico and Peru, although enormous for its time, became almost insignificant when compared to the later discoveries in California, Australia and the Klondike. Yet none of the latter would perhaps measure up to the heroic vision of El Dorado as conceived by the *conquistadores.*

There is, however, a modern nation, the Republic of South Africa, that, if it does not entirely fulfill the promise of El Dorado, surely comes as close to doing so as is possible in this world. If the shades of the *conquistadores* could be called forth from the past, they might well be stunned by the revelation that the southernmost nation in Africa (discovered, but not taken possession of, by the Portuguese navigator Bartholomeu Dias in 1488) now produces more gold in a single year than was yielded by the whole of Spanish America in the 200 years following its discovery and occupation. And more diamonds are brought forth annually from the mines of South and South-West Africa than were possessed by all the kings and emperors up to and including the time Queen Isabella pawned hers to finance the voyages of Columbus.

Of the $80 billion worth of gold* estimated to exist in the world today, more than $25 billion, or nearly one-third, has come from the South African Rand since gold was first discovered there in 1886. South Africa currently produces nearly 75 percent of the Western world's annual supply of the yellow metal. If production figures for the Communist world were available, South Africa would still contribute something close to 60 percent of the world's total output. South Africa is also the world's leading supplier of diamonds, both industrial and gem stones, and also produces more than half of the world's supply of platinum.

South Africa is also the world's third-ranking producer of uranium and has major deposits of other minerals, including coal, copper, iron, manganese and asbestos. Virtually every other mineral is also found in South Africa in commercial quantities except oil. Certainly all this mineral wealth in a country containing only 0.8 percent of the world's land area and 0.5 percent of total world population qualifies it as a modern El Dorado. But the Republic of South Africa, even without its unchallengeable position as the treasure house of the world, is a

*At $35 per ounce.

land of such diversity that it would still be considered a most unusual nation by any other standard.

Much of what the Western world hears about South Africa is, unfortunately, distorted by emotional reactions to the much criticized (and generally little understood) *apartheid* or "separate development" program of the South African Government and by international Communist propaganda, which seeks to cause as much mischief as possible in southern Africa. Make no mistake about it, the Russian and Chinese imperialists would dearly love to seize so rich a prize for their respective empires.[2] They hope to do this in the classic Leninist tradition, by first fomenting civil war and political chaos in all of southern Africa, and then imposing military, political and economic control over weak and inexperienced black revolutionary governments of their own creation.

So far, the attempts of the Soviets and the Chinese to sustain significant guerilla movements in South Africa, South-West Africa, Rhodesia and the Portuguese territories of Angola and Mozambique have been singularly unsuccessful, despite the repeated infiltration of Communist arms and Moscow- or Peking-trained terrorists.[3] On the propaganda front, however, the Communists have had better luck; they have assiduously fostered the simplistic image of a southern Africa in which a handful of white "colonialists" brutally oppress legions of helpless Blacks.

This propaganda line, repeated constantly by pro-Marxist politicians and academicians, is reinforced by much of the U.S. news media, which tends to lean over backwards to avoid charges of "racism" in its reporting. Consequently South Africa and its neighboring states consistently get a "bad press" in the United States, so consistently, in fact, that one is perhaps justified in being suspicious of the total accuracy or objectivity of such reporting. Unfortunately, the inflammatory rhetoric heard at the United Nations is too often the primary source of news concerning South Africa.

Whenever the press comment on a situation or country is almost totally negative, and such is the case with South Africa and her neighbor states, one cannot help but remember that the most successful method of propaganda involves nothing more than continuously slanted or one-sided reporting. There are, undeniably, many unfortunate aspects to the *apartheid* program, but they are being opposed not only by the outside world but by many white South Africans themselves. Like its economic condition, the socio-political situation of South Africa is anything but static. Some very positive things have been accomplished in recent years to improve the well-being of all the varied peoples of South Africa, and it is almost a certainty that much more is to come in this area. We should remember that less than 20 years ago rigid racial segregation (without the many compensations found in the *apartheid* program!) was a way of life in a great part of the United States. Time does not run backward, or even stand still, for either the United States *or* South Africa.

There are several other reasons why I believe that at least part of the criticism of South Africa is Red-inspired; one of them is because Portugal's rule of Angola and Mozambique is also invariably characterized in the same simple terms of whites oppressing Blacks, yet a less race-conscious "white" nation than Portugal can hardly be found. The late Dr. Antonio Salazar, the iron-willed but mild-mannered economics professor who was the Portuguese Chief of State for some thirty-seven years prior to his death in 1969, frequently reminded his people that they were a mulatto nation with the blood of the Moors in their veins. He insisted that intermarriage in the overseas territories, as at home, conferred full citizenship for the Blacks. And he encouraged such intermarriage; he wanted more mulattoism, not less. "If we didn't have our African people and were not intermarried with them, what would we be but another little province of Spain?" he demanded.[4]

Many of the officers as well as the soldiers of the Portuguese military forces are Black, and any Black resident of Angola or Mozambique who can pass a literacy test is granted the full rights of citizenship, including the right of suffrage. Yet the Communist puppets and sympathizers in the United Nations and elsewhere constantly raise the cry that Portuguese rule in Africa must be ended because of its "colonialist and racist" nature.

As for South Africa, it is charged, among other things, that it is a country ruled by fascists and "neo-nazis." Yet South Africa was *the first* country to recognize the new state of Israel in 1948 and has strongly supported Israel ever since. South Africa also maintains the most cordial and noncritical relations with Angola and Mozambique, even though the South African approach to the problem of maintaining racial harmony is entirely different from that of Portugal.

South Africa is also on excellent terms with many of its neighboring Black states, including Botswana, Lesotho, Swaziland, Zambia and Malawi. Cordial diplomatic and trade ties are also being maintained between South Africa and Madagascar. Talks have been initiated between South Africa and several of the former French-colonial states in central Africa in the hope that full diplomatic recognition and economic cooperation will eventually result from such dialogues. All this is part of South Africa's new "outward-looking" foreign policy of providing both trade and economic aid to Black African states.

During a recent official visit to South Africa of Dr. Hastings Banda, the Black president of Malawi, South Africans were treated to the sight of their Afrikaner Prime Minister, Mr. Johannes Vorster, seated between two Black ladies at the state banquet honoring Dr. Banda and thoroughly enjoying himself. All of the foregoing hardly fits the oft-drawn picture of South Africa as a neo-nazi police state.

Perhaps the real reason why the Communists are so anxious to gain a foothold in southern Africa was revealed by none other than Bram Fischer, South Africa's number-one Communist. According to a Johannesburg press report, Mr. Fischer was once asked if it was the gold that was the primary objective of Soviet subversion in southern Africa. "We would trade you all the gold in Africa for Cape Point," was Mr. Fischer's remarkably candid answer. Regardless of the accuracy of that story, it is obvious that a Soviet naval base at the southern tip of Africa would be of enormous advantage to them. With the Soviet forces in Egypt and the Middle East already in a position to establish control over the Suez Canal and the Eastern Mediterranean, a Russian naval and air force at the Cape would give them a stranglehold on all east-west shipping and particularly on the absolutely vital flow of oil from the Middle East to Western Europe.

At any rate, discounting Communist propaganda, the past, present and future of South Africa is far more complex than any simple case of white versus Black. But while virtually everyone recognizes the enormous economic potential of this most unusual nation, there are, understandably, some reservations about its political future. Before going any further, however, let me state my belief that the political risk of investing in South Africa is probably less than the economic risk of investing in most of the countries presumed to be politically safe (including perhaps even the United States) at this time. Actually, when considering an investment, one must balance the total risk, political, economic and monetary, against the overall potential for capital gain and income.

Furthermore, as I have stressed often enough, the investor must take the long view and not be disconcerted or misled by transient contemporary events or the erratic performance of the short term. Over the long run, I believe that political, as well as economic, conditions in South Africa will get better rather than worse. And since the price of gold is going to continue to rise over the long term, it looks like a winning combination.

The author confesses to strong feelings about individual freedom, and I would never recommend South African stocks or invest in them myself if I thought that by doing so I was encouraging or supporting tyranny. But this is certainly not the case. In fact, the mines and other industrial corporations in South Africa have been instrumental both in opposing the more discriminatory features of *apartheid* and in providing the best opportunities for the economic and cultural advancement of non-whites. In a country that is critically short of skilled labor, as is South Africa, it makes good sense to the mining and industrial enterprises to encourage the training and promotion of non-whites, whether the political administration agrees or not.

Industrial and technological enterprises are probably the most powerful force working to end race discrimination in South Africa. The sheer economic inefficiency and waste of segregation and all other forms of race discrimination make it incompatible with modern commercial and industrial organization. Even the government-owned railway system, out of inescapable necessity, is ignoring the old laws barring the employment of non-whites for skilled jobs. The General Motors Corporation of South Africa, whose labor force is 52 percent non-white, has been quietly doing the same thing for years.[5] There have been literally hundreds of similar cases in recent times, all indicating that large cracks are appearing in the failing walls of segregation, but I will cite only one more: the case of Mr. Harry Oppenheimer.

Mr. Oppenheimer is not only the richest man in South Africa, but probably one of the richest in the world. He controls a mining and industrial empire worth more than $3 billion, is a director of more than 100 companies and is chairman of at least 50 of them, the most important being the giant Anglo-American Corporation of South Africa, a holding company that controls the major share of gold (and diamond) production in South Africa. Harry Oppenheimer is also an outspoken foe of *apartheid,* as it is currently practiced.

When Mr. Oppenheimer's daughter Mary was married in 1965, most of the 3,000 guests who attended the ceremony were Black, although they could not come to the reception because of an *apartheid* law barring the serving of liquor to Blacks on white premises. In 1968, Mr. Oppenheimer agreed to become the chancellor of Cape Town University, which then numbered 266 non-whites among its 6,392 students. When the government tried to make him enforce its segregation rules on all extracurricular activities, Oppenheimer flatly refused.

"What is the use of our civilization" he said, "if we are not prepared to share it with men and woman of all races?"[6]

Well, the reader of course must make his own decision, but the author, for one, has no qualms whatever about investing in Mr. Oppenheimer's gold mines.

HISTORY AND GEOGRAPHY OF SOUTH AFRICA

The land that is South Africa today was first discovered by the Portuguese in the fifteenth century as they rounded the

Cape of Good Hope on their way to explore the Eastern oceans. Western civilization, however, did not actually come to southern Africa until 1652, when Jan van Riebeck led a small party of Dutch settlers ashore with instructions from the East India Company to establish a provisioning station for the company's vessels voyaging between Holland and the East Indies. In 1688, a party of French Huguenots, fleeing from religious persecution in Europe, arrived at the Cape and were readily assimilated by the small but thriving Dutch community. Also among the earliest arrivals were German mercenaries employed by the Dutch East India Company, and German and Swedish refugees from the Thirty Years War then raging in Europe.

The first English settlers, some 3,500 of them, did not arrive until 1820, and then they settled in the eastern part of the Cape, retaining their cultural identity and remaining more or less separate from the Dutch-German-Huguenot community. Three times before, however, in 1781, from 1795 to 1803, and again in 1806, British military and naval forces had forcibly occupied the Cape as strategic moves in the worldwide wars with Revolutionary and Napoleonic France. It was in part because of recurrent friction with the British that the original Dutch-assimilated population of the Cape, or "Boers" as they then began to call themselves, were led to leave the Cape area and begin the "Great Treks" up the coast and into the interior.

From 1835 to 1840, a large part of the Boer population left the Cape and moved northward, traveling in covered wagon trains, much as did the American pioneers moving into the western territories of the United States. In 1838, the Boers met and, after a series of bloody battles, defeated the well-organized forces of the Zulu king, Dingaan, who was then leading his people in a slow migration southward from central Africa. The Boer leader, Andreas Pretorius, proclaimed an independent "Republic of Natal" in the coastal area around Durban (see *Fig. 31,* MAP OF SOUTHERN AFRICA), but the British, who were then in full occupation of the Cape, sent their forces up the coast and, in 1843, forced the annexation of Natal as a British colony.

The Boers moved on again, this time westward and deeper

into the interior, and, in 1854, Britain recognized the independence of a Boer-established "Orange Free State." But in 1877, the British annexed the Boer-occupied Transvaal territory north of the Orange Free State. This action led to the first Anglo-Boer War (1881), in which Britain was defeated and forced to recognize the independence of both the Orange Free State and a new Transvaal Republic. But in 1886, the famous gold strike at Langlaagte in the Transvaal opened the Witwatersrand gold fields and brought thousands of new settlers to the Transvaal, including many British and others of non-Boer origin. Johannesburg was founded in 1886 and quickly grew from a raw mining camp to a bustling metropolis.

In 1895, a small force of British mercenaries, secretly sponsored by Cecil Rhodes and led by L.S. Jameson, made a daring but abortive attempt to seize the Rand gold fields.[7] Although thwarted by Boer forces, Jameson's raid greatly increased the ongoing tension between the Boers and the British, and a second South African War errupted between the two Boer Republics and Great Britain in 1899.[8] But unlike the first, the second Boer War ended in defeat for the Boers (in 1902), with the result that both the Transvaal and Orange River Republics became British colonies. However, the great South African general Jan Smuts managed to win a measure of self-government for the Transvaal and Orange River colonies by 1906.

In 1910, all four South African colonies, the Cape Province, Natal, Orange River and the Transvaal, were joined to form the Union of South Africa, with Louis Botha as its first Prime Minister. South Africa joined the Allies in the war against Germany in 1914, and sent expeditionary forces under the overall command of General Smuts to engage the German colonial forces in (German) South-West Africa and German East Africa. South-West Africa was quickly brought under control, but the campaign in German East Africa was a long and grueling one that lasted until the end of the war in 1918. After the war, South Africa was granted an indefinite "mandate," or right, to administer the former German colony of South-West Africa by the League of Nations. This obligation is still maintained by South Africa.

In 1925, Afrikaans, the colorful Dutch-African idiom of the

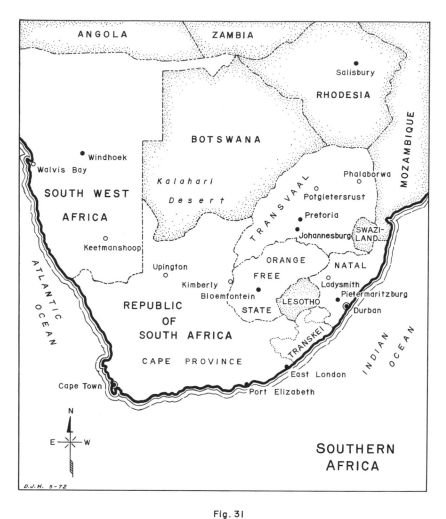

Fig. 31

Boers was made the other official language (besides English) of South Africa, replacing the regular Dutch.

The historic Statute of Westminster, enacted by the British Parliament in 1931, granted sovereign independence to the Union of South Africa, as it did to many other British colonies, changing the British Empire to a "Commonwealth" of nations.

As a member of the Commonwealth, South Africa voted to enter World War II in 1939 on the side of Great Britain. South African military forces were engaged around the globe, performing notable service, particularly in the North African and Italian campaigns.

The end of the Second World War marked the beginning of an industrial revolution in South Africa that was to transform it into the economic and commercial giant that it is today. However, the final ties to Britain were severed in 1961, when South Africa left the Commonwealth and declared itself a Republic.

The Republic of South Africa is definitely not a small country. All told, it encompasses an area of 472,359 square miles,* which is five times the size of Great Britain, or larger than Germany, France, Italy and Portugal together. It is one of the very few modern industrial nations with a relatively low population for its size. Counting all ethnic and national groups, the population density of South Africa is less than 40 per square mile, compared to 570 per square mile for Great Britain and 860 for the Netherlands. Much of South Africa, however, is arid or semiarid in climate and unsuitable for a high density of population.

The greater part of the country has an average elevation in excess of 4,000 feet above sea level. There are four well defined geographical areas, based on elevation:

A narrow coastal belt with an average elevation of less than 1,000 feet.

The Little Karoo, a narrow tableland in the south, separated from the coastal plain by the Langeberg and Outerquia mountain ranges and having an average altitude of 1,500 feet.

*Not counting South-West Africa, which would add another 317,817 square miles.

The Great Karoo, separated from the Little Karoo by the Swartberg and Suurberg ranges, and having an average elevation of from 2,000 to 3,000 feet.

The Highveld, consisting of the northern part of the Cape Province, the Orange Free State and most of the Transvaal, having an elevation ranging from 4,000 to 6,000 feet. Johannesburg, Transvaal, South Africa's largest city, is located at an altitude of 6,000 feet.

Rainfall ranges from more than 40 inches along the east coast to less than 5 inches in the western desert regions. Rainfall on the Highveld varies between 15 and 30 inches per year, making it somewhat arid and of limited use for agriculture. The prairie grasses of the Highveld, however, support an extensive cattle industry.

South Africa is a land of sunshine and, despite the fact that winter nights on the Highveld can be quite chilly, with frost common, daily sunshine with mild temperatures is the rule. On the other hand, summers on the Highveld are cooler than one might expect, because of the altitude. The coastal areas of the east are largely tropical, while the western Cape Province enjoys a Mediterranean climate with dry hot summers and mild wet winters.

THE SOUTH AFRICAN ECONOMY

South Africa has by far the strongest economy in the whole of Africa and one of the highest growth rates of any Western industrial nation. Although the Republic believes in and respects the profit motive and the free enterprise system, the State has had to involve itself in numerous major industries, including coal, oil and gas, iron and steel, electric power production, and rail, water and air transport, because private capital was considered inadequate to finance these basic requirements for an advanced industrial state.

The state-owned railway system operates more than 14,000 miles of track, 4,000 of which are electrified. There are approximately 15,000 miles of paved motor roads, with some 6,000 miles built to international standards for main arterial highways linking all major cities. More than 2 million motor vehicles are licensed in South Africa, and this is more than three-quarters of all motor vehicles on the entire African continent.[9] The Republic of South Africa produces more than three times as much steel as the rest of Africa combined. And despite her modest population and largely arid or marginal agricultural land, South Africa produces more than 20 percent of all the food and fibre raised in Africa. Similar comparisons can be made with nearly all other industries.

But although South Africa is one of the world's major trading nations, like all rapidly developing countries she consistently imports more than she exports. Nevertheless, the Republic is a highly desirable trading partner, for unlike the great majority of nations running trade and balance-of-payments deficits (including the United States), South Africa does not require foreign aid, or special "drawing rights" from the IMF, or loans from the World Banks or any special consideration from her creditors. South Africa is quite willing, and most able, to cover all her deficits promptly with cash—for the world's *cash* is still gold.

A major factor in the outstanding economic growth of South Africa is fiscal conservatism. There is close and continuous control over all government expenditures and a strong tradition of balanced budgets. All expenses of state and local governments are covered as far as possible by current revenues only. On the national level, *the annual budget has shown a surplus in every year since 1932.* Furthermore, all state-owned enterprises are expected to operate at a profit.

Foreign Investment in South Africa. The Republic of South Africa welcomes foreign investment, and outside capital committed to South African enterprises exceeds $4 billion. Great Britain still controls the major share of foreign capital, having some $2 billion invested, with more than half of this amount committed to general commercial and industrial enterprises and the balance in gold mining. The United States is next, with about 20 percent of total foreign capital, most of it involved in gold mining. However, many large American banks, including the Chase Manhattan and Morgan Guaranty, have offices and/or branches in South Africa; and more than 200 American industrial and commercial corporations have subsidiaries, branches or other major facilities in the Republic, including

General Motors, Ford Motor Company, Eastman Kodak, Texas Instruments, Weyerhauser Company, Kimberly-Clark and U.S. Steel.

France, or, more accurately, French citizens, control about $300 million in South African holdings, mostly in the manufacturing industries. Most other major industrial nations, including Japan, West Germany, Italy, Switzerland, Spain, the Netherlands, Canada, Norway and Sweden hold substantial investments in South Africa. There is no question but that a great deal of "smart money" has been put into South African enterprises in recent years.

It should be noted here, however, that while direct capital investment from the outside, such as the building or financing of new plants and other facilities, is obviously of considerable benefit to and strengthens the economy of a developing country, investment by individuals in existing, previously capitalized enterprises is completely neutral. When an individual buys a South African stock, he or she neither supports nor hinders either the South African Government or the corporation doing business in South Africa. Except for initial offerings and specific floatations for capital improvement or expansion, a share of common stock represents someone else's investment, generally made years before.

When one buys a share of stock, the money paid does not go to the country or corporation involved, but to the investor who previously held the stock (less a small cut for the broker who handles the transaction of course!). When an American buys a South African gold stock, the odds are that nine out of ten times it will be bought from another American. Much of the direct financing of South African mining ventures is traditionally done through the huge mining finance houses, such as the Anglo-American Corporation or the London-based Consolidated Gold Fields or Union Corporation. So anyone choosing not to buy South African gold stocks as a matter of principle, should at least be aware that such a choice has no effect whatever on either South Africa or its gold mining industry; some other individual or corporation, whether American or foreign, will always be in possession of each share of stock outstanding.

The Government of South Africa has never departed from its

traditional policy of permitting the unqualified repatriation of earnings (dividends) from investments made in South African enterprises by nonresidents. However, South Africa does have a withholding tax of 15 percent on such dividends and it also has limited currency and exchange controls, and how these two factors affect the nonresident investor will be discussed in the next chapter.

THE PEOPLE OF SOUTH AFRICA

At the beginning of 1972, the estimated total population of the Republic of South Africa was 19,220,000. The "Bantu," as the Black peoples of African origin are called, are by far the most numerous group, comprising approximately three-fifths of South Africa's inhabitants. Next in total number are the white peoples of European stock, followed by the "coloureds," a distinctive group of mulatto or racially mixed background. A fairly large community of Asians, consisting chiefly of immigrants from India, makes up the balance. Divided into primary racial groups the population of South Africa is (approximately) as follows:

Bantus	(Black)	13,000,000
Europeans	(White)	3,650,000
Coloureds	(Mixed)	1,950,000
Asians		620,000

But (as South Africans are quick to point out) theirs is really not a *multiracial* society, but a *multinational* one. There is no common culture, language or traditions, for example, uniting the various Bantu peoples. In fact, considerable animosity has at times existed between the principal Bantu nations.

The White Population. The white inhabitants of South Africa are themselves divided, in language, culture, politics and religion, the main division still being between the Boers (or Afrikaners as they now prefer to be called) and the English-language group. But although noticeable differences in attitudes and customs still exist between the Afrikaner majority (about 60 percent) and the English-speaking white South Africans, the old animosities of the nineteenth century and the

Boer Wars have long since been forgiven, if not forgotten. Nevertheless, the division appears to be as permanent as it is obvious, and Afrikaner and English-speaking children generally attend separate schools, even though they are required to learn both official languages.

In the commercial and industrial area, however, complete and unhindered cooperation between all white groups is the rule, even though, in addition to the predominant Afrikaner and English communities, South Africa accommodates several small but recognizable white cultural minorities, principally those of Portuguese, Greek and Italian origin.

South Africa has an aggressive program to encourage the immigration of Europeans, particularly those with technical or professional skills, and is currently welcoming such immigrants at the rate of about 40,000 per year.

The Black Peoples of South Africa. The Bantu (Black) peoples of South Africa are of mixed Hamitic and Negroid descent. Several centuries ago they began a slow migration southward from their original homes in the vicinity of the Great Lakes region of Central Africa. The Bantu crossed the northern boundaries of what is now the Republic of South Africa at about the same time that the white settlers at the Cape first began moving northward into the countryside. When considering the complex history, sociology and political life of this most unusual nation, it is well to remember that all of its major population groups are immigrants (except for the coloureds, who are only part immigrant!).

At any rate, the whites and Blacks arrived in South Africa at about the same time. The Bantu settled freely in various parts of South Africa, principally in the north and east, until the several frontier wars with the whites during the nineteenth century ended the black migrations and determined, for all practical purposes, the pattern of white and Black occupation as it exists today.[10]

The land rights of the Bantu were recognized soon after the formation of the Union of South Africa in 1910, by the terms of the Native Land Act (1913) that set aside 22.7 million acres for their exclusive occupation. A Native Trust and Land Act of 1936 reserved an additional 15.3 million acres for Bantu settlement. Altogether, the Bantu lands guaranteed under these acts totaled 65,652 square miles, or an area approximately equal to the U.S. state of Oklahoma.

The Bantu peoples of South Africa today consist of five large, and at least an equal number of smaller, groups, each with its own language, culture and traditions. There are at least seven distinct and separate Bantu languages, few of them related to any other. Many of the Bantu, however, also speak Afrikaans, English, or both, in addition to their own language. According to the latest available figures, the principal Bantu nations are:

Xhosa	–	3,600,000
Zulu	–	3,400,000
South Sotho	–	1,500,000
Tswana	–	1,450,000
Bapedi	–	1,200,000

The Coloureds. The nearly 2,000,000 "Coloured" people of South Africa form a unique but fairly homogeneous group, with a recognized national identity of their own. The Coloured South Africans (90 percent Afrikaans-speaking) are descended from some of the original Hottentot and Bushman inhabitants of the Cape area, who were joined by various other races, including some of the original white settlers, Asian slaves and indentured laborers imported from Ceylon and the Malay peninsula and sailors of all races who called at the Cape over the years.[11]

The Coloured community has enjoyed phenomenal economic success in recent years, giving rise to a substantial class of Coloured business and professional men. They own and operate many small shops and factories. The Coloured citizens of South Africa are also noted for their abilities as fishermen and seamen and for their love of the sea. Today they dominate South Africa's extensive fishing industry. As might be expected, the Coloured peoples of South Africa are concentrated mainly in Cape Town (in which they constitute a majority) and in other port cities of the Cape Province. The great majority of the Coloureds are Christians belonging to either the Dutch Reformed or Anglican Churches and their culture and way of life is basically Western and little different from the whites of South Africa.

A minority of the Coloureds, loosely referred to as Cape Malays, are of the Moslem faith, having retained a considerable degree of their Eastern heritage. The Cape Malays are renowned as craftsmen and artisans.

The Indians. South Africa's Asian community is composed primarily of peoples of Indian origin, with both Hindu and Moslem subdivisions well represented. The Indians first came to South Africa in the 1860's to work as indentured laborers on the sugar plantations of the Natal. Their numbers were later increased by the arrival of many artisans, traders and merchants. Today the Indian population forms a prosperous part of the South African population, numbering many successful merchants, brokers, doctors, lawyers, building contractors and industrialists in their ranks. The Indians are concentrated mainly in the Natal Province, with more than a third of them living in the port city of Durban, in which they are a majority. A moderate-sized but distinctive Chinese community and several other Asian ethnic identities are also part of the overall Asian population.

The Principal Cities of South Africa. The most recent estimated population figures show that the five leading cities of South Africa are:

City	White	Bantu	Coloured	Asian	Total
Johannesburg	450,000	675,000	65,000	35,000	1,225,000
Cape Town	350,000	85,000	450,000	10,000	895,000
Durban	225,000	250,000	30,000	265,000	770,000
Pretoria	215,000	210,000	9,000	10,000	444,000
Port Elizabeth	105,000	130,000	75,000	6,000	316,000

And if the social and political situation of South Africa were not complex enough, the country has *two* capital cities, a legislative capital at Cape Town and an administrative capital at Pretoria in the Orange Free State.[12]

South-West Africa. The South African-administered territory of South-West Africa (317,817 square miles) has a population of approximately 620,000, consisting of some 450,000 Bantu people, mostly of the Ovambo and Herero tribes, 100,000 whites of European origin and the remainder of Hottentot or Bushman descent. The extremely low population density of South-West Africa is due to its severely arid climate. The topography ranges from rugged mountains and tablelands in the west and south to vast areas of scrubland and desert in the northeast. South-West Africa sends six elected members to the South African Legislative Assembly and four appointed members to the South African Senate. The Government of South Africa has a continuing program of substantial economic assistance to further the development of South-West Africa.

The southern coastal plateau is rich in diamonds, which are the principal mineral export of South-West Africa. Since the end of World War II, South Africa has been involved in a chronic dispute with the United Nations over South Africa's right to continue the administration of South-West Africa. In the light of the fact that South-West Africa is one of the Western world's primary sources of industrial diamonds, it is perhaps understandable that the Communist bloc and their sympathizers in the United Nations have been most vocal in demanding (unsuccessfully) that South Africa be deprived of this territory and that it be turned over to a U.N. or "neutralist" administration.

Politics and the Apartheid Program. Unquestionably, the most readily identifiable feature of South African political life is the system of *apartheid* (literally "separateness"). South African whites insist that *apartheid* is not merely a system of racial segregation (although segregation is surely one of its obvious features at present), but a policy allowing for the "separate development" of each of the prominent national groups according to its specific needs and desires. Rightly or wrongly, the white South Africans contend (and they run the government) that South Africa's extraordinary multiplicity of distinct national identities precludes the country from ever becoming an "integrated" society, in the sense that a single political system can be shared by all.

The whites feel that under such an arrangement the majority in any given area would dominate all other groups and, on a national basis, that they, the whites, would be victims of Black racism encouraged by Communist agitators. They point to events in the Congo, Zambia and other Black African states as evidence of this. They also feel that the social and cultural interests of the various groups are so diverse and so well entrenched that the creation of a single South African national and cultural identity is neither practical nor desirable. It is believed that while the various nationalities and races can continue to enrich each other's culture as they have in the past, there will never be a "melting pot" philosophy as in the United States because, while immigrants to the United States invariably arrived relatively rootless and cut off from the land of their origin, South Africa's peoples arrived in united groups or as whole nations, retaining intact their complete history, culture and social organization.

The whites, despite their own diversity, see themselves as united by the common bond of Western (European) civilization. The Bantu peoples on the other hand, while accepting many of the economic and technical benefits of Western civilization, are, to a large degree, still attached to their own widely varied but distinctly African social and cultural patterns and organizations. The coloured and Indian communities are also presumed to be primarily concerned with their own interests and problems.

The white-dominated South African Government envisions the country as an association of autonomous, self-governing and largely self-sufficient national communities. The Bantu in particular are to be set up in their own national homelands or "Bantustans." The idea for the Bantustans was actually developed by the British during the Union period of South Africa. The Native Land Acts began this process and, before South Africa left the Commonwealth, the independent Bantu States of Lesotho* and Swaziland had already been created.

In 1963, the Transkei, a national homeland for the 3.5 million Xhosa peoples of South Africa was granted internal self-government. The Transkei, which is larger in area than Belgium, has its own national legislature, its own flag and national anthem and its own constitution. This constitution brings into

*Formerly known as Basutoland

effect a distinct Transkei citizenship, which embraces not only the Bantu normally residing on Transkei territory, but all Xhosa-speaking Bantu living and working in other parts of the Republic. At the same time, all citizens of the Transkei remain citizens of South Africa.

Six other Bantustans are either being planned or are in the process of development, so that each major Bantu nationality will eventually be accommodated with a self-governing homeland similar to the Transkei. The South African Government will retain control of foreign affairs, defense and other areas of overall national interest, but it insists that self-government within the Bantu homelands will not be a sham but the real thing. Not only are Blacks to assume all legislative and administrative posts within each Bantustan, but the South African Government has already acknowledged (in principle) their right, when they have achieved a sufficient level of development, to have individual representation at the United Nations. Lesotho and Swaziland have already been granted U.N. representation as sovereign nations.

Furthermore, the central government is making extraordinary efforts to ensure that the Bantu states will become economically viable as well as politically successful. Not only is a great amount of direct financial aid being channeled into economic development within the Bantustans, but generous tax incentives are being offered to industries that build plants on or near Bantu territories. All retail businesses and services within the Bantustans, however, must be owned and operated by Blacks.

It is of course conceded that probably no more than 50 or 60 percent of the Bantu will become or remain permanent residents of the various Bantustans; the balance will continue to live and work in the areas under white administration, where they are vitally needed to help maintain the national economy. A Coloured People's Representative Council and a Council for Indian Affairs have also been created to represent the special interests of those communities. Five of the 16 universities in South Africa have been established for the specific use of non-whites, although significant numbers of non-whites are also accommodated at the white universities.

Only the future, of course, will tell whether South Africa's plan to create a functional multinational society will succeed. At present it has the approval of the great majority of whites and even a substantial number of the Bantu. Many Black leaders and politicians feel that the Bantustans offer the most practical way for their people to achieve political and economic maturity and yet retain their African cultural identity. On the other hand, great numbers of Blacks (not to mention the coloureds) have become thoroughly Western in their outlook and the segregation and discrimination practiced in the white-administered areas is undoubtedly a source of deep resentment and frustration to them. However, many responsible observers feel that once the program of establishing the Bantu homelands is completed, and the racial balance between the Bantu and other nationalities outside of the Bantustans has been more or less equalized, the irksome restrictions now imposed on non-whites will gradually disappear.

At any rate, there is already an active opposition to segregation, both from the minority Progressive Party and from the antiapartheid white press. Even the predominantly Afrikaner Nationalist Party, which has dominated South African politics since 1948, is becoming less and less rigid in its positions as the political and economic realities of the present age are realized.

Apartheid, in the sense of multinationalism, is very probably going to remain the basis for South African socio-political life for the foreseeable future. But the injustices and inefficiencies of segregation will undoubtedly be greatly relaxed if not entirely eliminated in the years ahead. The great majority of whites are city dwellers, accustomed to seeing Blacks not as tribal savages but as modern urbanites like themselves. Many whites now work alongside Blacks and, if such familiarity does not always lead to mutual respect, it does tend to reduce racial fears and hostilities.

Whites in general are still paid anywhere from six to ten times as much as Blacks for doing the same work, but the wages of non-whites have been increasing about three times as fast as those of whites in recent years.[13] However some firms, including Polaroid and Barclay's Bank, have openly adopted policies of equal pay for equal work. Even some agencies of local government, such as the city of Port Elizabeth, have accepted this idea in principle.

The pragmatic Afrikaner Prime Minister of South Africa, Mr. Vorster, whose "outward looking" foreign policy of offering trade and aid to Black African states has proven so successful, has already warned the dwindling but still powerful segregationist wing of his Nationalist Party that the time for "practical politics" had arrived. That statement could mean anything, but Mr. Vorster's aides insist that it was the Prime Minister's way of notifying the party that big changes are ahead.[14]

South Africa has all the ingredients necessary for it to become a super economic power on a worldwide basis, in the fashion of Germany and Japan. To do this, however, she will have to utilize the abilities and energies of all her people to the fullest extent. But South Africa is not the United States and her path will not be the same as ours, nor should we expect it to be. Nevertheless, the evidence thus far suggests that this most unusual nation is destined for unusual achievement.

Political disturbances in South Africa have been almost nonexistent since the Sharpeville riots of 1961. But this surely does not mean that future racial or national outbreaks of a serious nature will always be avoided. If such disturbances do occur, they will undoubtedly have a pronounced negative effect on the price levels of South African securities. However, like the event itself, this effect will nearly always be quite temporary. The thing to do in such cases, if one has both the financial resources and the nerve, is to take advantage of the opportunity to buy favorite South African equities at a sharp discount.

Generally one must act when the news appears the worst, for that is when the selloff invariably reaches its greatest intensity. In any case, don't ever be panicked by newspaper headlines or anything else as inconsequential and give away a sound holding at a fat discount to someone with a cooler and wiser head. Never act in haste or out of fear in managing your investments. One of the best rules for investing is still BUY RIGHT AND SIT TIGHT. If you have bought a good stock at a fair price there is seldom any valid reason to sell it before its potential for growth is fully realized.

The reader will understand of course that the chapter now

concluded is by no means a complete or exhaustive review of the very complex socio-political situation of South Africa; it would be difficult to do justice to that subject in an entire volume this size. Yet I felt the need for this brief sketch, however inadequate, to open the door, at least for any reader not yet introduced to it, to this land that will most assuredly play a very prominent role in the events of the next decade. But if my comments on South Africa appear somewhat contradictory at times, it is because the Republic of South Africa is quite obviously a land of contradictions.[15] It is a nation moving ahead at a tremendous pace while still, in too many ways, bound to an unhappy and obsolete past. But investments are made for the future, not the past, and a lot of money has been invested by outsiders in South Africa's future. I think it is a safe bet.

Notes:

CHAPTER XIII

1. The term *El Dorado* is literally translated as "the gilded man," and is derived from a part of the legend that held that the priest-king of this fabled land was supposed to go about in garments encrusted with gold. What the *conquistadores* were actually searching for was "the land of the gilded king."

2. Imperialist governments are those that seek to extend military, political and/or economic domination or control over nations and territories other than their own. The fact that it may be Marxist- or Socialist-oriented does not in any way mitigate the imperialistic nature of such domination. In fact, current evidence suggests that Communist imperialism may be the most oppressive of all.

3. See Nathaniel Weyl, *Traitor's End; the Rise and Fall of the Communist Movement in Southern Africa* (New Rochelle, N.Y.: Arlington House, 1970).

4. Dr. Salazar's comments are from an article by George Weller in the *Chicago Daily News,* August 8, 1970. Both reporter and journal are highly respected for their objectivity.

5. *Time,* Nov. 1, 1971.

6. *Chicago Daily News,* March 23, 1971.

7. Rhodes and Jameson hoped that they would receive assistance from the British and other non-Boer miners on the Veld.

8. During the second Boer War, a young British war correspondent by the name of Winston Churchill distinguished himself, not only by his dramatic front-line dispatches, but by his daring escape from a Boer prisoner-of-war camp at one point in the campaign.

9. Although only about 6 percent of the motor vehicles in South Africa are presently owned by Blacks, this represents more Black-owned automobiles than in all the rest of Africa.

10. For a good history of the Bantu Peoples see, Donald R. Morris, *The Washing of the Spears* (New York: Simon & Schuster, 1965).

11. The original native inhabitants of the Cape were decimated by

two smallpox epidemics shortly after the arrival of the European colonists. Some of the Bushmen retreated into the mountain regions of the Western Cape and into the remoteness of South-West Africa, where their descendants survive to this day. Others, along with some of the Hottentots, fled into the interior, only to be massacred or enslaved by the advancing Bantu. The relative few who remained at the Cape later intermarried with some of the European and Asian arrivals to form the basis of the coloured South African community of today.

12.   The Cape Parliament survives from the days of British rule, while Pretoria was the old Boer capital of the Orange Free State. The present dual-capital arrangement remains as an acknowledgement of political "equality" between the Afrikaner and English-speaking communities.

13.   The disparity of compensation between white and Black workers is actually not quite as extreme as the bare statistics indicate, because urban Blacks are eligible for extra fringe benefits, including very-low-cost public housing and free medical care. There are also middle- and upper-middle-class Bantu business and professional men and even a few Bantu millionaires.

14.   *Time,* November 1, 1971.

15.   For a revealing look at South Africa's ambivalent and contradictory socio-political nature see Allen Drury, *A Very Strange Society* (New York: Trident Press, 1967).

XIV

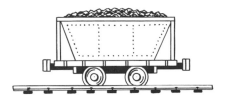

INVESTMENT IN SOUTH AFRICA: PROBLEMS AND POSSIBILITIES

"It is more important to avoid losing than to win."

—FRED C. KELLY

GOLD was known to exist in the Transvaal as early as 1854, but the fabulous Main Reef group of gold-bearing conglomerates, from which developed the enormous Witwatersrand gold mining industry, was not discovered until 1886. An Australian prospector named George Harrison is credited with making the first strike, when he stumbled on an outcropping of the Main Reef at Langlaagte farm on the southern slope of the Witwatersrand, the high-plateau country of Southern Transvaal. As the Main Reef was excitedly traced from farm to farm and outcrop to outcrop, it soon became apparent that this was not going to be another case of "poor man's mining," where anyone with a pan or a pick could hope to strike it rich on his own.

Unlike the placers and quartz mines of Canada, Australia and the American West, the gold of South Africa is found in thin conglomerate bands, or "reefs," that tilt downward at an angle of about 60 degrees initially and level off to about 30 degrees at substantial depth. And although the reef systems lie in a great arc some 300 miles long, they average only three to four feet thick and, in many places, narrow to where they are no more than a few inches in depth. Like widely separated pages in a book, the several reefs lie one on top of another, sloping downward at varying angles.

In many ways, the geology of the Witwatersrand or "Rand" resembles that of a coal mining area, except that the seams or "reefs" of the Rand slope downward at a more extreme angle than is usually the case with coal deposits. Unfortunately, although the conglomerate bands, or reefs, can usually be traced with considerable accuracy, the amount of gold within them varies widely. Therefore, before an area can be mined it must first be geologically tested and mapped by numerous multiple borings, generally an expensive and time-consuming process. There is, however, an offsetting advantage in that ore bodies and reserves of ore can be much more accurately determined by boring the reefs than is the case when exploring a typical quartz lode by the same method.

What quickly became apparent on the Rand, however, was that large-scale mining operations were essential if the widely disseminated, but enormous, deposits of the reef systems were to be profitably developed. In the early years, crisis after crisis occurred as the mines reached depths that exceeded the technology available at the time for further development. Yet each problem was met and overcome with new advances in mine engineering. Until 1891, something like a third of all gold in the crushed ore of the Witwatersrand mines was being wasted by imperfect methods of treatment. The McArther-Forrest cyanide process that came into general use about that time not only reduced wastage to a mere 5 percent or so, but made possible the mining of lower-grade ores. But this, in turn, called for still more extensive mining operations and much larger processing plants.

The growth of the South African gold mining industry reached a temporary peak just prior to World War I, as did that of the United States. But then the dislocations of the War itself, the postwar inflation and the exhaustion of many of the original mines of the Rand combined sharply to curtail existing production as well as further development. For a time it seemed that South Africa's extraordinary gold boom had burnt itself out and that the inevitable declining phase had begun. The devaluations of the 1930's, however, gave the Rand a new lease on life and gold production soared to another record high by 1940, with many new mines being opened and existing mines reaching for still greater depths.

Although World War II and its accompanying inflation severely reduced gold output for a time, a new wave of expansion got under way in the late forties and early fifties. The 1949 devaluation of sterling offset the immediate effects of the war-time inflation and the new demand for uranium provided additional incentive for investment in new mines and facilities. Postwar developments, however, were concentrated in the Carletonville area, southwest of the original Witwatersrand gold fields surrounding Johannesburg; at the Klerksdorp Field, still further to the southwest in the Transvaal; and in the newer Orange Free State Gold Field surrounding the cities of Welkom and Virginia. Such well-known mines as President Brand, President Steyn, Free State Geduld, West Driefontein, Western Holdings, Hartebeestfontein, St. Helena and Welkom were brought into production during this period.

Although South Africa was not spared the worldwide postwar inflation of the IMF-dollar standard, which continually (until 1968) increased production costs against a fixed price for gold, total gold output, overall mine earnings and total dividends paid to stockholders reached all-time records during the postwar years. For the most part, this expansion in the face of a monetary-financial condition that was devastating the gold mining industries of the United States and Canada was possible because the latest advances in mining technology could be employed on an ever-increasing scale to reach deeper and deeper for the seemingly endless resources of the reefs. Unlike the typical quartz lode mines found in the United States and Canada, with their far more limited and less accessible ore bodies, many South African mines were able to counter rising costs by simply increasing the overall tonnage of ore recovered and treated and by introducing greater efficiencies into their operations.

Although we have already charted the pronounced upward course of South African gold production from 1950 to 1970 in

Fig. 17, which presented it (along with that of the United States and Canada) in terms of its value in U.S. dollars (at $35 per troy ounce), it is still more revealing to see it presented in terms of actual production in millions of fine ounces. *Fig. 32* is therefore included here to show this remarkable growth in nonmonetary terms.

Fig. 32

SOUTH AFRICAN GOLD PRODUCTION

In Millions of Fine Ounces

1950–1970

Year	Output
1950	11.6
1951	11.5
1952	11.8
1953	11.9
1954	13.2
1955	14.6
1956	15.9
1957	17.0
1958	17.6
1959	20.0
1960	21.4
1961	23.0
1962	25.5
1963	27.4
1964	29.1
1965	30.5
1966	30.9
1967	30.5
1968	31.0
1969	31.1
1970	32.1

Furthermore, the exhaustion of many of the older mines has been more than made up for by the output of fewer, but larger and more productive, new mines. The latest such cycle began in the 1960's, when several large mines were opened in the recently developed Evander Gold Field, 60 miles east of Johannesburg. This group includes the Kinross, Bracken and Winkelhaak mines.

Nevertheless, because of the importance of gold mining as a major source of foreign exchange, the South African Government has been concerned over the closing of a considerable number of marginal mines in recent years, despite the substantial overall increase in gold output recorded during the 1960's. Consequently, a Gold Mines Assistance Act (hereafter referred to as GMA) was passed, which authorized subsidy payments to marginal gold mines, beginning April 1, 1968. Under the terms of the act, mines are eligible for benefits if, without such financial assistance, they would be forced to close within eight years. A complex formula determines the actual rate of payment, based partially on the average price received for gold during the year. Mines applying for state assistance must demonstrate that a significant increase in life expectancy and gold production is likely if such aid is granted.

Also, in 1970, the South African Government agreed to provide a direct loan of $10 million to help open a promising new gold mine in the West Rand. Shaft sinking began in 1971 and initial production is scheduled for early 1974, with full output of 100,000 tons per month expected by mid-1975.

THE OUTLOOK FOR THE SEVENTIES

Total output from South African gold mines for 1970 reached a record level (as it has in each year but one since 1951) of 32.16 million troy ounces valued at $1,125,750,000, from the mining and milling of 74.5 million tons of ore. Obviously, such statistics indicate an enormous industry that dwarfs that of the United States and Canada, and this is surely the case. By comparison, South Africa produced nearly 20 times as much gold as did the United States and more than 13 times the amount produced by Canada for the year 1970. The South African gold mining industry directly employs approximately 500,000 people, including (on the average) about 50,000 whites and 450,000 non-whites, the great majority of the latter coming from the Bantu communities. But despite the fact that gold is the principal export (in terms of overall monetary value) of South Africa, the gold mining industry, rather surprisingly, contributes only about 10 percent to the nation's gross national product.

At the beginning of 1971, there were 46 active gold mines in

South Africa, all members of the South African Chamber of Mines. One of them, the West Rand Consolidated, produces both gold and uranium as primary products. Nine other mines produce uranium in commercial amounts as a by-product, while the remaining 36 are straight gold producers. Of the entire group of 46 operating mines, a surprising total of 19 of them were eligible for GMA benefits in 1971. Under the terms of the Gold Mining Assistance Act, the Government of South Africa is permitted to make direct loans to mining companies for expansion and improvements and grant tax reductions or exemptions in addition to offering direct subsidy payments. Approximately $15 million was expended under this program for 1970.

Although production would probably remain at or near the 1970 level throughout the decade of the seventies, *even without a substantially higher international price for gold,* higher prices are obviously going to bring increased production as well as greater profit margins and larger dividend payments. Nevertheless, the importance of higher gold prices was indicated by the South African Chamber of Mines, which estimated (in 1970) that for each $1.00 of increase (above $35 per ounce) in the basic world price for gold, an additional 8 million ounces of gold could be profitably mined. A previous official study indicated that some 528 million ounces remained to be produced from existing or developing mines, even without a substantial rise in the price received for gold. Higher gold prices will obviously bring about a significant increase in this estimate. At any rate, South Africa will undoubtedly be extracting the wealth of the golden crescent until well into the twenty-first century.

However, despite the fact that the overall outlook for the gold mining industry in South Africa is quite favorable, there are some definitely negative factors affecting the mines, both individually and as a group. Among the negatives are chronic shortages of skilled labor, continuing inflation, declining ore reserves and grades in many of the older mines, and the need for ever-deeper mining with its associated problems of high temperatures, increased rock pressures and water infiltration.

The shortages of skilled labor are due in part to the intransigence of many of the white labor unions, which still resist the training and promotion of non-whites for technical and supervisory positions. Present trends however indicate that this particular problem will be eliminated in time through the immigration of more artisans and technicians from Europe (and, as I suggested earlier, even from Japan) and by the continued easing of the *apartheid* barriers to the training and promotion of Bantu and other non-white workers. Economic common sense, if nothing else, will eventually overcome even the most deep-seated ethnic or racial fears and prejudices.

The Contract Labor System. Nevertheless, the overall labor situation in the South African gold mining industry is quite different from that of North America. In the vertical quartz mines typical of the United States and Canada, only a very limited number of miners can work in a hard-rock drift or tunnel at one time. Hard-rock mining is a slow, difficult and expensive process and the space allowed for operations is always limited. In this type of mining, very little waste rock is handled; the orebody is generally a fairly compact mass and the problem is mainly to break it up and haul it to the surface for treatment.

Mining the reef deposits of South Africa, however, calls for an entirely different technique of mining, and its labor requirements are much higher. For example, largest of the South African gold mines, in terms of gold produced, is the West Driefontein property, which employs on the average 15,000 Bantu and 1,500 Europeans. Compare this total of 16,500 employees to that of the leading Canadian producer, Campbell Red Lake, which employed a grand total of 264 people in 1971, both above and below ground. A South African reef mine has to handle a great amount of waste material in relation to the actual amount of gold-bearing ore recovered. Main and auxiliary shafts frequently have to be sunk thousands of feet in depth, and many miles of tunnels and haulageways have to be constructed, before a gold-bearing reef is encountered. And the reefs themselves, although no more than three or four feet thick, may extend for many miles in length and breadth and tilt downward at a steep angle, making access for mining a difficult problem requiring the continuous construction of additional tunnels and galleries.

A South African mine generally consists of a large group of

contiguous claims covering a surface area anywhere from two to five miles in length and a mile or two in width. Some of them, however, are more or less symmetrical in shape but still cover approximately the same area. The enormous size and complexity of these mining enterprises and the availability of a large pool of Bantu labor, willing to work but unskilled in the use of tools and largely unacquainted with modern technology, has brought about the present contract-labor system. Under this arrangement, potential miners are recruited from most of the 50 black tribes of southern Africa, representing all seven of the principal Bantu nations. They come not only from South Africa itself, but also from Lesotho, Swaziland, Malawi, Rhodesia, Zambia, Mozambique, Angola, the Congo and even further to the north.

The younger Bantu men usually arrive at the mines fresh from their tribal environment and without funds. Therefore, they must be housed, fed, trained and equipped by the mining company before they can begin actual work in the mines. They must even be taught a rudimentary new language called *"Fanakalo"* so that, coming as they do from so many different tribes and nations, they can have a basic means of communication with each other and with European miners and engineers. *Fanakalo* was specifically created for use in the mining industry. The contract miners agree to work for periods ranging from four to 18 months, and during the contract period all their needs are provided for by the employing company, including food, lodging, clothing, medical care, transportation, schooling and training, tools and equipment.

In addition, a vast array of sports and recreational facilities are furnished, and this is no sham or token; the Chamber of Mines requires that they be first-class in every respect. When their tours of duty are finished, the Bantu contract miners can return to their tribes or countries of origin with their accumulated wages, which are enough for them to purchase a bride (still a requirement in many parts of Black Africa), acquire some cattle or otherwise get a start in life. They also take with them many new skills, a basic familiarity with tools and technology and a new sophistication regarding health and hygiene.

The contract-labor system has been extraordinarily successful thus far and has benefited not only the mining companies
but also the Bantu peoples themselves. There is no question but
that this system is absolutely essential to the continued operation of the South African gold mines. Some further development or evolution of the system may be necessary to meet the
inevitable changes of coming years, but there appears to be no
real possibility that the system itself can be discarded entirely
in favor of conventional employment practices, at least not for
the foreseeable future.

At any rate, the contract-labor system now appears to be
thoroughly accepted by the Bantu miners. A large number return again and again for additional tours of duty, and many
become more or less permanently employed, either as lower- or
middle-level technicians or in clerical work after sufficient
training. The white miners and engineers are representative of
both the Afrikaans- and English-speaking communities, but
they work on an hourly or salaried basis and are considered to
be permanent rather than contract employees. While the pay of
European employees is much higher than that of the Bantu, the
contract miners receive a greater amount of nonmonetary benefits from their employing company at no cost. Nevertheless,
the wages of Bantu contract miners have been increased at a
rate more than three times that awarded the white miners in
recent years.

Although it appears reasonable to assume, at this time, that
labor conditions in the mining industry will continue their
long-established tradition of stability and harmony, it must be
expected that labor compensation, for both white and Bantu,
will undoubtedly continue to rise.[1] This will be offset, however,
not only by higher revenues from an increased price for gold,
but by technological improvements and increased operating
efficiencies.

Technological Problems and Innovations. In the author's
opinion, certain technical and engineering problems are going
to be more of a challenge in the next decade than either labor
relations or South African inflation. The inevitable problem of
declining ore reserves is facing quite a few of the 46 operating
mines and there really isn't much one can do about that situa-

tion. But even the newer mines cannot avoid the difficulties of ultradeep mining, which include extra shoring and timbering to resist the enormous rock pressures developed at great depth, and ventilating problems because of extreme temperatures and great distances involved.[2] Water infiltration is also a constant problem since most of the mines now extend well below sea level, not to mention the ground-water table.

All of the foregoing factors naturally contribute to a constant upward pressure on operating costs that can depress profits and dividends, particularly in the marginal mines. It is clear, therefore, that even though the riches remaining in South Africa's "golden crescent," the 300-mile arc stretching from Evander through Johannesburg to Klerksdorp and ending on the plains of the Orange Free State, are sufficient to allow for operations at a very high rate for two, three or even four more decades, the problem for the investor is still one of selectivity. Here as everywhere else, the successful investor must buy the right stock at the right time. Just being located in South Africa does not automatically make a gold mine a good investment. Actually, no more than one-quarter of the 46 mines in operation during 1971 qualify as being suitable for long-term investment holding at this time, and they will be pointed out in the next chapter.

On the positive side, the South African Chamber of Mines is engaged in an extensive and continuous research program to develop new mining techniques and equipment that might help offset rising costs. Two of the most encouraging projects undertaken thus far are the development of a small portable ore crusher, or mill, that can be set up to work underground, and a mobile rock-cutting machine. Pilot models of both machines have already been built and are undergoing tests in mines near Johannesburg.

A successful small ore crusher would save the mines millions in construction and operating costs. If a series of such minimills could be set up underground to replace the large surface units presently in use, the finely crushed ore could be brought to the surface on conveyor belts or even through small pipelines.[3] This would save enormous sums now required to construct, maintain and operate large-diameter shafts, skip hoists and rail haulageways.

The rock-cutting machine would replace the drilling and blasting process currently necessary to tunnel and mine rock formations. Although experimental models of this machine have had preliminary trials, the Chamber of Mines is trying now to interest manufacturers, both in South Africa and abroad, in turning out production models, so that testing and evaluation on a large scale can be carried out. If the dangerous, expensive and work-interrupting blasting procedure could be eliminated, or even substantially reduced, a major reduction in operating costs would be possible in virtually all types of mines.

At present, mining executives and engineers remain skeptical about the feasibility of both the mini-mill and the rock cutter. They point out that such machines would have to be extraordinarily rugged and reliable to withstand the tremendous stress and pounding to which they would be subject during prolonged operation under actual working conditions. However, if there is one thing our technological age has taught, it is that nothing of this nature is impossible. Continued technological advance in the mining industry is inevitable and perfection of the two machines mentioned would be a very bullish factor, not only for South African mines but for those of North America as well. However, reliable production models of these machines will, in any case, not be available for several years.

Uranium Production. The worldwide demand for uranium that developed during the late forties and through the fifties played an important part in the postwar expansion of the South African gold mining industry, since many of the mines opened during that period were developed to take advantage of the significant uranium content of their gold ores. This was particularly true of the mines opened in the Orange Free State. But, unfortunately for some of these mines, the great uranium boom collapsed early in the sixties, due to overproduction and the failure of the demand for nuclear-power fuel to expand as fast as originally forecast. Those mines that depended on uranium sales as well as on gold production to remain profitable have, for the most part, either temporarily or permanently suspended operations.

In considering the ten remaining gold-uranium producers, the author's recommendation is that they be evaluated strictly as gold producers, discounting any actual or potential income from uranium. Regardless of the uniqueness of this heavy metal, it is, after all, just another industrial commodity, and one for which demand has been weak and erratic in recent years. The majority of the gold producers with uranium-content ore, including Welkom, President Steyn, President Brand and Hartebeestfontein, have been obliged to stockpile large quantities of their uranium-bearing "slimes" or tailings (after the gold has been extracted), because the international market for uranium has been so unfavorable. Consequently, even if the market for uranium does improve substantially during the seventies as expected, these large above-ground stockpiles of semi-processed uranium ore will overhang the market, perhaps for several years.

There is, however, one recent development that could substantially alter this condition. In 1970, South Africa claimed to have developed a new process for manufacturing the nuclear fuel itself (U-235) that was "competitive" with methods currently employed by the nuclear nations of the West, the United States, Great Britain and France. So far, South Africa has produced and sold only the uranium concentrate; the actual nuclear fuel has to be manufactured by the purchasing country.

One of the reasons for the depressed state of the uranium market during the sixties is that the manufacture of nuclear fuel from uranium is a fantastically expensive process, requiring an enormous investment in processing plant and equipment. The resulting high cost of the refined uranium fuel discourages its wider use, particularly in the less wealthy nations. If South Africa has really developed a low-cost method of manufacturing nuclear-reactor fuel that can be put into practical, large-scale use, she could not only capture a substantial part of the world market for such fuel, but a lower cost would also very probably encourage its greater use.

South African uranium producers would surely benefit from having, for the first time, a domestic market as well as an expanded world market. Windfall profits would accrue to those mines with large stockpiles of uranium ore, already written off through prior gold operations.[4] Increased earnings would be developed from future production. However, only time will tell whether or not the South African process will eventually lead to full-scale production facilities and, in any case, such facilities would take several years to construct. As yet, there is no evidence that South African experiments along this line have been carried beyond the laboratory stage.

But whatever happens, my view is still that the uranium potential of any South African mine should be regarded as a possible extra or bonus, but it should not be relied on to justify the purchase of a particular stock. The real leveraged profits along with the greatest margin of investment safety for the next decade will be in gold. Gold is depression-proof, uranium is not. *Gold is money,* uranium is a commodity. Any gold mine that depends on regular uranium sales to remain profitable, either now or in the future, I regard as highly speculative.

Platinum and Diamonds. As was noted earlier, in addition to being the world's leading producer of gold, South Africa also holds first position in the output of two other very important and very precious minerals, diamonds and platinum.

Although gem-quality diamonds have a marginal use as monetary-hedge investments, gem stones themselves make up only a small part of overall production.[5] The great majority of diamonds are sold in the industrial market to be used in the manufacture of cutting, drilling and grinding tools. The extraordinary hardness of the diamond makes it virtually irreplaceable for these purposes. A continuing supply of industrial diamonds is absolutely essential in any technologically advanced society. Practically the entire diamond output of South Africa, and of South-West Africa as well, is controlled by a single corporation, DE BEERS CONSOLIDATED MINES LTD. This corporation also controls very nearly all of the cutting and marketing arrangements throughout the world. Therefore, I suppose it would be accurate to say that De Beers is a world-wide diamond monopoly. It is, however, a *publicly owned,* worldwide diamond monopoly.

Platinum also enjoys limited favor as a monetary-inflation hedge investment, in the form of jewelry and, more recently in the United States, in the form of art medals or nonofficial commemorative coins. It is also held as private bullion in the

United States, although probably on a very small scale.* But although platinum is far more scarce than gold and costs three times as much per ounce on the average, it has no recognized monetary status in any part of the world.[6] As in the case of diamonds most of the world's platinum is utilized for industrial and technological purposes. Platinum and platinum compounds have many vital uses in the chemical and scientific industries. One of the fastest-growing demands for chemical compounds derived from platinum is in the antipollution field, where platinum catalysts are used in the construction of filters for the control of harmful exhaust emissions from internal combustion engines.

South Africa's major platinum producer is POTGIETERS-RUST PLATINUM LTD., which supplies more than half of the Western world's requirements for this vital precious metal.

Despite the limited secondary use of both diamonds and platinum as stores of value, these two precious items are still overwhelmingly industrial commodities. Consequently, diamond and platinum stocks are unsuitable as hedges against monetary troubles, inflation, depressions and devaluations. During a financial depression, or through any period of restricted industrial growth or production, the markets for these two commodities could undergo sharp declines, with a corresponding decrease in earnings, dividends and share prices for their respective stocks. A period of rapid industrial growth on a worldwide basis would of course be very bullish for these stocks. However, platinum prices in particular tend to fluctuate widely even under normal business conditions.

Perhaps the best way to participate in the future of diamond and platinum equities is to invest in one of the South African mining finance houses, such as the Anglo-American Corporation, or in one of the large mining investment trusts, such as the American-South African Investment Company, which is listed on the New York Stock Exchange. Both of these two companies hold substantial positions in diamond and platinum stocks, in addition to their gold shares. Many of the other finance houses

*U.S. Treasury regulations do not forbid the holding of platinum bullion as a store of value as they do in the case of gold.

and investment trusts also include diamond and platinum stocks in their portfolios.

HOW TO INVEST IN SOUTH AFRICAN GOLD STOCKS

There are three basic ways to invest in South Africa's gold resources: the mining finance house, the mining investment trust and the mining company itself. Shares in all three types of institution are readily available to American and other non-South African investors.

1. The Mining Finance House. Nearly all of the gold mines of South Africa are controlled by mining finance houses, which are large investment banking firms organized for the purpose of financing and underwriting mining and industrial development in southern Africa. The institution of the mining finance house came into being because of the enormous initial cost and substantial risk involved in bringing a large reef gold mine into production and because of the reluctance of individual private investors to commit capital to new enterprises in underdeveloped or frontier countries.

Seven large mining finance houses controlled and managed 43 of the 46 mines in production as of 1971.* They do not actually own all of the stock in these mines, of course, but own large blocks of such stock in addition to having special management agreements with the mines they control.[7] The mining finance houses also buy and sell gold shares as well as shares in some of their other investments, generating capital and capital gain for further investment commitments or to contribute to income. Besides their gold-mine holdings, the finance houses generally have substantial investments in copper, coal, diamonds, various other minerals, petroleum, industrial and commercial ventures and real estate. And although the majority of their funds are invested in South African enterprises, the mining finance houses also have holdings in some of the other states of southern Africa and in the United Kingdom, Australia and North America as well. Gold actually represents a minority

---

*Two of these mines, East Daggafontein and South African Land and Exploration, both controlled by Anglo-American Corporation, are scheduled to end operations in 1972.

interest in all the finance houses, including the largest, Anglo-American Corporation, which in 1971 had about 25 percent of its total assets in gold shares.

Following is a list of the seven largest mining finance houses *(Fig. 33)*, together with the number of mines they control, the percentage of assets invested in gold mining and the percentage of total income derived from gold investments for the 1970–71 period.

Fig. 33

LEADING MINING FINANCE HOUSES
OF SOUTH AFRICA—1971

Mining Finance House	No. of Mines Controlled	Percent of Investment In Gold	Percent of Income From Gold
ANGLO-AMERICAN CORPORATION OF SOUTH AFRICA LTD.	12	24	28
GOLD FIELDS OF SOUTH AFRICA LTD.*	8	83	68
UNION CORPORATION	8	28	44
ANGLO-TRANSVAAL CONSOLIDATED INVESTMENT CO. LTD.	5	26	14
BARLOW-RAND LTD.**	4	18	11
GENERAL MINING AND FINANCE CORPORATION LTD.	4	18	23
JOHANNESBURG CONSOLIDATED INVESTMENT CO. LTD.	2	9	8

*Consolidated Gold Fields Ltd. owns 49 percent of GFSA.

**Successor to Rand Mines Ltd. after June 1971 merger of Thos. Barlow & Sons and Rand Mines.

The trend in recent years has been for the finance houses to increase greatly in size through mergers and acquisitions and, consequently, to become more and more diversified in their holdings. The percentage committed to gold has been in a slow but steady decline, on the average, not only because of the growing size and diversity of their portfolios, but also because of the lack of suitable opportunities to finance new gold mining ventures. Old mines are being liquidated at a far greater rate than new mines are being developed.

However, if you are in a high tax bracket, or for any reason prefer low income and would rather have the majority of earnings from your equities reinvested for capital gain rather than distributed as dividends, then by all means buy the finance houses and investment trusts rather than the individual mines. Just remember that the finance houses are more broadly diversified, and anyone investing in them is investing in the general economic future of southern Africa and the Republic of South Africa in particular, as well as acquiring a modest position in South African gold mining. Those wishing to concentrate primarily on gold should consider the investment trusts.

2. *The Investment Trust.* Investment trusts are merely holding companies having as their principal asset investment positions in the shares of operating companies. The gold mining investment companies of South Africa concentrate their commitments in operating gold mines and have a much higher percentage of their assets in such shares (generally from 50 to 100 percent) than the finance houses. However, some of the principal investment trusts are in turn controlled by mining finance houses. The five most important investment trusts of South Africa, along with the percentage of assets committed to gold during the period 1970–71, are as shown in *Fig. 34.*

Fig. 34

LEADING GOLD MINING INVESTMENT TRUSTS

OF SOUTH AFRICA—1971

Investment Company	*Percent of Assets in Gold Mining*
AMERICAN-SOUTH AFRICAN INVESTMENT CO. LTD.	72
ORANGE FREE STATE INVESTMENT TRUST	100
WEST RAND INVESTMENT TRUST	100
U.C. INVESTMENTS LTD.	48
MIDDLE WITWATERSRAND LTD.	56

The investment trust, like the finance house is characterized by a low dividend yield and the reinvestment of the major portion of earnings. Long-term capital gain through an increase in its net asset value is one of the objectives of the investment trust. Undoubtedly, the investment trust best known to American investors is AMERICAN-SOUTH AFRICAN, which has approximately 72 percent of its assets in gold shares. Since it is the only South African investment trust listed for trading on an American stock exchange,* we will review ASA in detail later in this chapter. But first let us note the general position of the individual mining companies as investments.

3. The Mining Company. The individual mining company has both the highest yield and, in general, the best possibility for leveraged capital gain. However, these advantages must be balanced with the greater risks of investing in individual mines. A single mine is vulnerable to surprise bad news. Flooding, for example, is an ever-present danger for South African mines and one that can cripple or permanently close an active and profitable mine overnight. West Driefontein, the world's richest gold mine, was struck by a serious flood in 1968 when an underground dyke suddenly gave way, inundating the entire eastern half of the mine. It was many months before this mine could be dewatered and production returned to normal. But at least West Driefontein did recover, although it was a very close call. Other mines have not been so lucky.

A few years before the flooding, West Driefontein suffered another disaster not unknown to South African mining—an earth subsidence. The collapse of a large underground section of the mine, honeycombed with tunnels and galleries, caused a severe surface settlement, which in turn resulted in major damage to the company's ore-processing facilities. The entire plant had to be rebuilt at a different location. Although South African gold mines have, on the whole, a remarkable safety record and a history of overcoming the most severe challenges of ultradeep mining, the difficulties and dangers themselves are always present.

---

*The other investment trusts are also available to Americans, but must be purchased through the Over-the-Counter market.

Therefore, it is prudent to distribute the total investment capital alloted to South African gold shares among several different mines and, preferably, among more than one of the newer gold fields, *Evander, Far West Rand, Klerksdorp* and the *Orange Free State Area.* If available investment capital does not permit investment in at least three or four different mines, then the investor should concentrate on buying one or more of the investment trusts or finance houses.

Although South African mines generally offer high yields and sell at relatively low P.E. ratios, these yields must be evaluated in the light of the estimated remaining life of the mine and its trend of profits. The authoritative *Mining Journal* of London gives these definitions of estimated working life for South African gold mines:

Long	–	Over 20 Years
Medium	–	11 to 20 Years
Short	–	6 to 10 Years
Breakup	–	1 to 5 Years

The high yields usually offered by short-life mines may appear tempting, but the investor should discount an amortization factor from the available yield, for the mines themselves do not set aside any amount for depletion but traditionally pay out all of their net earnings in dividends. Therefore, remember that part of the dividend yield of a mine represents a return of capital as well as a disbursement of earnings. Consequently, a mine with a life expectancy of say ten years offering a seemingly high dividend yield of 10 percent is really no bargain at all, because all the investor will get back (discounting all other factors) is his invested capital, minus both the South African and U.S. income taxes that would be levied against this so-called dividend. This example assumes that the investor does not or is not able to sell the stock at a profit but holds it for the entire remaining life of the mine, in which case he or she would suffer a substantial capital loss, despite the illusion of a "high" dividend yield.[8]

As a general rule, the longer the estimated life of a mine, the less one has to allow for amortization of capital. In the case of long-life mines, the amortization factor can be ignored, for all practical purposes, and the entire dividend can be regarded as income.

On the other hand, the rich long-life mines will benefit least from devaluations (although they will still benefit substantially). The short- and medium-life mines will benefit from devaluations to a greater degree, both from the direct improvement in earnings that would result and also because a higher gold price may allow them to mine marginal ore and thus extend their working lives. A mine with marginal profits and large reserves of low-grade ore will benefit the most from upward movements in the price of gold, but holding stocks in such mines is risky, because if the price of gold is not sufficiently increased in time to offset ever-rising operating costs, the company could be wiped out; mines of this type go under every year.

Therefore, the safest course for long-term investors is to distribute capital alloted for South African gold investment among several of the top-grade, long-life mines (those that are rated "INVESTMENT GRADE" in the reviews that follow in Chapter XV), or buy one or two of the investment trusts and/or finance houses. The higher-leveraged speculative stocks should be bought only on substantial price concession and only by those investors who can afford the risk and who have first established strong investment positions in both North American and South African gold stocks.

Because South African gold mining stocks are available only through the Over-the-Counter market and are not listed on North American stock exchanges, they are not really suitable for active trading. The OTC market is safe enough but it is not as liquid as the regular exchanges. Furthermore, accurate and up-to-date trading statistics are not readily available from the OTC market. The best way to trade actively in South African gold mining would be through the shares of the American-South African Investment trust, which is the only South African equity listed for trading on an American stock exchange. This stock, which is listed on the New York Stock Exchange, should be regarded as being in the TRADING-INVESTMENT category as described in Chapter X. It can also be considered an excellent long-term investment holding.

American South African is a rather unique holding company. It is registered in South Africa and normally deals only in stocks sold through Johannesburg, but it is not itself listed on the Johannesburg Stock Exchange. In fact, South African residents are not permitted to buy or hold shares in this trust. The company was formed in 1958 to provide an opportunity for American citizens to invest in South African gold shares through a company listed on the New York Stock Exchange, with all the advantages that such a listing offers. However, these shares are now also quoted in London and Amsterdam and traded in most of the other European stock exchanges.

AMERICAN-SOUTH AFRICAN INVESTMENT CO. LTD. (ASA)
Capitalization

FUNDED DEBT	None
COMMON STOCK	Authorized: 6,000,000 Shares.
	Issued: 2,400,000 Shares.
EXCHANGE LISTING	New York Stock Exchange
PRICE RANGE (1971)	53⅞–31¾
DIVIDEND (1971)	$0.70 ($0.35 semiannually)*
NET ASSET VALUE	$30.17 (Based on Johannesburg S.E.
PER SHARE (1971)	prices for holdings as of Aug. 31, 1971).

*Less 15 percent South African nonresident withholding tax.

History.   Incorporated in 1958, American South African is a closed-end investment trust holding a portfolio of South African mining stocks. Company policy since its incorporation has been that a minimum of 50 percent of its net assets should be committed at all times to the ordinary (common) shares of South African gold mining companies. At the close of 1971, approximately 72 percent of net assets were in gold mining shares, 17 percent in diamonds (DE BEERS) and the remainder in miscellaneous South African copper, platinum and industrial stocks. In 1969, authorized capital was increased to 6 million ordinary shares from 2.4 million. As of December 31, 1971, no plans had yet been announced to issue or exchange any of the additional shares.

Fundamental Position.   The company is specifically exempt from South African taxes on the dividend income from its investment portfolio. Only other income, such as interest received, is subject to South African income tax. Realized gains from portfolio investments are also exempt from taxation. The company is allowed to transfer its gross income freely in U.S. dollars, including profits from the sale of portfolio assets. And since it does not do business in the United States, ASA is also exempted from U.S. corporate income and capital gains taxes. (The individual U.S. shareholder must, of course, pay personal income tax on dividends received from ASA, and U.S. capital gains tax must be paid on any profits resulting from the sale of ASA shares.)

Since dividends paid by gold mining companies may be presumed to be, in part, a repayment of capital resulting from the depreciation and depletion of the mining property itself, the company excludes from income an estimated portion of dividends received from its holdings as an allowance for amortization of capital. This excluded portion is used to reduce the cost of the related investment. Dividend distributions to shareholders are paid out of net income; capital gains are reinvested in additional equity positions.

The South African Government levies the usual 15 percent nonresident withholding tax on dividends paid to ASA shareholders.

Within the limits of its charter, the company follows an active and aggressive investment policy and doubled its net asset value in the ten years preceding 1971.

Portfolio (as reported August 31, 1971).

FAR WEST RAND AREA:	Shares
Blyvooruitzicht Gold Mining	860,000
Doornfontein Gold Mining	980,000
East Driefontein Gold Mining	617,585
Kloof Gold Mining	746,400
West Driefontein Gold Mining	470,000
Western Areas Gold Mining	426,200
Western Deep Levels	218,300

KLERKSDORP AREA:

Buffelsfontein Gold Mining	376,600
Hartebeestfontein Gold Mining	49,400
Southvaal Holdings	807,300
Southvaal Holdings—Options	63,500
Vaal Reefs Exploration & Mining	559,600
Western Reefs Exploration & Development	322,200
Zandpan Gold Mining	543,300

ORANGE FREE STATE AREA:

President Brand Gold Mining	355,300
President Steyn Gold Mining	373,100
St. Helena Gold Mines	500,000

EVANDER AREA:

Winkelhaak Mines	702,200

DIAMONDS, COPPER & MISCELLANEOUS:

De Beers Consolidated Mines (diamonds)	2,457,700
Palabora Mining (copper)	200,600
Potgietersrust Platinum	110,000
Transvaal Consolidated Land & Expl.	465,900
Vereeniging Estates	29,900

Total value of portfolio based on Johannesburg Stock Exchange prices, August 31, 1971—$69,670,515

Financial Position. Under the terms of its charter, the company may not issue senior securities or borrow money. ASA is also exempt from the U.S. interest equalization tax on its purchases of foreign shares. U.S. purchasers of American South African stock are also exempted from this tax, unless they specifically purchase foreign-held shares (ASA fn).

Regular ASA shares purchased through the New York Stock Exchange are purchased from other U.S. persons and are therefore exempt from IET.

INCOME STATISTICS ($ Per share)*

Year	Net Income Per Share	Div's	Price Range High Low	Net Asset** Value Per Share
1960	$0.77	$0.20	17 – 9	$16.72
1961	0.87	0.20	13-3/8 – 9	17.26
1962	0.67	0.20	16-5/8 – 10-3/8	20.71
1963	1.09	0.30	19-3/4 – 13-1/4	22.08
1964	1.17	0.50	25-1/8 – 14-5/8	23.82
1965	1.25	0.60	39-1/8 – 20-3/4	25.30
1966	1.28	0.70	44-5/8 – 27-3/4	28.35
1967	1.30	0.70	58-7/8 – 30	28.57
1968	1.20	0.70	82 – 49-1/4	35.44
1969	1.32	0.70	69-7/8 – 26	33.60
1970	1.56	0.70	49-1/2 – 27-3/4	32.42

*Adjusted for 2-for-1 stock split in 1966.

**Average value based on Johannesburg S.E. prices for portfolio holdings.

Rating: TRADING-INVESTMENT

Comment: Although ASA is surely a prime vehicle for either trading or long-term investment in South African golds, and has had an excellent growth record for the past decade, share prices have tended to fluctuate widely in recent years, ranging from below net asset value to well above net asset value. It is interesting to note that in its early years ASA consistently sold at *less* than its net asset value, which goes to prove, I guess, that investors are often slow to recognize a bargain! Obviously, an investment trust should not be bought at too great a premium over its portfolio value. This is a fine stock, but avoid chasing it during periods of emotional buying in the gold group.

FINANCIAL-MONETARY SITUATION OF SOUTH AFRICA

All South African gold mines are required to sell their entire gold output to the South African Reserve Bank at a fixed price equal to the gold value of the South African monetary unit, the rand. The Reserve Bank, in turn, sells any gold in excess of its needs on the world's markets, at its discretion. If a portion of this gold is marketed at a higher level than the fixed South African monetary price, the resulting profits or "premiums" (less marketing costs, etc.) are distributed to the mining companies on a prorated basis determined by the mining company's percentage of total sales to the Reserve Bank. Thus the mines benefit from a higher gold price, even though obliged to sell through a central marketing agency.

Through most of 1971, premium payments have tended to increase individual mine earnings from 20 to 30 percent above the prior two years. Marginal and short-life mines understandably benefit most from premium payments. For the U.S. shareholder, such increases in profits are very often reflected in increased dividends or dividends maintained that would otherwise have been reduced, particularly for the lower-medium and short-life mines. Long-life and developing mines, however, will divert at least part of any increase in profits toward reducing development costs and loans outstanding, if possible.

The reader should note here that overall gold output for South Africa is probably (as of 1971) at or near its peak. The average life of a South African gold mine is only about 20 years. Even though some mines have produced, or are expected to produce for up to 30 years or more, others run out of payable ore in as little as ten years. It must be expected that declining grades and the breakup of older mines will increasingly tend to offset new mine openings and expansion schemes. Sharply higher gold prices will not significantly extend the lives of those mines unable to develop additional ore reserves, low-grade or otherwise, and there are many mines in this category. But a much higher gold price will of course greatly increase the earnings and dividends of such mines for their remaining periods of operation.

As overall production declines, however, additional upward pressure will be put on the price of gold in world markets, and this will accrue to the benefit of the surviving mines. This factor alone indicates that the investor should limit South African holdings to investment trusts, which continually rotate and upgrade their portfolios, or concentrate specifically on long-life and upper-medium-life mines (which will be reviewed in the next chapter).

A portfolio of medium- and lower-medium-life mines would undoubtedly offer a higher dividend yield, and perhaps even have the possibility of a greater percentage of immediate capital gain, *if* the price of gold is sharply increased in the near future. But if the overall rise in the world price for gold is held to a gradual pace over the next decade, the opportunity for large capital gains on the shares of marginal mines will very probably be lost. Although I confidently expect the price of gold to rise to a minimum of $100 per ounce by 1980 and perhaps even to $150, how this objective is achieved will very largely determine the course of profitability for gold mining investments.

If the rise in the price of gold is gradual over the next decade, much of the potential profit for marginal mines will be offset by inflation, higher wage rates and the increased costs of deeper mining. And by the time some degree of world monetary stability is achieved, along with a permanently higher price for gold, many of the medium- and lower-medium-life mines could be out of business. On the other hand, if a doubling or tripling of the present $45 average world gold price were to occur suddenly and within a very few years, startling capital gains and large dividend increases might accrue to the holders of the lower-life, lower-grade South African gold shares. But the holders of long-life and upper-medium-life mines will benefit *either way.* And the holders of gold-coin investments will, of course, also benefit whether the world price of gold rises suddenly or gradually.

Devaluation of the Rand.   The December 19, 1971, devaluation of the U.S. dollar, raising the "official" world price for gold from $35 to $38 per troy ounce, was paralleled by a devaluation of the South African rand from $1.40 per rand to $1.33 per rand. The South African Reserve bank's fixed price for the metal was consequently increased from R 25 to R 28.50 per ounce. However, the double drop caused by the devaluation of the rand against the dollar and the dollar against gold, coupled with the up-valuation of major European currencies, served to increase the free-market price of gold by nearly 27 percent, in South African terms, above the general level of a year earlier. The full impact of this change will be felt during the year 1972 and will obviously be beneficial.

For the near term, some confusion has arisen in making adjustments between the variations in price between identical shares traded on the London and Johannesburg Exchanges and in the American Over-the-Counter market. There have already been slight increases in dividend payments to American shareholders resulting from these changes in currency parities. There will no doubt be additional "official" devaluations of the dollar* and other currencies, including the rand, before the present idiotic IMF fiat-gold exchange system breaks down completely.

The second phase of the world monetary crisis that began in 1967 with the devaluation of the British pound sterling will see the end of the present stage of meaningless "devaluations" and futile attempts to bring about a workable system of fixed currency parities without actual gold convertibility. The world will sooner or later enter a period of floating exchange rates and this will obviously be an even more difficult time for the repatriation of dividends and the accurate valuation of South African Share prices in terms of floating U.S. dollars. But the investor holding long-life high-quality issues can remain calm in the knowledge that monetary price must eventually adjust to true value.

World monetary stability will eventually be reestablished after the price of gold has risen to a level where a return to a meaningful international gold standard becomes possible for the major trading nations of the world. Perhaps at that time the rand will be fixed at parity with an emerging gold-backed Common Market "Eurocurrency" monetary unit (perhaps to be designated the "ECU"). South Africa already has strong economic and financial ties with the major European states and a close monetary relationship would be a natural development.

In any case, the purchasing power of gold in absolute terms, as well as in monetary parities, will be greatly increased by the time a new world monetary system inevitably arises out of the

*The dollar and other paper currencies will actually continue to float against gold as long as they are not made redeemable in gold, no matter what the "official" rate is claimed to be.

ashes of the monetary disaster that is presently overtaking us. The question of whether the Common Market plus Japan can eventually support a minimum gold price double or triple the present level, if the United States chooses to allow the dollar to float more or less permanently, must be answered affirmatively, because the following factors will combine to assist them in maintaining a high "official" world monetary price if they choose to do so:

1. Increasing industrial and commercial demand, which will soon absorb all current production.
2. Gradually declining world output.
3. Growing world population, adding to both monetary and technological demand.
4. Advancing technology, which will develop new uses and requirements for gold.
5. Further expansion of Common Market and Japanese economies.
6. Additional economic and financial growth of presently underdeveloped areas of the world.
7. Expanding world trade.

It must also be remembered that the U.S. Treasury, contrary to popular economic mythology, has not actually supported the price of gold since 1957, the last year a true balance-of-payments surplus allowed us to buy more gold than we sold. We can hardly claim to have "supported" the old $35 price by *selling* some $14 billion worth of gold on balance during the postwar years. What we were actually doing was suppressing the price of gold during this time.

South African Tax Policies.   The South African Government levies a graduated corporate income tax against the profits of gold mining companies, a tax that is quite complex in structure. New mines pay no taxes at all until the total initial investment is recovered and older high-grade mines are often able to reduce their tax liabilities by entering into joint ventures, leases and tribute arrangements with lower-grade or marginal mines. Expansion projects of older mines can be charged against current income to reduce taxes. Such tax-shelters are often of limited duration, however, and their sudden expiration can significantly affect earnings at times.

The best source of detailed and up-to-date information concerning tax positions, estimated lives, ore reserves and grades, and significant developments affecting the outlook for individual mines, and for the investment trusts and finance houses as well, is the publication that will be described in the next paragraph. But first it must be mentioned that there is a South African withholding tax (currently 15 percent) levied against all dividends paid to nonresident shareholders of South African stocks. American shareholders are obliged to report the full dividend declared on their South African stocks, but may deduct the South African tax withheld when filing U.S. income tax returns.

The Quarterly Review of South African Gold Shares. The purpose of this book is to "open the door" to gold as an area of investment, but obviously it cannot provide continuous coverage of the various stocks introduced; for that type of information we must rely on periodicals. Fortunately, there is a highly respected publication that provides this service with regard to South African gold mining stocks, investment trusts and mining finance houses. This is the *Quarterly Review of South African Gold Shares,* published by the *Mining Journal,* 15 Wilson Street, London, EC2M, 2 TR, England.

The *Quarterly Review* is not an advisory service or market letter, but a very professional and very current survey and analysis of all South African gold stocks. Printed in magazine format, each issue contains more than 70 pages of concise information, comment and background material. A full page is devoted to each stock. The *Review* is the equivalent of a Standard and Poor's guide for South African gold shares. A full year's subscription (four issues) by airmail is currently £8.50 or R 16.50 or $22.00 (U.S.).* The author feels that this publication is indispensable to the serious investor maintaining a significant position in South African gold stocks.

---

*But please write to them for the latest rates before subscribing, as they may well have changed, due to further devaluations, etc., by the time you read this.

Notes:

Chapter XIV

1. South Africa has had a compulsory arbitration law for years and major strikes are virtually nonexistent. The South African Chamber of Mines negotiates industry-wide contracts and establishes the conditions of employment for both white and Bantu labor.

2. Temperatures tend to increase with depth, as one gets closer to the molten interior of the earth. Without enormous ventilating systems, not only would the miners suffocate from lack of oxygen, but the heat would be unbearable in the lower levels of these mines, which often reach a depth in excess of two miles.

3. If the finely crushed ore were mixed with mine water, the resulting slurry or slime could easily be pumped to the surface through 12-inch-diameter pipelines. This would not only be far less expensive than hauling and hoisting large chunks of rock, which is the present practice, but it would also assist in keeping the mine dewatered.

4. Stockpiled uranium ores, or residual "slimes," still have to be processed into uranium concentrate before they can be sold, and this refining expense is, of course, a charge against the mining company's potential or actual profit from the sale of such stockpiled uranium.

5. Investing in diamonds, however, is an area that is reserved for experts, or at least it requires expert guidance. The average investor would be unable to tell a good diamond from a mediocre or poor one and the cutting, color and other aesthetic qualities greatly affect the price of a gem diamond.

6. During the early part of the nineteenth century, platinum was used as money in Russia (the world's second-largest producer of the metal) and, from 1828 to 1845, the Russians struck platinum coinage.

7. It is not necessary for a finance house to have a majority ownership of stock in a specific mine in order to exert management control. Most mines enter into management agreements with their particular finance house in order to obtain experienced management and direction. The finance house, in turn, re-

ceives a small percentage of the mine's earnings as its management fee.

8. During the last few years of operation, the share prices of a mine approaching its end naturally become quite cheap and the dividend yield can become very high in relation to the stock price. Furthermore, upon the actual termination of operations a final or "breakup" dividend may be paid, which is a distribution of all remaining financial assets of the mining company, plus whatever can be obtained from the salvage value of plant and equipment, the sale of landholding, etc. Since these breakup dividends can sometimes be quite large, knowledgeable speculators can and do make good profits by buying short-life and breakup mines at a big discount, collecting rich dividends for a few years and then hoping for a generous final distribution. But this is a game strictly for specialists in this line—don't try it unless you really know what you are doing!

XV

THE LEADING GOLD STOCKS
OF SOUTH AFRICA

"We expect gold to be a major contributor to the economic life of our country for a long time to come."

—DR. ADRIAN A. VON MALTITZ,
PRESIDENT, SOUTH AFRICAN CHAMBER OF MINES

THE primary markets for South African gold shares are London and Johannesburg, where investors are traditionally more concerned with dividend yield than with capital appreciation. Consequently, South African golds generally sell at far more reasonable P.E. ratios and provide much more generous dividend returns than their U.S. and Canadian counterparts. North American stocks have, since the early 1960's, tended to sell at P.E. ratios that anticipate higher future earnings and dividends from a major increase in the price of gold. Furthermore, Canadian and U.S. issues have a far more limited number of shares in their capitalizations, which gives them a scarcity factor seldom found in the larger and more generously capitalized South African gold mining enterprises.

South African gold stocks have long been favored by British investors. In his recent book, *Investment and the Return to Equity Capital in the South African Gold Mining Industry*

(Cambridge, Mass.: Harvard Univ. Press, 1967), Dr. S. Herbert Frankel, a professor of economics at Oxford, demonstrated that the total return on South African gold shares (dividends plus capital repaid and market appreciation) exceeded the average of blue chip stocks on the London Stock Exchange for the entire period from the beginning of commercial gold mining in South Africa (1887) until the research for the book was completed in 1965. A similar comparison with the Dow Jones stocks of the New York Exchange resulted in the South African gold group surpassing the New York industrials in overall profitability in 1926 and remaining in the lead until 1962.

Since 1962, however, a largely artificial (in the author's opinion) American stock market boom, fueled by the debasement of the U.S. dollar and an unbelievable expansion of public and private debt, has made further comparisons distorted and unreliable. I personally feel that the 1960's boom can be compared very closely to the *ersatz* prosperity of the 1920's. Both periods were fired by cheap money and a mindless orgy of fiat credit. *When* this second "new era" ends exactly as the first, in panic and disaster, we may see a period of three to five years when gold shares are the glamor stocks of Wall Street, not to mention the London and Continental exchanges.

The Over-the-Counter Market. With the exception of the American-South African Investment Co., U.S. residents seeking to purchase South African gold shares must obtain them through what is called the "over-the-counter" (OTC) market. The OTC market is a rather loosely organized network of broker-dealers or "houses" operating under the rules of the National Association of Securities Dealers, Inc. (NASD). Actually, the term describes an over-the-telephone or over-the-wire market for all securities that are not traded on a regular listed exchange and for all securities dealers who are not members of such exchanges. However, neither part of the above definition is wholly exclusive, as nonmembers of exchanges among the NASD may sometimes deal in listed stocks as well as unlisted issues and stock exchange member firms may also make markets in some of the more prominent unlisted issues.

Over-the-counter, therefore, is more a method of trading

than a specifically defined organization for trading like the listed exchanges. The over-the-counter market is primarily a retail market rather than a continuous auction market. OTC dealers buy and sell securities to individuals, to each other and to the regular exchange members. The OTC dealer's compensation is obtained from the small "spread" between the "bid" price, or the price they are willing at a given time to pay for a stock, and the "asked" price that they are willing to sell it for. This spread may range from ¼ to ¾ of a point, depending on the price of the stock and other factors. The exchange-member brokerage firm on the other hand is compensated for its services on a standardized commission basis fixed by the exchange.

The OTC market actually handles a far greater number of stocks than all of the open-auction markets, such as the New York, American and Midwest exchanges combined. More than 20,000 stocks are traded over-the-counter, while there are only 1,945 issues listed on the New York Stock Exchange and 1,350 on the American.*

Because a stock is traded over-the-counter rather than on a listed exchange does not in itself mean that the stock in question lacks merit or is not trustworthy. Many of America's finest corporations do not have their stocks listed for trading and are therefore available only through the OTC market. Most bank and insurance stocks are traded over-the-counter, as are the great majority of foreign securities and even U.S. Treasury obligations.

There are several reasons why companies may be traded over-the-counter rather than listed on one of the major exchanges, but the two principal ones are that they either do not wish to or cannot submit all the periodic reports required by the U.S. Securities and Exchange Commission to maintain a listing and, secondly, that there may not be sufficient stock available in the company concerned to provide at all times the minimum floating supply required by the exchanges to maintain a continuous auction market for the stock. The OTC market also provides an opportunity for the stocks of small companies and

*As of December 31, 1971.

new and unseasoned companies, as well as foreign companies, to be made available to the U.S. public.

The main difficulty for investors in over-the-counter stocks is keeping abreast of the current price quotations for such stocks. Unfortunately, the newspapers that print daily lists of over-the-counter trades, such as the *Wall Street Journal,* are forced by space limitations to concentrate primarily on the best known and most actively traded domestic issues. The *Journal* provides daily quotations for only a few of the South African gold stocks. The weekly *Barron's* publishes a somewhat longer list, but it is still not complete. Therefore you may have to rely on your broker to keep you posted, as he can usually get you a quotation in a few minutes through his wire services.

Therefore, if you cannot find your stocks quoted daily or weekly in the papers, a good plan is to check with your broker on a regular basis, once or twice a week, for quotations on the South African stocks in your portfolio. Keep a permanent record of these quotations, or chart them if you wish, so that you will always have an up-to-date and overall view of what your stocks are actually doing. During periods of unusual activity in the gold group it would of course be advisable to ask for quotations on a daily basis.

Orders for over-the-counter stocks are placed in the usual manner through your own broker, who in turn contacts several OTC houses who customarily "make a market" for or deal in the stock concerned. This is to assure that you get the best possible price for the stock. Your own broker adds his usual commission to OTC transactions as well as to listed issues.

As a general rule, it is a little harder to get in or out of an OTC stock than a listed one during highly volatile market periods. The supply-demand situation of a typical OTC issue is much less flexible than a listed stock and consequently any unusual increase in buying or selling pressure on an OTC issue can cause sharp and sudden changes in its price level. Therefore, the best time to buy the over-the-counter golds is during dull and inactive periods in the gold group. Remember that the OTC gold stocks will follow the trend of the listed ones, so watch the big board gold group to determine the market conditions for the OTC gold issues.

South African gold stocks can of course be sold most readily when the overall market for golds is strong or reaching a buying climax. However, during weak markets for golds or markdown phases in the gold group, prices for the less liquid OTC gold issues can drop very abruptly, even though their overall swings are usually less intense than the listed golds.

Ordinary Shares and American Depositary Receipts.   The "ordinary" (i.e., common)* shares of South African gold mining companies, investment trusts and finance houses are represented by certificates issued by each corporation in the usual manner. However, American investors desiring a position in these stocks may also have the option of purchasing them in the form of "American Depositary Receipts" or ADR's. For the convenience of U.S. investors, certain New York banks, such as the Morgan Guaranty Trust Co., have made arrangements to act as the custodian or depositary for large blocks of popular foreign stocks, including most of the South African gold shares. These depositary banks can then issue their own certificates (the ADR's) on a share for share basis, with each ADR certificate representing a like number of ordinary shares held in trust by the depositary. ADR's are available through your broker via the OTC market.

The advantage of the ADR's is that no foreign-exchange transactions are necessary to purchase or transfer them. When you buy the ordinary shares of South African corporations, the transfer and registration of the certificates is made in Johannesburg or London, which means a delay of from six to eight weeks after purchase before you actually receive the stock certificates. Furthermore, the dividend checks received on ordinary shares are denominated in South African rands and therefore must be sent for collection to a bank dealing in foreign exchange, and this too involves a delay (generally from two to three weeks) before payment in U.S. funds is returned.[1]

But when ADR's are purchased, the transfer and registration is effected at the depositary bank in New York and can therefore be completed in a much shorter time. Also, dividends paid

---

*The term "ordinary" is customarily used in lieu of common for British and South African stocks.

on the ADR's (which are at the same rate as declared on the ordinary shares) are denominated in U.S. funds, which of course means that ADR dividend checks can be negotiated immediately.[2] Generally there is little or no difference in price between the ordinary shares and the ADR's of a particular company. Specifically, the advantages of ADR's over ordinary shares for American investors are:

1. ADR certificates are more convenient to obtain and transfer, since they are registered within the United States.
2. ADR dividend checks are denominated in U.S. funds and are therefore immediately negotiable.
3. The U.S. interest equalization tax does not apply to ADR's.

Consequently, ADR's are more suitable than ordinary shares for relatively short-term holding, for periodic trading as part of the trading-investment strategy and for holding in margin accounts or custodial accounts with brokerage firms.

However, it is at least conceivable that the U.S. Government could seize or block the assets behind the ADR's, namely the foreign shares held in trust by the depositaries, if it was decided that some grave national emergency warranted such a step. The value of the ADR's themselves could be considerably altered by such an action, to put it mildly. (Perhaps they would be redeemed in government bonds!) The seizure of foreign assets by governments in wartime is, of course, commonplace. The British Government confiscated all foreign securities and assets it could get its hands on in 1940, and the U.S. Government seized or blocked enemy financial holdings and assets in both World Wars. And, of course, during the great worldwide financial crisis of 1933, the United States Government demanded the surrender of gold bullion, gold coin and silver bullion. Therefore, I do not think it inconceivable to suggest that a future world monetary-economic crisis could see a move by the U.S. Government to seize foreign financial assets to help shore up a collapsing dollar.

The main point here is that it would be far easier for a government to seize or block the depositary holdings of one or two banks than to try to round up ordinary shares in individual hands scattered throughout the country. I sincerely hope that the day never comes when such a step will be thought necessary. But, if it does, there may be a significant advantage in holding ordinary shares rather than ADR's. The ordinary shares represent an actual and direct equity in the issuing corporation. Consequently, such shares could be sold anywhere in the world—assuming you could get them there. Therefore, if you want to anticipate the worst and are planning to use South African golds strictly for long-term investment holding, your preference would be for the ordinary shares.

The Interest Equalization Tax. The U.S. Interest Equalization Tax (IET), as described in Chapter XII, applies to South African ordinary shares purchased abroad, but does not apply to such shares if they are purchased from another American. So if you wish to avoid this tax, make sure that your broker requests AMERICAN-OWNED stock when placing your orders for ordinary shares of South African corporations. The words AMERICAN-OWNED should appear on the *confirmation of purchase* statements you receive from your broker, because the confirmation so marked is the evidence that the South African stock in question is exempt from IET (you can't tell from the certificate).

If you do not specify AMERICAN-OWNED when purchasing South African ordinary shares it is possible that your order could be filled through London or Johannesburg and you would then be stuck for the tax. And purchases made abroad may not necessarily be any cheaper than corresponding American-owned shares or ADR's.

However, there may be cases where neither American-owned ordinary shares nor ADR's are available for certain South African corporations and, if you wanted such stock, you would have no choice but to buy abroad (assuming exchange controls did not prevent it) and pay the tax. The tax could be recovered if the stock was later sold abroad, but that too has its problems. Don't, in any case, sell stock in Johannesburg unless you want to spend the money there.

The Blocked Rand. Like all rapidly developing countries, South Africa has a tremendous need for capital. The Republic has also had a more or less continuous balance-of-payments deficit for the last decade. Consequently, the South African Government has instituted exchange controls and the rand is a partially blocked currency. Although the repatriation of dividends and other earnings on South African investments is freely permitted, the return of *capital* is not allowed except by special arrangement. So if you sell anything in South Africa, you will not be able to have the proceeds returned to you in dollar exchange. The London and Canadian markets are still open, but I feel that it is only a matter of a very short time before all major trading nations will institute some form of exchange control.

Therefore, concentrate on buying and selling in the American market as much as possible. If you are forced to buy abroad (and are allowed to do so) it would still be preferable to *sell* in the U.S. and consider the IET as just part of the overhead. There is always a chance that a sale made in London or elsewhere could be suddenly blocked before the proceeds could be returned. In the normal course of events, however, your broker would not sell your stock abroad unless specifically requested to do so.

SELECTING SOUTH AFRICAN GOLD STOCKS FOR INVESTMENT

For most American investors, the South African gold stocks in their portfolios should be regarded primarily as long-term investment holdings. The problem then is the usual one of selectivity and timing—buying the right stock at the right time. We have already discussed timing in some detail in Chapter IX, and there is not much I can add with regard to South African gold stocks in particular except that whenever medium- and long-life mines sell down to a level where they yield* 8 to 10 percent or more, they should be bought with great confidence, and when they rise to a point where yields are generally less than 5 percent, they should be regarded with some suspicion.

Unfortunately, however, I can make no hard and fast rules

---

* *Yield* is the rate of dividend expressed as a percentage of the market price of a stock. To determine yield, one divides the (most recent) annual dividend by the current market price. Thus, a stock selling for $20 per share and paying a dividend of $1.20 per share has a yield of 6 percent.

for the treacherous monetary and financial climate we have already entered. The previous comment is based on the experience of the 1960's and may no longer be entirely valid in the face of a rapidly collapsing dollar. Perhaps the only safe path for the '70's will be to buy quality gold issues whenever one has the money, or over a fixed period of time, thus averaging the overall investment base.

The averaging technique, whereby one commits more-or-less-equal sums of money at fixed intervals over a period of time, without regard to the general price levels of stocks, has long been accepted as an effective method of building long-term investment portfolios, even though such an approach would seldom provide opportunities for trading profits.

However, a combination plan whereby one buys gold shares at regular intervals, regardless of the general price level, but varies the *amount* of money committed so that larger sums are employed when prices are relatively low (based on P.E. ratios and yields) and smaller amounts are invested during advanced markets, would probably be the best solution to the problem of acquiring long-term investment portfolios for the 1970's. This combination plan would also allow for a modest amount of intermediate-term trading, if the investor is so inclined.

Under the combination plan, if the investor were going to commit, say, $1,000 per quarter as his average, he would increase the amount invested to $1500 during those quarterly investment periods when (and if) P.E. ratios and yields were generous, and decrease the amount committed to $500 for those quarters when prices for gold shares were on the high side. If prices for these stocks had made an extreme advance since the last investment commitment, the investor would make no new purchases but instead realize a modest profit on any issues that appeared obviously overbought and overpriced.

Investment Grade Stocks.   Fortunately, when it comes to the problem of buying the right stocks, we can be less equivocal than in the matter of timing. Due to the sedimentary "reef" structure of the South African gold fields, the probable life of a particular mine can be estimated with considerable accuracy, by dividing the probable ore reserves (as determined by borehole testing) by the current and estimated future milling rate. Of course rising costs and other difficulties can bring about a reduction in any estimate of this type and rapidly rising gold prices on the other hand could extend the lives of certain older mines. However, for our purposes, the 1971–72 estimates of the authoritative *Mining Journal* of London can be accepted without further discussion.[3]

Since we are going to include only certain finance houses, the investment trusts and operating mines in the long- and medium-life category in our recommended investment portfolios, a minor revision in the estimated lives of certain mines would not significantly alter the investment potential of such portfolios. I am not denying that money can be made in some of the short-life mines, but I feel that they are primarily for professional speculators and those who can follow the gold market very closely. For most of us, the "safety of capital" principle would indicate that we avoid all high-risk situations. At any rate, the author is not going to recommend or review any South African mines that are now (1971–72) in less than the *medium-life* category.[4]

Using the *Mining Journal's* estimates for probable life-spans, a financial "table of organization" for the South African gold mining industry can be constructed as shown in *Fig. 35*.

The first step in determining what South African gold stocks or "Kaffirs"* to consider for inclusion in a gold investment portfolio is to eliminate the obvious: the finance houses that do not have a significant percentage of investment capital committed to gold, and all operating mines having an estimated life expectancy of less than 11 years. This preliminary screening leaves a total of 25 stocks to choose from, including seven from the finance house/investment trust group and 18 developing or operating mines (see *Fig. 36*). Naturally, not all of these stocks are of equal merit, and their individual problems and possibilities will be touched on in the reviews that conclude this chapter.

The remainder of the finance house/investment trust group are not recommended as *gold* holdings, because of their broad

---

*Taken from a South African colloquialism for a Black South African. Hence any stock "native" to South Africa is a Kaffir, although the term is applied primarily to South African gold shares.

Fig. 35

FINANCIAL ORGANIZATION
OF
THE SOUTH AFRICAN GOLD MINING INDUSTRY

December 31, 1971

Anglo-American Corporation of South Africa Ltd.

ASSOCIATED FINANCE HOUSES:
Charter Consolidated
De Beers Consolidated
Rand Selection Corp.

INVESTMENT TRUST SUBSIDIARIES:
Orange Free State Investment Trust
West Rand Investment Trust

MINING SUBSIDIARIES:	Location	*Est.* *Life*	*Financial* *Position*
East Daggafontein Mines	(FER)	B	GMA
Free State Geduld Mines	(OFS)	S	
President Brand Gold Mining Co.	(OFS)	M	
President Steyn Gold Mining Co.	(OFS)	M	
South African Land & Expl. Co.	(ER)	B	GMA
Southvaal Holdings	(K)	D	
Vaal Reefs Expl. & Mining Co.	(K)	L	
Welkom Gold Mining Co.	(OFS)	S	
Western Deep Levels	(FWR)	L	
Western Holdings	(OFS)	S	

Anglo-Transvaal Consolidated Investment Co. Ltd.

INVESTMENT TRUST SUBSIDIARY:
Middle Witwatersrand

MINING SUBSIDIARIES:			
Hartebeestfontein Gold Mining Co.	(K)	M	
Loraine Gold Mines	(OFS)	S	
Virginia Orange Free State Gold Mining Co.	(OFS)	S	
Zandpan Gold Mining Co.	(K)	M	GMA

Barlow-Rand Ltd.

MINING SUBSIDIARIES:			
Blyvooruitzicht Gold Mining Co.	(FWR)	S	
Durban Roodepoort Deep	(CR)	S	GMA
East Rand Proprietary Mines	(CR)	S	GMA
Harmony Gold Mining Co.	(OFS)	S	

Gold Fields of South Africa

ASSOCIATED FINANCE HOUSE:
Consolidated Gold Fields

MINING SUBSIDIARIES:

Doornfontein Gold Mining Co.	(FWR)	M	
East Driefontein	(FWR)	D	
Kloof Gold Mining Co.	(FWR)	L	
Libanon Mining Co.	(WR)	S	
Venterspost Gold Mining Co.	(WR)	B	
Vlakfontein Gold Mining Co.	(FER)	B	
West Driefontein Gold Mining Co.	(FWR)	M	

General Mining and Finance Corporation, Ltd.

ASSOCIATED INVESTMENT COMPANY:
Sentrust Beperk

MINING SUBSIDIARIES:

Buffelsfontein Gold Mining Co.	(K)	M	
South Roodepoort Main Reef Areas	(WR)	B	GMA
Stilfontein Gold Mining Co.	(K)	S	GMA
West Rand Consolidated Mines	(WR)	S	GMA

Johannesburg Consolidated Investment Co. Ltd.

MINING SUBSIDIARIES:

Elsburg Gold Mining Co.	(SWR)	D	
Randfontein Estates Gold Mining Co., Witwatersrand	(WR)	D	
Western Areas Gold Mining Co.	(SWR)	M	

Union Corporation, Ltd.

ASSOCIATED INVESTMENT TRUSTS:
Geduld Investments
U.C. Investments

MINING SUBSIDIARIES:

Bracken Mines	(EV)	S	
Grootvlei Proprietary Mines	(ER)	B	
Kinross Mines	(EV)	L	
Leslie Gold Mines	(EV)	S	
Marievale Consolidated Mines	(FER)	B	
St. Helena Gold Mines	(OFS)	M	
Winkelhaak Mines	(EV)	L	

Independent

MINING COMPANY

Witwatersrand Nigel	(FER)	B	GMA

Notes:

1. Location References:
    CR – Central Rand
    ER – East Rand
    EV – Evander
    FER – Far East Rand
    FWR – Far West Rand

K   – Klerksdorp
OFS – Orange Free State
SWR – South of West Rand
WR   – West Rand

2. Estimated Life References
    D   – Developing (New mine under development)
    L   – Long   (More than 20 years)
    M   – Medium   (11 to 20 years)
    S   – Short   (6 to 10 years)
    B   – Breakup   (1 to 5 years)

3. GMA—indicates mine receiving state aid under the Gold Mining Assistance Act.

4. SUBSIDIARY status indicates management control but does not necessarily include statutory ownership of a majority interest in the company concerned.

diversification, although they may be in other respects investment grade issues. The balance of the operating mines (listed in *Fig. 37* for the convenience of the reader) must be considered as ranging from SPECULATIVE to HIGHLY SPECULATIVE. Some of these stocks, particularly the ones with a life expectancy on the upper end of the SHORT category (8–10 years), such as Free State Geduld and Western Holdings, could be bought on substantial price concession and held for 2 to 4 years as income producers and as speculations on a rapid rise in the price of gold, but I would have to see 15 percent or more in probable yield to justify such purchases. In general, however I would not be interested in the SHORT-LIFE group—there is risk enough in some of the MEDIUM-LIFE stocks.

Fig. 36

SOUTH AFRICAN GOLD MINING STOCKS
SUITABLE FOR INVESTMENT HOLDING
December 31, 1971

FINANCE HOUSES:
Anglo-American Corporation of South Africa
Gold Fields of South Africa
Union Corporation

INVESTMENT TRUSTS:
Middle Witwatersrand
Orange Free State Investment Trust
U.C. Investments
West Rand Investment Trust

DEVELOPING MINES:
East Driefontein Gold Mining Co.
Elsburg Gold Mining Co.
Randfontein Estates Gold Mining Co., Witwatersrand
Southvaal Holdings (U)

LONG-LIFE MINES (More than 20 years)
Kinross Mines
Kloof Gold Mining Co.
Vaal Reefs Exploration & Mining Co. (U)
Western Deep Levels (u)
Winkelhaak Mines

MEDIUM-LIFE MINES (11 to 20 years)
Buffelsfontein Gold Mining Co. (U)
Doornfontein Gold Mining Co.
Hartebeestfontein Gold Mining Co. (U)
President Brand Gold Mining Co. (u)
President Steyn Gold Mining Co.
St. Helena Gold Mines
Western Areas Gold Mining Co.
West Driefontein Gold Mining Co. (u)
Zandpan Gold Mining Co. (U)*

Notes:
(U) -Indicates mines where uranium sales could contribute significantly to future earnings.
(u) -Indicates mines where uranium earnings would be of only minor importance.
*Zandpan Gold Mining Co. has entered a merger agreement with Hartebeestfontein, with the latter to be the surviving company. The plan is awaiting government approval.

Fig. 37

SOUTH AFRICAN GOLD MINING STOCKS
NOT RECOMMENDED FOR INVESTMENT HOLDING

SHORT-LIFE MINES (6 to 10 years)
Blyvooruitzicht Gold Mining Co. (U)
Bracken Mines
Durban Roodepoort Deep
East Rand Proprietary Mines
Free State Geduld Mines
Harmony Gold Mining Co. (u)
Leslie Gold Mines
Libanon Mining Co.
Loraine Gold Mines
Stilfontein Gold Mining Co.
Virginia Orange Free State Gold Mining Co. (U)
Welkom Gold Mining Co. (u)
Western Holdings
West Rand Consolidated Mines (U)

BREAK-UP MINES (1 to 5 years)
East Daggafontein Mines
Grootvlei Proprietary Mines
Marievale Consolidated Mines
South African Land and Exploration Co.
South Roodeport Main Reef Areas
Venterspost Gold Mining Co.
Vlakfontein Gold Mining Co.
Witwatersrand Nigel

Notes:
   (U) -Indicates mines where uranium sales could contribute signifi-
       cantly to future earnings.
   (u) -Indicates mines where uranium earnings would be of only
       minor importance.

The Individual Stock Reviews.   The reader should keep the
following points in mind when referring to the reviews of
individual South African gold stocks that follow in this
chapter:
   1. Figures stated in terms of South African rands may be
      converted to U.S. dollars on the following basis: 1 rand =
      US $1.40 (this was the exchange rate that prevailed prior
      to the Smithsonian devaluations of December 1971).
   2. The PRICE RANGE quoted for the stock is based on U.S.
      over-the-counter transactions for ordinary shares, stated
      in U.S. dollars per share.
   3. DIVIDENDS are stated in terms of U.S. dollars before
      South African withholding taxes, foreign exchange varia-

tions, transfer fees and/or ADR depositary charges are deducted.

4. The capitalization noted under ORDINARY SHARES ISSUED is, in most cases, partially represented by American Depositary Receipts (ADR's).
5. Statistical data is taken directly from the latest annual and quarterly reports of the companies concerned and is presumed to be accurate.
6. The ESTIMATED LIFE indicated is as determined by the *Mining Journal* of London.
7. The RATING assigned to each stock is an opinion of the author.
8. The COMMENTS concerning each stock are based on the author's interpretation of the company's reports and other significant data.
9. The reviews in this book are bound to become less relevant with the passage of time and, consequently, before making purchases the latest annual or quarterly report of the company concerned or the most recent issue of the *Quarterly Review of South African Gold Shares* should be consulted to update and supplement the reviews presented here.

ANGLO-AMERICAN CORPORATION OF SOUTH AFRICA, LTD.

ACTIVITY	Finance house
ORDINARY SHARES ISSUED	129,820,000*
PREFERRED SHARES	4,759,000
CAPITALIZED DEBT	R 7,023,000 (repayable 1971/74)
	R 92,000 (repayable 1982)
	R 8,289,000 (repayable Dec. 1972)
PRICE RANGE*	1969: 6¼—10⅞
	1970: 6⅝—9¼
	1971: 4¾—8½
DIVIDENDS	1966: $0.18, 1967: $0.18, 1968: $0.19½
	1969: $0.22½, 1970: $0.22½, 1971: $0.22½
DIVIDENDS PAID	November and May
NET ASSET VALUE (per share)*	1966: $5.63, 1967: $6.75, 1968: $9.97, 1969: $8.47, 1970: $7.03
	*After 10 for 1 stock split in 1969

Rating: INVESTMENT GRADE

Comment: Anglo-American is a finance, exploration, management and investment organization that heads an international group of mining, industrial and investment companies that it administers or manages but, in most cases, does not actually control. However, substantial investment positions are maintained in most of the associated companies. Anglo-American has large holdings in De Beers Consolidated, the diamond trust, and Charter Consolidated, a United Kingdom-based finance house. The chief area of mining investment is still southern Africa, although the company is also engaged in widespread prospecting and development elsewhere in Africa and in North and South America, Europe, Australia and the Far East as well.

The most important acquisition in recent years has been the controlling interest in Engelhard Hanovia, a U.S. corporation, which in turn owns 44 percent of Engelhard Minerals and Chemicals, the largest refiner and supplier of precious metals in the United States.

Anglo-American's gold investments are held primarily through its associated portfolio companies: Orange Free State Investment Trust and West Rand Investment Trust. Overall investment and income distribution for 1968, 1969 and 1970 was as shown in the following table:

INVESTMENT AREA	Percent of Investment			Percent of Income		
	1968	*1969*	*1970*	*1968*	*1969*	*1970*
Gold	26	21	24	34	32	28
Diamonds	33	33	25	23	22	18
Platinum	1	1	1	1	1	2
Copper	5	7	7	13	15	22
Other Mining	7	8	10	9	8	12
Industrials	20	22	25	12	13	11
Finance	8	8	8	8	9	7
	100	100	100	100	100	100

The chairman announced in December of 1971 that portfolio holdings were little changed in composition or value from the previous year.

Anglo-American is a solid holding for conservative investors. Although not a major gold investment it does provide a substantial gold hedge to balance its interesting worldwide industrial and mining portfolio.

GOLD FIELDS OF SOUTH AFRICA

ACTIVITY	Finance and portfolio company
ORDINARY SHARES ISSUED	16,211,477
CAPITALIZED DEBT	R 6,000,000
PRICE RANGE	1970: 10¾–18⅜,*
	1971: 9¼–19¾
DIVIDENDS	Year ending June 30, 1971: $0.63*
DIVIDENDS PAID	February and August
NET ASSET VALUE	Year ending June 30, 1971: $19.12*
(per share)	

*All figures dated on or before June 30, 1971, refer to the West Witwatersrand company prior to amalgamation.

Rating: INVESTMENT GRADE

Comment: Gold Fields of South Africa (GFSA) is a major new finance and investment house created in 1971 through the amalgamation of the West Witwatersrand Investment Trust with a subsidiary of the London-based Consolidated Gold Fields finance house. In order that the new company should not be subsidiary to a non-South African corporation, Consolidated Gold Fields has limited its interest in GFSA to just under 50 percent. The new Gold Fields company has become a major South African mining finance and investment house with net assets of approximately R 221 million. GFSA will be responsible for the promotion, financing and administration of the Gold Fields group of mines, which includes Doornfontein, East and West Driefontein and Kloof.

The new GFSA will also have interests in a number of base-metal projects through its 54-percent-owned subsidiary, Vogelstruisbult Metal Holdings. There are additional positions in various industrial and real estate ventures.

However, the main part of the Gold Fields portfolio is represented by the former assets of the West Witwatersrand Investment Trust. The West Wits portfolio had been concentrated in mines of the West Rand and the Far West Rand. Aside from the possibility of a new mine south of Doornfontein, there is not much chance for additional investment by West Wits-GFSA in new gold mining properties and the long-term trend of new investment for the combined company will probably be directed toward base metals and related projects. Nevertheless, gold output from the mines in the West Wits portfolio will most likely continue to rise until 1975 or so.

Although GFSA had not, as of Dec. 31, 1971, published an annual report since the West Wits merger, the *Mining Journal* estimates that the combined corporation had (in 1971) approximately 83 percent of its assets in gold mining enterprises and derived about 68 percent of its income from gold, including management fees and commissions. The respective figures for 1972 are expected to be slightly higher.

With its strong position in gold and its moderate capitalization, GFSA would fit into any long-term investment portfolio, particularly at a price close to its net asset value.

UNION CORPORATION, LTD.

ACTIVITY	Finance house
ORDINARY SHARES ISSUED	50,000,000
CAPITALIZED DEBT	R 4,000,000 (repayable 1974–83)
	R 5,371,000 (miscellaneous loans)
PRICE RANGE	1969: 4¼–7¾
	1970: 4½–7¼
	1971: 3¾–5¼
DIVIDENDS	1967: $0.13; 1968: $0.13; 1969: $0.16;
	1970: $0.17
DIVIDENDS PAID	December and June
NET ASSET VALUE	1967: $5.01; 1968: $5.86½; 1969: $6.10;
	1970: $5.77

Rating: INVESTMENT GRADE

Comment: Gold has been the most important area of interest of Union Corporation for many years, although in 1970 the percentage of income from gold slipped below 50 percent. However, considering indirect holdings through associated investment and finance companies, gold is still the central field of investment for Union.

Directly and indirectly, the Evander mines, Bracken Leslie

and Winkelhaak are the most substantial holdings. St. Helena and Southvaal are also well represented. In finance, the major positions are in U.C. Investments, Bay Hall Trust, Charter Consolidated, Selection Trust and Geduld Investments. The most important industrial holding is a 30–40 percent interest in South African Paper and Pulp. In the "other metals" category, Impala Platinum is the central attraction, with Union holding a 46.75 percent interest in this company.

Union Corporation is active in exploration throughout the world, but the main emphasis remains on southern Africa. The following table shows investment distribution in recent years:

INVESTMENT AREA	Percent of Investment			Percent of Income		
	1968	1969	1970	1968	1969	1970
Gold	37.4	25.7	27.9	47.9	50.4	44.4
Other Metals	9.0	22.5	24.1	19.2	17.2	25.2
Industrials	19.6	23.6	17.4	14.0	14.8	14.8
Finance	29.9	24.4	22.3	16.4	14.9	13.2
Miscellaneous	3.5	3.8	8.3	2.5	2.7	2.4
	100.0	100.0	100.0	100.0	100.0	100.0

Union is a well-diversified organization with strong positions in both gold and platinum. Future prospects depend on developments in these two metals.

MIDDLE WITWATERSRAND, LTD.

GROUP	Anglo-Transvaal
ACTIVITY	Portfolio and exploration company
ORDINARY SHARES ISSUED	8,980,578
CAPITALIZED DEBT	R 615,000
PRICE RANGE	1969: 3¼–6½
	1970: 4⅛–8¼
	1971: 2¾–6¼
DIVIDENDS	1969 through 1971: $0.12½ (annually)
DIVIDENDS PAID	February and August
NET ASSET VALUE (per share)	1969: $3.76½; 1970: $3.29
Rating:	SPECULATIVE
Comment:	Middle Wits is an investment holding company

associated with and under the administration of Anglo-Transvaal Consolidated. Although gold was formerly the main area of investment, with large portfolio holdings of Hartebeestfontien and Buffelsfontein, the company has broadened its interests in recent years. The following table indicates the reported investment and income spread for 1969 and 1970:

AREA OF INVESTMENT	Percent of Investment		Percent of Income	
	1969	1970	1969	1970
Gold and Uranium	47	56	42	50
Base Metals and Other Minerals	33	32	38	37
Mining Finance	18	9	19	11
Industrials	2	3	1	2
	100	100	100	100

As indicated by the table, non-gold-mining accounted for 32 percent of investment and 37 percent of income during 1970. Associated Manganese, Consolidated Murchison (copper), Associated Ore and Metals, Messina Development (Transvaal), Palabora Mining (platinum), Potgietersrust Platinum and Prieska Copper Mines Ltd. are important holdings. The last named is the most significant non-gold holding and MIDWITS has a 24 percent interest in this developing company, which has estimated ore reserves of 47 million tons averaging 1.74 percent copper and 3.87 percent zinc.

The mining finance section of the portfolio is represented chiefly by a sizable holding of shares in the parent Anglo-Transvaal Corporation.

Middle Witwatersrand will undoubtedly respond to higher future gold prices but the main interest in this stock is its large holding of Prieska Copper. This mine is scheduled to begin production in 1973 and, given favorable prices for copper and zinc, the shares of Middle Wits could benefit significantly in the latter half of the seventies. MIDWITS is best described as a combination gold hedge and copper-zinc-platinum speculation.

ORANGE FREE STATE INVESTMENT TRUST, LTD.

GROUP	Anglo-American
ACTIVITY	Investment holding company
ORDINARY SHARES ISSUED	10,943,406
CAPITALIZED DEBT	Nil
PRICE RANGE	1969: 10½–17¼
	1970: 9¾–14¼
	1971: 10¼–16⅞
DIVIDENDS	1966: $0.98; 1967: $0.98; 1968: $0.98;
	1969: $1.05; 1970: $1.08½
DIVIDENDS PAID	March and August
NET ASSET VALUE	1970: $16.88
(per share)	

Rating: INVESTMENT GRADE

Comment: Orange Free State (OFSITS) is an investment holding company managed by the Anglo-American Corporation. As its name implies, the company's holdings are concentrated primarily in operating gold mines of the Orange Free State field. Although investments are now being made in other areas, Orange Free State mines accounted for 90 percent of portfolio investments, in terms of quoted market values, as of December 31, 1970. The following table shows the OFSITS portfolio reported on that date:

GOLD MINES	LOCATION	SHARES
East Driefontein	FWR	709,000
Free State Geduld	OFS	2,100,000
Harmony	OFS	1,800,000
Kloof	FWR	160,000
Loraine	OFS	2,400,000
President Brand	OFS	2,808,000
President Steyn	OFS	3,000,000
St. Helena	OFS	1,925,000
Welkom	OFS	2,450,000
West Driefontein	FWR	10,000
Western Holdings	OFS	1,575,000
Southvaal Holdings	K	854,000
Southvaal Options	K	1,759,000

MISCELLANEOUS

Sentrust	40,000
Gold Fields of S.A.	181,000
Anglo-American Industrial Corp.	40,000
Witwatersrand Deep	31,000
Carlton Centre Debentures	R 1,000,000

Although OFSITS was able to increase its dividend slightly in recent years, it must be expected that a conservative dividend policy will be followed in the future as the company attempts to generate additional capital for investing outside of the Orange Free State area. The primary problem facing OFSITS is that its major holdings are in mines that are, for the most part, at or past their peaks. However, the company believes that additional investment opportunities will be found outside of the fully developed Orange Free State field.

In any case, diversification is vital, because income from the Free State mines, with the exception of St. Helena and President Steyn, has already begun to decline. This company will respond favorably to an early and sharp increase in the price of gold but its long-term future is more ambiguous. OFSITS is probably still suitable for investment, but only if bought at a low price in relation to its earnings and dividends.

U.C. INVESTMENTS, LTD.

GROUP	Associated with Union Corporation
ACTIVITY	Investment holding company
ORDINARY SHARES ISSUED	19,500,000
CAPITALIZED DEBT	R 1,266,000 (repayable 1974)
PRICE RANGE	1969: 2½–4¾
	1970: 2⅞–4½
	1971: 1⅞–2¾
DIVIDENDS	1967: $0.14½; 1968: $0.15½; 1969: $0.16; 1970: $0.16½; 1971: $0.16½
DIVIDENDS PAID	March and September
NET ASSET VALUE (per share)	1968: $3.53; 1969, $3.32; 1970: $3.12
Rating:	SPECULATIVE

Comment: The percentage of gold investment in the U.C. portfolio has been declining for some years and is currently less than 50 percent. Aside from a small position in St. Helena, the company's (1971) gold holdings were concentrated in the Evander mines and consisted of Bracken, 7.75 percent; Kinross, 16.3 percent; Leslie, 7.25 percent; and Winkelhaak, 12.35 percent of estimated portfolio value respectively. Kinross and Winkelhaak are the best of the Evander mines and have long lives ahead of them. U.C.'s substantial position in these stocks will have a major bearing on its future.

The largest non-gold holding was an 11.69 percent interest in Impala Platinum, which accounted for 19.0 percent of portfolio value in 1970. Mining finance and investment, principally shares of Union Corporation and Geduld Investments account for 5.56 and 7.4 percent of portfolio value respectively. Among industrial issues, the primary holding was South African Pulp and Paper, accounting for 7.5 percent of total portfolio valuation. The trend of U.C.'s investment portfolio is shown in the following table:

PERCENT OF TOTAL MARKET VALUE
at December 31

INVESTMENT AREA	1967	1968	1969	1970
Gold	63.14	58.48	37.23	44.00
Platinum		3.12	16.32	19.00
Industrials	17.53	14.08	18.51	12.94
Mining Finance	11.08	15.47	15.06	13.21
Diamonds	1.29	1.82	1.71	1.27
Other Mining	0.35	0.70	1.58	1.67
Miscellaneous	6.61	6.33	9.59	7.91
	100.00	100.00	100.00	100.00

The future of U.C. rests basically on its gold and platinum holdings. The possibility of extensive use of platinum in antipollution devices for automotive engines is significant.

WEST RAND INVESTMENT TRUST, LTD.

GROUP	Anglo-American
ACTIVITY	Investment holding company
ORDINARY SHARES ISSUED	11,008,606
PREFERRED SHARES	6,000,000 (redeemable 1974)
PRICE RANGE	1969: 10¾–19⅞
	1970: 11–15½

	1971: 9⅞–18¾
DIVIDENDS	1966: $0.59½; 1967: $0.59½; 1968: $0.-59½; 1969: $0.63; 1970: $0.66½
DIVIDENDS PAID	March and August
NET ASSET VALUE	Dec. 31, 1970: $16.50
(per share)	
Rating:	INVESTMENT GRADE

Comment: WRITS is a holding company of the Anglo-American group concentrating its investments in gold mining companies of the Far West Rand and Klerksdorp fields.

West Rand is in a better position than its sister holding company of the Anglo-American group, OFSITS, in that it has had the opportunity to invest in much newer mines in recent years. The WRITS portfolio, shown in the following table, has impressive holdings of such future stars as East Driefontein, Kloof, Vaal Reefs and Western Deep.

WEST RAND INVESTMENT TRUST HOLDINGS
Based on Report Dated Dec. 31, 1970

GOLD MINES	*LOCATION*	*SHARES*
Blyvooruitzicht	FWR	1,700,000
Buffelsfontein	K	2,000,000
Doornfontein	FWR	650,000
East Driefontein	FWR	4,500,000
Elsburg	SWR	350,000
Hartebeestfontein	K	1,700,000
Kloof	FWR	2,500,000
Libanon	WR	100,000
Southvaal Rights	K	700,000
Stilfontein	K	10,000
Vaal Reefs	K	2,250,000
Venterspost	WR	50,000
West Driefontein	FWR	2,000,000
Western Areas	SWR	1,050,000
Western Deep Levels	FWR	3,200,000
Zandpan	K	1,654,000
MISCELLANEOUS		
Ellaton Corp.		59,000
Gold Fields of S.A.		1,300,000
Western Ultra Deep		434,000
Loans to others		R 3,145,000

One of the interesting features of the WRITS portfolio is that it has strong representation in the high-grade uranium producers among its gold holdings. While not significant in 1972, it could become important in the latter part of the decade. West Rand also has an important interest in a possible new gold mine south of Doornfontein, through its large holdings of Gold Fields and Western Ultra Deep Levels. These two finance companies control the mineral rights in this area.

West Rand Investment Trust must be considered one of the very best South African gold portfolio investments.

BUFFELSFONTEIN GOLD MINING CO. LTD.

GROUP	General Mining
LOCATION	Klerksdorp
PRODUCTION	Gold, Sulphuric Acid, Pyrite, Uranium
ORDINARY SHARES ISSUED	11,000,000
CAPITALIZED DEBT	R 402,000
URANIUM LOAN	R 3,257,000 (Repayable Dec. 31, 1972)
MILLING	Began 1957. Current monthly rate: 230,000 tons.
Estimated Life:	UPPER-MEDIUM
PRICE RANGE	1969: 6½–12½
	1970: 6¼–8¼
	1971: 3½–6¾
DIVIDENDS	1967: $0.50½; 1968–1970: $0.52½; 1971: $0.47
DIVIDEND PAYMENTS	February and August
Rating:	SPECULATIVE

Comment: Buffels is a major gold-uranium producer, with the largest uranium plant in South Africa. Unfortunately, the near-term outlook for uranium is not very promising. Furthermore, repayments on state uranium-development loans currently require R 540,000 per quarter and although the uranium loans will be repaid by the end of 1972, the company's sales contracts for uranium also expire at that time. Therefore, the company is preparing to stockpile excess uranium oxide once again, which will cost an estimated additional R 6 million over the next five years.

The gold prospects of Buffelsfontein, upon which the company will have to be judged, are somewhat ambiguous at present (1971–72). Much depends on prospects in the new southern section of the mine which is currently under development.

The company's financial resources have been severely strained, due to current and projected uranium expenditures and the costs of developing the deeper levels of the mine and opening the southern section. A loan of R 5 million had to be negotiated in August 1971 to see the company through the difficult period envisioned for the next two or three years. The dividend rate was also reduced in 1971 from US$0.47 for the year ending June 30, 1971, to US$0.25 for the year ending June 30, 1972.

Although Buffelsfontein apparently has sufficient reserves of gold-bearing ore to put the mine in the UPPER-MEDIUM category, it is obvious that, barring some unexpected recovery in the uranium market or a sharply higher near-term price for gold, the company will be financially handicapped for the next few years. Long-term prospects, however, are favorable. This stock may become a good bargain if the immediate difficulties are overdiscounted.

DOORNFONTEIN GOLD MINING CO. LTD.

GROUP	Gold Fields
LOCATION	Far West Rand
PRODUCTION	Gold only
ORDINARY SHARES ISSUED	9,828,000
CAPITALIZED DEBT	Nil
MILLING	Began 1953. Current monthly rate: 118,000 tons.
Estimated Life:	UPPER-MEDIUM
PRICE RANGE	1969: 3–5
	1970: 3½–5¼
	1971: 3¼–5½
DIVIDENDS	1967: $0.35, 1968: $0.32
	1969: $0.32, 1970: $0.37½,
	1971: $0.29½
DIVIDEND PAYMENTS	February and August
Rating:	INVESTMENT GRADE
Comment:	Despite the fact that ore-reserve grades have

been increased during 1970 and 1971, there has not been a corresponding rise in the millhead grade, because of increased ore dilution due to the longwall stoping method of mining now employed in the deeper levels of the eastern section of the mine to minimize the risk of rock-pressure bursts. The eastern section is the main source of tonnage at present (1971–72) but No. 1 auxiliary subvertical shaft and No. 2 subvertical shaft in the center section have been sunk to final depth and will allow the deep levels of the central section to be put into production. Nevertheless, the fall in millhead grade and overall tonnage tended to offset higher gold premiums earned in 1971 and brought about a modest reduction in dividends.

The life of this mine is UPPER-MEDIUM, but it has been extremely sensitive to inflationary pressures. Its operating costs per ounce of gold recovered are the second highest on the Witwatersrand, exceeded only by West Driefontein, where extensive dewatering operations, still required as a result of the 1968 flooding, have pushed costs above their natural levels. Higher gold prices and the devaluation of the rand should allow this mine to maintain profits and dividends at the current level for the next year or two, but long-term prospects depend on the world price for gold outpacing domestic inflation and rising costs. Doornfontein would really stand out as a "depression" stock.

EAST DRIEFONTEIN GOLD MINING CO. LTD.

GROUP	Gold Fields
LOCATION	Far West Rand
PRODUCTION	(assumed) Gold only
ORDINARY SHARES ISSUED	44,620,000
"A" SHARES ISSUED	2,780,000
CAPITALIZED DEBT	R 2,502,000
MILLING	To begin 1972. Maximum rate scheduled to be reached in 1976: 181,000 tons per month.
Estimated Life:	DEVELOPING (assumed LONG)
PRICE RANGE	1969: 2¼–5½
	1970: 2½–3¾
	1971: 2⅜–4½
DIVIDENDS	Nil

Rating: INVESTMENT GRADE

Comment: Development work on this mine suffered a severe setback in late 1968, when the No. 4 shaft of adjacent West Driefontein mine was flooded out. East Drie. had a lease arrangement to use this shaft for part of its own underground development and the flooding of East Driefontein works was also extensive. Complete rehabilitation was not accomplished until early 1972, and the entire operation required the pumping of about 45 billion gallons of water from the flooded areas.

The gold-bearing reefs underlying the East Driefontein property have been tested by 30 boreholes and it is estimated that the claim area contains some 77 million tons of ore averaging 18 grams of gold per ton. The estimated life of this mine is definitely LONG. Maximum mining depth will eventually exceed 10,000 feet.

Because of the long delay in regaining control of the flooded area served by West Drie. No. 4 shaft, work has been accelerated on the East Drie. No. 2 shaft and ore from this area will be available for treatment when the East Driefontein mill is opened for production early in 1972. Initial capacity will be 100,000 tons per month, rising to a maximum rate of 181,000 tons per month by the end of 1976.

However, the delay and extra cost resulting from the 1968 flooding will require the raising of more capital. It is calculated that an additional R 20 million will be needed to bring the mine to the self-financing stage. But although this may require further capitalization, it should not seriously detract from the long-term promise of the mine. As of December 31, 1970, R 30,348,222 had already been expended on this project.

Dividends are expected to begin in 1974 and the mine will be in a tax-exempt status for many years.

Despite its large capitalization, this company will probably be a safe and rewarding holding for the future, but one need not be in any hurry to buy it. Buy only on generous price concession or during general weakness in the gold group. For the patient long-term capital gains investor, this would be a suitable acquisition.

ELSBURG GOLD MINING CO. LTD.

GROUP   Johannesburg Consolidated

LOCATION   South of West Rand

PRODUCTION   (assumed) Gold only

ORDINARY SHARES ISSUED   31,500,000

CAPITALIZED DEBT   R 5,500,000 (due 1974)

LOAN TO WESTERN AREAS   R 2,320,000 (interest free)

MILLING   Began 1968. Capacity: 91,000 tons per month.

Estimated Life: DEVELOPING (assumed MEDIUM-LONG)

PRICE RANGE   1969: ¾–1¾

    1970: ¾–1¼

    1971: ⅞–1⅝

DIVIDENDS   Nil

Rating: INVESTMENT GRADE

Comment: Based on borehole testing, the Elsburg property contains about 19 million tons of ore with an average grade of 26 grams of gold per ton, indicating a life expectancy of about 20 years at capacity production rate of 91,000 tons per month. Pending further development of the Elsburg holdings, the Elsburg mill, which was completed in 1968, has been operating primarily with ore contributed from the adjacent Western Areas mine. This arrangement allows Elsburg to retain most of the premium payments earned on the combined Elsburg-Western Areas ore treated at the Elsburg mill.

In the final quarter of 1971, some 12,600 tons of development ore from Elsburg were treated at the company's mill. The balance of about 250,000 tons was contributed from Western Areas. From 1972 on, increasing amounts of ore will come from the Elsburg property until the full 91,000 tons per month capacity of the Elsburg mill can be satisfied from its own ore. Development of the Elsburg property has been slower and more costly than originally estimated and has left the company short of funds.

Additional short-term borrowing may be required, but this should have little effect on the long-term outlook for the mine. The assessed loss of R 38,300,000, as of March 1971, allows for a substantial tax-free period in the years ahead. The company has not yet begun payment of dividends and it must be expected that loan repayments will cut into gross income for the next few years. This is another one for the patient investor to buy low and hold for the long pull.

HARTEBEESTFONTEIN GOLD MINING CO. LTD.

GROUP	Anglo-Transvaal
LOCATION	Klerksdorp
PRODUCTION	Gold and Uranium
ORDINARY SHARES ISSUED	9,000,000
CAPITALIZED DEBT	R 2,092,000
URANIUM LOAN	R 3,904,000 (repayable by Dec. 1973)
MILLING	Began 1955. Capacity: 218,000 tons per month (45,000 tons reserved for Zandpan).
Estimated Life:	UPPER-MEDIUM
PRICE RANGE	1969: 1⅞–6¼
	1970: 1¾–3¼
	1971: 3⅛–4¾
DIVIDENDS	1967: $0.56; 1968: $0.28; 1969: $0.14; 1970, 1971: $0.11
DIVIDENDS PAID	February and August
Rating:	INVESTMENT GRADE

Comment: Hartebeestfontein can best be described as a promising turnaround situation. After five years of continuously declining earnings and dividends, the company has entered a merger agreement with the neighboring Zandpan mine, also part of the Anglovaal group, that may significantly benefit shareholders in both companies. The plan calls for Harties to purchase the entire assets of Zandpan for R 15.15 million, to be paid by Hartebeestfontein assuming the debts of Zandpan, amounting to some R 8 million and issuing to Zandpan 2.2 million shares of Harties valued at R 7.15 million. Formal application for approval of this merger has been made to the South African Government. If successful, the completed merger will bring about lower overheads, more rapid development of new areas and more efficient uranium production. It may also be expected that Harties will be able to apply the R

28 million tax loss carried by Zandpan to combined operations.

As for Harties itself, the overall situation there appears to be stabilizing. Costs continue to rise but are being more than offset by an improving grade of ore and increased premium payments. Uranium profits were higher in 1971 than in 1970, but still resulted in a loss of 6 cents per share for the year. High capital expenditures for a major shaft sinking will be terminated by the end of 1972 and uranium earnings should also be sufficient to cover uranium loan repayments by that time. Consequently, the prospect for 1973 and beyond is for substantial dividend increases, even without the Zandpan merger, that will add considerably to this interesting UPPER-MEDIUM life producer.

KINROSS MINES, LTD.

GROUP	Union Corp.
LOCATION	Evander
PRODUCTION	Gold only
ORDINARY SHARES ISSUED	18,000,000
CAPITALIZED DEBT	R 3,000,000
MILLING	Began 1967. Current capacity: 122,000 tons per month.
Estimated Life:	LONG
PRICE RANGE	1969: 1½–2¾
	1970: 1⅝–2¼
	1971: 1¾–2½
DIVIDENDS	1968: $0.04; 1969: $0.14; 1970: $0.19½; 1971: $0.16½
DIVIDENDS PAID	May and September
Rating:	INVESTMENT GRADE

Comment: Kinross is the newest and deepest mine of the Evander field and current geologic evidence is that this mine will complete the development of the district. Ore values in the Evander area tend to be erratic, which means that an unusually high amount of development work is required to maintain ore reserves. Prior to 1971, operations were confined to the southeastern part of the property, but a further shaft sinking to open up the northwest section is under consideration. It can also be anticipated that the new shaft sunk in the northern section of adjacent Winkelhaak mine will be utilized on a tribute or lease basis for underground development at Kinross.

The dividend for 1971 was slightly reduced to retain cash for future capital expenditures and to provide loan repayments. Kinross will not be subject to income tax for several years, until its R 19,290,000 tax loss is written off. Earnings could therefore rise sharply in response to increased premium payments, as unit costs have so far been held down. The erratic nature of the Evander ore, however, indicates a cautious approach; buy on weakness for long-term holding.

KLOOF GOLD MINING CO. LTD.

GROUP	Gold Fields
LOCATION	Far West Rand
PRODUCTION	Gold only
ORDINARY SHARES ISSUED	22,241,650
"A" SHARES	7,998,350
CAPITALIZED DEBT	R 6,718,614
NATIONAL FINANCE CORP	
LOAN	R 3,500,000
MILLING	Began 1968. Current capacity: 163,000 tons per month.
Estimated Life:	LONG
PRICE RANGE	1969: 3–6½
	1970: 3–5½
	1971: 3⅞–6⅛
DIVIDENDS	1970: $0.07; 1971: $0.11
Rating:	INVESTMENT GRADE

Comment: Kloof suffered a temporary setback in 1971 because of a serious underground fire that broke out in June. By December of 1971, however, production had been returned to 95 percent of normal. Premium payments received by the company in 1971 would have more than offset the effects of inflation had it not been for the fire, but until further development work, including the construction of additional subvertical shafts, is completed, there will not be a significant expansion of production. Capital expenditures, consequently, are likely to remain high until after 1975 or 1976 and dividends could continue to be modest until after that time. A sharp advance in the world price of gold, resulting in still higher premium payment, could of course beneficially alter this situation.

Borehole indications and explorations from subvertical shafts reveal increased tonnages of high-grade ore. If further development confirms these initial indications, the probability is that the milling rate will be increased to 245,000 tons per month and this will obviously be reflected in higher earnings and dividends.

The original estimate of resources, made prior to production, projected an overall reserve of 90 million tons of ore with a value above 14 grams per ton, indicating a LONG life for Kloof. And an assessed loss for tax purposes of R 54,563,000, as of September 1971, guarantees a substantial period of tax-free operation for the company. Kloof must be considered as being in the first rank as a long-term gold investment, despite its substantial capitalization.

PRESIDENT BRAND GOLD MINING CO. LTD.

GROUP	Anglo-American
LOCATION	Orange Free State
PRODUCTION	Gold only
ORDINARY SHARES ISSUED	14,040,000
CAPITALIZED DEBT	Nil
MILLING	Began 1954. Current capacity: 190,000 tons per month.
Estimated Life:	UPPER-MEDIUM
PRICE RANGE	1969: 10¼–14¾
	1970: 10–13¾
	1971: 9¾–11¾
DIVIDENDS	1967: $1.19; 1968: $1.19; 1969: $1.61; 1970: $1.61; 1971: $1.47
DIVIDENDS PAID	May and November
Rating:	INVESTMENT GRADE

Comment: President Brand has been one of the stars of the rich Orange Free State group, but, beginning in 1971, the company entered a period of high capital expenditures that will put increased pressure on profits and dividends for the next two to four years. An agreement has been made for President Brand to purchase adjacent President Steyn's No. 3 shaft for R 9.5

million, the total price to be paid by September 1973.

President Brand's wholly-owned subsidiary, Free State Saaiplaas, became liable for taxation in 1971, which reduces
Brand's dividend income from this source. Also, the high dividends of 1969 and 1970 were derived in part from a distribution
of accumulated profits from F. S. Saaiplaas, following favorable settlement of a court case. In December 1971, the chairman
of President Brand pointed to declining ore grades at both the
Brand mine and Saaiplaas, increased tax liabilities and rising
costs as indicating further reductions in earnings and dividends. Rising premium income could of course counteract
these adverse trends.

A 181,000-ton-per-month uranium plant, completed in 1971
to treat high-grade uranium slimes from President Brand and
Welkom, has not been commissioned because of the unfavorable market for uranium. The plant can be activated on short
notice, but uranium earnings will not be extensive in any case.

President Brand's estimated life is in the UPPER-MEDIUM
category, which makes it suitable for long-term investment
holding if it can be purchased low enough to discount the near-
term negative factors. Capital expenditures should decline substantially after 1973.

PRESIDENT STEYN GOLD MINING CO. LTD.

GROUP	Anglo-American
LOCATION	Orange Free State
PRODUCTION	Gold only
ORDINARY SHARES ISSUD	14,000,000
CAPITALIZED DEBT	Nil
MILLING	Began 1954. Current capacity: 209,000 tons per month.
Estimated Life:	MEDIUM-LONG
PRICE RANGE	1969: 3¼–5⅞
	1970: 3–5¼
	1971: 4¾–7
DIVIDENDS	1960 through 1971: $0.21 per year
DIVIDENDS PAID	May and November
Rating:	INVESTMENT GRADE
Comment:	Several favorable developments add to Presi-

dent Steyn's already bright lustre. An agreement has been made for Pres. Steyn to develop an area adjacent to its southern boundary on a royalty basis, and this area, which is owned by Sentrust-Lydenburg and Plats General mining companies, has yielded very high values from borehole testing. The leasing companies are to receive 25 percent of the profits after tax while President Steyn retains the balance. President Steyn's No. 4 shaft, from which the company's own high-value area will be exploited, may be commissioned in late 1972 and, consequently, an increase from the 1971–72 output of 209,000 tons per month to an anticipated maximum of 272,000 tons per month may occur much sooner than the original 1976 target date. If extra plant capacity is needed for this purpose, an agreement has been negotiated with President Brand for surplus facilities at Free State Saaiplaas to be made available to President Steyn after 1972.

This company is in sound financial shape and current and future capital expenditures can be financed largely from profits and tax savings. Boreholes east of the No. 4 shaft indicate very high values in this area. In December 1971, President Steyn's chairman reiterated the company's policy of using premium earnings for capital purposes and maintaining the dividend rate at the usual R 0.15 (US $0.21) where it has remained for 11 consecutive years.

Uranium royalties were ended in 1965 and the uranium treatment plant at the mine site was dismantled. Large quantities of uranium-bearing slimes are still being stockpiled, but the company has not entered into any of its neighbors' uranium agreements, which indicates that the prospects for extra income from this source are not considered very promising.

Despite the modest dividend likely to prevail for the next few years, President Steyn's long-term attractions recommend it for inclusion in all types of portfolios.

RANDFONTEIN ESTATES GOLD MINING CO., WITWATERSRAND LTD.

GROUP	Johannesburg Consolidated
LOCATION	West Rand
PRODUCTION	(assumed) Gold and Uranium

ORDINARY SHARES ISSUED	5,413,553
GOVERNMENT LOAN	R 8,000,000
MILLING	Began 1889 (original mine).
Estimated Life:	DEVELOPING (presumed LONG)
PRICE RANGE	1970: 1½–2⅝
	1971: 1⅜–2¼
DIVIDENDS	Nil
Rating:	SPECULATIVE

Comment: Randfontein is beginning a totally new operation south of the original Randfontein property, which has ended production. However, the mill and other facilities at the old mine will be used to treat ore from the new property.

The offer of a government loan of R 8 million in March 1970, on favorable terms, was instrumental in making this venture economically feasible. Capital requirements to open this mine are estimated at R 13 million initially, followed by an additional R 6 million over the following five or six years. The experience of other developing mines suggests that this estimate may be on the low side. The company currently has available R 5 million from stock subscriptions and this, plus the state loan of R 8 million, should be sufficient to bring the mine to production.

Ultimately, three shaft systems are envisioned, but at present only No. 1 is under construction, together with an associated ventilating shaft. No. 1 shaft system should be commissioned by mid-1973 and production should begin in early 1974, building up to 68,000 tons per month in the following year and a half.

Until 1970, Randfontein had been paying clean-up dividends from the old mine and from sundry rents, royalties and tributes, but these payments have been stopped due to the need to reinvest capital in the new mine.

Borehole testing indicates an interplay of both gold and uranium values in different sections of the new lease area and this will undoubtedly present some difficult technical and financial problems and choices. But with its present low capitalization of only 5.4 million shares, the company makes an interesting long-term speculative holding. If the prices for *both* gold and uranium are strong in the second half of the decade of the '70's and in the '80's, as many believe they will be, this stock may offer a chance to get in cheaply on the ground floor.

ST. HELENA GOLD MINES, LTD.

GROUP	Union Corp.
LOCATION	Orange Free State
PRODUCTION	Gold only
ORDINARY SHARES ISSUED	9,625,000
CAPITALIZED DEBT	Nil
MILLING	Began 1951. Current Capacity: 181,000 tons per month.
Estimated Life:	UPPER-MEDIUM
PRICE RANGE	1969: 6¾–10¼
	1970: 7¼–10¾
	1971: 8¾–12½
DIVIDENDS	1966: $1.05; 1967: $0.91; 1968: $0.78½; 1969: $0.95; 1970: $0.98; 1971: $0.96½
DIVIDENDS PAID	May and November
Rating:	INVESTMENT GRADE

Comment: St. Helena is a mature mine that has been an excellent performer, and its position at the end of 1971 continued to be favorable. Despite a continuing shortage of skilled labor, the company increased its milling rate in both 1970 and 1971 and, in the latter year, profits advanced substantially as increased premium earnings helped to offset rising operating costs. Proven ore reserves of 8.9 million tons, averaging 18 grams of gold per ton at the end of 1971, were being maintained at a level slightly above the rate for the prior five years.

Major development work after 1971 will be in the area of No. 8 shaft, and it is possible that a part of Ongegund 13 farm will eventually be included in the St. Helena lease area and worked from No. 8 shaft.

With its substantial ore-reserve position and encouraging development work, earnings and dividends at St. Helena should continue to increase if premium income can keep pace with or grow faster than unit costs. In addition, the period of heavy capital expenditures has largely been passed. The mine is still in the UPPER-MEDIUM category and the capitalization is not excessive. Consequently, St. Helena should be a safe and productive holding for the remainder of the decade.

SOUTHVAAL HOLDINGS, LTD.

GROUP   Anglo-American

LOCATION   Klerksdorp

PRODUCTION   (assumed) Gold and Uranium

ORDINARY SHARES ISSUED   14,168,959

SHARES UNDER OPTION   6,831,041 (until 12-31-71)

SHARES TO BE SUBSCRIBED   5,000,000 (by 12-31-72)

CAPITALIZED DEBT   Nil

LOAN TO VAAL REEFS   R 4,170,000

MILLING   Output to be treated by Vaal Reefs

Estimated Life: DEVELOPING (presumed LONG)

PRICE RANGE   1969: 1¾–2⅞

            1970: 1⅞–3¼

            1971: 2¼–4⅛

DIVIDENDS   Nil

Rating: INVESTMENT GRADE

Comment: Southvaal is a new company established on what was formerly the "south lease" of the Vaal Reefs property, or that part of Vaal Reefs lying south of the Vaal river. The decision to split the original Vaal Reefs lease area into two separate mines was determined, in part, by the substantial tax advantages resulting from such an arrangement. Under the terms of the expansion agreement, Vaal Reefs is entitled to 40 percent of the profits from Southvaal mining and, in return, is required to treat all Southvaal ore at Vaal Reefs plants. Furthermore, Vaal Reefs is obligated for certain capital expenditures on the Southvaal properties, including the construction of a new 150,000-ton shaft on the Pretoriuskraal 53 area Southvaal has acquired from Western Holdings in exchange for 1 million Southvaal shares. Work on this shaft will begin in 1974.

After exercising all its options and rights, Vaal Reefs will have a direct 25-percent interest in Southvaal, in addition to its 40 percent royalty arrangement. Authorized capital shares of Southvaal, after the exercise of all rights and options, will be increased to 26 million shares, with 6.5 million being held by Vaal Reefs and 1 million by Western Holdings.

On the Southvaal property itself, the two shafts of the initial system have been sunk to final depth and brought into production. Development and testing of the reefs in this area has consistently shown high values. A gradual increase in production to 180,000 tons per month over the next five years is scheduled. No uranium production is presently contemplated and uranium oxide will probably be stockpiled if it becomes available in the course of gold production.

Southvaal is a good long-term capital gains holding, although dividends are probably still several years away unless much higher premiums for both gold and uranium are coming sooner than is generally expected. The patient investor will wait to buy this one until a general correction in the gold market, or some other event, provides an unusual opportunity.

VAAL REEFS EXPLORATION AND MINING CO. LTD.

GROUP	Anglo-American
LOCATION	Klerksdorp
PRODUCTION	Gold and Uranium
ORDINARY SHARES ISSUED	19,000,000
CAPITALIZED DEBT	Nil
URANIUM LOAN	R 4,307,000 (repayable by Dec. 1973)
LOAN FROM SOUTHVAAL	R 4,170,000
OTHER SHARE HOLDINGS	5,000,000 Southvaal
	1,500,000 Southvaal rights (for 1.5 million Southvaal shares).
MILLING	Began 1956 (Vaal Reefs) & 1941 (Western Reefs). Combined current capacity: 367,000 tons per month.
Estimated Life:	LONG
PRICE RANGE	1969: 9¼–16½
	1970: 9⅛–12½
	1971: 7⅝–11¼
DIVIDENDS	1966 through 1971: $0.70 per year
DIVIDENDS PAID	February and August
Rating:	INVESTMENT GRADE

Comment: Prior to the 1970–71 merger and expansion schemes, Vaal Reefs controlled what were virtually two separate mines: the original mine north of the Vaal river and the section south of the river known as the south lease. The south lease was established as a separate company, SOUTHVAAL, with Vaal Reefs retaining a large direct interest, as well as a 40-percent claim on Southvaal mining profits. In 1971, Vaal Reefs completed a merger with adjacent Western Reefs on the basis of one Vaal Reef share for every two Western Reef shares tendered. The above statistical section refers to combined operations of both mines.

Vaal Reefs holds 5 million Southvaal shares and has the right and obligation to acquire a further 1.5 million shares by December 31, 1972. This will give Vaal Reefs a direct 25-percent ownership in Southvaal in addition to its 40-percent royalty arrangement with the latter company. In addition, Southvaal has been expanded by the acquisition of the Pretoriuskraal 53 area from Western Holdings. To exploit both the Pretoriuskraal section and the entire western part of Southvaal, Vaal Reefs will sink a new 150,000-ton-per-month-capacity shaft on this property beginning in 1974. All these efforts will extend Vaal Reefs' already long life and lead to a truly giant operation, well equipped to resist inflation. The mine already has the highest milling rate of any South African gold operation by a considerable margin.

Output from the Western Reefs mine, currently 170,000 tons per month, is expected to taper off after 1975 and production from the new Pretoriuskraal shaft will be phased in at that time. Capacity at the original Vaal Reefs mine (the north lease) is to be expanded to 240,000 tons per month following completion of the new No. 4 shaft. All this is in addition to planned Southvaal production of 180,000 tons per month, which means that the combined Vaal Reefs-Western Reefs mills could eventually be treating as much as 600,000 tons per month.

Vaal Reefs uranium plant has been reconditioned to meet any demand for uranium above existing contract levels; however, the chairman warned that (as of 1972) uranium demand was still depressed and that part of the mines' output of uranium oxide would have to be stockpiled. Ore from Southvaal is not being treated for uranium until demand improves.

For 1971, Vaal Reefs maintained the usual R 0.50 (US $0.70) dividend on the increased capitalization. From 1973 on, profits will start to flow from Southvaal and dividends will most likely be increased. Vaal Reefs should certainly be rated very highly as a long-term gold investment, particularly in view of the relatively modest capitalization of the company's very substantial assets.

WEST DRIEFONTEIN GOLD MINING CO. LTD.

GROUP   Gold Fields

LOCATION   Far West Rand

ORDINARY SHARES ISSUED   14,082,160

CAPITALIZED DEBT   Nil

MILLING   Began 1952. Current capacity 218,000 tons per month.

Estimated Life: MID-MEDIUM

PRICE RANGE   1969: 12¼–18¾
1970: 12–19¼
1971: 15¼ 21¾

DIVIDENDS   1967: $1.33; 1968: $1.36½; 1969: $0.98; 1970: $1.40; 1971: $1.51

DIVIDENDS PAID   February and August

Rating: INVESTMENT GRADE

Comment: West Drie's reputation as "the world's richest gold mine" has been well deserved. Despite an inordinate share of problems and difficulties, the company has been an outstanding performer and its shares are still one of the better gold commitments for the income-oriented investor.

The dewatering of No. 4 shaft area, flooded since November 1968, was finally completed in January 1972 and access was regained to all levels of both East and West Driefontein mines served by this shaft. Actually, West Driefontein managed remarkably well despite the three-year loss of the high-value No. 4 area, and paid record dividends in 1970 and 1971. Dividends for 1972 promise to be even higher. This spectacular performance is due largely to the very high grade ore currently being obtained from the rich Carbon Leader Reef in the western section of the mine.

However, to achieve a better balance of mining and milling, it has been decided to sink a new subvertical shaft in the eastern section of the mine to open an area of lower-grade ore to add to production. Meanwhile, an agreement has been reached with East Driefontein to mine East Drie. ore adjacent to No. 4

shaft on a royalty basis. This agreement will run until March 31, 1973, and after that time it is expected that production will become available from the new eastern subvertical shaft. Capital expenditures are expected to decline in the future and rising premium earnings should also have a very favorable effect on earnings and dividends for the next few years.

A uranium plant and a sulphuric acid plant are also operating at capacity, but earnings from these sources are expected to remain modest.

West Driefontein's operating costs have been extraordinarily high due to the pumping expense of the dewatering project but, now that pumping has returned to normal, there could be a considerable reduction in overhead that should also be reflected in higher earnings and dividends.

With a life estimate in the MID-MEDIUM area, the company should be an excellent income holding, plus a devaluation hedge, until 1976 or so. Beyond that point the situation will depend on whether or not additional ore reserves can be developed and on merger and tribute possiblities.

WESTERN AREAS GOLD MINING CO. LTD.

GROUP	Johannesburg Consolidated
LOCATION	South of West Rand
PRODUCTION	Gold only
ORDINARY SHARES ISSUED	20,675,000
CAPITALIZED DEBT	R 4,778,000
SHARE HOLDINGS	1,297,000 Elsburg
MILLING	Began 1961. Current Capacity: 204,000 tons per month.
Estimated Life:	MID-MEDIUM
PRICE RANGE	1969: ¾–2½
	1970: ⅞–1¾
	1971: 1½–2¾
DIVIDENDS	1966 through 1969: $0.07; 1970 through 1971: $0.08½ per year
DIVIDENDS PAID	February and August
Rating:	SPECULATIVE

Comment: Although developed ore reserves more than doubled in the five years preceding 1971, rising to 6,099,000 tons averaging 11.2 grams of gold per ton, rapidly escalating costs and inflationary trends have prevented this mine from living up to its original expectations.

It is hoped that development in the area of the new southern subshaft may confirm the higher grade originally revealed by borehole testing of this area. But, as of late 1971, this hope had not yet been fulfilled.

Current profits are being aided by tribute payments from Elsburg. However, capital expenditures and loan liabilities will probably continue to restrict earnings and dividends at Western Areas, although the company was able to provide a modest increase for 1971 despite two serious underground fires that depressed overall earnings for the year. The company will become liable to income tax beginning in 1974.

Premium income is very important to Western Areas, although the company's shares could also respond to a general improvement in grade. The latter may be possible as a result of the opening of the southern section of the mine, according to a statement made by the chairman in March 1972. With an estimated life of about 15 years (from 1972), the shares of this mine are primarily a speculation on a sharply higher price for gold coming before 1975 or 1976.

WESTERN DEEP LEVELS, LTD.

GROUP	Anglo-American
LOCATION	Far West Rand
PRODUCTION	Gold only
ORDINARY SHARES ISSUED	25,000,000
CAPITALIZED DEBT	R 1,806,000
MILLING	Began 1962. Current capacity: 265,000 tons per month.
Estimated Life:	LONG
PRICE RANGE	1969: 8¼– 13½
	1970: 8½– 10¾
	1971: 7⅜– 11½
DIVIDENDS	1966: $0.35; 1967; $0.63; 1968: $0.77; 1969 through 1971: $0.91
DIVIDENDS PAID	February and August
Rating:	INVESTMENT GRADE

Comment: After steadily expanding profits from the start of gold production until 1970, the trend apparently levelled off in 1971. Nevertheless, production and grade are being maintained at a high rate. Recovery grade was 18.5 grams per ton as opposed to 19.05 grams in 1970. Production and recovery grade are expected to remain steady in 1972.

Western Deep has commissioned a new uranium plant, at a cost of R 4.5 million, with a capacity of 63,500 tons per month. Production from this plant is being stockpiled for future sales, but income from this source is not expected to be significant.

Capital expenditures at Western Deep are still high and will total R 14 million in 1972. Part of this cost is required for the sinking of additional subvertical shafts to open the mine to still greater depths, although production at the 1971–72 rate can be maintained from existing No. 2 and No. 3 main shaft systems. The life of this mine is definitely LONG, probably approaching 30 years, although prospects in the deep southern section and in the extreme western area have not revealed very high values from preliminary borehole testing.

The good dividend record of the period 1965–71 is largely the result of tax-free production. However, the company will probably become liable for taxation some time in 1973 and, barring a substantial increase in the price of gold before then, this will undoubtedly be reflected in temporarily lower earnings, dividends and share prices.

The shares of Western Deep Levels would make a sound long-term holding but they should obviously be bought *after* the effects of taxation have been thoroughly discounted.

WINKELHAAK MINES, LTD.

GROUP	Union Corp.
LOCATION	Evander
PRODUCTION	Gold only
ORDINARY SHARES ISSUED	12,000,000
CAPITALIZED DEBT	R 500,000
MILLING	Began 1958. Current capacity: 155,000 tons per month.
Estimated Life:	MEDIUM-LONG
PRICE RANGE	1969: 1½– 3¼

	1970: 1⅞– 2⅞
	1971: 2½– 4⅛
DIVIDENDS	1966: $0.23½; 1967: $0.16½; 1968: $0.14;
	1969: $0.14; 1970: $0.15½; 1971: $0.16½
DIVIDENDS PAID	May and November
Rating:	INVESTMENT GRADE

Comment: Winkelhaak is one of the most promising gold mining investments in South Africa. Prior to 1971, operations had been confined to the southern area of the mine where a considerable degree of faulting interferes with efficient reef exploitation. Nevertheless, gold production and profits for the final quarter of 1971 reached record levels. Beginning in 1972, production was begun from the new No. 5 shaft in the northern section of the mine, where values are expected to be higher and faulting of the reefs much less in evidence. The No. 5 shaft area is virtually a whole new mine under development, and mill capacity will probably be increased within two or three years.

The life estimate of the mine may be extended when development of the northern area proceeds, but MEDIUM-LONG, or about 20 years, appears to be a minimum expectation as of 1972. The period 1972 through 1973 will probably be one of consolidation, although modest dividend increases, even for these years, are quite possible. Surplus earnings have been retained to retire outstanding loans, including the capital loan of R 500,000. No large capital expenditures are pending.

Investors planning to add individual South African mines to their portfolios could hardly do better than by beginning with this one.

ZANDPAN GOLD MINING CO. LTD.

GROUP	Anglo-Transvaal
LOCATION	Klerksdorp
PRODUCTION	Gold and Uranium
ORDINARY SHARES ISSUED	13,020,285
CAPITALIZED DEBT	R 4,000,000
MILLING	Began 1963. Current capacity: 82,000 tons per month.
Estimated Life:	MID-MEDIUM
PRICE RANGE	1969: 1½– 3¼

1970: 1½– 3
1971: 2⅞– 4¼

DIVIDENDS   Nil

Rating: SPECULATIVE

Comment: The principal factor affecting the destiny of this mine is its proposed merger with adjacent Hartebeestfontein, awaiting state approval in 1972. The plan calls for Hartebeestfontein to absorb Zandpan in exchange for 2.2 million shares of Harties, plus the assumption by Harties of Zandpan's existing capital debt of R 4 million and short-term loans amounting to R 8 million. The two mines would become a single integrated operation, and considerable saving in operating expenses and taxation should accrue to the combined companies.

The stock of Zandpan itself is not recommended for investment holding. Since beginning operations, Zandpan has been a struggling enterprise. The company has had to borrow large sums to maintain operations and finance capital expenditures; R 4 million was obtained from the National Finance Corporation and another R 3.3 million from Anglo-Transvaal. In 1970, the South African Government took the unusual step of granting the company state gold mining assistance, even though Zandpan was technically not qualified for such aid because its ore reserves were sufficient for more than eight years operation. The state assistance, granted for a period of two years, enables work to continue on the new No. 2 shaft, where it is hoped gold values will be higher.

Zandpan has been a good high-grade uranium producer but gold values tend to be erratic. Unfortunately the market for uranium has been depressed for some years and much of the company's output has had to be stockpiled.

Development of the area to be served by No. 2 shaft should eventually give a clearer picture of Zandpan's potential. Proven ore reserves at the beginning of 1971 were 1,817,000 tons containing 14.5 grams of gold and 0.40 kilograms of uranium per ton.

Notes:

Chapter XV

1. Your local banker, however, can usually forward foreign checks for collection and the equivalent in U.S. funds will eventually be deposited to your account.

2. The depositary agency or bank deducts a fee of $0.01 per share from all ADR dividends disbursed, as compensation for its services.

3. The *Mining Journal*'s estimates are subject to periodic minor revisions to keep them current at all times (see *Quarterly Review of South African Gold Shares*).

4. All active South African gold mines are reviewed in every issue of the *Quarterly Review*.

Part 4

Portfolio Selection
and Management

XVI

HOW TO BUILD AND MANAGE
A GOLD INVESTMENT PORTFOLIO

"To restore the dollar will be a very painful process, but the alternatives are political repression, socialism and worldwide inflation."

—JACQUES RUEFF

THE quotation that introduces this chapter was made by M. Rueff in 1968, but the process of restoring the dollar through balanced budgets, deflation, liquidation of excessive debt and a return to a meaningful gold standard has not yet even been considered, let alone begun. Therefore, we endure the alternatives. Eventually the United States and other major industrial nations will be forced to abandon the Keynesian folly and restore sound money, domestically and internationally. Meanwhile, the best defense against both the eventual "pain" of restoring the dollar and the alternative of its further destruction is, in the opinion of the author, a gold investment portfolio consisting of gold coins and gold mining stocks, with the latter being selected from both North American and South African sources, following the principles and guidelines noted in earlier chapters of this book.

Since I have already set forth my views on gold coin investing in some detail in a previous work,* I will limit my comments

*Donald J. Hoppe, *How to Invest in Gold Coins,* New Rochelle, N.Y.: Arlington House, 1970.

here to the matter of proportion. I prefer a minimum ratio of
10:2; that is, for every $1,000 committed to gold mining stocks,
an additional $200 could be invested in gold coins. If one de-
cides to include common silver coins in the monetary hedge
portfolio then $50 more per $1,000 would be assigned for this
purpose. However, the investor can omit the silver and add
additional common gold coins, if it is so desired, and get the
same basic protection. The ideal portfolio mix for the investment climate of the 1970's would therefore be as follows:

Gold Mining Stocks	Gold Coins	Silver Coins (optional)
$ 1,000	$ 200	$ 50
2,500	500	175
5,000	1,000	250
10,000	2,000	500
25,000	5,000	1,750
50,000	10,000	2,500
100,000	20,000	5,000

Of course, the proportion of gold coins may be increased if
the investor feels more competent in this area of investment.
Coins are strictly a long-term capital gains investment, however, and there is no leverage involved unless one buys them on
margin, which I definitely *do not* recommend. And obviously
there will be no income yield from a coin portfolio. But the
remaining advantages of a gold coin position, as outlined in
Chapter VIII, indicate their usefulness in a gold investment
portfolio, not the least of which is furnishing a readily accessible reservoir of store-of-value assets.

Naturally, when discussing investment portfolios, it is assumed that the investor is adequately protected in other ways,
such as through holdings in personal real estate, sufficient insurance protection, a satisfactory cash balance, a favorable
debt position, etc., and that the funds available for investment
are truly *surplus* and will not be needed next month or even
next year for noninvestment purposes.

The model portfolios presented in this concluding chapter
are designed to accommodate the long-term investor desiring

a gold investment position requiring the minimum of supervision. Therefore, if you do not wish to attempt any trading operations on your own or do not want to employ any part of the *Trading-Investment Plan* described in Chapter X, then the best choice would be to build and maintain a *long-term* investment portfolio of issues selected both from those rated INVEST-MENT-TRADING among the North American mines and from the stocks rated INVESTMENT GRADE in the South African Group.

All stocks, in both groups, rated SPECULATIVE are avoided in the long-term portfolios, not necessarily because they have less potential, but because they have a higher risk factor and require a much closer degree of supervision than the INVEST-MENT-rated stocks. The reader is still encouraged to try to select his or her own particular portfolio, after reading the reviews in this book and updating them as far as possible from further reading in the periodicals recommended. With only three North American stocks and 25 South African issues qualifying for an INVESTMENT rating, it is not too formidable a job.

For the reader's general guidance, however, the author includes in this chapter model portfolios ranging from $1,000 to $100,000 that he would select for long-term investment holding, based on the conditions and information prevailing as of December 31, 1971. No mention is made in these model portfolios of the number of *shares* in each position, for two reasons: (1) the variability of share prices makes it inadvisable to attempt to set an "ideal" price for each stock, as specific prices would obviously have to be based on conditions prevailing at the single point of time in which they were written, rather than when they were being read and (2) the investor should become accustomed to thinking in terms of *amounts* of capital committed to particular positions, rather than being overly concerned with the number of shares acquired. After all, 500 shares of a $2 stock is no more valuable than 20 shares of a $50 stock, yet the human tendency is to attach a greater importance to the larger number of shares. However, a portfolio is not balanced by the number of shares in various positions but by the percentage of total capital allotted to each stock or group of stocks.

Initial Commitments.   Investors having no prior position in gold stocks can move initially with a little more aggressiveness than typical for the "averaging" methods of accumulation described in the previous chapter. An initial position should range from one-quarter to one-half of total portfolio that the investor can afford to acquire. If the gold market has been quiet for some time and gold stocks are down substantially from previously recorded highs, then up to one-half of the planned portfolio value can be acquired as a single initial position, with the remainder accumulated through the averaging technique. However, if the market for gold shares has been very active and prices are on the high side, restrict the initial position to one-quarter of the total value of the portfolio amount you ultimately plan to acquire.

THE MODEL PORTFOLIOS

Fig. 38
MODEL $1,000 PORTFOLIO

Stock	*Amount*
Campbell Red Lake Mines	$ 500
West Rand Investment Trust	500
	$1,000

Fig. 39

MODEL $2,500 PORTFOLIO

Stock	*Amount*
Dome Mines, Ltd.	$1,000
American-South African Investment Co.	1,000
President Steyn Gold Mining Co.	500
	$2,500

Fig. 40

MODEL $5,000 PORTFOLO

Stock	Amount
Campbell Red Lake Mines	$1,500
Homestake Mining Co.	1,500
West Rand Investment Trust	1,500
President Steyn Gold Mining Co.	500
	$5,000

Fig. 41

MODEL $10,000 PORTFOLIO

Stock	Amount
Campbell Red Lake Mines	$ 1,000
Dome Mines, Ltd.	2,000
Homestake Mining Co.	2,000
American-South African Investment Co.	2,000
West Rand Investment Trust	2,000
Vaal Reefs Exploration & Mining Co.	1,000
	$10,000

Fig. 42

MODEL $25,000 PORTFOLIO

Stock	Amount
Campbell Red Lake Mines	$ 2,500
Dome Mines, Ltd.	2,500
Homestake Mining Co.	2,500
Union Corporation, Ltd.	2,000
West Rand Investment Trust	3,000
Kloof Gold Mining Co.	2,000
President Steyn Gold Mining Co.	2,500
Vaal Reefs Exploration & Mining Co.	3,000
Western Deep Levels	2,000
Winkelhaak Mines, Ltd.	3,000
	$25,000

Fig. 43

MODEL $50,000 PORTFOLIO

Stock	Amount
Campbell Red Lake Mines	$ 5,000
Dome Mines, Ltd.	4,000
Homestake Mining Co.	5,000
Anglo-American Corp. of South Africa	3,000
Union Corporation, Ltd.	3,000
West Rand Investment Trust	4,000
East Driefontein Gold Mining Co.	2,500
Kinross Mines	2,000
Kloof Gold Mining Co.	3,500
President Steyn Gold Mining Co.	4,000
Randfontein Estates, Witwatersrand	2,000
Vaal Reefs Exploration and Mining Co.	3,500
Western Deep Levels	3,000
West Driefontein Gold Mining Co.	2,500
Winkelhaak Mines, Ltd.	3,000
	$50,000

Fig. 44

MODEL $100,000 PORTFOLIO

Stock	Amount
Campbell Red Lake Mines	$ 10,000
Dome Mines, Ltd.	9,000
Homestake Mining Co.	12,000
Anglo-American Corp. of South Africa	4,500
Gold Fields of South Africa	4,500
Union Corporation, Ltd.	4,000
Orange Free State Investment Trust	3,500
West Rand Investment Trust	5,000
Doornfontein Gold Mining Co.	3,000
East Driefontein Gold Mining Co.	3,500
Hartebeestfontein Gold Mining Co.	4,000
Kinross Mines	2,500
Kloof Gold Mining Co.	5,000
President Steyn Gold Mining Co.	5,500
Randfontein Estates, Witwatersrand	3,500
St. Helena Gold Mines	4,000
Vaal Reefs Exploration and Mining Co.	5,500
Western Deep Levels	4,000
West Driefontein Gold Mining Co.	3,000
Winkelhaak Mines, Ltd.	4,000
	$100,000

Although the large percentage of capital committed to South African stocks in the model portfolios generally assures an above-average dividend yield for the entire portfolio, those investors requiring the highest possible return on their investments for current income can improve the yield of the selected portfolio by substituting dividend-paying stocks for some of the non-dividend-paying developing mines and by increasing the amount of capital concentrated in the shares of corporations paying the more generous dividends. Such substitution, however, will tend to reduce the long-term capital gains potential of the portfolio. To illustrate portfolios oriented toward high dividend yield, while still maintaining adequate long-term devaluation and inflation protection, *Alternate Portfolios* for $10,000, $25,000 and $50,000 amounts are included for the reader-investor's consideration.

Fig. 45

ALTERNATE $10,000 PORTFOLIO
(Higher Income Variation)

Stock	Amount
Campbell Red Lake Mines	$ 1,000
Homestake Mining Co.	1,000
West Rand Investment Trust	2,000
Hartebeestfontein Gold Mining Co.	1,000
President Brand Gold Mining Co.	1,500
St. Helena Gold Mines	1,500
West Driefontein Gold Mining Co.	2,000
	$10,000

Fig. 46

ALTERNATE $25,000 PORTFOLIO
(Higher Income Variation)

Stock	Amount
Campbell Red Lake Mines	$ 2,500
Homestake Mining Co.	2,500
Orange Free State Investment Trust	2,000
West Rand Investment Trust	2,500
Hartebeestfontein Gold Mining Co.	1,500
President Brand Gold Mining Co.	2,000
St. Helena Gold Mines	2,500
Vaal Reefs Exploration and Mining Co.	3,000
Western Deep Levels	3,000
West Driefontein Gold Mining Co.	3,500
	$25,000

Fig. 47

ALTERNATE $50,000 PORTFOLIO
(Higher Income Variation)

Stock	Amount
Campbell Red Lake Mines	$ 5,000
Dome Mines, Ltd.	4,000
Homestake Mining Co.	4,000
Anglo-American Corp. of South Africa	2,500
Gold Fields of South Africa	2,500
Orange Free State Investment Trust	3,000
West Rand Investment Trust	5,000
Doornfontein Gold Mining Co.	2,000
Hartebeestfontein Gold Mining Co.	2,000
President Brand Gold Mining Co.	3,000
President Steyn Gold Mining Co.	3,500
St. Helena Gold Mines	3,500
Vaal Reefs Exploration and Mining Co.	3,500
Western Deep Levels	3,000
West Driefontein Gold Mining Co.	3,500
	$50,000

North American Portfolios. Quite obviously our model portfolios depend rather heavily on the high-quality South African mines, and this results from the inescapable fact that South Africa is by far the area with the greatest potential for profit in gold investment. However, there undoubtedly will be some American investors who simply will not be comfortable with a large part of their investment capital committed to South African enterprises. It must be admitted that for those easily upset by radical political propaganda and newspaper sensationalism, owning South African shares may prove to be somewhat of a trial for the next few years. Radical left-wing political groups, both in the United States and elsewhere, have already hinted that the ending of the U.S. military involvement in Indo-China will allow them greatly to increase their political and propaganda campaign against southern Africa.

It is the author's view, however, that long before this decade is ended, the political leadership of the United States will be so desperately involved in trying to find solutions for our own pressing monetary, economic and social problems that the present compulsion to meddle in the affairs of southern Africa will have passed into its well-deserved oblivion. Investors in South African gold shares have been handsomely rewarded in the past and I believe the future holds even greater promise. Nevertheless, the first part of the present decade could see some political irritation between the United States and South Africa, promoted by the radical left.

So if an investor is going to get ulcers every time some radical troublemaker or ultraleft political hack tries to draw attention to himself or distract the public's attention from his real purpose by fulminating against South Africa, then perhaps he had better concentrate on North American gold stocks and save the wear and tear on his nerves. I must point out, however, that avoiding the supposed political risk by eliminating South African shares from the portfolio greatly increases the financial risk and decreases the investment potential, as North American gold stocks, with few exceptions, do not offer anywhere near the promise found in the better South African issues.

The leading North American gold stocks are of course very well suited for regular trading operations or for holding in a portfolio based on the *Trading Investment Plan* outlined in Chapter X. However, aside from the "big three": Campbell Red Lake, Dome, and Homestake, there is an obvious shortage of North American gold shares that can accurately be described as long-term investment-quality issues. Nevertheless, using the most promising choices from among the SPECULATIVE issues, a satisfactory portfolio could be put together that, with careful supervision, should at least offer a basic protection against major devaluations and further monetary collapse. Consequently, four exclusively North American gold stock portfolios, ranging from $5,000 to $50,000 are illustrated as our final exhibits.

Fig. 48

ALTERNATE $5,000 PORTFOLIO
(North American Shares Only)

Stock	Amount
Aunor Gold Mines	$ 500
Campbell Red Lake Mines	1,000
Dickenson Mines	500
Dome Mines	1,000
Homestake Mining Co.	2,000
	$5,000

Fig. 49

ALTERNATE $10,000 PORTFOLIO
(North American Shares Only)

Stock	Amount
Aunor Gold Mines	$ 500
Campbell Red Lake Mines	1,500
Dickenson Mines	1,500
Dome Mines	1,500
Eagle Gold Mines	500
Homestake Mining Co.	2,500
Kerr Addison Mines	1,000
Pato Consolidated Gold Dredging	1,000
	$10,000

Fig. 50

ALTERNATE $25,000 PORTFOLIO
(North American Shares Only)

Stock	Amount
Agnico Mines	$ 1,000
Aunor Gold Mines	1,500
Camflo Mines	1,000
Campbell Red Lake Mines	3,500
Dickenson Mines	2,000
Dome Mines	3,000
Eagle Gold Mines	2,000
Homestake Mining Co.	4,000
Kerr Addison Mines	2,500
Madsen Red Lake Gold Mines	1,500
Pato Consolidated Gold Dredging	3,000
	$25,000

Fig. 51

ALTERNATE $50,000 PORTFOLIO
(North American Shares Only)

Stock	*Amount*
Agnico Mines	$ 2,500
Aunor Gold Mines	2,500
Camflo Mines	2,500
Campbell Red Lake Mines	5,500
Dickenson Mines	5,000
Dome Mines	7,500
Eagle Gold Mines	3,000
Homestake Mining Co.	9,000
Kerr Addison Mines	4,000
Madsen Red Lake Gold Mines	2,500
Pato Consolidated Gold Dredging	4,500
Pamour Porcupine Mines	1,500
	$50,000

Managing an Investment Portfolio.   No matter how carefully or fortuitously an investment portfolio is initially acquired, some degree of subsequent management and supervision is absolutely essential. If there is one thing in this life that is consistent, it is that nothing can remain consistent or static for very long. Sooner or later everything changes, and many forms of change are largely unpredictable. Therefore, even long-term investment portfolios require continuous supervision. The investor should certainly continue to keep well informed and up-to-date on financial and economic developments in general, on developments affecting the gold mining industry and on the fortunes and prospects of the more important individual mines. And obviously we must be aware of all new developments affecting the stocks in our portfolios or that we may be holding at the moment. All this requires a careful reading of the financial press and of the periodicals recommended in this book. You may lock up your stocks—but don't forget them.

When, for any reason, you must sell something, sell the stock or stocks that have gone up the *least* or performed the poorest, not the stocks in which you might have the best profits. *Sell the losers, not the winners,* when liquidating part of a long-term investment portfolio. That way the portfolio gets stronger rather than weaker. If you develop the bad habit of selling only those stocks that have made good gains, because you can't bear to "take a loss," you may eventually be stuck with an entire portfolio of losers that would have to be acknowledged sooner or later anyway.

It is seldom a good idea to "average down," that is to continue to buy more shares of a declining stock just for the sake of establishing a better average price for the total of such shares in the portfolio by offsetting the purchases made earlier at a higher price level. Before buying a declining stock, make sure that the decline is due to external market factors rather than the result of some fundamental circumstance adversely affecting the company itself. Be especially cautious with a stock that declines while the rest of the gold group remains firm or is advancing.

In general, the long-term portfolio investor should be basically a fundamentalist rather than a technician. The major concern of the fundamentalist investor is to buy the most promising stocks, while the technically oriented trader is more involved with trying to anticipate intermediate market movements. Of course, the long-term investor also tries to "buy low," but the merit of the stock itself is of much greater importance to him than temporary changes in the public's attitude toward gold shares.

Therefore, the long-term investor will watch for basic changes in the outlook for his stocks rather than be overly concerned with day-to-day or week-to-week market action. Only when the long term trend for gold changes from "up" to uncertain or down will market conditions become a more significant factor for the long-term portfolio investor, and this will not occur until several years after a major devaluation of the dollar and worldwide monetary adjustments have brought an obvious return to financial and monetary stability. At that time, gold shares will no longer have any special "hedge" value or protection and can be regarded as one would any other mining enterprise.

Important negative factors to watch for are failure to maintain ore-reserve tonnage at a level to insure several years of future production, a steady decline in estimated ore reserves over a period of several years, gradually falling ore grade and the decline of a MEDIUM-life mine into the SHORT-life category in the case of South African mines. Don't hesitate to weed out periodically any stocks in your portfolio that begin to show fundamental weaknesses of this type or that are not living up to their original promise. However, a drop in earnings or a cut in dividends may not in itself be an automatic signal to eliminate a particular holding, if such a setback is the result of temporary technical or financial dislocations. A decline in reported earnings or dividends *may* actually be a bullish sign, if the retained capital is being expended on new developments or acquisitions. Sometimes a setback in earnings, particularly when caused by some fundamentally positive development, offers an excellent opportunity to acquire the shares concerned at a bargain level.

Above all, know what is going on. Read the financial press; read the *Northern Miner* if you have a good position in Canadian shares; read the *Mining Journal* and the *Quarterly Review of South African Gold Shares* for news of the South African Mines, and read the annual and quarterly reports of your companies. A good plan is to keep a clipping file or scrapbook of news articles and other items of information concerning all companies either represented in your portfolio or under consideration. This will give you a broad overall view of the general progress (or lack of it) at each specific company. A single news item in itself can sometimes be misleading, but when placed in context with the trend of events over a period of two or three years it can be more accurately evaluated.

Investment Advisers and Advisory Services.   There are perhaps a dozen major investment advisory services and market letters that have devoted a good deal of space in recent years to gold and gold mining stocks. Some of them have been warning of the present monetary-financial mess for almost a decade and during that time have been imploring their subscribers to put at least part of their funds into gold investments. In this they have surely performed a most valuable service.

Of course, not all of these services are of equal merit. Furthermore, among the more general market letters there are some which tend to get enthusiastic for gold stocks only when the market for them is in a highly emotional and advanced state. But when calmness returns for a time and the gold market subsides to a more reasonable level, this type of advisory service tends to ignore the golds and turns its attention to whatever else has become the most widespread speculative mania of the moment. Obviously, such tactics are definitely contrary to the principles outlined in this book.

However, among the monetary-gold oriented investment advisory services there are some which rate high marks, not only for their investment suggestions, but for their astute reporting and evaluation of international monetary developments. I read several of these services on a regular basis, in addition to the basic periodicals recommended, in order to help keep current on international monetary and economic developments. In addition, I contribute articles to some of these services from time to time. In general, those services which take a long-term investment approach, based on a continuing fundamental analysis and review of the world monetary-economic situation, are recommended, while market letters concerned primarily with short-term speculative moves and situations should be avoided.

However, I am not going to recommend any specific advisory service or services here—not even the ones I have contributed to or plan to contribute to. Basically, I feel that matching an investor to an investment advisor or advisory service is a highly subjective propostion, much like finding your personal lawyer or physician. Experience has taught me that each investment advisory service or market letter, regardless of its objective merits, has what could be described as a recognizable personality. Consequently, the subscriber's personality must be compatible with the "personality" of the advisory service, or else the subscriber will not only not benefit very much from the particular service, but may actually be confused or misled by it.

Therefore, you will have to do your own screening from among the many worthwhile investment advisory services and letters (as well as from those not so worthwhile!). I suggest short trial subscriptions to those services you may have heard favorable comments about or that may intrigue you through their advertising. If you do eventually find an advisory service (or services) that gives you a feeling of confidence and provides you with sufficient background material and financial news coverage to reduce the fog of uncertainty, it will no doubt help you in making investment decisions and reaching your financial objectives.

In any case, I do recommend subscriptions to the *Wall Street Journal,* the *Northern Miner* and the *Quarterly Review of South African Gold Shares* as excellent sources of the *objective* information needed by the long-term investor to successfully manage a gold investment portfolio.

Among individual brokers and analysts there are many knowledgeable specialists in gold mining stocks, such as Peter Kiernan of Fahnestock and Co.; C. Austin Barker of Hornblower and Weeks—Hemphill Noyes; Deson Sze of Harris, Upham and Co.; William L. Graham, Jr. of David A. Noyes Co.; and Elmer L. Carsello of Clark, Dodge and Co., to name just a very few. Please remember, however, that ideally the person best suited to manage *your* financial affairs is *you yourself.* And this book is surely not the ultimate word on the subject, but has been written only as a guide to help its readers become more proficient at helping *themselves.*

Mutual Funds and Gold Stocks.   A few American mutual funds have taken to holding substantial blocks of gold shares in recent years, but I don't know of any ordinary fund that regularly maintains a sufficient quantity of such shares in its portfolio to make it of interest or consideration as a gold-hedge investment. However, since the late 1960's, several funds have been organized specifically to maintain portfolios primarily or exclusively concentrated in gold investments. Most of the foreign-based of these gold funds include gold bullion positions among their assets. Consequently, American investors are not allowed to own them, according to the U.S. Treasury, although this ruling has never been openly challenged in the U.S. courts. Among the best known of the foreign gold funds are the Munich-based Midas Fund and the Toronto-based Canadian-South African Gold Fund, both of which are obliged by their charters to keep a minimum of 25 percent of their assets in gold bullion.

There are a few American-based gold funds, such as the International Investor's Fund of New York, that do not hold bullion positions but keep the majority of their assets in gold shares. In 1971, International Investor's had assets of about $4,000,000, with about 80 percent of that amount committed to gold mining and gold mining financial shares. If you think that such funds would be your best choice, I'm sure your broker will be happy to help you make a selection.

However, a mutual fund is a form of indirect rather than direct ownership of gold shares and this book is concerned with the *direct* ownership and management of gold-oriented investments. May I observe again that the most ideal and potentially profitable arrangement is for the investor to acquire the skill to manage his or her own affairs. It is my hope that this book will aid in that purpose.

APPENDIX I

PRESIDENTIAL PROCLAMATION OF MARCH 6, 1933

Declaring Emergency Executive Control Over All
Banking And Currency Transactions

WHEREAS there have been heavy and unwarranted withdrawals of gold and currency from our banking institutions for the purpose of hoarding; and

WHEREAS continuous and increasingly extensive speculative activity abroad in foreign exchange has resulted in severe drains on the Nation's stocks of gold; and

WHEREAS these conditions have created a national emergency; and

WHEREAS it is in the best interests of all bank depositors that a period of respite be provided with a view to preventing further hoarding of coin, bullion or currency, or speculation in foreign exchange, and permitting the application of appropriate measures to protect the interests of our people; and

WHEREAS it is provided in Section 5 (b) of the Act of October 6, 1917 (40 Stat. L. 411) as amended, "That the President may investigate, regulate or prohibit, under such rules and regulations as he may prescribe, by means of licenses or otherwise, any transactions in foreign exchange and the export, hoarding, melting or earmarking of gold or silver coin or bullion or currency, and

WHEREAS it is provided in Section 16 of the said Act "that whoever shall willfully violate any of the provisions of this Act or of any license, rule or regulation issued thereunder, and whoever shall willfully violate, neglect or refuse to comply with any order of the President issued in compliance with the Provisions of this Act, shall, upon conviction, be fined not more than $10,000, or, if a natural person, imprisoned for not more than ten years, or both."

NOW, THEREFORE, I, *FRANKLIN D. ROOSEVELT,* President of the

United States of America, in view of such national emergency and by
virtue of the authority vested in me by said Act and in order to prevent the export, hoarding or earmarking of gold or silver coin or
bullion or currency, do hereby proclaim, order, direct and declare
that from Monday, the sixth day of March to Thursday, the ninth
day of March, Nineteen Hundred and Thirty-three, both dates in-
clusive, there shall be maintained and observed by all banking institutions and all branches thereof located in the United States of
America, including the territories and insular possessions, a bank
holiday, and that during said period all banking transactions shall
be suspended. During such holiday, excepting as hereinafter provided, no such banking institution or branch shall pay out, export,
earmark or permit the withdrawal or transfer in any manner or by
any device whatsoever, of any gold or silver coin or bullion or currency or take any other action which might facilitate the hoarding
thereof; nor shall any such banking institution or branch pay out
deposits, make loans or discounts, deal in foreign exchange, transfer credits from the United States to any place abroad, or transact
any other banking business whatsoever.

During such holiday, the Secretary of the Treasury, with the approval of the President and under such regulations as he may prescribe, is authorized and empowered (a) to permit any or all of
such banking institutions to perform any or all of the usual banking functions, (b) to direct, require or permit the issuance of clear-
ing house certificates or other evidences of claims against assets of
banking institutions, and (c) to authorize and direct the creation in
such banking institutions of special trust accounts for the receipt
of new deposits which shall be subject to withdrawal on demand
without any restriction or limitation and shall be kept separately in
cash or on deposit in Federal Reserve Banks or invested in obligations of the United States.

As used in this order the term "banking institution" shall include
all Federal Reserve Banks, national banking associations, banks,
trust companies, savings banks, building and loan associations,
credit unions, or other corporations, partnerships, associations or
persons, engaged in the business of receiving deposits, making
loans, discounting business paper or transacting any other form of
banking business.

IN WITNESS WHEREOF, I have hereunto set my hand and caused the
seal of the United States to be affixed.

(Seal)

Done in the City of Washington, this 6th day of March—1 A.M. in the year of our Lord One Thousand Nine Hundred and Thirty-three, and of the Independence of the United States the One Hundred and Fifty-seventh.

FRANKLIN D. ROOSEVELT

By the President:
CORDELL HULL
Secretary of State.

APPENDIX II

EXTRACT FROM EXECUTIVE ORDER OF APRIL 5, 1933

Forbidding the Private Holding of Gold Coin,
Gold Bullion and Gold Certificates

By virtue of the authority vested in me by the Act of March 9, 1933, I, Franklin D. Roosevelt, President of the United States of America, do declare that said national emergency still continues to exist and pursuant to said section do hereby prohibit the hoarding of gold coin, gold bullion and gold certificates within the continental United States.

For the purposes of this regulation, the term "hoarding" means the withdrawal and withholding of gold coin, gold bullion or gold certificates from the recognized and customary channels of trade.

All persons are hereby required to deliver on or before May 1, 1933, to a Federal Reserve bank or a branch or agency thereof or to any member bank of the Federal Reserve System all gold coin, gold bullion and gold certificates now owned by them or coming into their ownership.

Whoever willfully violates any provision of this Executive order or of these regulations or of any rule, regulation or license issued thereunder may be fined not more than $10,000, or, if a natural person, may be imprisoned for not more than ten years, or both; and any officer, director, or agent of any corporation who knowingly participates in such violation may be punished by a like fine, imprisonment, or both.

The following exceptions are made to the delivery requirements of this order:

(a) Such amounts of gold as may be required for legitimate and customary use in industry, profession or art within a reasonable time, including gold prior to refining and stocks of gold in reasonable amounts for the usual trade requirements of owners mining and refining such gold.

(b) Gold coin and gold certificates in an amount not exceeding in the aggregate $100 belonging to any one person, and gold coins having a recognized special value to collectors of rare and unusual coins.

(c) Gold coin and bullion earmarked or held in trust for a recognized foreign Government or foreign central bank or the Bank for International Settlements.

The President of the
United States of America

FRANKLIN D. ROOSEVELT

APPENDIX III

EXECUTIVE STATEMENT
OF JANUARY 31, 1934

Relating to the Devaluation of the Dollar

1. Acting under the powers granted by Title 3 of the act approved May 12, 1933 (Thomas Amendment to the Farm Relief Act), the President today issued a proclamation fixing the weight of the gold dollar at 15-2/21 grains, nine-tenths fine. This is 59.06 plus percent of the former weight of 25-8/10 grains, nine-tenths fine, as fixed by Section I of the Act of Congress of March 4, 1900. The new gold content of the dollar became effective immediately on the signing of the proclamation by the President.

Under the Gold Reserve Act of 1934, signed by the President Tuesday, January thirtieth, title to the entire stock of monetary gold in the United States, including the gold coin and gold bullion heretofore held by the Federal Reserve Banks and the claim upon gold in the Treasury represented by gold certificates, is vested in the United States Government and the "profit" from the reduction of the gold content of the dollar, made effective by today's proclamation, accrues to the United States Treasury. Of this "profit" two billion dollars, under the terms of the Gold Reserve Act and of today's proclamation, constitutes a stabilization fund under the direction of the Secretary of the Treasury. The balance will be covered into the general fund of the Treasury.

In his proclamation of today the President gives notice that he reserves the right, by virtue of the authority vested in him to alter or modify the present proclamation as the interests of the United States may seem to require. The authority by later proclamations to accomplish other revaluations of the dollar in terms of gold is contained in the Gold Reserve Act signed on Tuesday.

2. The Secretary of the Treasury, with the approval of the President, issued a public announcement that beginning Feb. 1, 1934, he will buy through the Federal Reserve Bank of New York as fiscal agent, for the account of the United States, any and all gold delivered to any United States Mints or the Assay Offices in New York or Seattle, at the rate of $35 per fine troy ounce, less the usual Mint charges and less one-fourth of one percent for handling charges. Purchases, however, are subject to compliance with the regulations issued under the Gold Reserve Act of 1934.

The President of the
United States of America

FRANKLIN D. ROOSEVELT

APPENDIX IV

EXTRACT FROM EXECUTIVE STATEMENT OF AUGUST 15, 1971

Suspending Convertibility of the Dollar

In the past seven years there has been an average of an international monetary crisis every year. Who gains from these crises? Not the workingman; not the investor; and not the real producers of wealth. The gainers are international money speculators. Because they thrive on crises, they help create them.

In recent weeks, the speculators have been waging an all-out war on the American dollar. The strength of a nation's currency is based on the strength of that nation's economy—and the American economy is by far the strongest in the world. Accordingly, I have directed the Secretary of the Treasury to take the action necessary to defend the dollar against the speculators.

I have directed Secretary Connally to suspend, temporarily, the convertibility of the dollar into gold or other reserve assets, except in amounts and conditions determined to be in the interest of monetary stability and in the best interests of the United States.

Now, what is this action, which is very technical? What does it mean for you?

Let me lay to rest the bugaboo of what is called devaluation.

If you want to buy a foreign car or take a trip abroad, market conditions may cause your dollar to buy slightly less. But if you are among the overwhelming majority of Americans who buy American-made products in America, your dollar will be worth just as much tomorrow as it is today.

The effect of this action, in other words, will be to stabilize the dollar.

Now this action will not win us any friends among the international money traders. But our primary concern is with the American workers, and with fair competition around the world.

To our friends abroad, including the many responsible members of the international banking community who are dedicated to stability and the flow of trade, I give this assurance: the United States has always been—and will continue to be—a forward looking and trustworthy trading partner. In full cooperation with the International Monetary Fund and those who trade with us, we will press for the necessary reforms to set up an urgently needed new international monetary system. Stability and equal treatment is in everybody's interest. I am determined that the American dollar must never again be a hostage in the hands of international speculators.

The President of the
United States of America

RICHARD M. NIXON

APPENDIX V

INTERNATIONAL CURRENCY ADJUSTMENTS ANNOUNCED DECEMBER 31, 1971

Resulting From "The Smithsonian Agreement"

Country and Currency	Old Parity	New Parity	Percent Change Against Old Parity
United States (dollar)	$35.00	$38.00	–8.57
The Group of Ten			
Belgium (franc)	0.0200	0.0223	+ 11.57
Canada (dollar)	0.9250	floating	—
France (franc)	0.1800	0.1955	+ 8.57
Italy (lira)	0.001600	0.001719	+ 7.48
Japan (yen)	0.002777	0.003246	+ 16.88
Netherlands (guilder)	0.2762	0.3082	+ 11.57
Sweden (krona)	0.1933	0.2078	+ 7.49
Switzerland (franc)	0.2451	0.2604	+ 6.36
United Kingdom (pound)	2.4000	2.6057	+ 8.57
W. Germany (deutschmark)	0.2732	0.3103	+ 13.57
Western Europe			
Austria (schilling)	0.0385	0.0429	+ 6.22
Denmark (krone)	0.1333	0.1433	+ 7.45
Finland (markka)	0.2381	0.2439	+ 2.44
Greece (drachma)	0.0333	0.0333	0.00
Norway (krone)	0.1400	0.1505	+ 7.49
Portugal (escudo)	0.0348	0.0367	+ 5.50
Spain (peseta)	0.0143	0.0155	+ 8.57

Pacific Area

Australia (dollar)	1.1200	1.1910	+	6.34
New Zealand (dollar)	1.1200	1.1952	+	6.71

Near and Far East

India (rupee)	0.1333	0.1376	+	3.16
Iraq (dinar)	2.8000	3.0637	+	8.57
Israel (pound)	0.2857	0.2506	−	14.00
Kuwait (dinar)	2.8000	3.0637	+	8.57
Malaysia (dollar)	0.3267	0.3547	+	8.57
Pakistan (rupee)	0.2100	0.2100		0.00
Saudi Arabia (riyal)	0.2222	0.2431	+	8.57
Singapore (dollar)	0.3267	0.3547	+	8.57

Africa

Ethiopia (dollar)	0.4000	0.4375	+	8.57
Ghana (new cedi)	0.9800	0.5506	−	84.00
Malawi (pound)	2.4000	2.6261	+	8.57
Rep. of South Africa (rand)	1.4000	1.3068	−	6.65
Uganda (schilling)	0.1400	0.1400		0.00

Latin America

Mexico (peso)	0.0800	0.0800		0.00

Notes:

1. *U.S. parity* expressed in terms of officially declared Treasury price for gold.

2. *Canadian dollar* remained in floating status after the Smithsonian agreement. Old parity shown is from May 31, 1970, the last day of fixed parity for the Canadian dollar.

3. *New Parities* for other currencies expressed in terms of devalued ($38 per ounce of gold) U.S. dollars.

4. *Old Parities* shown are those (officially) in effect as of April 30, 1971, before the monetary crisis of 1971 began.

5. Old IMF rule limiting currency fluctuations to 1 percent (on either side of fixed parity) abandoned under the Smithsonian agreement in favor of a new 2¼ percent margin (up or down), allowable before central bank support of a particular currency becomes mandatory.

6. Most Latin American countries employ multiple-exchange-

rate systems and have no single stated parity for their currencies against the dollar. However, many of them did make additional adjustments in response to the Smithsonian agreement. Brazil, in a series of continuous small devaluations reduced the value of the cruzeiro by about 8.7 percent between May and December of 1971. Chile devalued its trade escudo by about 25 percent. Colombia reduced the dollar value of its peso by 4 percent. Uruguay devalued its peso by imposing a surcharge of P 120 on certain trade transactions. The Dutch Antilles and Surinam revalued their currencies against the dollar by 5 percent and Venezuela revalued the bolivar by 2.3 percent.

7.   The Appendix V table shows official quotations current as of December 31, 1971, only and is intended to show the immediate effects of the Smithsonian agreement. Readers are reminded that exchange rates are subject to frequent change and should consult banking sources or the financial press if up-to-date quotations are required for any purpose.

Glossary

Virtually every field of study requires the use of specialized terms, and in this book we have been involved with no less than three basic areas of knowledge: economics and finance, investing and the stock market, and gold—its mining, processing and utilization. The interests of the gold-oriented investor require a familiarity with the principal terms of all three of these distinct but related areas. In using such words in the course of this book I have tried, as far as possible, to use them in a definitive context. However, since a formal table of definitions is often quite useful to the reader of technically oriented works, this brief list of the most frequently encountered specialized words of economics and finance, the stock market and the gold mining industry, not only in this book but in the general literature concerned with its three related subjects, is also included.

American Depositary Receipts (ADR's) certificates issued by an American bank or trust company representing an equivalent amount of foreign shares held in trust by the issuing depositary bank. This arrangement is designed to facilitate American trading in foreign securities.
Afrikaans an African-Dutch idiom that is the other official language of the Republic of South Africa, in addition to English.
Afrikaner a white Afrikaans-speaking South African of Dutch or Dutch-French-German descent (see also Boers).
arbitrage the practice of taking advantage of, and profiting by, minor differences in price that sometimes occur between equivalent or

equally exchangeable items. Applies to stocks, bonds and commodities, as well as to coins and currencies.

assay to laboratory-test or analyze a small sample of ore for its valuable mineral content.

Au the chemical symbol for gold.

bank credit purchasing power created by bank loans to individuals and organizations without corresponding or offsetting bank deposits by other individuals or organizations.

bank note paper currency issued by a bank. Actually, a promissory note issued by a legally authorized bank for use as a money substitute. Formerly, bank note currency was redeemable in standard money on demand.

bear market a market with a definite declining trend of significant duration.

bears those who believe stock prices will go down and economic conditions will get worse—the pessimists.

Big Board a popular term for the New York Stock Exchange (the largest in the United States).

bimetallism a monetary standard under which the monetary unit is defined and redeemed in terms of both gold and silver.

Boers the name formerly given to the original Dutch-French-German settlers of South Africa and their descendants (see Afrikaner).

bond a certificate of debt issued by a corporation or government, bearing a fixed rate of interest and a specified maturity date.

borehole a small-diameter hole drilled from the surface or from an underground tunnel or position to sample an orebody. The drill is constructed so that a cylindrical section or "core" of rock or ore can be removed for assaying.

breakup the final stage in the life of a mine, in which operations are gradually terminated and remaining assets are sold.

broker an agent who accepts and executes orders to buy or sell securities and commodities.

brokerage firm an organization that acts as an agent for persons wishing to buy or sell securities or commodities and that charges a commission or fee for this service. Most brokerage firms or "houses" maintain membership in one or more of the major exchanges.

bullion a monetary metal (gold or silver) in an uncoined state; the pure metal, usually stored in bars or ingots—.999 fine.

bull market a market with a pronounced rising trend of extended duration.

bulls those who believe stock prices will go up and economic conditions will get better—the optimists.

capitalized debt long-term corporate debt that is acknowledged by the issuance of interest-bearing negotiable certificates, such as bonds, debentures and loan shares.

coin (historic) a piece of precious metal, intended for use as money, stamped with marks or inscriptions showing that it was issued by an authority or government that guarantees its weight and purity.

coin (modern) a piece of metal marked and issued by a governmental authority to be used as money. Such metal tokens represent the fractional parts of the monetary unit.

common stock how the word "stock" came to be used to describe participating shares in corporate enterprises is something of a mystery. Possibly it came about because such shares were originally traded in exchanges or markets set up for the trading of livestock. As far back as the Middle Ages, at least, men bought and sold shares or participations in various mercantile ventures, sea voyages, etc. The rewards of a family business or a partnership go to those who do the work. The rewards of a larger or "public" business or enterprise can be shared with those who supply the capital as well. A share of common stock, therefore, represents a portion of direct ownership in a corporate venture. It is the foundation of the capitalist system. A common stockholder is entitled to share directly in the rewards of the business (if there are any) in proportion to his holdings, while his possible loss is limited to the amount of his investment.

conglomerate a rock composed of a mixture of materials: pebbles, sands, miscellaneous minerals, etc., cemented together by geologic heat or pressure. The gold-bearing "reefs" of South Africa are conglomerates.

credit money money that derives its value from the credit of the issuing agency (literally, from trust in its solvency and honesty.)

currency tangible money, both paper and coin.

debase to reduce the intrinsic value (bullion content) of a coin while maintaining its face value.

debt money same as credit money. Paper currency derived from the monetization of government debts.

deflation a reduction in the amount of currency and/or bank credit available to an economy without a corresponding decline in the ability to produce wealth.

demonetize when referring to a coin or note: to withdraw legal-tender status. When said of metal: to cease using it to define the monetary unit.

devaluation a redefinition of the monetary unit that makes it worth less in terms of bullion or foreign exchange.

development   work done in a mine to open up and prove orebodies; tunnels and shafts constructed to gain access to orebodies.

diamond drilling   borehole exploration using a diamond-tipped drill and drilling rig.

dilution   the amount of waste rock that must unavoidably be processed along with payable ore. Usually expresed in terms of percentages.

discount rate   the rate of interest, set by the Federal Reserve Board, at which the Federal Reserve System will advance money to member banks. The discount rate is periodically adjusted in hopes of influencing economic activity.

economics   the social science concerned with the conditions and laws affecting the production, distribution and consumption of wealth (that is, all material goods of economic utility). Prior to the twentieth century the subject was often referred to as "political economy."

face value   the numerical sum stamped on a coin or note, in terms of monetary units, as determined by the issuing authority.

fault   a vertical or horizontal displacement of a geologic strata or formation.

Federal Reserve Board   the Board of Governors of the U.S. Federal Reserve banking system.

fiat credit   credit created or extended in excess of any tangible relationship to the actual wealth in existence; credit based on an abstract idea or theory rather than on recognizable physical assets or collateral.

fiat money   money that derives its value only from the arbitrary power of the state to compel its acceptance; it is not defined or redeemed in any metal or commodity, and is without intrinsic value— money that is money because the government says it is. See *legal tender.*

finance   the science of raising and expending revenues, public or private; the management of monetary affairs.

funded debt   long-term debt of a company with replacement terms and dates arranged and interest rates settled (see also *capitalized debt*).

fineness   the ratio of pure metal (gold or silver) to total weight, in bars, ingots or coins, usually expressed as a decimal percentage. U.S. standard gold coins were .900 fine, or 90 percent gold and 10 percent alloy.

fine ounce   a troy ounce of pure gold. The standard gold bar of commerce is 400 fine ounces or 33.3 troy pounds (equal to about 27.4 pounds avoirdupois; see *troy weight*).

fractional notes paper money with a face value less than the monetary unit.

free coinage a policy or law providing that anyone who deposits (gold or silver) bullion in the mint is entitled to receive in exchange coins of equal weight in grains pure of the metal deposited (less whatever small fixed seigniorage charge or ratio is established).

gold standard a metallic standard based on gold.

grade the amount of gold or other valuable minerals contained in an ore, usually expressed in terms of ounces per ton in North America and grams per ton in South Africa.

Gresham's Law a principle formulated by Sir Thomas Gresham (1519–79) who noted that when coins of equal face value but different intrinsic value are put into circulation together, the coin with the higher intrinsic value will be hoarded and only the coin of lower intrinsic value will remain in circulation. (It is sometimes put in the form of an aphorism: "Bad money drives out good money.") Despite the delusions of the New Economics, the events of recent years demonstrate rather convincingly that Gresham's Law is not about to be repealed.

haulageway a large tunnel in a mine through which ore is hauled, usually by narrow-guage railway, either directly to the surface or to a main elevator shaft.

headframe the structure erected over a mine shaft to support the elevator cables and sheaves.

hedge to protect oneself from expected or unexpected financial hazards by making offsetting purchases of appropriate securities or commodities.

hoarder a person who saves large quantities of common coin in the belief that the intrinsic value is greater than the face value; one who acts in accordance with Gresham's Law.

inflation a process whereby the volume of currency and/or bank credit in an economy is increased faster than the creation of new wealth can justify, resulting in escalating wages and prices.

intrinsic value the actual commodity value of the metallic content of a coin.

invest to buy and hold with the expectation of obtaining a profit or increasing wealth through subsequent advances in value; to convert money into some form of wealth other than money.

Kaffirs South African gold mining shares. The term is derived from an Afrikaans colloquialism for a native black South African.

Keynesian economics economic policies based on the theories of the late British economist John Maynard Keynes (1883–1946), that overall economic activity can be decisively influenced by changes in a government's spending and tax policies and, particularly, that an economic decline can be corrected by large increases in deficit government spending.

legal tender   whatever is declared by law to be, and therefore must be accepted as, legal satisfaction for the repayment of debts and the fulfillment of contracts denominated in money. (Not all money is legal tender for all debts. Minor coins are legal tender only in small amounts. You cannot, for example, force any one to accept a sack of pennies in payment for a $100 debt.)

level   a term denoting the various depths of a mine's horizontal workings, analogous to the "floors" in a building.

leverage   a financial arrangement or inherent factor that increases the potential for profit of an investment or speculation, usually at the cost of also increasing the potential for loss. Just as a lever multiplies mechanical effort, leverage, in market terms, multiplies financial effort.

longwall stoping   a method of mining similar to that used in coal mining. It increases the mining rate, but limits the selectivity with which it can be achieved.

margin   the amount of cash a buyer is required to place in the hands of a broker when buying stocks on partial credit. If you buy a stock for cash, the certificate can be delivered to you in a few weeks. But if the purchase is on margin, that is, not paid for in full, the broker loans you the balance of the money required and he retains custody of the stock.

margin account   an account with a brokerage firm in which the investor or speculator is allowed to buy stocks on partial credit. In a margin account, you are required to sign an agreement giving the broker the right to sell your stock if it should decline to a point where the loan made on it is no longer safely covered by its market value.

margin call   a little note from your broker stating that your margin loan is no longer adequately protected by the market value of your securities—and if you do not deliver to him very quickly enough additional cash to insure that protection, he is going to sell the margined stock and retire said loan.

margin rate   the percentage of cash legally required for a margin purchase. Margin rates are established by the Federal Reserve Board, as it deems prudent.

metallic standard   refers to a money system that defines and redeems the monetary unit in terms of a fixed amount of metal, either as standard coin or bullion.

minor coin   small-denomination coin not having bullion value. (As a result of the coinage act of 1965, all U.S. coins except the debased [40-percent-silver] Kennedy halves were reduced to minor coin.)

monetary standard the measuring value of the monetary unit, be it an actual commodity (gold or silver), credit (debt), or the legislative fiat of the state.

monetary unit the standard money, in terms of which all other types of money are defined. (In the United States, the dollar; France, the franc; Italy, the lira; etc.)

money almost anything that is generally accepted as a medium of exchange or means of deferred payment. In modern times, it includes currency; checking accounts; bank deposits; gold reserves; certain short-term government debt instruments, such as Treasury bills and notes. Originally, a commodity generally agreed upon as the common medium of exchange.

neo-Keynesian economic theories or policies superficially based on, thought to be based on, or borrowing haphazardly from the Keynesian doctrines. An economic theory or policy relating to but not exactly parallel to the original Keynesian theories.

negotiable said of a security or note when it can be freely bought and sold in private financial markets.

nominal value same as face value.

numismatics the study of coins, medals, and all forms of money, on a systematic or scientific basis.

odd lot fewer than 100 shares of a stock for which the customary unit of trading is 100 shares. Any amount of shares less than the recognized unit of trading.

ore a rock or conglomerate containing a valuable mineral or minerals in significant or commercially payable quantities.

over-the-counter a rather loose term for the whole area of trading in securities not listed on a stock exchange.

pillar ore that has to be left in place in a stope or stoping area to provide roof supports.

preferred stock a form of stock on which dividends are paid at a fixed rate, if they are earned by the company. The preferred stock dividend must be paid before any money can be distributed to common stockholders but the amount of dividend due the preferred shareholders is limited to the fixed rate. There is no limit, on the other hand, to the amount of dividends that can be paid to common shareholders, except the availability of profits.

pressure burst occasionally, the extreme pressures developed at great depths in a mine can cause a supporting pillar to fail or, literally, burst—a very dangerous occurrence.

price-earnings ratio (P/E ratio)   an arbitrary figure used to gauge the valuation of a common stock, derived by dividing the current price by the previous 12 months earnings. Example: if the earnings of a given stock were $1.00 per share and the price of that stock was currently $15 per share, the P/E ratio would be 15. If the P/E ratio is high, the stock may be overvalued and if it is very low the stock may be undervalued. A P/E ratio of 10 is considered fair or "normal" for a mining stock, but most North American gold issues consistently sell at considerably higher ratios, because they are in short supply and investors are anticipating a much higher price for gold.

prime rate   the minimum rate of interest at which the largest banks will loan money to private or corporate customers with the best credit rating. The prime rate varies according to supply and demand conditions for lendable funds and bank credit.

redeemable   said of paper money when it can readily be exchanged for bullion or intrinsic-value coin at a fixed rate.

reef   a gold-bearing conglomerate in the form of a thin but widely distributed seam. The typical orebody configuration of the South African gold fields.

reserves (ore reserves)   the estimated tonnage of payable ore opened up and proved by development work.

revaluation   a redefinition of the monetary unit that makes it worth more in terms of bullion or foreign exchange.

round lot   the recognized unit of trading for a stock or commodity. For most stocks the standard round lot is 100 shares.

seigniorage   1. a small minting fee that is obtained from the difference between the intrinsic value and the face value of standard and subsidiary coin. 2. the profit accruing to a government when the face value of its currency greatly exceeds the cost of producing it.

short sale   if you sell a stock that you have borrowed (your broker actually borrows it for you) in the hope of replacing it at a lower cost later on, you have made a short sale.

silver standard   a metallic standard based on silver.

Special Drawing Rights (SDR's)   a scheme whereby the members of the International Monetary Fund (IMF) are granted special credits or "rights" that can be utilized to settle balance-of-payments deficits. The amount of special credit granted is related to each member nation's "pledge" or deposits of gold and currency with the IMF. Under this plan, a creditor nation is obliged to accept these nonredeemable SDR "credits" whenever offered in lieu of gold.

specie   the standard metallic money, gold, silver, as opposed to paper notes, nonstandard coin, etc.

speculate   to buy and sell with the hope of profiting from significant fluctuations in price.

standard coin   intrinsic-value coin with a face value equal to its bullion value (under a metallic standard).

stope, stoping   the process of extracting ore after it has been made accessible by development work. A stope is a working area being mined or formed by mining.

subincline shaft   a shaft constructed at an incline or angle from one of the lower levels of a mine. An inclined shaft that does not reach the surface.

subsidiary coin   intrinsic-value coin with a face value more than the bullion value (at the official rate).

subvertical shaft   a vertical shaft beginning on one of the lower levels of a mine. A vertical shaft that does not reach the surface.

troy weight   the system of weights and measures used for gold and other precious metals. The troy units of measurement are grains, pennyweights, ounces and pounds and are determined as follows:

> 24 grains — 1 pennyweight (dwt)
> 20 dwt.   — 1 ounce
> 12 ounces — 1 pound

One ounce troy is equal to 1.097 ounces avoirdupois and 1 troy pound is equal to .82285 pounds avoirdupois (there are only 12 ounces to the troy pound vs. 16 ounces to the avoirdupois pound).

yield (securities)   dividends or interest calculated as a percentage of the purchase price. In the case of stocks, one divides the annual dividend per share by the purchase or quoted price per share to determine yield.

yield (mining)   the actual amount of gold (or other metal) extracted from the total tonnage of ore mined and milled or processed by a mining company, sometimes expressed in terms of ounces or grams per ton.

Bibliography

The literature of the stock market is enormous. However very little of it relates specifically to the subject of gold investment. The brief bibliography presented here includes only those works that were of direct help in the preparation of this book. Standard stock market reference and statistical works are not included. The author was also greatly assisted by various issues of the periodicals cited in the list of periodicals following this bibliography.

GENERAL HISTORY OF GOLD

Allen, G. *Gold, History from Ancient Times to the Present Day.* New York, 1965.
Green, Timothy. *The World of Gold.* New York: Walker & Co., 1968.
Rist, Charles. *The Triumph of Gold.* Translated by Philip Cortney. New York: Philosophical Library, 1961.
Sutherland, C.H.V. *Gold, Its Beauty, Power and Allure.* New York: McGraw-Hill, 1969.

GOLD. COINS

Hoppe, Donald J. *How to Invest in Gold Coins.* New Rochelle, N.Y.: Arlington House, 1970.
Gold Coin Catalogues
Friedberg, Robert. *Gold Coins of the World, Complete from 600 A.D. to the Present.* 3rd ed. New York: The Coin and Currency Institute, 1970.
Schlumberger, Hans. *Gold Coins of Europe Since 1800.* New York: Sterling Pub. Co., 1968.

Yeoman, R.S. *A Guidebook of United States Coins.* Racine, Wis.: Whitman, annual editions.

GOLD MINING AND GOLD INVESTMENT

BUREAU OF MINES BULLETIN 650: *Mineral Facts and Problems* (Gold Section) 1970 ed. U.S. Government Printing Office.

Frankel, S. Herbert. *Investment and the Return to Equity Capital in the South African Gold Mining Industry, 1887–1965.* Cambridge, Mass.: Harvard Univ. Press, 1967.

Hoyt, Charles D. *Gold, Preprint from 1970 U.S. Bureau of Mines Minerals Yearbook.* U.S. Government Printing Office (published annually).

Northern Miner Editorial Staff. *Canadian Mines Handbook.* Toronto: The Northern Miner Press, annual editions.

Northern Miner Editorial Staff. *Mining Explained.* Toronto: The Northern Miner Press, 1969.

HISTORY OF GOLD MINING

Paul, R.W. *California Gold, the Beginning of Mining in the Far West.* Lincoln, Neb., 1967.

Rosenthal, Eric. *Gold, Gold, Gold; The Johannesburg Gold Rush.* London: MacMillan, 1970.

Wagner, Jack R. *The Gold Mines of California.* Berkeley, Cal.: Howell-North, 1970.

MONEY, INFLATION, AND FINANCIAL DELUSIONS

Bakewell, Paul. *Thirteen Curious Errors About Money.* Caldwell, Ida.: Caxton, 1962.

Groseclose, Elgin. *Money and Man.* New York: Frederick Ungar, 1961.

Mackay, Charles. *Extraordinary Popular Delusions and the Madness of Crowds.* London, 1841. Reprint ed., with a foreword by Bernard M. Baruch. New York: L.C. Page Co., 1932; 11th printing, 1960.

Rand, Ayn. *Capitalism: The Unknown Ideal.* With contributions by Nathaniel Branden, Alan Greenspan and Robert Hessen. New York: New American Library, 1966.

Rickenbacker, William F. *Death of the Dollar.* New Rochelle, N.Y.: Arlington House, 1966.

_____. *Wooden Nickels, or, the Decline and Fall of Silver Coins.* New Rochelle, N.Y.: Arlington House, 1968.

Rueff, Jacques. *The Age of Inflation.* Chicago: Henry Regnery, Gateway Ed., 1964.

White, Andrew Dickson. *Fiat Money Inflation in France.* Reprint ed. Irvington, N.Y.: Foundation for Economic Education, 1959.

SOUTH AFRICA, HISTORY AND BACKGROUND

Drury, Allen. *A Very Strange Society.* New York: Trident Press, 1967.
Morris, Donald R. *The Washing of the Spears.* New York: Simon & Schuster, 1965.
Weyl, Nathaniel. *Traitor's End; the Rise and Fall of the Communist Movement in South Africa.* New Rochelle, N.Y.: Arlington House, 1970.

PERIODICALS

For the General Investor:
    Barron's (Weekly)
    200 Burnett Road
    Chicopee, Mass. 01021
    Mining Journal, Ltd. (Weekly, by Airmail)
    15 Wilson Street, Moorgate
    London, EC2M 2TR, England
    The Northern Miner (Weekly)
    Circulation Dept.
    77 River Street
    Toronto 247, Ontario, Canada
    Quarterly Review of South African Gold Shares
    c/o *Mining Journal*
    15 Wilson Street, Moorgate
    London, EC2M 2TR, England
    The Wall Street Journal (Daily)
    Various regional editions—New York,
    Midwest, West Coast.
For the Gold Bug, Treasure Hunter and Prospector:
    American Gold News (Monthly)
    P.O. Box 427
    San Andreas, Cal. 95249
    California Mining Journal (Monthly)
    2539 Mission Street
    Santa Cruz, Cal. 95060
For the Gold Coin Collector-Investor:
    Coin World (Weekly)
    P.O. Box 150
    Sidney, Ohio 45365
    Numismatic News (Weekly)
    Iola, Wisconsin 54945

Index

Abd-el-Malik, Caliph, 38
Abydos, 26
Abyssinia, 26
ADR. *See* American Depositary Receipts
Aegina, 31
Afrikaans, 425–427, 433
Afrikaner Nationalist Party, 438, 439
Afrikaners, 431–432
Agnico Mines Ltd., 411, 412
Ajax Mine (Colo.), 350
Alabama, 348
Alaska, 83, 246, 322, 351, 360, 363, 397
Alaska Juneau (mining company), 325
Alexander the Great, 23, 31
Alexius Comnenus, 37
Algeria, 152
Allen, Robert S., 166
Allies, 59, 64, 68, 91, 155, 425
American Depositary Receipts, 478–480, 489
American Gold News, 368
American Revolution, 73, 75, 347
American Stock Exchange, 310, 355, 379, 476
American-South African Investment Co. Ltd., 207, 332, 337, 387, 456, 459, 460, 462–466, 475
Amsterdam, 463
Anaconda Company, 332
Anderson, Robert B., 166, 167, 168
Anglican Church, 433
Anglo-American Corporation of South Africa Ltd., 423, 430, 456, 457, 458, 484, 487, 489–491, 495, 498, 507, 508, 512, 513, 517
Anglo-American Industrial Corp., 496
Anglo-Boer War, 425
Anglo-Transvaal Consolidated Investment Co. Ltd., 458, 484, 493, 494, 504, 519, 520
Angola, 419, 420, 421, 450
Annco Mines, 326
antoninianus, 34
apartheid, 243–244, 419, 420, 422, 423, 435–439, 449
Appalachian (gold) lode, 347–348, 349
Arab empire, 38, 40
arbitrage, 56
Argentina, 219
Argonaut Mine (Calif.), 350
Arizona, 347, 349, 360
as, 32
asbestos, 418
Asians (So. Africa), 431, 434, 436
assignat, 53, 54, 108, 125, 181
Associated Manganese Co., 494
Associated Ore and Metals Co., 494
Association, The, 369
Assyria, 25, 30, 50

Atlee, Clement, 148
Augustus, 33, 38
Aunor Gold Mines Ltd., 389–390
Aurelian, 34
aureus, 32–33, 34, 43
Australia, 56, 242, 243, 244, 245, 246, 322, 350, 357, 417, 443, 457, 490
Australian Gold Rush, 349
Austria, 59, 65, 106, 107, 159, 299
Austria-Hungary, 57, 58, 59
Austro-Russian Treaty, 159
Ava Gold Mining Co., 405
averaging down, 536
Aztecs, 72, 417

Babylonians, 30
Baffinland Iron Mining Ltd., 404
Baghdad, 38
Baird Township, Ont., 404
Balmer Township, Ont., 392, 394
Bance del Giro, 52, 58
Banco della Piazza del Rialto, 51-52
Banda, Dr. Hastings, 421
Bank Holiday, 111–112
bank notes, 44, 45, 48, 49, 55, 79–81, 88–90; definition of, 79
Bank of England, 55, 64, 94, 107, 109, 149, 186, 202, 214
Bank of France, 94
Bank of the Republic of Colombia, 409
Banking Act of 1865, 88
Banking and Currency Committee, House, 87
Bantu, 431, 432–433, 434, 436–437, 438, 447, 449, 450–451
Bantustans, 436–437, 438
Bapedi (Bantu nation), 433
Barcelona, 38
Barclay's Bank, 438
Barker, C. Austin, 539
Barlow, Thos., & Sons, 458
Barlow-Rand Ltd., 458
Barron's, 380, 477
Basle, 178
Basutoland. *See* Lesotho
Bay Hall Trust Co., 493
Beer Hall Putsch, 123
Belgium, 57, 158, 436
Berlin, 59
bezant, 36–37, 38, 42
Bible, 25
bimetallism, 44, 45–48, 49, 54, 56, 77, 78, 82–84, 209
Bingham, Utah, 360
Bismarck, Otto, Prince von, 57
Black Hills, S.D., 349
Bland-Allison Act, 82, 83
Blue Star Mine (Nev.), 350
Bluffy Lake Iron Mines, 397
Blyvooruitzicht Gold Mining Co., 498